TRAINING

TRAINING
PROGRAMMES
FOR
27 SPORTS
USING
HEART
RATE
MONITORS

SPORTS INCLUDED:

triathlon, duathlon, multisport,
rowing, kayaking, road cycling,
mountain biking, distance running,
rugby union, rugby league, soccer,
netball, basketball, hockey, skiing,
surfing, golf, tennis, squash, cricket,
softball, volleyball, martial arts,
motor racing, sail boarding,
general fitness, fat loss

Precision Training

TRAINING
PROGRAMMES
FOR
27 SPORTS
USING
HEART
RATE
MONITORS

Jon Ackland

REED

The author wishes to thank the following for their kind permission to reproduce diagrams and data in this book:
Sally Edwards: graphs from The Heart Rate Monitor Book *on pages 17, 18, 21, 42, 58, 62.*
Peter Janssen: graphs from Training, Lactate, Pulse Rate
on pages 22, 23, 26, 27, 42, 44, 53, 54, 58, 62, 65, 66, 196.
The National Heart Foundation: diagram on pages 32–3.
Charles F. Ehret and Lynn Waller Scanlon: data from Overcoming Jet Lag *on page 74.*
Polar Electro Heart Rate Monitors Oy: data on page 19, cover photo.
Every heart rate monitor graph in this book has been produced using Polar Heart Rate Monitor technology (Polar Sport Tester, Polar Vantage NV, Polar Xtrainer, Polar Advantage Interface with precision performance and training advisor software, and Polar Interface and software).

Published by Reed Books, a division of Reed Publishing (NZ) Ltd, 39 Rawene Rd, Birkenhead, Auckland. Associated companies, branches and representatives throughout the world.

The opinions expressed in this book are intended as a guide only. The author accepts no responsibility for any injury or loss sustained by an individual or team as a result of using the material contained herein.

ISBN 0 7900 0618 9

The author asserts his moral rights in the work.
First published 1998

Designed by Graeme Leather, Island Bridge
Cover designed by Sunny H. Yang

Printed in New Zealand

DEDICATION

When an athlete stands on the Olympic dais to accept a medal, they feel the satisfaction and pride that their hard work and sacrifice has taken them to their goal. They also accept the medal on behalf of the many unsung heroes without whose support their dream could never have been realised. Writing a book is a little like that.

My unsung heroine is my partner, Kerri, whose support, patience, strength and outright belief in me give me the freedom to pursue my dreams and write books like this one. Whatever either of us does, we both do.

Therefore, WE would like to dedicate this book to our mothers, Maureen Ackland and Anne McMaster. We love you; thanks for all your unselfish dedication to us.

This book is also dedicated to Russell and Denise Maylin, whose support over the last few years has been unfailing and whose friendship we rely on.

As always, to my dad Jim and my sister Jill and my good buddy and ever faithful companion, Corduroy (our Newfoundland dog).

ABOUT THE AUTHOR

Jon Ackland is an exercise physiologist who has been working in the sports performance and training field for the last 15 years. As an 'applied sports scientist', he provides athletes and coaches with the training advice, testing and performance feedback needed to set up and refine high performance training systems.

Jon is the director of Performance Lab International, a company that helps athletes and coaches all over the world to improve performance. The company's goal is to provide 'cutting edge', quality information and training plans for all levels presented in a practical, commonsense format. In the four years that Performance Lab has been operational, its success in working with athletes and coaches has included two world records, eight national records, two world championships, numerous national titles, top Olympic performances, and many top ten placings in the world.

Jon holds a degree in science and a diploma of exercise science. Prior to setting up Performance Lab, he worked for the New Zealand Institute of Sport; under Jim Blair's supervision, with teams involved in New Zealand Rugby, Olympic yachting, America's Cup, Whitbread Around the World Yacht Race, New Zealand Basketball, New Zealand Hockey and New Zealand Skiing; and with many other top athletes of numerous sporting codes. His personal sporting background includes competitive school athletics, one national and three North Island rowing titles, five Ironmans and two representations at the World Ironman Triathlon championships in Hawaii.

Also by the same author:
The Power to Perform
The Performance Log

CONTENTS

FOREWORD

Twenty years ago, I got the idea of developing a wireless heart rate monitor. A sports coach was wanting to measure athletes' heart rates more accurately than by palpating and in real time during the sports performance. He knew that heart rate provides useful information, but in order to use it wisely, that information must be accurate.

Developing a heart rate monitor was a very interesting task and I set to work. With the skills and knowledge of our engineers at the University of Oulu in Finland, and persistent work and strength of will, we developed a wireless Polar Heart Rate Monitor that measures heart rate ECG-accurately. Today, Polar Heart Rate Monitor is a well-known trademark sold all over the world.

In athlete training, the same rules are valid as in research and business: to get success, one must strive to do better. The usefulness of measuring heart rates in training has increased as the physiological research has proceeded. An increasing number of sports benefit from heart rate control. Heart rate monitors are a feedback tool that gives the temporary as well as the long-term state of the body and by means of this, an athlete learns many things than not even the coach can teach. The coach can at most help in interpreting the information.

Precision Training contains information that will help sports people to make the right interpretation of this information, in the best possible form. The book deals with the use of heart rates in sports training in a thorough way and, from a coach's point of view, is clear and intelligible.

Polar Electro Oy is a leader in developing, manufacturing, marketing and selling wireless heart rate monitors. In cooperation with researchers, coaches and athletes, we will continue to keep developing more and more versatile and useful devices. The multi-faceted book that you have in your hands is an indicator of this fruitful cooperation. Jon Ackland has written this book for those who want to succeed.

Professor Seppo Säynäjäkangas
Inventor of the portable wireless heart monitor

ACKNOWLEDGMENTS

Special thanks to Caroline Rutherford and Brendon Downey for their tireless effort and dedication at Performance Lab - it's great to work with professionals. Thanks for all the typing, indexing, cups of tea and all the other bits you guys do each day that keep everything functioning.

Thanks as well to:

Brett Reid, for 'ghost writing' parts of this book.

Torsten Lonnberg of Polar Heart Rate Monitors, Oy, for his continuing support.

Clayton Scott and Leisure World, for your support.

Peter Janssen of Reed Publishing, for all your help.

Peter Dowling and Alison Southby, my editors at Reed, for a fantastic job yet again.

Graeme Leather of Island Bridge, for his perseverance and a great design job.

Sunny Yang, for her awesome final design work.

Steve Clark.

Some of New Zealand's leading sports experts lent their advice on the training aspects of the programmes at the rear of the book. For their time, wisdom and assistance, my thanks to:

Mark Sutherland, strength & conditioning coach.

Martin Dowson, Sports Performance Centre, Auckland Institute of Technology.

Tracey Paterson, consultant to NZ Netball.

Andrew Turner, consultant to the Warriors and Auckland Rugby.

Haydn Smyth, basketball legend.

Finally, thanks to:

Jason (the vet) Thrupp, Zane Kean, Chris & Liz McFadden, Paul Gunn, Dave Sherwood, Rob Heyway, Dr Dene Egglestone, Dr Steven Legg, and Steve Lock.

PREFACE

If you were going to write a book on training, why would you choose to focus on heart rate monitors? Isn't that a little specific or even pedantic?

Well, when I first thought about writing a book on heart rate monitors, I was actually quite excited. Of all the things in my career that I love, the thing I am most passionate about, next to training athletes, is ... gadgets! I have every kind of electronic sports training equipment you can think of!

But there is a sound reason for my interest in heart rate monitors: they herald the beginnings of a transition in training for sport. Heart rate monitors are the forerunners of more and more sophisticated data collection devices on training and competition.

Why is this important? Because over the next few decades, athletes and players will be able to improve their performances greatly by measuring training and competition, learning what works and what doesn't, and individualising their training more than ever before. The meeting between the computer/electronics age and sport holds great potential and excitement. So it was timely for me to write about what is happening with heart rate monitors and sports.

Furthermore, I had noticed that the heart rate monitor books available did not fully relate training to using your heart rate monitor. Coming from my background, you can't discuss heart rate monitors without discussing training. I wanted to write a book about how a heart rate monitor can fit into and be effective for training and competition.

To tackle this topic, in the first part of the book I discuss the key issues relating to heart rates and heart rate monitors. In the second part, I look at how training and sports performance work , and finally, bring together heart rate monitors and training into sport-specific programmes. This helps the athlete/player to understand heart rates, heart rate monitors and training, and gives them a programme that will optimise their performance. Of course, you can also make use of the programmes without a heart rate monitor too.

The final chapter contains over 260 programmes for 27 different sports, so there should be one to suit you. Some of this material will be familiar to readers of *The Power to Perform*, and it may be useful to refer to this book for more detail about your programme.

The key ingredients that I want you to get out of *Precision Training* are:

1. Understanding the 'Big Picture ' on sports performance.
2. Understanding heart rates and heart rate monitors
3. Understanding quality, not quantity is most effective to achieve your maximum potential in anything.
4. Understanding the logic of progressions in training. (i.e. walk before you run, before you sprint).
5. Having fun; dream dreams, set goals, believe you can do it and it will happen.

I hope you enjoy the book. Train hard, train smart, live long and perspire!

Jon Ackland

PART
one

THE HEART AND THE HEART RATE MONITOR

THE HEART

The heart is a muscle located under the rib cage (nearly in the centre of the chest) which pumps blood around the body. Why would it want to pump blood around the body? Because your blood contains oxygen, and oxygen is the fuel that makes the muscles function (even at rest). Without oxygen the muscles wouldn't work and would die — and so would you, for that matter.

The blood also transports and delivers other items that are necessary for healthy living, such as white cells and proteins, and it removes waste products.

Not surprisingly, the harder an athlete/ player works, the more fuel (oxygen) muscles require. This means the heart must work at a higher rate, i.e. beat faster. That's why resting heart rates are low and exercising heart rates are high. In one sense, then, heart rate is the body's 'rev counter' — it measures how much work the body is doing.

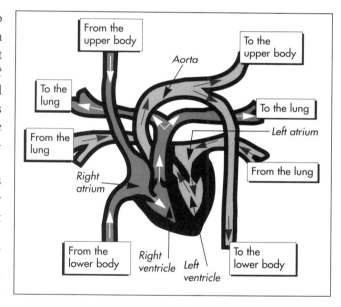

FIGURE 1.1: The heart

The complete sequence of a heart beat follows a specific rhythm, which is actually a sequence of electrical activities in the heart. These electrical activities form a pattern represented by a continuous, repetitive electrical wave (see fig 1.2).

MONITORING THE HEART

The electrocardiograph (ECG for short) has been used in hospitals for a long time. ('Electro' means electric, 'cardio' means heart, and 'graph', surprisingly enough, means graph.) The ECG records in wave form the electricity generated by the heart. With each beat of the heart, this wave repeats itself over and over again in a rhythmical sequence. If the rhythmical sequence changes, the heart is not beating correctly.

Heart rate (e.g. 72 beats per minute) is a measure of the main 'electrical pulse' of the heart that occurs on each beat. Naturally, if you can measure the wave, you can measure the heart rate: hence, the invention of the heart rate monitor.

Originally conceived to measure effort and fitness, the first portable, wireless heart rate monitor was produced by Dr Seppo Säynäjäkangas in Finland in the early 1980s to help athletes/players train more effectively.

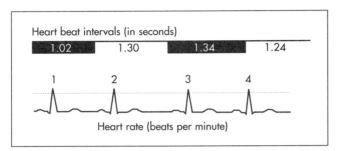

Figure 1.2:
The ECG — graphing the electrical activity of the heart

A heart rate monitor has two parts — a chest strap that contains two electrodes, and a receiver, or watch, that is strapped to the wrist. The electrodes pick up the electrical pulse from the athlete's heart, and this pulse is then transmitted wirelessly to the wrist watch (receiver). The wristwatch displays the pulse or heart rate, thus informing the athlete/player about the body's physiological response to exercise.

Heart rate monitors have had an enormous impact on training and sport, and have brought technology and sports/training science within the reach of all sports people.

WHY USE A HEART RATE MONITOR?

♥ The heart rate monitor acts as a 'rev counter' to give a precise measure of exercise intensity. You know exactly how hard you are working, making you less likely to commit training errors (e.g. overtraining, injury).

♥ Training can be more easily designed for the individual — you exercise at your pace, not someone else's. This means higher quality training and less wasted training.

♥ Your progress can be accurately measured — for any given speed, your heart rate drops as you get fitter. Resting heart rate also drops.

♥ It's easy to see improvement. This is very motivational.

♥ It gives you an objective view of how hard you are working.

♥ It is a good indicator of fatigue (heart rate elevated in the morning) and many other training variables.

♥ You can be more specific about your training.

FIGURE 1.3:
The heart rate
monitor receiver
resembles a
wristwatch.

The heart rate monitor can:
- ♥ display heart rate.
- ♥ set target training zones — the zones that you will train in (on some models, the monitor beeps if your heart rate is above or below the training zone).
- ♥ record average training heart rate for the training session.
- ♥ record heart rate at intervals.
- ♥ record heart rate for the full duration of the workout.
- ♥ display time, alarm, and stop-watch functions.

There are many other features. For more information, turn to Appendix 5.

PUTTING IT ALL TOGETHER

♥ Heart rate is the body's 'rev counter', measuring how hard the body is working.

♥ Heart rate monitors register the electrical activity that shows how fast the 'rev counter' is going.

♥ Heart rate monitors come in two parts — chest straps with electrodes and wristwatch receiver.

♥ Heart rate monitors improve quality of training.

CHAPTER 2

HEART RATES

RESTING HEART RATE

Resting heart rate is the number of times your heart beats when your body is at rest. The heart rate is low because your body is doing little except maintaining normal bodily functions. It is not necessary to pump extra blood (and oxygen) around the body to meet energy demands.

Resting heart rate is best taken in bed, lying down, upon waking. If you wake to an alarm, you may need to rest for a few minutes before taking your heart rate — the shock of the alarm will raise it! If you need to go to the toilet when you wake up, this can also raise your heart rate. True resting heart rate (i.e. when the body is least active) occurs in the early hours of the morning, around 3:00–5:00 a.m., but it is still quite low when you wake up.

To take your heart beat, place your fingers (not your thumb) on your wrist (palm side) at the base of your thumb; count the number of pulses for 15 seconds and multiply by 4.

Resting heart rate can be measured sitting or lying down during the day or in the evening. Some people (particularly those with stressful jobs) may find it more effective to take their heart rate at night, when they are more relaxed (in the morning, the mere thought of work can be enough to hype them up!). Similarly, the excitement of race day is likely to raise your resting heart rate above normal.

The average resting heart rate is around 70 beats per minute (bpm). Fit athletes/ players often have resting heart rates around 40–50 beats per minute. Five-time Tour de France winner Miguel Indurain has a resting heart rate of 28 beats per minute!

As the following table shows, resting heart rate can be affected by a number of conditions.

Variable	Initially	Short-term	Long-term
Fatigue/overtraining	Up	Up	Down
Anxiety/Stress	Up	Up	Down
Heat	Up	Up	Same
Cold	Up	Up	Down
Altitude	Down	Up	Same
Illness	Up	Up	Down
Fitness	Same	Same	Down

ASSESSING AVERAGE RESTING HEART RATE

Sports people tend not to take things lying down, but in the case of your resting heart rate, you can make an exception.

By measuring your heart rate each morning for a couple of weeks, you will be able to establish your average resting heart rate. For example:

	M	T	W	T	F	S	S
Heart rate	56	54	55	56	54	56	57

Total heart rates = 388, divided by seven days = 55.4. This gives you an average heart rate for the week of 55.

MAXIMUM HEART RATE

Maximum heart rate (HR^{max}) is the highest heart rate that you can achieve. This obviously occurs at maximum intensity or effort. Maximum heart rates can vary

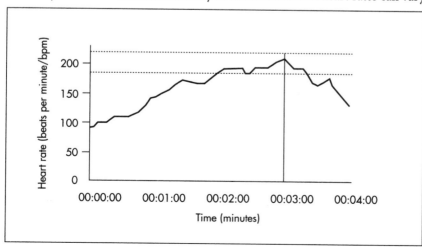

FIGURE 2.1: Maximum heart rate test (800-m run)

from 130–220 beats per minute, depending on the person. I've seen young athletes finish maximum effort tests at 210!

HEART SIZE, FITNESS AND HEART RATES

The heart is a muscle, and like all muscles it isn't the same size in everyone. Also, being a muscle, it can be trained. This will increase its size. But how can you tell what size your heart is?

In a large heart, the left ventricle is larger. The left ventricle is a compartment that pumps blood around the body. If it is larger it can pump more blood per heart beat (thereby delivering more oxygen to the muscles). And the more blood that can be pumped per beat, the less often the heart has to beat.

So? Larger hearts have a lower heart rate. For example, two athletes/players may be exercising at the same speed, but because one has a larger heart, their heart rate will be lower:

Runner 1: speed = 5 min/km; HR = 170 bpm.

Runner 2: speed = 5 min/km; HR = 150 bpm.

Okay, but what does this really mean? In most cases, not much.

Some people have inherited larger hearts, but this usually has no bearing on performance. These people just tend to 'rev' lower than others. Nevertheless, élite athletes/players do tend to have larger hearts than the rest of the population, and therefore, lower training and competition heart rates.

Interestingly, I have trained with many athletes with lower training heart rates than me (I rev high), but I often used to end up waiting for them at the finish line!

Heart size can also change with training. Just as weight training can increase muscle size, cardiovascular training (training that makes you puff) can make your heart get bigger.

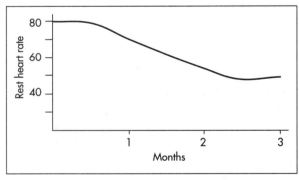

FIGURE 2.2: Drop in morning resting heart rate over three months as a result of increased fitness through training

When you exercise, your muscles demand more oxygen (that is, more blood), so the heart has to beat more often. After a period of time, it adapts by increasing in size so that it can pump more blood per beat and, therefore, will not have to beat as often. So, as you get fitter, your resting and exercise heart rates drop.

I once went for a run while very unfit and did a course I often run in 30 minutes at an average heart rate of 180. A few months later, having done a lot of training in between, I ran the same course in 30 minutes but at a heart rate of 154. I was much fitter!

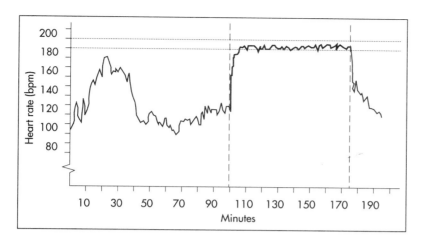

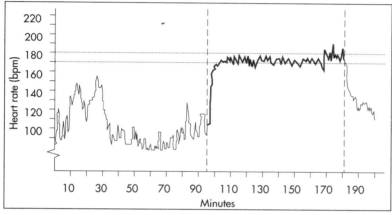

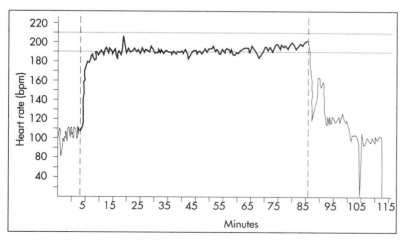

FIGURE 2.3:
Comparison between three cyclists in a team time trial, riding at the same speed. Note the differences in heart rates at the same speed, indicating different heart sizes.

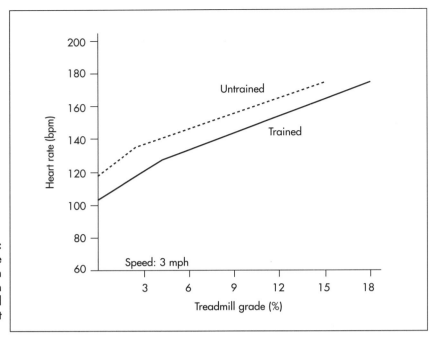

FIGURE 2.4:
Drop in exercise
heart rates through
training shown
during a treadmill
test

It is important to remember that most of this change occurs in the first six to eight weeks of training. This sometimes gets sports people into trouble because they usually establish their training heart rates when they start training. As a result, over the first six to eight weeks as their heart gets bigger it becomes harder and harder to get into the higher training zones (and they end up training in the wrong zones). This sometimes makes athletes/players think that they are overtrained or lazy.

Instead of worrying about being lazy, they should pat themselves on the back, because if their heart rates are dropping, the cardiovascular training is working and they are getting fitter! Now is the time to get their heart rates reassessed so that they can train correctly.

Below is an example of how an athlete's heart rates can change over the first six to eight weeks of training.

Start of training	*After eight weeks of training*
Sprint = 175–190 (3 min/km)	Sprint = 165–190 (3 min/km)
Race pace = 170–175 (4 min/km)	Race pace = 160–165 (4 min/km)
Up-tempo = 160–170 (5 min/km)	Up-tempo = 150–160 (5 min/km)
Easy = 130–160 (6 min/km)	Easy = 120–150 (6 min/km)

Needless to say, if, after eight weeks, this person continued training at a race pace of 170–175 bpm, they would be doing the wrong sort of training and would end up very overtrained!

It is also important to understand that heart rates vary considerably between individuals. So don't worry about others' heart rates; concentrate on your own.

Indeed, heart rates vary so much that the standard formulae for maximum heart rate — 220 minus age for men and 226 minus age for women — only apply to about 60 percent of people.

I have a maximum heart rate (running) of 204, but my maximum heart rate based on 220 minus age would be 189 — 15 beats lower. I have tested a healthy 45-year-old whose maximum heart rate (cycling) hit 203 — that's 28 beats higher than expected!

Heart rates are not necessarily going to be within the expected range because people's hearts can be significantly larger or smaller than average.

Here are two examples where the standard calculations didn't work.

♥ A health/fitness exerciser phoned me because over the previous six months his training had not produced the results he wanted. He was very meticulous about his training, and had calculated the training heart rates based on the standard formula. His aerobic training zone, based on the 220 minus his age (55) calculation for maximum heart rate, worked out at 129–139. In fact, his actual maximum heart rate (165) was around 190 — his aerobic training zone should have been 138–158! This meant that for the previous six months all his training had been at an intensity that was too low to create any noticeable cardiovascular improvement. That wasted a lot of time and effort.

♥ Another athlete was training for a cycle race. This athlete calculated his aerobic training zone based on a theoretical maximum of 195 (220 minus age); the zone worked out to be 137–159. However, his actual maximum, due to a genetically large heart, was 170, giving training heart rates for the required zone of 122–140. This meant that he struggled to get to his calculated training heart rates and had to 'push' very hard to train at the predicted aerobic training level. Obviously, his training heart rates were too high; he ended up becoming overtrained.

These examples illustrate two important points. First, listen to your body. If the training feels too easy, it is too easy. If it feels too hard, it is too hard. Second, the standard calculation of maximum heart rate (220/226 minus age) does not work for everyone, so be careful.

If in doubt, either do your own maximum heart rate test (see page 114) or get an exercise testing lab to assess it.

Heart rate and age

As you get older, your training heart rates and maximum heart rate drop. This is irrespective of your state of conditioning. However, it appears that the rate at which both rates drop may be slower for sports people who have exercised regularly throughout their lives than for those who have discontinued exercise.

This may be because a sedentary person's heart muscle loses its elasticity, whereas a sports person who continues to exercise will not lose that elasticity to the same degree. In other words, use it or lose it!

On average, training and maximum heart rates drop by about one beat per year. This can be seen below in the calculation of maximum heart rate.

For a male, 220 minus age (in years) = maximum heart rate; for a female, 226 minus age. For example:

20-year-old male: 220 – 20 = 200; female: 226 – 20 = 206
40-year-old male: 220 – 40 = 180; female: 226 – 40 = 186
60-year-old male: 220 – 60 = 160; female: 226 – 60 = 166

However, as we have seen, heart rates can vary considerably from this calculation. Thus, although heart rate does drop as you get older, the rate at which it drops varies considerably between individuals.

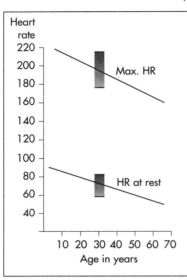

FIGURE 2.5:
Drop in training, maximum and resting heart rates due to age

PUTTING IT ALL TOGETHER

♥ Resting heart rate — the heart rate when you are least active.

♥ Maximum heart rate — the heart rate when you are most active.

♥ Heart size and fitness — some people have naturally large or small hearts resulting in higher or lower heart rates than usual.

♥ Heart size changes as we get fitter so heart rates (resting and exercise) drop.

♥ Heart rates and age — as you get older your heart rate drops.

HEART RATE AND ITS RESPONSE TO ILLNESS, MEDICATION AND STRESS

ILLNESS

Illness has exactly the same effect on heart rate as overtraining — it pushes it up. If your resting heart rate is 10 percent above what it usually is, then you should have an easy day's training. If it is much higher than this, have a day off. It all comes down to listening to your body — if you feel tired, you are tired.

Heart rate goes up when you are ill because your body is having to work harder to combat the illness. In cases of long illness, your heart rate will be raised early in the illness (the first weeks or months). It may then return to normal or drop below normal even though you are still ill. This is due to central nervous system depletion (see Overtraining, page 80).

FIGURE 3.1:
Changes in resting heart rate due to heavy workouts, racing and illness.

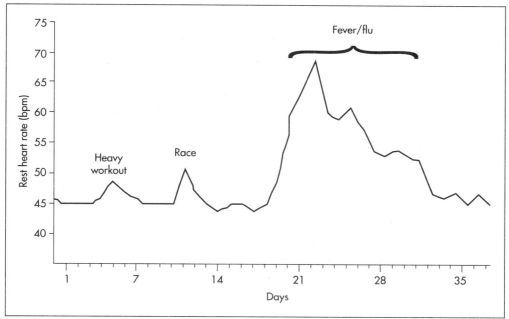

27

Taking time off when you are ill

To have a day off or not to have a day off when you are sick? The easy answer is that most people should have a day off.

If you train four times or less per week, have a day off. If you are training more than four times per week, you need a different strategy. I have found that when athletes/players who train a lot get sick, they invariably get sicker if they either train harder or stop training!

The only explanation I have for this is that if you train a lot, your body gets used to the regularity of training — it's a part of normal, daily life. If you stop training 'dead', that is as much a shock to the athlete's body as too much training.

If sports people who train more than four times per week feel ill (heart rate up 10 percent or more), train very lightly (such as 20 minutes of low intensity on your bike for a cyclist — absolutely no high intensity). This makes your body 'think' you are still training, but allows recovery at the same time.

Exceptions to this, however, are fever and continued injury. If you have a fever or are causing more harm to yourself, stop training!

MEDICATION

Various medications influence heart rate. Beta blockers, used to control blood pressure, will lower resting, training and maximum heart rates.

Some sportspeople use beta blockers, such as atenolol, to enhance performance. How do beta blockers do this? Beta blockers reduce heart rate, which makes your hands more steady in sports like shooting, archery and bowls. (Many shooters will try and shoot between heart beats, when their hand is most steady.) Some other anti-hypertensive drugs, depending on the type, can also bring heart rates down. Of course, using such drugs in this manner contravenes International Olympic Committee rules.

Erythropoietin (EPO) is another drug that athletes use illegally to enhance performance. EPO increases the number of oxygen-carrying red blood cells in a person's bloodstream. This improves oxygen uptake, thereby lowering heart rate (fewer beats are needed to get the same amount of oxygen to working muscles).

Anti-asthmatic drugs (like Ventolin) can raise heart rates for a brief time due to an adrenalin-like effect. The same applies to pseudoephedrine, which is found in some flu and cold medications.

Diuretics, used illegally by sports people to reduce weight, and by people with high fluid retention or heart trouble, can also push up heart rate. Even coffee can elevate your heart rate for a brief time.

The effects of some medications on heart rate:

Medication	Raises heart rate	Lowers heart rate
Beta blockers	–	✓
Other anti-hypertensives	✓	✓
Anti-asthmatic	✓	–
Diuretics	✓	–
Pseudoephedrine	✓	–
Amphetamines	✓	–

ANXIETY OR STRESS

Mental stress will raise heart rate at rest and, sometimes, during exercise. Your resting heart rate can be elevated in the morning if you think you are going to have a very busy or stressful day. Stress levels may also increase your exercise heart rate, although in most cases exercise will help to reduce the stress.

In the case of severe long-term stress (mental burnout, nervous breakdown), heart rate may be elevated initially but then drop to normal or below normal over a period of weeks or months. This is because the body gets run down.

Here is an example, using two time trials that I did, of how stress can affect heart rate.

♥ For the first time trial (which was over 10 km) my stress levels were low. In addition, I wasn't nervous about doing it. I ran 10 km at a 3.7 min/km pace, at a heart rate of 182.

♥ Less than two weeks later my stress levels were high — I was very busy at work and I was coping with the death of a close friend. Under these conditions I ran a 20-km time trial on the Rotorua marathon course. I ran 20 km at a 4.5 min/km pace (0.8 min/km slower than the 10-km trial) at a heart rate of 185 (three beats higher than the 10 km).

If you are a runner you will know that that is a big speed difference (the difference between a 37-minute 10 km and a 45-minute 10 km), and moreover there was a higher heart rate at a slower speed. I had done very little training during the intervening fortnight, so I wasn't physically tired.

Whether it was the stress that raised my heart rate or whether it had worn me out, I don't know. But I do know it made a big difference to my heart rates (and performance). Whether it's physical stress (exercise) or mental stress, it affects performance.

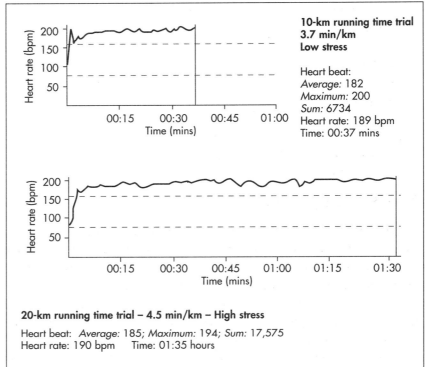

A warning, though: make sure you assess the stress and your heart rate reading in context. The following story about an Ironman competitor illustrates how the situation can be misread. But first, quickly ask yourself this question: 'How would I feel getting up on a normal training morning compared to a race morning that I have trained 12 months for?' Chances are you would feel more nervous on race morning, right? And what would that do to your resting heart rate? Yep, raise it.

Back to the story. This particular athlete woke up on race morning, took his resting heart rate, and found that it was elevated. Thinking that he was either tired or sick, he pulled out of the race!

Almost certainly the elevated heart rate was because of the excitement of race morning. By failing to be aware of this, the athlete threw away 12 months of training. Put another way, he lost 65 working days: at $20 per hour, that's $10,400!

Sports people who might normally have resting heart rates of between 45 and 60 bpm can find they are up to 70–100 for the 24 hours before a competition, and up to 70–140 just prior to their competition start. This is nothing to worry about: it's just the body getting ready to go fast, to compete.

Of course, if your heart rates begin to increase too early, it may mean you are getting 'psyched up' too early. This will probably impair your competition performance as you will be a little jaded by the time you race/play.

You should, therefore, try and keep heart rates around normal levels until very close to the start of the race.

HEART RATES AND HEART ABNORMALITIES

Your heart rate monitor is like an ECG machine (in American television dramas, where they often make those important 'beeping' sounds, they're called EKGs). ECGs allow your doctor to look at your heart ('engine') function without having to actually 'lift up the bonnet' (which is far more painful!).

When the heart beats it generates electricity. This electricity creates a 'wave' that can be recorded on the ECG. In a healthy heart, this wave repeats itself over and over again as your heart pumps blood around your body.

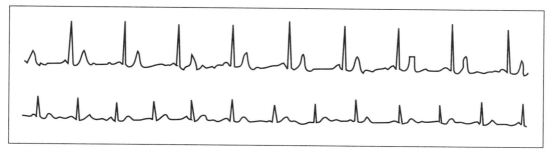

FIGURE 3.3: Normal ECG graphs

If for some reason the heart does not contract or 'beat' normally, the electrical activity that the heart generates shows variations. This changes the 'wave' on the ECG.

While an 'abnormal' wave may indicate some minor heart abnormality that is of no concern (some very fit sports people have minor abnormalities due to the fact that they have very large, strong hearts), an abnormal ECG can be an early warning of serious heart problems.

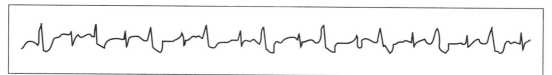

FIGURE 3.4: Abnormal resting ECG graph

How does this relate to your heart rate monitor? Your heart rate monitor acts like an ECG machine by picking up the electrical activity of your heart. If the numbers that show up on your monitor are erratic, either now and then or continuously, this may indicate an abnormality that should be checked by your doctor before you resume exercise.

If you are exercising and see a sudden change in heart rate, slow down immediately. Don't stop suddenly, though, and don't panic. There are other factors that can cause sudden changes on your heart rate monitor.

For instance, check your signals aren't being interfered with by someone else's heart rate monitor (or some other wireless transmitting device, or overhead power lines). Sometimes the skin on your chest where the strap goes is too dry (there must be sweat or water between your skin and the electrodes for them to pick up the electrical pulses from your heart). This would generally only occur at the start of a workout. Wet your skin and the electrodes, and recheck.

If problems still occur, get the batteries in the transmitter and watch checked. They may need to be changed. Sometimes the battery in the transmitter is loose. To check this, shake the transmitter. A rattle indicates a loose battery (runners often have this problem!).

If none of the above apply, accept that you may have a heart abnormality. See a doctor as soon as possible.

FIGURE 3.5: Abnormal resting ECG graph — note the difference in the shapes of the 'spike' and periods where the heart does not beat.

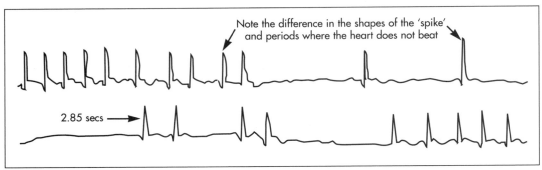

Note the difference in the shapes of the 'spike' and periods where the heart does not beat

2.85 secs ⟶

FIGURE 3.6: CPR procedure: in order to do effective CPR and Life Support, a course should be undertaken.

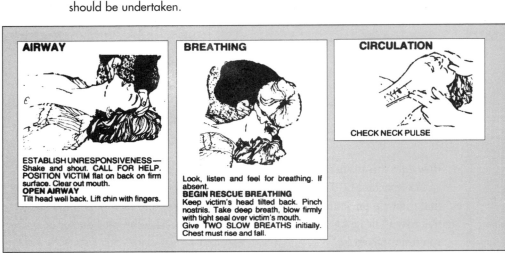

AIRWAY

ESTABLISH UNRESPONSIVENESS — Shake and shout. CALL FOR HELP. POSITION VICTIM flat on back on firm surface. Clear out mouth.
OPEN AIRWAY
Tilt head well back. Lift chin with fingers.

BREATHING

Look, listen and feel for breathing. If absent.
BEGIN RESCUE BREATHING
Keep victim's head tilted back. Pinch nostrils. Take deep breath, blow firmly with tight seal over victim's mouth. Give TWO SLOW BREATHS initially. Chest must rise and fall.

CIRCULATION

CHECK NECK PULSE

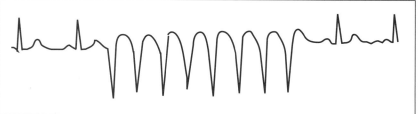

FIGURE 3.7
Abnormal ECG graph — ventricular tachycardia

FIGURE 3.8:
Abnormal ECG graph — ventricular fibrillation

Heart abnormalities, particularly serious ones, are often accompanied by signs other than a wildly fluctuating heart rate. These signs include feeling dizzy, nauseous, or light-headed; a loss of feeling down the left arm; chest pains; or a heart rate that continues to remain abnormal at rest. If you experience any of these conditions lie down, relax, and get someone to call an ambulance or a doctor.

Remember, though: abnormalities are more likely to occur the older you get. Under the age of 35, abnormalities are unlikely. Long-term colds or flu viruses can sometimes infect the heart and, in a perfectly healthy individual, create a temporary but serious abnormality. A few years ago, a yachtsman I tested (an Americas Cup grinder actually) had a flu virus that he had not fully recovered from. It infected the heart muscle and an abnormality showed up on the ECG. The grinder had to train lightly for a few weeks until it went away.

Here's another true story that underlines the need to be wary of fluctuating

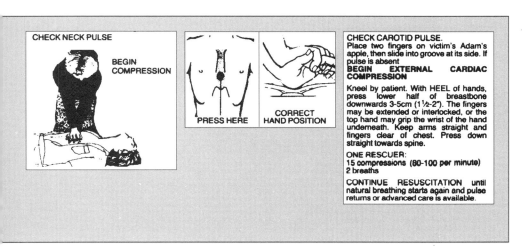

readings on your heart rate monitor. A cyclist, having bought a heart rate monitor, found it wasn't working properly (heart rates fluctuated inconsistently all the time). He sent it back to the retailer and got a new one but this monitor also failed to work properly, giving the same fluctuating readings as the first. This second monitor was also sent back. While the cyclist was waiting for the third monitor to arrive at the shop, he collapsed and died of a heart attack during a race. It wasn't the heart rate monitors that were faulty, it was the rider's heart!

Always check any abnormality with your doctor, and if you are over 35 years of age, have a medical check-up once a year (if you are over 50, get a check-up every six months). It could save your life. You should also learn CPR: it could save someone else's life.

LOSS OF BLOOD

Obviously, if there is less blood in your body, your heart needs to pump more frequently to make up for the shortfall. In other words, the blood needs to be recirculated more often.

Fit sports people often act as blood donors, giving around 0.5 litres per visit. After this donation, it takes 2–3 weeks for the haemoglobin to return to its normal level. During this time, heart rates can be slightly elevated and recovery will be slower. Therefore, it makes sense to avoid taking part in major competitions within 3–4 weeks of donating blood.

PUTTING IT ALL TOGETHER

♥ Illness in general raises heart rate.

♥ Medication — various medications increase or decrease heart rate.

♥ Anxiety or stress — increases your heart rate.

♥ Heart abnormalities can sometimes be picked up by a heart rate monitor.

♥ Loss of blood — if you donate blood the reduced blood volume means a higher heart rate until your body replaces it.

CHAPTER 4

HEART RATE AND FACTORS THAT CAN AFFECT IT DURING TRAINING

HEART RATES AND INTERVALS/SPEEDWORK

When starting a workout or interval, intensity can move up almost instantaneously. A runner can be moving along at a 5 min/km pace within 10 strides; a cyclist can be riding at 26 kph within 20 pedal revolutions. Heart rate, however, takes a while to get up to speed — it can take 2–4 minutes to increase to the point where it is accurately measuring intensity.

Most sports people exercise too hard when they use a heart rate monitor for interval/speedwork training. Why? Because they forget about the lag time between when they start the interval/speedwork and when the heart rate matches the training intensity. Where does the mistake occur?

If an athlete/player knows that they need to exercise at a heart rate of, say, 160 bpm to be working at the right intensity, they will often go as hard as they can at the start of the interval to get their heart rate up to that level as fast as possible. They think that if they sprint at the start of their interval to get their heart rate up, they can settle into a slightly lower intensity once they reach 160 bpm. Unfortunately, sprinting to get their heart rate up quickly means they are training at too high an intensity at the start of the interval.

How do you fix this? Simple. Begin the interval at the intensity that you 'feel' is correct. Hold the same pace throughout the whole interval and let the heart rate come up as you move through the interval.

You can tell when the intensity is correct because heart rate will begin to plateau at the correct level. If it plateaus at a slightly lower level than planned, you know you need to do the next interval harder. If it is too high, slow down for the next interval.

In summary: sprinting to get your heart rate up quickly is the best way to overtrain using a heart rate monitor. Don't do it.

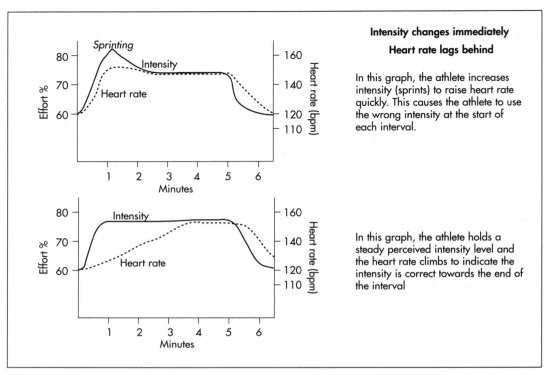

Intensity changes immediately
Heart rate lags behind

In this graph, the athlete increases intensity (sprints) to raise heart rate quickly. This causes the athlete to use the wrong intensity at the start of each interval.

In this graph, the athlete holds a steady perceived intensity level and the heart rate climbs to indicate the intensity is correct towards the end of the interval

FIGURE 4.1:
Heart rates and intervals

HEART RATE MONITORS AND RESTS BETWEEN INTERVALS/SPEEDWORK

Heart rates can be very useful in determining rest periods between intervals. Most sports people use an arbitrary time between interval/speedwork efforts to gauge recovery, e.g. 5 x 6-minute intervals at 150–160 bpm with a 1-minute rest between. Instead of an arbitrary recovery time, e.g. 1 minute, the rest period can be the time it takes for your heart rate to drop to a predetermined level, e.g. 110 bpm. This level is usually around 20–60 beats below the heart rate for high aerobic intensity intervals (steady-state race pace); it depends in part on your age.

Using heart rate to determine recovery between interval/speedwork efforts can be very useful as it takes into account fatigue and environmental variables. For example:

Variable	Time for HR to drop 60 beats
Normal	1 min
High level of fitness	30 secs
Fatigue	90 secs
Altitude	90 secs
Heat	90 secs

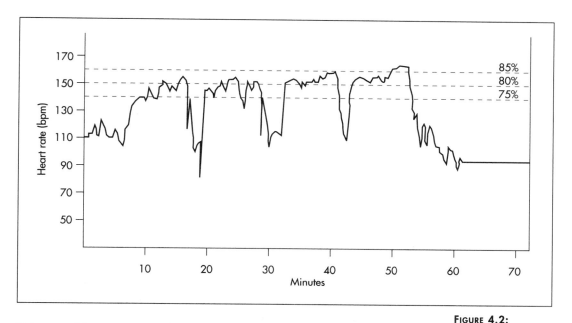

Using an arbitrary rest period would mean insufficient recovery, for example, for an athlete who trained at altitude. This could lead to overtraining.

Using heart rate to determine recovery provides information on the tiredness of the athlete/player. It also means the interval/speedwork is comparable across different conditions. Improvements in fitness can also be ascertained, i.e. it takes less time for heart rate to drop to the required level. Another effect is that intervals/speedwork can involve decreasing rest periods over a number of weeks building up to a race or game.

Weeks out from race or game	Rest period (minutes)	Equivalent heart rate drop from 180 bpm (beats)
12	5	60
8	4	50
6	3	40
4	2	30
2	1	20

Heart rate drop-off is reduced in the same way that an arbitrary rest period would be reduced (note that the heart rate drop-off is quicker when you are fitter).

Heart rate monitors can provide other useful information when doing speedwork. For example:

Usual rest period (60-beat drop-off) = 60 secs

Target heart rate for intervals = 180–185 bpm

Interval	HR	HR drop-off time	Assessment
4 x 5 mins	180–185	60 secs	Good.
4 x 5 mins	180–185	40 secs	Very good. You are getting fitter!
4 x 5 mins	170–175	60 secs	Legs tired. Do active recovery (can't get to 180–185 bpm).
4 x 5 mins	180–185	80 secs	Tired. Do half your intervals.
4 x 5 mins	180–185	2 mins	Very tired or ill. Go home.

HEART RATES AND HILLS

Here's a real 'no brainer': heart rate goes up when you go up hills because your body has to work harder.

A question that's often asked is: does heart rate need to be kept down on hills? The answer (within reason) is: no. For instance, if you are climbing a 'mega' hill and your heart rate is near maximum and you feel like you are going to collapse, then you don't need to be Einstein to know that's not clever. But a heart rate elevated by 30–40 bpm is fine for short periods of time going up hills.

You can take 'staying in the training zone' too literally. I have heard of people getting off their bike and walking up the hills to keep their heart rate down. Although this might be okay in some situations, e.g. if you're very unfit, in most cases keeping your heart rate down on hills is not a reality. So long as you don't raise your heart rate to near maximum levels, going up a hill with a heart rate higher than usual (above your training zone) for short durations is fine. You are strength endurance training the muscles and if you keep your heart rate down on hills, you don't get the 'strength'.

HEART RATES AND DIFFERENT SPORTS

A sports person will have different heart rates for different sports, for the same level of effort. Here are some heart rates for five different sports when training at 80 percent effort:

Running:	170	Cycling:	160
Rowing:	160	Swimming:	150
Kayaking:	145		

The reason heart rate varies between sports is the differing number of muscles used. Put simply, the more muscles you use in your sport, the higher your heart rate will be.

Running requires more muscles than cycling because not only must the athlete/player use muscles to move forward, they also require muscles to hold them upright (not the case in cycling). Because running requires more muscles than cycling, it requires more 'fuel' (oxygen) and, as a result, more oxygen-carrying blood. More blood required equates to a higher heart rate. Swimming, on the other hand, primarily uses arm muscles, which are smaller than leg muscles, so swimming heart rates are lower than 'leg sport' heart rates.

Of course, very efficient or inefficient techniques in any sport may complicate this. For example, someone who is inefficient in cycling but efficient in running may have the same heart rate for both sports when training at the same perceived effort. However, for the same perceived intensity, heart rates usually vary between sports.

INSUFFICIENT RECOVERY

RESTING HEART RATE

If an athlete/player has had insufficient recovery from the previous workout(s), resting heart rate may become elevated. But how elevated does it need to be before you reduce training?

If resting heart rate is up to 10 percent above normal, have an easy day. If it's 10 percent or more above normal, have a day off. For example:

$HR^{rest} = 50$; normal $HR^{rest} = 56$; day off
$HR^{rest} = 52$; train normally $HR^{rest} = 60$; day off/ill?
$HR^{rest} = 48$; very well, recovered/getting fitter

An elevated resting heart rate means you are overly fatigued. Training in this state will be ineffective, and a waste of time and energy. Listen to your body and take it easy.

HEART RATES, INSUFFICIENT RECOVERY AND TRAINING

If you are tired, you may find that you cannot achieve your training heart rates during speedwork. Or you may achieve the heart rates but struggle more than usual to do so. If you are a runner, this means that your legs are too tired to allow you to go fast enough to achieve the right heart rates. The best course of action? Back off and have an easy day.

If the desired heart rates cannot be reached, or are reached only with abnormal effort, then you have not recovered. If you continue, you are prolonging the time it will take before you have recovered enough to train effectively again. There is also more chance of overtraining and injury.

Elevated heart rates (compared to normal) at the same speed also mean that you are tired. If training heart rates are up by more than 5–10 bpm, have an easy day or go home and rest. Training while tired may mean that your body absorbs less training than when it is fully recovered. For example:

Athlete/player A

	M	T	W	T	F	S	S
Daily training absorbed (%)	100	90	60	50	40	0	100
	T	T	T	T	T	D/O	T
Fatigue	L	L/M	M	M/H	H	–	L

Total training absorbed for week: 73.3% (100 + 90 + 60 + 50 + 40 + 100) ÷ 6

Athlete/player B

	M	T	W	T	F	S	S
Daily training absorbed (%)	100	90	0	100	100	0	100
	T	T	D/O	T	T	D/O	T
Fatigue	L	L/M	–	L	L	–	L

Total training absorbed for week: 81.6% (100 + 90 + 100 + 100 + 100 + 0) ÷ 6

Note : Expected number of training days was 6.
Key: T = training day; D/O = day off; L = low fatigue; M = medium fatigue; H = high fatigue.

As you can see in the above table, athlete/player B had a day off on Wednesday as well as Saturday. This resulted in athlete/player B having a more effective training week compared with athlete/player A, who got tired on Wednesday but continued to train until taking a day off on Saturday.

In total, athlete/player B absorbed 8.3 percent more training during the week than athlete/player A. That's 132.8 percent more training over a 4-month training build-up — the difference between first and tenth in a race (and maybe first and last!).

Indeed, one difference between champions and the rest of the competition is that champions know when to stop training. Although many people know how to train, it's the sports people who know when not to train who are usually the best.

FLUID LOSS/DEHYDRATION

During exercise the body produces heat, which leads to perspiration. The sweat on the skin evaporates and has a cooling effect on the body.

Excessive fluid loss through sweat and respiration (water vapour released into the air through breathing) can lead to problems. If there is too much fluid loss, the body does not sweat properly and is not cooled very well. If this happens, the body will start to overheat. This can lead to some serious consequences.

A loss of more than 2–3 percent of bodyweight through fluid loss will drastically affect performance. It will also drive up body temperature. If this continues for too long, it can be life-threatening. Over 1–2 hours, a 70-kg athlete/player can lose 3 percent of bodyweight in fluid. This equates to over 2 kg.

The easiest way to check on fluid loss is to weigh yourself (without clothes) before and after each workout. The difference in weight will be due to fluid loss. Put simply, a 1-kg loss in weight should be replaced by 1,000 ml in fluid (0.1 kg equates to 100 ml).

Weighing yourself before and after exercise is a good way to test the effectiveness of your hydration strategies. A weight loss obviously means you are not drinking enough! A trap, though, is that after prolonged activity you must account for a weight loss due to a loss of glycogen (muscle fuel) as well as water. You only replace 65 percent of weight loss during racing as the rest of the weight loss, 35 percent, is glycogen.

And remember, it can take 24–36 hours to rehydrate fully. This will obviously affect the quality of the workouts done within this time.

Therefore, when training and racing, fluid should be replaced regularly (150–250 ml every 10–15 minutes). As well as water, replace electrolytes which aid muscle function. You can buy commercial drinks that contain fluid, carbohydrates and electrolytes to maintain fluid balance, provide energy and keep muscles functioning well.

The following table illustrates the difference that adequate rehydration during training or racing makes:

Duration (mins)	Weight before (kg)	Weight after (kg)	Drink during (ml)	Weight difference (kg)	Drink after (ml)
60	70.0	69.2	0	0.8	800
60	70.0	69.8	600	0.2	200
60	70.0	70.0	800	0.0	0

If you lose too much fluid the water content of your blood decreases, which means the volume of your blood drops. This in turn means the heart has to work harder (pump more often) to get the required amount of blood around the body. Thus, heart rate goes up when you lose fluid and that means you work harder to maintain the same speed compared to when you are hydrated.

Figure 4.3 shows what happens during a workout at 70 percent VO_{2max} (65–75 percent effort) when the temperature is 20 °C. Two runners were tested: one drank 250 ml every 15 minutes, while the other drank nothing. The test ended for each runner when they were exhausted (pleasant, eh!).

The runner who didn't drink had a higher heart rate that climbed steadily as dehydration increased. His test lasted 30 minutes less than that of the athlete/player who drank.

FIGURE 4.3:
Heart rate and fluid intake

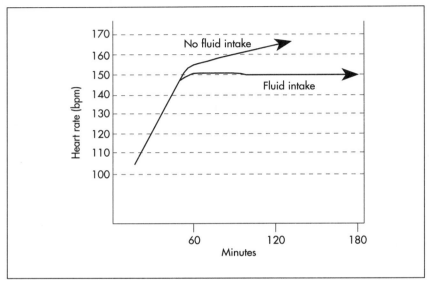

There are many famous dehydration stories: the marathon runner staggering into the stadium and weaving her way around the 400-metre track at the 1984 Los Angeles Olympics; Mark Allen's struggle to finish and win an early Nice triathlon; Paula Newby Fraser stopping close to the end of the 1995 Hawaiian Ironman.

The most famous story of all occurred on 6 February 1982, at the Ironman in Hawaii. Julie Moss leads the women's race but collapses 800 m from the finish line. She stands and walks towards the finish line but collapses several times; she is seriously dehydrated. She collapses one last time 20 m from the line, still in the lead, and crawls towards the finish line. As she does this, the second-placed woman, Kathleen McCarthy, passes her and wins the 225-km race. Moss's struggle is broadcast on ABC's 'Wide World of Sports' and thousands around the world are inspired by her determination.

As you can see, even the big names make this mistake. Planning a careful fluid/nutrition race strategy, monitoring your body and your heart rate and always being alert to dehydration (never underestimate it) can give you safe, happy, fast racing (See *The Power to Perform* for more information). I set my heart rate monitor interval times to go off every 15 minutes: 1 beep to remind me to drink taking 2–3 sips depending on conditions then, 15 minutes later, 2 beeps to drink and eat and then back to 1 beep again after another 15 minutes. This stops me from forgetting during the race, when I have other things to concentrate on.

In summary, if you don't drink enough to replace fluid loss during training and racing:

♥ heart rate goes up;

♥ performance goes down;

♥ health risks increase.

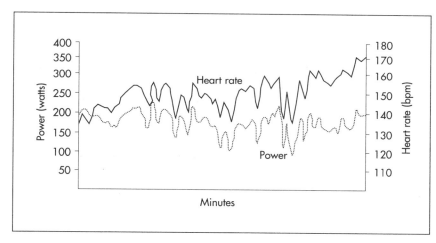

FIGURE 4.4:
Relationship between heart rate and power, in cycling, leading to dehydration

NUTRITION

Better forms of fuel provide better performance potential and often a lower heart rate for the same speed. This is most evident in training. For example, in one study, one group of athletes had extra carbohydrate supplementation during exercise, while the other group had normal nutrients with no supplementation. Both groups exercised for 120 minutes at 70 percent VO_{2max} (approximately 80 percent effort). The group who took the supplementation had lower exercise heart rates for the same workload, and achieved a 7 percent greater workload.

Now for a controversial topic. It is becoming more widely believed that not everyone operates best on the same fuel. It seems that some athletes/players tend to operate better on fats, while others tend to operate better on carbohydrates.

This may be based on a genetic tendency or it may be just what your body is used to. Maybe the 'eat carbohydrates to go fast' cry of the 1970s and 1980s is not completely true.

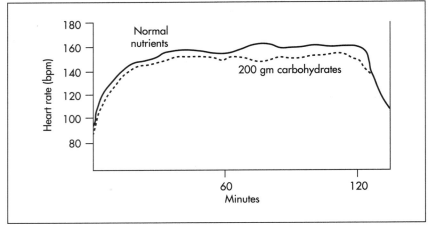

Figure 4.5:
The effect of nutrition
on heart rate

In addition, the widely reported percentages of fat/carbohydrate/protein for the optimal sports diet may be okay as an average, but they may not be ideal for everyone. We are, after all, individuals.

A very simple test is to ask yourself or a friend what they would most like to eat or drink during a very long workout (3–5 hours) or when they get very tired from the accumulated training of several days or weeks. Some athletes/players talk about high-fat foods and others talk of high-carbohydrate foods. In my experience, a lot of speed and power athletes prefer carbohydrates as their main fuel source when tired and a lot of endurance athletes prefer higher fat content foods when tired.

A particular athlete/player may operate better and at lower heart rates on either carbohydrates or fats. Telling an athlete/player who operates best on fats to eat less fat and more carbohydrates may decrease their performance rather than increase it. This does pose an ethical dilemma, of course. What happens if you eat a high-fat diet all your life — are you more prone to heart disease? The facts say you are. Perhaps it's best to talk to a nutritionist.

MUSCLE FATIGUE

Muscle fatigue can affect heart rate, with mild muscle fatigue generally pushing training heart rates up. At high training intensities, however, different effects are felt.

Let's say you go out to do some intervals/speedwork, or you are doing a maximum heart rate test or anaerobic threshold test. You find that no matter how hard you try, during the speedwork you can't get up to your usual interval heart rates, and in the max test or the anaerobic threshold test your muscles (legs in cycling) give out much earlier than usual. You're 'legless'.

You expected to have a heart rate of 180, and you can't get above 170. This is an indication that your muscles have not fully recovered from a previous training session.

In this situation, the athlete/player doing intervals or speedwork should drop the interval workout and do some easy training. The tests should be postponed until the muscles are fully recovered.

Cardiac drift

Cardiac drift is the upward drift in heart rate that occurs during long, continuous aerobic training. For instance, you may start a bike ride at a heart rate of 160, at a speed of 28 kph. Later in the bike ride you may find that your heart rate drifts up to 165 or 170, even though you are maintaining the same speed. This gradual increase in heart rate is due to fatigue, increased body temperature and, possibly, slight dehydration.

Why does cardiac drift occur?

The first two factors that cause cardiac drift are relatively straightforward. If you are not fit (or not fit for the duration of the workout), as you get tired your heart rate drifts up. Increased body temperature will also raise your heart rate (e.g. a hot environment). The effects of dehydration, however, need a little more explanation.

Your working muscles demand oxygenated blood to function. To meet the increasing demand made by tiring muscles, the heart must either increase the amount of blood pumped each beat (stroke volume) or the number of beats per minute. Either way, more blood is supplied (cardiac output increases). If, however, you become dehydrated, the heart's options for supplying blood are cut to one. With less fluid in the body, the volume of blood is lower, so the heart cannot supply more blood per beat (stroke volume) except by increasing heart rate to balance supply. Hence, cardiac drift occurs.

How marked is cardiac drift?

A fit, experienced athlete/player may show very little cardiac drift during a workout — usually no more than five beats per minute. This may not even be noticed. In reality, cardiac drift generally has little impact on training heart rates unless the athlete/player is:

♥ unfit.

♥ training in hot weather.

♥ dehydrated.

WARM-UPS

Warm-ups are aimed at gradually bringing the body up to the exercise pace or intensity level at which you will be training or racing. Warm-ups reduce the chance of injury and increase the effectiveness of the workout (particularly for higher intensity workouts).

The main goals of the warm-up are to increase muscle temperature, metabolic rate, blood flow and lubrication of joints, and to improve muscle contractile capacity. The higher the training intensity of a workout, the longer the warm-up should be: for instance, 15–20 minutes for intervals/speedwork, 20–30 minutes for races. Breaking out in a sweat means that your warm-up is satisfactory, for this indicates that you have raised your body's internal temperature.

If in the first 2–20 minutes of your workout you feel less comfortable than usual (breathing too hard, out of breath), particularly in speedwork, you may not have warmed up enough. Stretching should follow the warm-up.

WARMING UP WITH A HEART RATE MONITOR

Warm up gently for 5–15 minutes at a comfortable heart rate. Then, after stretching, start slowly increasing the exercise intensity until your heart rate reaches the level you expect it to reach during the workout. If you are doing speedwork, you should then back off and recover in preparation for the session. With lower intensity training you can generally move straight into the workout.

WARM-DOWNS

A warm-down is a drop in exercise intensity designed to promote recovery. It helps prevent blood pooling in your extremities, which can make you feel light-headed (common after speedwork). In a cyclist, for example, blood pools in the blood vessels in the legs and not enough returns to the heart. As a consequence, the heart beats faster in an attempt to increase blood flow and you feel dizzy.

During a workout, exercise-induced waste products are accumulated in the body, and they remain there even after exercise is completed. When you stop exercise cold, the waste products in the body take much longer to dissipate, as your metabolic rate (the basic speed at which your body functions) drops to resting level very quickly.

Ideally, you should lower your training intensity slowly by engaging in a light activity which does not stress the body, i.e. an activity that does not produce further waste products. At low training intensities, exercise waste products are removed at a much faster rate as your metabolic rate is still higher than at rest. This will improve the rate of recovery, making you fresher and able to train more effectively in the following workout.

The higher the training intensity used in the workout, the longer the warm-down: for example, 20–30 minutes for intervals and races.

Warming down after a race can take a lot of discipline — you would often much rather have a drink, eat or talk — but get that warm-down done first!

WARMING DOWN WITH HEART RATE MONITORS

After your workout, you should gradually bring your intensity/heart rate down to a recovery heart rate (100–120 for most people, although it tends to be lower the older you are). Once heart rate has dropped to this level, continue exercising for 10–15 minutes at this intensity to allow full recovery before stretching.

PUTTING IT ALL TOGETHER

A SUMMARY OF HEART RATE RESPONSE OF TRAINING

Variation	Initial	Short-Term	Long-Term
Intervals	Slow to rise in response to intensity	Matches intensity	N/A
Rests between intervals	Good indication of recovery period		
Hills	Up	Up	Up
Different sports	Depends on the number and size of the muscles used		
Insufficient recovery	Up	Up	Down
Fluid loss	Up	Up	Up
Nutrition	Depends on type of food the athlete is suited to		
Muscle fatigue	Up/down	Up/down	Down
Cardiac drift	Up	Up	N/A
Warm-up	Up	Up	N/A
Warm-down	Up but low	Up but low	N/A

CHAPTER 5

HEART RATE MONITORS AND FACTORS THAT CAN AFFECT HEART RATE DURING COMPETITION

RACE/GAME WARM-UPS

Warming up for races and games involves between 20 and 60 minutes of exercise in the sport you are about to compete in. If you are racing in a multisport/triathlon type of race where two or more different sports are performed during the same race, warm up in each of them. This will allow you not only to warm up all competition-specific muscle groups but also to check your equipment.

When warming up for a multisport event, always work backwards from the last sport to the first sport. For example, a triathlon warm-up should proceed in this order: run, cycle, swim. This is because you need to do the most thorough warm-up for the first event as in the following events you will already be warmed up extensively by the preceding disciplines. If you start the first event cold it will take 5–20 minutes of competition to warm up, which obviously affects your race performance — and you won't feel good either!

Competition/game warm-ups should begin 20–30 minutes before the competition start. Ease in with about 5 minutes of light, low heart-rate activity specific to the competition followed by about 5 minutes of easy, specific stretches. Continue your warm-up after stretching with light-activity, building intensity gradually to competition-pace heart rate over 5–10 minutes. You need to spend several minutes at competition-pace heart rate to be fully warmed up. The intensity is then dropped back to light-activity heart rate (for another 5–10 minutes) to keep warm. This should continue until the competition starts. Allow sufficient time for full recovery before the race begins.

Do not warm up too early as you will have to spend too long staying warm before the competition starts. In fact, the closer the warm-up is to start time, with adequate recovery, the better. Spending 30 minutes warming up with several minutes at competition pace will not harm your performance. If you are well conditioned this will, in fact, enhance your performance significantly.

If you are doing a multisport/triathlon race, warm up with light activity at a low heart rate in each discipline except for the sport you are to race in first. In that discipline, warm up to race-pace heart rate and use it to stay warm before race start.

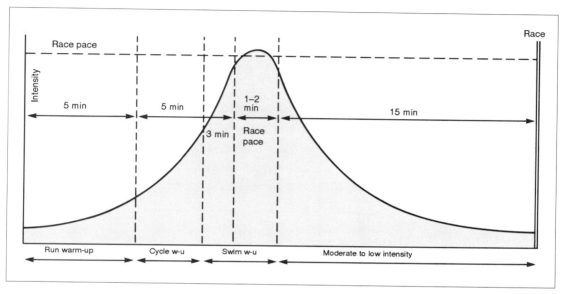

FIGURE 5.1:
Heart rates during race/game warm-ups prior to competition

HEART RATES AND COMPETITION

In shorter sporting events (<2 hours), and even in portions of longer events, competition heart rates may differ from training heart rates. During competition you may find that heart rates come up more quickly and are 5–10 beats higher than for the same perceived exertion (speed) in training.

As we've seen, resting heart rate may be elevated on race morning. Remember the guy who woke up on race morning and pulled out because he thought he was tired? The nervousness or anxiety that you feel before and during competitions seems to push your heart rate up. This is probably due to adenalin, a hormone the body produces when it is in a 'fight or flight' situation. Adrenalin 'hypes' the body up to prepare it for threatening (or 'life or death') situations. In other words, your body is preparing you for 'battle', or in this case, a competition.

When using heart rates for competition, make sure you know what your race/game heart rates are. 'Like' competitions or time trials can help you work this out.

I once experienced this difference in racing heart rates during a marathon. During training I discovered that 3-hour pace for me equated to a heart rate of 160. Accordingly, when I did my race-pace simulations in training, I trained at 160 heart rate. This worked well — my whole build-up went well, particularly my speedwork. Now it was time to race. I thought I'd be very clever. If a heart rate of 160 gave me 3-hour pace, all I needed to do was run the marathon at a heart rate of 160.

Come race day my heart rate at the start line was 100. When the gun went off, my heart rate quickly climbed to 160. I'd never seen my heart rate go up this quickly before but I thought, 'No problem, stick to the game plan.' As I continued, I felt as if I was going too slow. But I kept thinking, 'Stick to the game plan.'

By the 15-km mark I realised I was way off my intended 3-hour pace and had to accept a slower marathon time. Anxiety (adrenalin) had artificially elevated my racing heart rate. Running at a heart rate of 160 in the race was equivalent to running at a heart rate of 150 in training. I should have taken anxiety into account and added 10 beats to my training heart rate to get my racing heart rate.

This applies to most races under 2–3 hours in single-discipline sports, and under 4–6 hours in multi-discipline sports. In longer races you will tend to start with an elevated heart rate but it drops back to normal during the race.

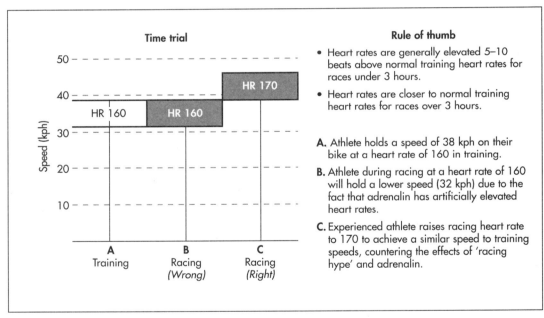

Time trial

Rule of thumb

- Heart rates are generally elevated 5–10 beats above normal training heart rates for races under 3 hours.
- Heart rates are closer to normal training heart rates for races over 3 hours.

A. Athlete holds a speed of 38 kph on their bike at a heart rate of 160 in training.

B. Athlete during racing at a heart rate of 160 will hold a lower speed (32 kph) due to the fact that adrenalin has artificially elevated heart rates.

C. Experienced athlete raises racing heart rate to 170 to achieve a similar speed to training speeds, countering the effects of 'racing hype' and adrenalin.

FIGURE 5.2:
Heart rates and racing

In Ironman triathlons, athletes may be horrified to discover that heart rates are well above what they expected when they come out of transitions and may remain elevated for 15–40 minutes after. Ignore this.

In summary, anxiety can elevate heart rates for competition and important speed sessions such as time trials. Add 5–10 beats for shorter races and/or test competition heart rates before the big day.

TIME TRIALS AND PACE JUDGEMENT

The best way to race triathlons, duathlons or any other form of time-trial distance event is to maintain an even pace or effort. An even pace enables you to use your energy in the most 'economic' way possible. Changes of pace or effort are expensive and drain your energy bank account quickly.

The even pace, of course, should be the fastest pace you can sustain for the entire race or time trial. This pace, for example, may be for a race of one hour at your anaerobic threshold pace.

Your race pace will have a corresponding heart rate (85 to 95 percent of HR^{max}). Once you know this heart rate, you can use it to help keep your effort strong and steady for an entire race or time trial. This is particularly useful when racing over hills or in windy conditions, as both situations contribute to race speed fluctuations which can confuse your perception of race pace.

When on the bike it is useful to link heart rate to cadence (how fast you are pedalling). This allows you to optimise gear changes as well as pace. Optimal time trial cadences are around 85–95 revs per minute (rpm), and around 90–95 rpm for most people.

An example of the heart rate/cadence link:

Optimal race-pace heart rate (tested) = 170–175.

Optimal cadence = 85–95.

Heart rate	Cadence	Analysis
172	87	Excellent. Hold effort.
180	89	Heart rate too high; you are going too hard. Change to easier gear.
140	92	Heart rate too low. Too easy. Change to a harder gear.

Note: You will need to watch heart rate and cadence constantly because both change as the course changes and you become fatigued.

Using heart rate to monitor effort on the bike is particularly useful for inexperienced cyclists, though notable improvements in performance have also been achieved by experienced riders using heart rate to gauge effort. Inexperienced cyclists often push too big a gear, causing severe leg fatigue. They end up 'legless' late in the race. This is because the lower the cadence (big gears), the more muscular the effort. The higher the cadence (small gears), the more cardiovascular the effort. The optimal cadence, of course, lies somewhere in the middle; for example, 90–110 rpm for a road race; 85–95 rpm for a time trial.

It is important for triathletes and duathletes to understand this because not only will monitoring heart rate on the bike help your bike time, but the less leg fatigue you can incur on the bike, the better you will go in the run (refer to *The Power to Perform* for more information).

This applies to time trial steady-state sports including time-trial cycling, triathlon or running.

FIGURE 5.3:
Heart rate vs
pedal cadence

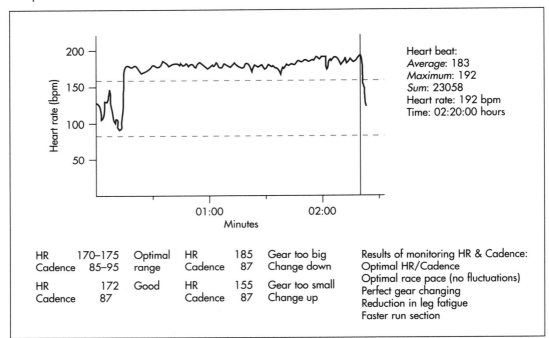

HR	170–175	Optimal	HR	185	Gear too big	Results of monitoring HR & Cadence:
Cadence	85–95	range	Cadence	87	Change down	Optimal HR/Cadence
HR		172	Good	HR	155	Gear too small	Optimal race pace (no fluctuations)
Cadence		87		Cadence	87	Change up	Perfect gear changing

Results of monitoring HR & Cadence:
Optimal HR/Cadence
Optimal race pace (no fluctuations)
Perfect gear changing
Reduction in leg fatigue
Faster run section

Heart rate monitors can be very good for working out or adjusting your race strategy. Note, though, that your racing heart rates tend to be 5–10 bpm higher during a race than in time trials because of race 'hype'.

VARIATIONS IN HEART RATES DURING RACING AND POSSIBLE CAUSES

Heart rate drops significantly during the race (see fig 5.4):

♥ started too fast.

♥ inadequate taper (legs too tired to hold pace for duration of race).

♥ not enough base distance work (specific to race).

♥ overtrained.

♥ hit the wall, bonked, legs 'blew up' in longer races.

Heart rate increases slightly during the race (see fig 5.5):

♥ started too slowly.

♥ ineffective warm-up.

♥ not enough speedwork (specific to race).

Heart rate increases significantly during the race (see fig 4.4):

♥ dehydrated (drink lots of water and check for other signs of dehydration).

Heart rate is too high at the start and remains too high for the duration of the race:

♥ too tired.

♥ overtrained.

♥ ill.

Heart rate 'jumps' or fluctuates greatly (150 to 220 bpm) in the space of a few beats:

♥ check transmitter and battery.

♥ wet your skin and the electrodes more.

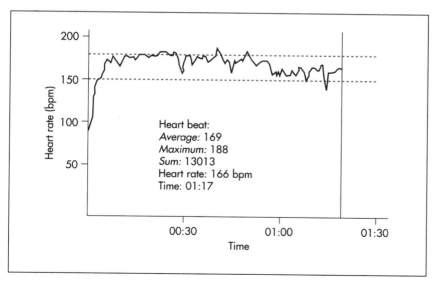

FIGURE 5.4:
This athlete started the race too fast. Note that heart rates drop off towards the end due to tired legs.

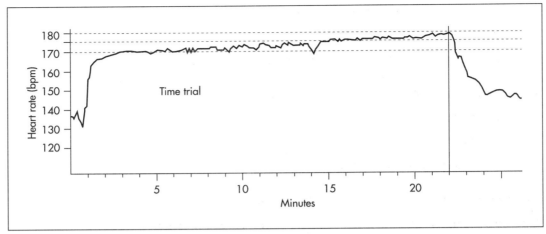

FIGURE 5.5: Rising heart rate during a race — this athlete started too slow!

♥ check signals aren't being affected by someone else's monitor or overhead power lines.

♥ accept that it could be a heart abnormality. Stop exercising and see a doctor as soon as possible.

Heart rate remains constant at usual race pace level:

♥ good race preparation and good race pace.

GLYCOGEN DEPLETION — HITTING THE WALL, GETTING THE BONK

Glycogen is energy stored in the muscle and it is your body's primary fuel source (after oxygen). During prolonged exercise, your body can reach a stage of glycogen depletion, after which it converts to using fat as the predominant fuel source. During this conversion you experience what is known as 'hitting the wall' or 'getting the bonk'. This can be very uncomfortable (in the case of hitting the wall, downright painful).

Hitting the wall is muscle-specific. In other words, you become glycogen-depleted only in the muscles being used. This is common in sports that involve continuous high intensities for over 2–4 hours.

The marathon has made hitting the wall a common experience. In this event it generally happens around the 30–35-km mark. You will find that quite suddenly your legs begin to tie up and it becomes painful to take each step. Unlike the romantic visions often portrayed of hitting the wall, it is not a mystical experience. It may not be the worst experience in the world, but it sure hurts like hell. Most athletes who are aiming to run a marathon hard will experience hitting the wall in some form. A lot end up walking.

When you hit the wall, you run out of glycogen in the muscles being used (in the marathon, your legs) and they cease to function effectively. The rest of you, however, is fine.

Bonking also involves glycogen depletion, but of a different kind. When you 'bonk' (not in the rude sense of the word), you run low on liver glycogen. This means that your blood glucose level drops. Rather than experiencing muscle-specific fatigue, the athlete/player will feel a more general fatigue.

In my experience, the symptoms of bonking are as follows. The first sign is a feeling of needing to slow the pace, and yawning. As you become more depleted you begin to feel an all-over tiredness. Further on, it becomes very difficult and painful to continue and you may start to fantasise about certain foods. You then begin to feel sleepy. (I once had an experience while running in a half-Ironman where I was quite literally almost asleep on my feet while at the same time fantasising about hamburgers.) Finally, you begin to feel dizzy.

I have known athletes to pass out while exercising. This is not only dangerous but it really hurts when you fall off your bike.

A friend of mine (Bob) was training on the Hawaiian Ironman bike course, checking it out for his wife who was competing a few days later, and he ran out of food. He eventually became so badly 'bonked', and so desperate, that he had to stop another athlete, who happened to be going by in the opposite direction, and beg him to share some of his food, which he very kindly did. He finally struggled back to his hotel and reported to his wife, Heather, that she shouldn't worry too much, it was just going to be the hardest bike ride of her life.

While out on a training ride for another Ironman, one member of our training group disappeared. When we realised that he had gone we turned back and eventually found him, rather tattered and torn, desperately riding to try to catch us. When we asked what had happened, he informed us that he had bonked, fallen asleep on his bike and crashed. We suspected there were better ways of catching some zzz's, but each to their own, I guess.

One year I found an Ironman competitor lying in such a peculiar position that I thought he had collapsed. He very coherently informed me, however, that he was a bit tired and was just having a little rest.

Bonking seems to be more common in cycling than in other sports but multi-discipline sportspeople also encounter it. It generally takes 4–10 hours to get into this state, and it occurs during long events at low intensity. Correct eating strategies during exercise, and effective training methods, will help you to avoid bonking.

Putting it All Together

Training variation:

♥ Race warm-ups — warm up to race-pace heart rate.

♥ Racing — racing heart rates are 5–10 beats higher than training heart rates for the same speed due to adrenalin.

♥ Time-trial racing can be improved by using a predetermined race-pace heart rate.

♥ Glycogen depletion — hitting the wall and getting the bonk drop racing heart rates and racing speeds due to lack of energy to supply the working muscles.

Weird Things

TO DO WITH YOUR HEART RATE MONITOR

Sex

If you have some free time on a Sunday afternoon, there are interesting (if odd) possibilities for heart rate monitor use. What about the simple act of making love? What happens?

I chickened out! I got another fearless stuntperson (whose identity will remain a secret for all eternity) to do the test.

Heart rates went from a resting value of 50 to a maximum of 145! That's nearly three times resting. This didn't involve any gymnastics or use of motorised devices: the subject was in a horizontal position of very low activity.

No prizes for guessing what happened at the peak heart rate during recording: let's just call it the 'big O'! The low total time of 15 minutes also indicated a certain lack of stamina in the discipline.

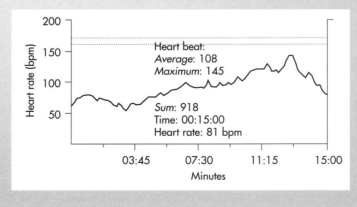

Heart rates and the environment

Heart rates and altitude

At higher altitudes, there is less oxygen per volume of air and the barometric pressure is consequently lower. The air therefore is 'thinner'.

As a sports person's exercising muscles require oxygen to work, less oxygen in the air means that the muscles do not function as well. This adversely affects performance.

Aerobic (endurance) ability is affected at altitudes above approximately 1,500 m (5,000 ft). Above that altitude there is an approximately 3-percent decrease in aerobic ability with every 300-metre increase in height above sea level.

For example:

Altitude	Aerobic ability
0 m	100%
1,976 m (6,500 ft)	90%
4,286 m (14,100 ft)	75%
6,992 m (23,000 ft)	50%

Performance changes at altitude for athletics in Mexico City (2,250 m; 7,400 ft):

Distance	Changes
100–400 m	Enhanced 1–2%
3,000 m steeplechase to 5,000 m	Impaired 5–6%
10,000 m to marathon	Impaired 6–7%

The athlete /player adapts to altitude stress by increasing haemoglobin and red blood cell production. This increases the oxygen-carrying capacity of the blood, which in turn increases performance potential compared to the unadapted state.

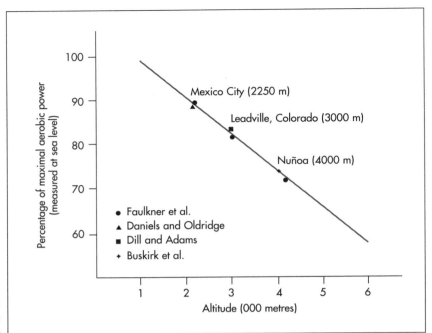

FIGURE 6.1:
Changes in aerobic
ability due to altitude

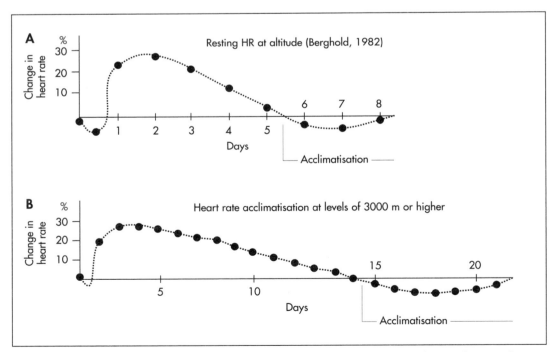

FIGURE 6.2: The effect of altitude on heart rate over (A) 8 days and (B) 21 days
of acclimatisation

The most rapid increase in red blood cells occurs in the first three to four weeks, and it may continue to increase gradually for up to a year.

It generally takes between 8–10 days to adapt to altitude (excluding taper). On arrival at altitude you will experience shortness of breath, and heart rate will soon become elevated by about 10 percent above your normal resting heart rate (although it may actually drop in the first few hours at altitude).

At altitudes over 3,000 m (10,000 ft) your resting heart rate can be 50 percent higher than normal. You may also experience headaches, nausea, lethargy, loss of appetite and sleep disturbances.

On the second day at altitude you will become progressively more tired. Training must now be conducted very carefully — it is very easy to overtrain. Any mistake in training will be very costly, and so training load (intensity/volume) is generally reduced during this period (intensity more so than volume).

FACTORS TO CONSIDER WHEN TRAINING AND COMPETING AT ALTITUDE

1. Hydration is very important. Dehydration is greatly exaggerated at altitude, so it is very important to ensure that you consume large quantities of fluid before, during and after training (mild dehydration can take up to 24 hours to rectify, and this may affect the next critical workout). You should weigh yourself before and after training (0.1 kg weight loss = 100 ml; 1 kg = 1,000 ml) and replace the weight lost with the equivalent amount of fluid. Unless you are using multivitamin supplements, urine colour should remain clear.

2. Regular blood tests are necessary leading up to arrival at altitude. There are a number of blood parameters to check. Ferritin (iron stores) and complete iron are particularly important as these are used to build the red blood cells that are produced as you adapt to altitude. Low iron stores can lead to an athlete/player performing poorly or getting sick soon after arrival at altitude. Foods rich in iron are, therefore, a very important part of the pre-altitude dietary plan (particularly for women). It may also be of use to measure baseline haemoglobin levels, full blood count and haematocrit (the volume of red blood cells per unit of blood). People often overlook the importance of vitamin B12 and folic acid in the production of red blood cells. These levels can be tested as part of a routine laboratory screening and should be carried out before going to altitude, as deficiencies may affect haemoglobin and red blood cell production quite significantly, thus affecting performance.

3. Don't sit around during the first few days at altitude. Light exercise stimulates breathing and circulation, slightly quickening your adjustment. Train very lightly during the first few days.

4. Rest and recovery should be emphasised. An athlete/player will require more recovery on arrival at altitude.

5. Eat smaller meals but more of them, since digestion can be more difficult at altitude. Emphasise carbohydrates for recovery.

6. Nutrition plays a large part in maintaining good health and form during altitude adaptation. This is worth following up with a sports nutritionist.

7. A stopover may help effective adaptation. Flying into a competition where adaptation includes adjusting to altitude, jet lag and heat at the same time may not be the most effective plan. It may be better to adapt to heat and recover from jet lag at sea level, and then go to altitude (jet lag recovery = 1 day for every time zone travelling east, 3/4 days per time zone travelling west; heat acclimatisation takes approximately 8–10 days). If heat acclimatisation is required, it may be better to heat-acclimatise artificially before leaving home. (*Note:* more research into jet lag and heat acclimatisation is needed before definitive guidelines on overcoming these conditions can be offered.)

8. You need to be very fit/conditioned before going to altitude.

9. Athletes/players are more susceptible to infection during the adaptation period to altitude. Be very careful with recovery, nutrition and health.

10. Athletes/players suffering from asthma may experience difficulty in acclimatising to altitude.

11. Make sure you are prepared for sudden changes in weather and temperature at altitude.

12. Use a humidifier on arrival at altitude (the air at altitude is dry and can dehydrate you, particularly when you are sleeping).

13. It appears that training at altitude is not the major cause of adaptation problems. Rather, it is the recovery from training (the 'live high, train low' theory).

There are a number of effects an athlete/player must consider when training during the 'adaptation to altitude' period. These are:

1. The aerodynamic effect. The air is thinner at altitude, so there is less wind resistance. This means you travel through the air faster (i.e. all other things being equal, a cyclist will travel faster at altitude than at sea level).

2. The cardiovascular effect. Due to the thinner air at altitude, less oxygen can be

taken in during the adaptation phase. Therefore, you will only be able to exercise at a slightly lower training speed from the aerobic (endurance) level (i.e. running at the same sea level-speed will be too intense and you will end up overtraining; training speed, therefore, must be modified for the altitude and the degree of acclimatisation).

3. The muscular effect. With a decreased aerobic ability at altitude, the cyclist's ability to apply strength endurance is reduced (a cyclist will move faster due to the thinner air but may not be able to push as hard on the pedals, thereby losing strength endurance during their weeks at altitude).

4. The motor pattern effect. The athlete/player's cardiovascular ability at altitude is initially impaired; this can result in their leg or arm cadence being slower than it was at sea level because they don't have the aerobic power to go fast. As a consequence their muscles 'learn' to move more slowly, i.e. the cardiovascular system gets trained at altitude but leg speed or stroke rate don't and may actually get worse!

WHAT DOES ALL THIS MEAN?

You need to maintain cardiovascular, muscular and motor pattern ability as close as possible to competition. Some athletes/players get around the problem of training at altitude by living at altitude (to get the altitude effect) and coming down to sea level (under 1,000 m) for strength endurance and speed training. Of course, if you have to compete at altitude, you must train at altitude.

It's also worth noting that there is currently no proof that altitude training enhances sea level performance, although a lot of athletes/players feel it works. However, if you are going to prepare at altitude for sea level performance, you need to know all the pluses and minuses. (For more information on how to train at altitude, see *The Power to Perform*.)

HEART RATE MONITORS AND ALTITUDE

Heart rate monitors are very useful for avoiding training errors at altitude. Uses include:

1. Measuring degree of adaptation to altitude

In the first few hours at altitude, heart rate will drop. After this, it will begin to rise. At 2,000 m your heart rate will be about 10 percent above your sea level heart rate. At 4,500 m it will be about 50 percent higher. As you acclimatise, resting and training heart rates will return to normal, or even lower. At this point, acclimatisation is complete. By measuring the number of days required for your heart rate to return to sea level rates, the time it takes to adapt can be calculated.

2. Matching altitude and sea-level intensities

Initially, it is easy to overdo training at altitude. The tendency is to push too hard because you are going so slowly due to the diminishment in your aerobic ability (you may be faster on the bike, however, because of the reduction in air resistance). By using your heart rate monitor you can train at the same intensities as at sea level, without succumbing to the desire to increase your speed. If you go directly to altitude, speedwork is not recommended during the first week. Once adaptation has taken place, training workloads similar to those carried out at sea level will be possible.

3. Setting correct rest periods between intervals

If you are doing speedwork at altitude, particularly intervals, rest periods need to be longer because recovery takes longer. To ensure your rest periods are not too short (or too long), don't begin exercising until your heart rate has dropped the same amount as it would at sea level (40–60 bpm for most athletes/players). During the adaptation phase it will take longer for your heart rate to drop than it would at sea level at the same intensity.

HEAT AND HUMIDITY

When you exercise, your muscle activity produces heat and raises your body temperature. Your body tries to keep its temperature down to maintain the equilibrium of your core and deeper tissues (the 'thermal balance').

Your body dissipates heat in a number of ways. It raises your heart rate to pump more blood to your skin, and radiates and conducts (loses) heat to the surrounding air. The hotter the surroundings, the higher your heart rate. Sweating also occurs to take the heat away. The sweat on the hot skin is evaporated as air

FIGURE 6.3:
The effect of heat
on heart rate

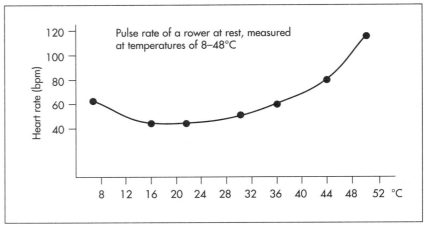

(wind) passes over it, cooling the body. The body is therefore able to retain a fairly constant temperature for optimal operation.

If the environmental temperature is high, it is harder for the body to lose heat, and if the humidity is high, sweat does not evaporate as well.

It takes seven to ten days to acclimatise to hot, humid climates, and two to three weeks to fully adapt. This acclimatisation period does not include tapering for competition, as you should be recovering in taper, not adapting.

When you travel to any country where the ambient temperature is above 25.6° C, acclimatisation is necessary. Even if the temperature is below 25.6° C, but hotter than where you normally train, some form of acclimatisation is advisable. But the acclimatisation must be specific to the competition environment, heat and humidity.

I heard one tragic story about an athlete who prepared for a running event in a hot environment by training in the heat. On race day, however, it was very hot and very humid. During the race the athlete collapsed and died. He had adapted to the heat but not to the humidity!

In case this scares you, there may have been other factors involved in the athlete's death, but the basic point is well illustrated.

The key to acclimatisation is to get used to exercising in the heat. It is not good enough simply to live in the hot environment. You must train in the heat (same environmental conditions, same training intensity and a similar training duration).

When you first arrive in a hot environment you will be very susceptible to fatigue, so reduce training volumes and intensities. Start with short, low-intensity workouts, and do them in the cooler times of the day (early morning and evening).

Over the next 7–10 days, gradually return to normal training volumes and intensities. Be very careful, though, not to do too much when you arrive at the competition venue. This can overtire you and impair the following workouts.

It is important to understand the relationship between temperature and humidity. Temperatures up to 25° C are safe, even in high humidity. However, when the temperature climbs to 27° C, an increase in humidity can be very dangerous.

High humidity (water vapour in the air) will not allow adequate evaporation of sweat from the body. Sweating is one way the body reduces its core temperature. If the core temperature gets too high you begin to experience the first symptoms of heat stress. If it continues to climb there is the potential for heat exhaustion or heat stroke.

Temperature is not the only contributing factor to heat stress. Other factors include lack of sleep, infection and glycogen depletion.

It is important that you understand the symptoms of heat stress.

Early symptoms are excessive sweating or cessation of sweating, dizziness, goose bumps, headaches, nausea and vomiting.

Imagine this nightmare. You race in a very hot, very humid environment. The duration of the race is four hours, and you are not really fit enough for it, nor are you heat acclimatised.

At the start of the race, your heart rate rises so more blood can be pumped to the skin and your sweat rate increases to aid cooling. Because you have not acclimatised, your body's ability to sweat is poor (it's not used to sweating that much). You are also unfit, so your body is working harder, and this is compounded by the extra work that the heat is making you do.

As a result, you're not sweating well and your body temperature is climbing. To make matters worse, the high humidity and the low wind level mean that the small amount of sweat that you are producing is not evaporating properly. The cooling is not working and you're getting hotter.

On top of this, you don't drink (you lose fluid during exercise through sweating and respiration, and you're not replacing it) so the water content in your body is starting to drop. That means the water level in the blood drops and the blood thickens. To keep the blood being pumped to the skin, the heart has to pump more — hence the higher heart rate. But the blood volume has dropped so much that the heart can't pump blood to the skin any more.

You begin to feel disorientated and have goose bumps (no blood going to the skin). The heart finds it too hard to pump the thickened blood and you have a heart attack.

In short: pay close attention to heat, humidity and hydration, and understand that not doing so can have serious consequences.

I had to sit an athlete down on Pay n' Save hill (Palani Road) during the Hawaiian Ironman in 1990 as he had developed quite a list and was weaving all over the road due to dehydration.

How to deal with the heat

1. If you are doing speedwork in hot conditions, initially do shorter intervals with longer rests. Alternatively, do speedwork in the cooler parts of the day.

2. In hot conditions, as all athletes/players know, the body loses a lot of fluid. This is particularly so during the first four days of training in a hot environment. It is critical, therefore, that you replenish fluid supplies in order to avoid dehydration.

    Drink before, during and after workouts, and steadily throughout the day.

This may seem excessive but thirst is not a good indicator of the need for fluids — if you feel thirsty, dehydration has begun — so it is best to establish a regular drinking pattern.

It is also a good idea in hot climates to weigh yourself before and after workouts to keep a check on fluid loss. Any weight loss is fluid loss (although during intense racing 35 percent can be due to loss of the muscle energy, glycogen, and 65 percent due to water loss.) Drink 1 litre of fluid for every kilogram of bodyweight lost during exercise.

A 2-percent loss in bodyweight after a workout or race (a 1.4-kg loss for a 70-kg athlete/player) represents a fluid loss due to thermal or exercise-induced dehydration. This decreases muscular strength and endurance considerably. Dehydration can affect training for 24–36 hours, as it takes time to rehydrate completely.

3. Wear loose-fitting clothing so that the air circulates around your body. This helps sweat evaporation and cooling.

4. Wear light-coloured clothing that reflects sunlight, rather than dark clothing that absorbs the sun's heat. Wearing a light-coloured cap in hot conditions can also help keep you cool.

5. Clothing that 'wicks' sweat away from the skin, such as polypropylene and cotton, is also good for evaporation. Materials that are impermeable to water or that hold water and become damp affect the cooling mechanism of sweating and increase the chance of heat injury.

6. Watch air-conditioned rooms. This can make the air very dry. If you sleep eight hours in an air-conditioned room you can get quite dehydrated (depending on the outside humidity). Put a glass of water or water bottle by your bed so you can drink in the night if you wish. Note, though, that air-conditioning in your room at night can help in your early heat acclimatisation; i.e. exercise and live in the heat, sleep in the cool.

7. Endurance athletes when racing (especially running) constantly check wind conditions. In head winds and side winds, the cooling effect of the wind is greater. A following wind will not have the same cooling effect, as

FIGURE 6.4:
The effect of cooling on heart rate

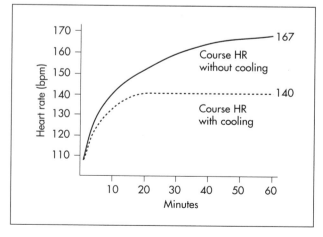

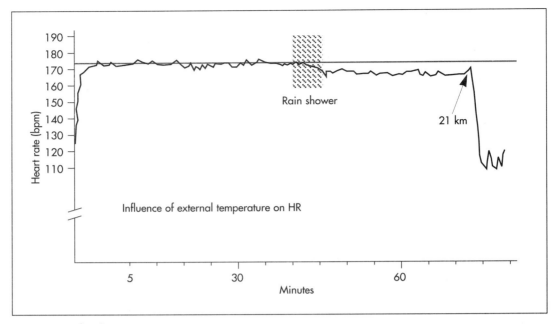

Figure 6.5: A rain shower cools the athlete, causing exercise heart rate to drop.

the evaporation of sweat is reduced (the speed of the wind passing over the body is slower as you are moving with the wind).

If you see your heart rate begin to climb inappropriately during a warm weather race/game, sponge yourself down. The extra water on the skin will evaporate and have a cooling effect. Putting water on the head is particularly good for cooling.

In the Hawaiian Ironman in Kona, there is an interesting first timers' trap. In the first 6 kilometres of the marathon the run is very sheltered from the wind due to buildings and trees. There is no wind to help cool the body and evaporate sweat. The athlete does not feel hot in these conditions, just grotty! They can't understand why they are feeling so bad and with the famous lava fields coming up, things look pretty 'ugly'. Often the athlete pulls out. What they don't realise is that if they put excess water on themselves to help evaporation and patiently wait for the lava where the wind is blowing, aiding cooling so they will feel better.

ARTIFICIAL HEAT ACCLIMATISATION

Artificial heat acclimatisation may be necessary if you cannot get to the competition venue early enough to acclimatise fully. This form of heat training has been carried out in heat chambers, greenhouses and heated training rooms. For many athletes, however, these techniques may not be available.

Another technique for inducing hot conditions artificially involves wearing excessive layers of clothing while exercising, especially on the head.

To create humidity, place wet towels near a heater in an enclosed room. But if you are training in a heated room, use a fan to aid the evaporation of sweat from the body.

HEART RATES AND HEAT

Heat affects heart rate in much the same way as altitude does.

Degree of heat adaptation

During heat adaptation, training and resting heart rates will be elevated above normal. Sweating also increases. Acclimatisation can be considered complete when heart rates return to normal. This should take 7–10 days.

A fully acclimatised athlete/player may have lower resting and training heart rates than normal.

Training intensities and heat

When you are training in the heat your body is under more stress, so training speeds or times for an unacclimatised athlete/player will be slower for the same intensity or effort. Adjust for this by using your heart rate monitor to train at the same intensity (not speed!) that you would use away from the heat. This reduces the chance of overfatigue or overtraining. It also allows adaptation to occur more smoothly, and maintains the continuity of the training.

Rests between intervals — how long?

As with altitude, heat will increase the time it takes an unacclimatised athlete/player to recover between intervals. However, the time it takes for heart rate to drop to a recovery level (e.g. a 40–60-bpm drop) will help compensate for the extra stress the heat places on the body. Monitoring heart rate between intervals to gauge recovery is, therefore, better than using arbitrary recovery times.

COLD

Cold temperatures cool the body. To maintain an optimal temperature in the cold, blood is drawn away from the body's extremities and the skin, and delivered to the core (heart, lungs, brain). That's why you get cold hands and feet in cold weather, and why, in extremely cold conditions, you can get frostbite of the fingers and toes.

Since the body does not have to pump as much blood to the extremities and the skin in cold weather, heart rate drops when temperature drops. Shivering may increase your heart rate again.

COPING WITH TRAINING AND COMPETITION IN COLD CONDITIONS

1. Dress in layers that provide an insulating barrier of air that helps retain body heat.

2. Ideally, the clothing should allow for the evaporation of sweat while still providing added protection against the cold.

3. The clothing closest to the skin should be polypropylene, as this helps 'wick' sweat away from the skin.

4. On top of polypropylene, a woollen shirt and/or sweater is useful, as it is warm and somewhat water-resistant.

5. Finally, an outer waterproof coat (one that breathes is best) is advisable.

If clothing becomes wet due to sweat or weather, the insulating qualities are decreased and body heat is lost. Manufacturers are now producing lightweight clothing with good qualities of insulation, freedom of movement and evaporation, making training and competing, even in harsh conditions, both possible and enjoyable.

The primary aim when training and competing at low temperatures is to prevent cold exposure and to avoid damp clothing. Cold weather, wind chill and wet clothing can be a deadly combination.

Alcohol consumption can also increase the rate of heat loss and cause a drop in blood glucose levels, resulting in a decrease in energy.

I remember a cycling championship one year that was held in very cold conditions. One of the cyclists became hypothermic and disorientated, and in a cold-induced, confused state rode off the race course by accident, continued 10 km down the road and collapsed in a ditch. Fortunately a passerby wondered why a state-of-the-art racing bike was lying abandoned on the side of the road, stopped to check things out, and found a very cold, unconscious cyclist lying in the ditch.

If you are stopping and starting during training, put on warm clothing during the breaks otherwise body temperature will drop, muscle function will be impaired and performance will decline. Warm-ups are extremely important during cold conditions.

Warm up longer and more thoroughly in cold conditions to prevent injury and a drop in performance.

POLLUTION AND SMOKING

Carbon monoxide (CO) can also have an effect on training heart rates. Carbon monoxide can be inhaled through smoking (active or passive) and through exhaust fumes from vehicles. When inhaled, carbon monoxide binds to haemoglobin in the blood. Haemoglobin carries oxygen around the body to the muscles, so this binding affects performance drastically. CO will bind to haemoglobin 200 times more easily than oxygen, and it is held in the bloodstream for many hours.

It only takes a small amount of CO to decrease the oxygen-carrying capacity of the blood. For example, one cigarette (or being around a smoker all day) can affect about 5 percent of your haemoglobin. Heavy smokers can have up to 15 percent of their haemoglobin bound to CO. This can have a huge effect on performance and, of course, heart rate. Why? Simple: with less oxygen in the system, the heart must work harder to supply enough blood to the working muscles.

Traffic pollution on a Los Angeles motorway averages 55 ppm (parts per million) of CO. If someone stays for an hour, while inactive, on or alongside the motorway, the CO concentration in their blood goes up 3 percent. After 8 hours, it's up 8 percent. Try driving home in heavy traffic for an hour and then having a workout afterwards. Blah!

In the graph shown in figure 6.6, a smoker who had not smoked for three hours did the following test: four minutes of exercise (ergometer; 75 watts), followed by four minutes' rest. Five workloads of four minutes were conducted with four periods of four minutes' rest between them. During the third and fourth rest periods one cigarette was smoked.

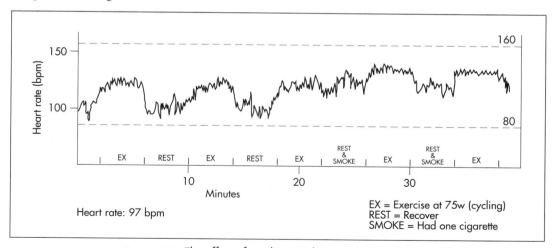

FIGURE 6.6: The effect of smoking on heart rate

The result? Heart rates during the first three workloads were 120–125, while during the two rest periods they were 90–95. Heart rates in the final two workloads (having had a cigarette before each) were 10 beats higher and in the two rest periods were 20 beats higher. The heart rates may also have been affected by the nicotine in the cigarette, which creates a temporary 'hyped up' effect.

I have a friend who has done many Ironman triathlons and during this 'world's hardest one-day sport event', he'll stop momentarily and light up to relax. Wow!!

PUTTING IT ALL TOGETHER

HEART RATE RESPONSES

Variation	Initial	Short-Term	Long-Term
Altitude	Down	Up	Normal
Heat	Down	Up	Normal
Cold	Down	Up	N/A
Humidity	Down	Up	Normal
Pollution & Smoking	Up	Up	Up

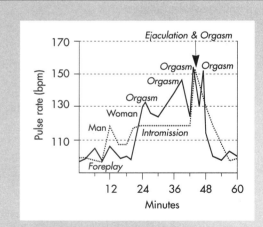

Weird Things
TO DO WITH YOUR HEART RATE MONITOR

More Sex

This heart rate monitor sex graph derives from a university study (Ford and Beach), which measured both male and female heart rates. You can see this was a big study — the participants worked very hard! The male hit the 'big O' once and the woman managed four of 'big O' calibre. Impressive — 60 minutes with a total of 5 orgasms!! The only question is what is intromission — are they in a 'holding pattern' or is that where the male goes out to get the jaffas?

CHAPTER 7

HEART RATES AND AIR TRAVEL

AIR TRAVEL AND JET LAG

You may have to travel long distances to a competition venue or during your working life, possibly flying across many time zones. This leads to a disruption in the normal daily rhythm of bodily functions. These rhythms are known as circadian rhythms and represent our 'body clock'.

Our internal clock controls physiological and psychological systems on a 24-hour, day/night cycle (although, if given free rein, the body actually settles into a 25-hour cycle). This clock is tucked away in two tiny portals in the brain called the suprachiasmatic nuclei. These, along with the pineal gland (also located deep in the brain), act as an internal clock that controls virtually every biochemical process in the body.

What causes our so-called body clock to regulate our functioning? Well, mainly the presence or absence of cues. For instance, the presence/absence of light, meals, physical activity and sleep all contribute to the maintenance of the circadian rhythm.

Functions that follow regular rhythms include sleep, body temperature, heart rate, blood pressure and metabolic rate. Notice the change in the number of times my heart beats in a period of four hours on a morning or evening shift due to circadian rhythms.

Four hours of working day—heart rate

Date	Shift	Average	Total
22/10	p.m.	68	16,320
23/10	a.m.	61	14,640
24/10	p.m.	67	16,080
25/10	a.m.	62	14,880
29/10	p.m.	74	17,760 (sick)
30/10	a.m.	66	15,840 (sick)

| 31/10 | a.m. | 64 | 15,360 |
| 01/11 | p.m. | 72 | 17,280 |

Average (a.m.) 14,960
Average (p.m.) 16,560 — 1600 times more, excluding the effects of sickness

Shifts: a.m. = 7.00 a.m.–3.30 p.m.,   p.m. = 11.30 a.m. –8.30 p.m.

Performance factors that also appear to have circadian rhythms are strength, power and reaction time.

Rapid travel across time zones leads to the desynchronisation of circadian rhythms and results in the feeling commonly known as 'jet lag' (though it would probably be more accurate to call it 'body-lag', as it is the body that lags behind). The symptoms of jet lag include malaise, tiredness during the day, appetite loss and disturbed sleeping patterns.

Even travelling through one time zone will affect your body clock, but the effects only become significant after a time change of three or more hours. The greater the distance travelled, and the more time zones crossed, the greater the jet lag.

Direction of travel is also important. It takes between 30 and 50 percent less time to adjust when travelling westward compared with travelling the same distance eastward. North/south travel has little effect.

To work out how long it may take to overcome jet lag, allow one day for every time zone crossed when travelling eastward, and 18 hours (0.75 of a day) for every time zone crossed when travelling westward. It seems easier for the body clock to adapt to longer days than to shorter days while travelling. This may be due to the effects of sleep. Of course, not all people react the same way.

RISK FACTORS FOR JET LAG

♥ Number of time zones crossed — the more time zones you cross, the greater the effects of jet lag.

♥ Direction of travel — travelling eastward shortens the day/night cycle. This is harder to adjust to than travelling westward, when the days are lengthened.

♥ Age — the older you are, the more difficult it is to cope with jet lag.

♥ Personality type — more outgoing people have less trouble adjusting to jet lag.

♥ Rhythms — the more rigid your lifestyle (waking, sleeping, eating, etc.), the more difficult the adjustment.

♥ Night owls vs morning people — night owls cope better than morning people.

JET LAG AND THE ATHLETE/PLAYER

Jet lag affects the athlete/player's body in many ways. The body's daily high and low points are altered, which in turn affects energy systems, reaction times and concentration levels.

This is partly due to the disruption of the production of the hormones involved in controlling body function. This disruption results in a greater likelihood of muscle cramps, tiredness, headaches, digestive disorders and kidney dysfunction.

When you are jet lagged, strength decreases, particularly at high speed, and muscle endurance declines. Psychological effects include a reduced feeling of well-being, low arousal, low motivation to train, and increases in malaise and irritability.

The tables in figure 7.1 show the time required for resynchronisation of various bodily processes, including heart rate, following jet lag.

The effect of jet lag on heart rate varies according to the following:

♥ Number of time zones crossed.

♥ Direction of travel.

♥ Personal rhythms.

♥ Individual fitness.

♥ Individual response to jet lag, including resynchronisation strategies.

Aside from time zones crossed and direction of travel, which we've already discussed, your own personal rhythms can greatly affect how you adjust to jet lag. People with more regimented lifestyles will find adjustment more difficult than people with more flexible routines. And the fitter you are, the faster you recover.

Finally, while different people respond differently to jet lag, using resynchronisation strategies can speed up recovery significantly.

Specific reasons why heart rate might be affected by jet lag and jet travel include:

♥ Disruption of circadian rhythms (usual heart rate high/low points in 24 hours have moved).

♥ The stress of flying — some people are more anxious about flying than others. This pushes heart rate up, particularly during take-off and landing procedures.

♥ Cabin pressure — the artificial altitude in the cabin (usually equivalent to

Eastbound flights

	Time zone changes (hours)					
	2	4	6	8	10	12
Adrenalin	2	4	6	8	8–10	8–10
Body temperature	3	6	9	12	12	12+
Bowel movements	3	6–7	9–10	12	12	12+
Heart rate	2	4	6	8	8–10	8–10
Performance (psychomotor)	3	6–7	9–10	12	12	12+
Reaction time (vigilance)	1–2	3–4	5	6–7	8	8
Sleep pattern	1	3–4	4–5	6–7	8–9	8-9

Westbound flights

	Time zone changes (hours)					
	2	4	6	8	10	12
Adrenalin	1–2	2–3	4	5–6	6–7	8–10
Body temperature	2	4	6	8	10	12+
Bowel movements	2–3	4–5	7	9	11	12+
Heart rate	1–2	2–3	4	5–6	6–7	8–10
Performance (psychomotor)	2	4	6	8	10	12+
Reaction time (vigilance)	1	1–2	2–3	3	4	5–8
Sleep pattern	1	2	3–4	4–5	5–6	8–9

FIGURE 7.1:
Typical number of days until resynchronisation after time zone changes

1,000–1,500 m) — can create mild oxygen deficiency, promoting lethargy. Different aircraft have different levels of pressurisation. A Boeing 747 Jumbo jet, for example, is pressurised to 1,400 m (4,700 ft; a 17 percent drop in available oxygen over sea level), whereas a DC9 is pressurised to 2,900 m (8,000 ft; a 33 percent drop). The higher altitudes simulated by cabin pressure result in the heart rate responding in the same way it does to altitude: it may drop initially but will increase after a few hours.

♥ Dehydration due to humidity — the low humidity in an aircraft cabin can lead to a dry mouth, sore throat and mild dehydration. Humidity in most aircraft is around 8–12 percent, which is very low. The longer the flight, the lower the humidity becomes. This is because the cruising altitude of aircraft has a humidity of almost zero. Most of the humidity in a long flight is the sweat and breath of the passengers (now you know why it's easy to catch a cold during a long flight). Fluid consumption, therefore, is very important to avoid dehydration.

Lower fluid volumes in the body mean the heart has to pump faster to maintain the correct supply of oxygen and blood. Thus, lower body fluid volumes may elevate heart rate. Increase fluid intake by drinking water, fruit juices or electrolyte drinks. A lot of athletes/players drink plenty of water on their flight and flush out electrolytes — this will impair muscle function to some extent, decreasing the quality of following workouts. Avoid alcohol and coffee because of their dehydrating effects.

♥ Air quality — aside from altitude and humidity, air quality can be discussed in terms of recirculation. The recirculation of the air in an aircraft affects its quality. Older aircraft replace 100 percent of the cabin atmosphere with fresh air every three minutes. Newer aircraft, to save fuel costs, replace 50 percent and recirculate 50 percent every six or seven minutes. Ventilation is usually two to three times higher in First Class than in Economy Class.

The quality of the air is important. Sitting in the smoking section or the transitional section between smoking and non-smoking (for those flights that still have smoking) means less oxygen is available. Stale air or air containing carbon monoxide from cigarette smoke may increase heart rate.

Taken together, all these factors can affect the time it takes for your heart rate to return to normal after jet lag, and your ability to recover from a long flight.

When a friend of mine flew to London recently we tested all the theories. As you can see the results, shown in figure 7.2, were marginal. The effect on heart rate of take-off and landing may be the result of mild nervous tension and the plane's acceleration, which tenses up the muscles.

The actual flight may show change but the only way to check this accurately is to measure cumulative heart rate during the flight (total number of beats in a flight) and compare this to a similar but non-flying situation.

My friend's morning resting heart rate was slightly elevated in the days

**Denise Maylin
Auckland–London on
Air New Zealand 747-400**

Window seat, front cabin

Normal resting heart rate is around 50

22:00	70	Ascent
23:00	68	
00:00	69	
01:00	sleep	
02:00	sleep	
03:00	sleep	
04:00	63	
05:00	63	
06:00	71	Breakfast
07:00	70	Descent
08:00	82	In transit
09:00	83	In transit
10:00	53	Boarded
11:00	58	Ascent
12:00	62	
13:00	62	
14:00	60	
15:00	66	
16:00	65	
17:00	63	
18:00	sleep	
19:00	sleep	
20:00	62	
21.00	66	
22:00	68	
23:00	68	Arrival

Following days

Morning 1	53
Morning 2	53
Morning 3	50
Morning 4	51

FIGURE 7.2:
The effects of air travel on heart rate — causing jet lag, lack of sleep, cabin pressure, low humidity

following the flight, but it is difficult to say whether this was induced by jet lag or just by having sat on an aeroplane for hours on end with little or no sleep.

PUTTING IT ALL TOGETHER

The following table summarises the effect of travel on heart rate.

Variation	Initial	Short-Term	Long-Term
Air travel	Down	Up	N/A
Jet lag	Up	Up	Normal

This heart rate graph records a young male doing his first 3,000-m free-fall parachute jump. Standing at the plane door about to jump into the 'blue void', his heart beat was 177 beats per minute. A normal heart rate for someone of his age when standing would be 70 — that means 107 beats of mortal terror created by adrenalin.

His heart rate dropped as he dropped, but when it came time to pull the rip cord, his heart rate shot up again (probably due to anxiety about whether certain apparatus would work). Again his heart rate dropped as he realised he was gently drawing closer to terra firma. Then, when he touched the ground, his heart rate shot up due to exhilaration.

Weird Things
TO DO WITH YOUR HEART RATE MONITOR

Jump out of a Plane from 3,000 m

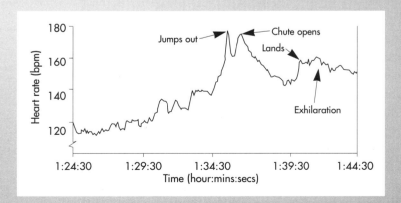

CHAPTER 8

HEART RATES AND OVERTRAINING

OVERTRAINING

ADAPTATION VERSUS OVERLOAD

Adaptation — your body's ability to adjust to exercise stress and get 'stronger' — is a far better training strategy than overtraining. In overtraining, the body cannot tolerate the exercise stress being placed upon it. This leads to fatigue (muscular and general), loss of performance and training burnout.

Overtraining needs to be differentiated from the short-term tiredness that occurs whenever training load increases. Overtraining is a state of prolonged fatigue characterised by decrements or plateaus in performance despite continued training. In chronically overtrained sports people, a decline in performance of 5 to 15 percent is not uncommon. One study showed a drop of 11 to 15 percent in training pace, and a 43 to 71 percent drop in training distance!

So, write this down now: training too much, too hard or too quickly will not lead to long-term performance gains. It will lead to injury, fatigue, illness and staleness.

In a study of élite runners, it was found that 60 percent overtrained at some point in their career. Too many athletes/players, especially the younger ones, are lost to sport because they train too hard too soon, break down, and lose interest. Alternatively, they are unable to train at the levels they once did because of continuing health or biomechanical problems.

While overtraining is a common problem in endurance athletes, particularly those training for ultra-distance races and those who race often or have too many games, it also occurs in sports people who try to fit training in around work and social obligations, leaving little time for recovery (physical and mental).

The main causes of overtraining are:

1. Inadequate recovery between training sessions.

2. Excessive amounts of high-intensity (and sometimes high-volume) training.

3. Sudden changes in training load (distance, duration or intensity).

Other training factors that contribute to overtraining are:

1. Intense strength training.

2. Frequent competition and travel.

3. Monotony in the training programme.

4. No off-season.

Non-training factors that contribute to overtraining include:

1. Inadequate nutrition.

2. Insufficient sleep and rest.

3. Anxiety about life events, e.g. exams, a new job.

4. Occupational stress.

5. Mental conflict.

6. Changes and irregularities in lifestyle.

7. Repeated failure to achieve goals.

Overtraining athletes/players may be doing no more training than their peers, but due to outside pressures, medical problems or even their personal tolerance to training, may be feeling fatigued. Remember, to achieve performance improvement the body must be allowed to adapt gradually to increased training volume and intensities. It is not absolute training duration (volume) and intensities that matter, but rather the amount of training and speedwork you personally can recover from — no recovery, no improvement!

Of course, your ability to recover depends largely on your training history. The more years you have been in the sport, the bigger your base, and the more training you can do and recover from.

SYMPTOMS OF OVERTRAINING

EMOTIONAL AND BEHAVIOURAL CHANGES

♥ Lethargy and excessive fatigue, especially at rest.

♥ Loss of purpose, energy and competitive drive; poor attitude, confusion, loss of enthusiasm to train.

♥ Feelings of helplessness and being trapped in a routine.

♥ Feeling emotionally unstable; excessive emotional reactions.

♥ Loss of libido (interest in sex).

♥ Increased anxiety and depressive feelings.

♥ Increased irritability and anger (mood changes).

♥ Sleep problems (difficulty getting to sleep, nightmares, waking often during the night).

♥ Decreased self-confidence.

♥ Poor concentration, inability to relax.

PHYSICAL CHANGES

♥ Weight loss, weight fluctuations and loss of appetite.

♥ Heavy, painful or 'weak-feeling' muscles.

♥ Excessive sweating.

♥ Increased susceptibility to infections and illness (colds, rashes, fevers).

♥ Increased number of persistent injuries.

♥ Reduced performance in training and racing.

♥ Above expected heart rate at rest, and during and after exercise.

♥ Drop in blood pressure on standing, elevated resting and post-exercise blood pressure.

♥ Swelling of lymph glands (sore throats).

♥ Gastrointestinal disturbances (diarrhoea and nausea).

♥ Hyperactivity.

♥ Inability to maintain training load.

♥ Chronic fatigue.

♥ Hormonal changes, e.g. testosterone/cortisol levels in males.

♥ Low serum ferritin levels.

♥ Slower heart rate recovery.

♥ Headaches.

♥ Deterioration of sports skills.

♥ Menstrual irregularities.

HEART RATES AND OVERTRAINING

Overtraining will initially increase resting and training heart rates.

Maximum achievable heart rate may be lower due to muscular fatigue. This is the first stage of the chronic overtraining syndrome. Later, moving into the depletion phase (the second stage of overtraining) heart rate drops to normal or below normal. Exercise heart rates may also be lower and muscular fatigue may prevent the athlete/player from getting anywhere near higher intensities.

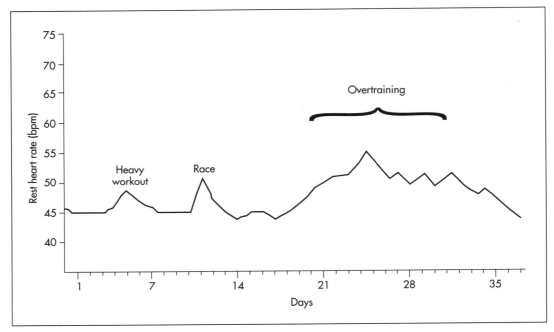

FIGURE 8.1: Elevated heart rates during overtraining

CHRONIC FATIGUE/OVERTRAINING AND THE CENTRAL NERVOUS SYSTEM

The chronic fatigue experienced by overtrained sports people seems to be caused by too much stress being placed on the central nervous system. There appear to be two stages in the 'Chronic Overtraining Syndrome'.

STAGE ONE

In the first stage, the athlete/player's body goes into a kind of 'overdrive', enabling it to cope with the excess load placed upon it. During overdrive the body seems to draw on the physical, emotional and mental reserves normally kept for emergencies. If you've ever reached that stage when under high stress (e.g. during exam time) you get a bit 'silly' and frenetic, you will know what this is like.

Indicators of central nervous system overdrive include:

♥ Reduced performance (training and racing).

♥ Higher than expected heart rate at rest and during exercise.

♥ Sleep problems.

♥ Emotional instability.

♥ Elevated blood pressure.

♥ Delayed recovery of heart rate after exercise.

If overtraining is caught in this overdrive stage, damage can be kept to a minimum and recovery can be swift.

STAGE TWO

If you carry on into the second stage of the Chronic Overtraining Syndrome, the 'depletion' stage, then you are heading for big trouble and a long, slow recovery. The body's energy reserves begin to run out and 'overdrive' is not sustainable any longer. The body's immune system can get very run down and you are more likely to pick up illnesses that may stay around for weeks or even months! This happens several days after exams, or a big race or game, when you feel really tired for a week, want to sleep more and sometimes get a cold.

Indicators of central nervous system depletion include:

♥ Reduced performance (racing and training).

♥ Lower than expected heart rate at rest and during exercise.

♥ Excessive sleeping.

♥ Unstable behaviour, depressive feelings.

♥ Low blood sugar response to exercise.

♥ Low blood pressure.

♥ Rapid recovery of heart rate after exercise.

In my experience, it takes as long to recover from overtraining as it took to achieve it.

A top athlete once trained so hard that he got into this state. He'd been through the 'hyped up' stage 1 phase and was firmly entrenched in stage 2. Every morning he took his resting heart rate — which was normal (bear in mind that in stage 2 your body is so run down that heart rate drops back to normal) — so he thought that he was fine and went out and trained hard. He stopped listening to his body which was telling him that he was shattered. Don't laugh, it's very hard for an athlete/player who is training all the time to recognise fatigue as they are used to being in a state of partial fatigue most of the time.

MEDICAL CONSIDERATIONS

It is important, of course, that overtraining is distinguished from normal fatigue and medical problems.

Medical factors that may affect the body and contribute to overtraining symptoms include:

♥ Illness — colds, glandular fever, post-viral infections.

♥ Inadequate nutrition.

♥ Anaemia (iron deficiency).

♥ Exercise-induced asthma (EIA).

♥ Physical changes due to ageing (you can't do what you used to); not coping because your present fitness level is not as high as previously.

♥ Psychological factors.

Back in 1985 when I used to row competitively, I began to feel very tired. This was during exam time and I was exhausted. I struggled through exams and afterwards was sleeping 14–16 hours per day. UGH!! Things didn't seem to be getting better either. I went to see the doctor and had blood tests but nothing showed up and I was told it was stress. Things got worse and worse. My summer job was physically demanding, I had to stop rowing, I couldn't run or cycle and I felt like I was losing my mind. I went to the doctor two or three more times but still nothing showed.

I was then sent off to talk to a psychiatrist so in March the following year, five months after this all started, I went back to the doctor again. The blood tests came back with an indication that I had glandular fever and the highest white blood cell count (showing infection) that the doctor had ever seen. I'd had glandular fever all along and they couldn't detect it. They'd told me it was stress (which it wasn't) and I'd continued to train hard because nobody had told me otherwise.

I spent three months flat on my back in bed, then went back to university and took a full year to recover back to competitive training and racing again. It was the worst time of my life. I'd lost all my energy and enthusiasm and felt like I was going mad. This illustrates one simple point when it comes to over-fatigue: if you feel tired — you are!!! No matter what anyone says, listen to your body!!!

Non-physical stressors that can affect performance:

♥ Schooling (at any level).

♥ Working environment.

♥ Living conditions.

♥ Training facilities.

♥ Financial situation.

♥ Social environment.

♥ Sport administration.

♥ Travel problems, disruption of circadian rhythms (e.g. jet lag).

Another triathlete friend of mind became very overtrained and couldn't understand why it was happening as she had done similar or even greater amounts of training in the past. It turned out that the ventilation to her new office blew in air from a street which had heavy traffic most of the day. She was told she had petrochemical poisoning. After the ventilation was fixed, she got better.

The body can become over-fatigued by one or more of the following five contributors:

1. Overtraining.
2. Stress.
3. Poisoning (alcohol, allergy).
4. Illness.
5. Bio-chemical/hormonal imbalance.

You must take all of these into account when balancing your training. Nobody except Clark Kent is Superman.

If medical factors do not appear to be causing chronic fatigue, overtraining can be tested for in males by measuring its effect on androgenic (male) hormones. Specifically, the testosterone/cortisol ratio is measured. If you are overtrained, the testosterone is depleted and the cortisol is therefore proportionally higher than normal.

During the off-season, basic medical screening can be done to establish baseline health levels and to ensure that there are no underlying medical problems that may affect health and performance or endanger your life.

THE NOT-SO-GREAT EIGHT

The eight big mistakes that can lead to overtraining are:

1. Increasing training load, volumes or intensity when you feel tired, or when you have had a steady decline in training performance (for over two weeks) because you mistakenly believe that if you train harder, you will get better.

2. The belief that you have to win everything all the time. You can't peak for every

race or game, all year round (or, in the case of some very competitive sports people, for every workout).

3. Too long a season.

4. High levels of competitive stress.

5. Frequent racing.

6. Intense training over an extended period of time.

7. Lack of effective recovery.

8. Lack of positive results/enjoyment.

HOW TO PREVENT OVERTRAINING

The best way to avoid overtraining is to listen to your body! The main ways to prevent overtraining are:

♥ Ensure careful planning of training schedules and seasons (particularly during the competitive season).

♥ Practise optimal training strategies and effective recovery techniques; effective nutrition.

♥ Pay attention to and ensure control of study, work and relationships.

♥ Avoid sudden increases in training load, both mileage/duration and speedwork (which needs to be gradually phased in). This is especially important at the beginning of build-up.

♥ Avoid too much speedwork and frequent competition. The more stress, intensity and time involved in training, the less speedwork and racing can be done.

♥ Avoid monotonous training (particularly during the high-volume phase). Break up the regimented structure of your training. I know a group of cyclists who have what they call the 'cappuccino' ride (or 'café training'). This is a long off-season Sunday bike ride that specialises in visiting cafés, sampling their wares, sitting in the sun, telling a few lies and generally having a laugh. Oh, and by the way, they complete a few kilometres as well.

♥ Be aware of all the other physical and psychological stressors which may affect your training. If possible, try and arrange a stress-free life away from your sport! If this can't be done, then at least be aware of your stress levels and train accordingly. Do not push on regardless. For example, if work stress goes up, then training must come down.

♥ Do not adopt a 'train harder' response to performance plateaus or performance drops. This often happens to athletes and players during long seasons. Training longer and harder will not get you out of a slump. On the contrary, you will just dig a bigger hole for yourself.

In most cases, a performance plateau or drop (if you haven't increased training and aren't ill) is due to excessive fatigue or a natural performance drop following a peak. This means a recovery period is required. Once recovery is complete, training loads can increase again.

Remember, rest is as important as exercise — no recovery, no improvement!

USE OF HEART RATE MONITORS TO AVOID OVERTRAINING

Heart rates in most overtrained sports people will tend to be higher at rest (but not always) and during exercise, and will drop more slowly following exercise. Remember, though, that heart rates can be elevated if you are ill, under stress, in high temperatures, dehydrated, or have recently exercised or eaten.

WAYS TO ASSESS OVERTRAINING RISK

Some easy tests for assessing whether you are at risk of overtraining are:

♥ Morning heart rate (see page 21).

♥ Training heart rate/speed (see page 88).

♥ Exercise economy tests (see *The Power to Perform*).

♥ Time trials (to monitor performance change).

♥ Perceived level of fatigue (see pages 291–4).

Other tests include:

♥ Blood tests (see your doctor).

♥ Physiological lab tests (talk to a local exercise testing lab).

PUTTING IT ALL TOGETHER

Heart rate and overtraining

Variation	Initial	Short-Term	Long-Term
Overtraining	Up	Up	Down

Note: Training can have only two effects:
1. It can make you fit (perform better).
2. It can make you tired.

CHAPTER 9

Heart rate responses — A quick reference

Summary of heart rate responses

Variation	Initial	Short-Term	Long-Term
Illness	Up	Up	Down
Stress	Up	Up	Down
Hills	Up	Up	Up
Insufficient recovery	Up	Up	Down
Fluid loss	Up	Up	Up
Muscle fatigue	Up/down	Up/down	Down
Glycogen loss ('hitting the wall')	Down	Down	N/A
Glycogen loss ('the bonk')	Down	Down	N/A
Cardiac drift	Up	Up	N/A
Altitude	Down	Up	Normal
Heat	Down	Up	Normal
Cold	Down	Up	N/A
Humidity	Down	Up	Normal
Air travel	Down	Up	N/A
Jet lag	Up	Up	Normal
Overtraining	Up	Up	Down
Pollution	Up	Up	N/A
Smoking	Up	Up	N/A
Loss of blood	Up	Up	N/A
Intervals	Slow to rise	Correctly indicates intensity	Correctly indicates intensity

Key: *Initial* = minutes to hours   *Short-Term* = hours to days
Long-Term = weeks to months

Notes:

1. Heart abnormalities: heart rate may fluctuate wildly (sometimes it may rise very high).
2. Age: the older the athlete is, the lower the heart rate.
3. Heart size: the larger the heart, the lower the heart rate.
4. Fitness: as you get fitter, your heart rate goes down.
5. Rests between intervals: heart rate is a good indicator of the recovery period required.
6. Racing: heart rate is artificially elevated by adrenalin.
7. Different sports: heart rate depends on the number and size of the muscles used.
8. Nutrition: heart rate depends on the type of food the athlete is suited to.

RESTING, TRAINING AND RACING HEART RATES

RESTING HEART RATES

HR at rest	Explanation
Normal	Recovered
Elevated	Fatigued
Lower	Fitter

TRAINING AND RACING HEART RATES

HR at rest	Training HR	Speed	Explanation
Normal	Normal	Normal	Everything is fine
Normal	Elevated	Elevated	Going too fast
Normal	Won't rise	Can't get up	Muscles tired
Elevated	Elevated	Low	Fatigued/ill
Normal	Becomes elevated	Drops	Dehydrated
Normal	Elevated	Low	Fatigued
Normal	Normal	Low	Muscles fatigued
Elevated	Normal	Normal	Mild stress
Elevated	Elevated	Normal	Stress/race hype
Normal	Drops	Drops	Hit the wall, bonked
Lower	Lower	Same or higher	Fitter

IF HEART RATES VARY SO MUCH IN SO MANY CONDITIONS, WHY DO WE USE THEM?

A lot of athletes/players and coaches won't use a heart rate monitor because they say there are too many variables to make it worthwhile. As we have discussed, heart rates are influenced by many factors: fatigue, heat, cold, nutrition, altitude, medication, illness, dehydration, anxiety and pollution. How can you be sure using a heart rate monitor is practicable given all these variables?

Simple: ask someone who has trained with a heart rate monitor for several years. Ask them if all these variables have stopped them from working out what heart rate to train at. The answer will be 'no'! Indeed, it is not so much a question of how you can use a heart rate monitor when there are all these variables, but how you can fail to use one. After all, what better way to contend with all the variables than by accurately measuring how hard you are working?

It should also be remembered that the variations in heart rate due to weather, illness and other factors are, in most cases, minimal. By using a heart rate monitor you get to understand better what is normal and what isn't. That allows you to make better training decisions.

Okay, so the many variables that can affect training make using a heart rate monitor more logical. But is training with a heart rate monitor effective? In a word — yes! Of course, many athletes have trained very successfully without a heart rate monitor. And equally, many athletes have trained unsuccessfully with one. It all comes down to the fact that a heart rate monitor simply provides extra information on how your body is responding to your training.

Think of a heart rate monitor like a rev counter in a racing car. Every racing car has a rev counter (tachometer). Why? Because when it comes to performance, you need all the information you can get.

Finally, to those of you who still aren't convinced — try training with a heart rate monitor for a while. You'll soon realise that they are an invaluable training tool which, when used correctly, can help you optimise training and racing.

WE ARE ALL INDIVIDUALS

Not everyone's heart rate responds in the same way. My heart rates very rarely go up when I am tired, either at rest or in training. They generally go down. Maybe that says something about the ability of my muscles to recover compared to my cardiovascular system. Maybe my muscles recover far more slowly.

Who knows, but in any case, remember that you are an individual, and while the heart rate responses listed in this book apply to many people, your heart rates may respond slightly differently in certain circumstances.

PUTTING IT ALL TOGETHER

♥ Heart rates respond in a wide range of ways to different variables.

♥ Heart rate monitors are useful because they provide more information on how your body is responding to training.

♥ Not everyone responds in the same way.

This is a landmark research study. All the variables were tied down and many trials were conducted in a double-blind cross-over study.

Who am I kidding? I just went and did this revolutionary study — an assessment of Disneyland and Universal Studio park rides, a.k.a. 'The Clash of the Titans'. Space Mountain and Indiana Jones the Ride were disqualified due to too much electrical interference with my heart rate monitor. So that left the two 'big boys': Disneyland with 'Splash Mountain' and Universal Studios with 'Jurassic Park the Ride'.

Weird Things
TO DO WITH YOUR HEART RATE MONITOR

Theme Park Rides

As you can see, the nine-storey drop in Jurassic Park raised my heart rate to a maximum of 130 beats per minute, but the drop into inky blackness off Splash Mountain took my rate to 150. My average heart rate during Jurassic Park was 86, as against 97 for Splash Mountain.

You may be able to extrapolate from this that I was having more fun at Splash Mountain. In actual fact both were great and I heartily recommend them.

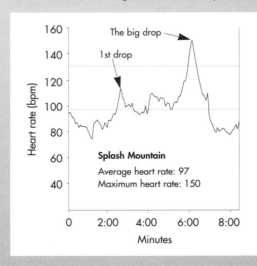

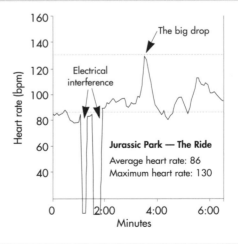

CHAPTER 10

TRAINING INTENSITIES

Let's talk about training. There are two main factors involved:

1. How long (volume).

2. How hard (intensity).

Excluding muscular effort, training can always be described by these two factors. 'I went for a 30-minute run (volume) at a heart rate of 165 (intensity).'

We will first discuss 'how hard'—the training intensities, and how they allow us to train effectively using a heart rate monitor. We'll come to the 'how long'—the designing of a training programme—later.

THE ENERGY SYSTEMS

First we need to know a little about how the body works. The body uses two main energy systems, one of which breaks down into two further parts. These systems are:

1. The ANAEROBIC energy system, which breaks down into the alactic (immediate) and lactic (non-oxidative) subsystems;

2. The AEROBIC energy system (oxidative).

The ANAEROBIC system is used during high-intensity exercise where energy demands exceed aerobic metabolism. In other words, this system is used when you are exercising without your muscles using oxygen; in sprinting, for example.

The ANAEROBIC ALACTIC system is used during very high-intensity exercise (maximum effort under 10–20 seconds) and supplies immediate energy. It does not require oxygen to function (anaerobic) and no lactic acid is produced (alactic).

The ANAEROBIC LACTIC system 'kicks in' just before the anaerobic alactic system runs out, and does not require oxygen to function (anaerobic). It does, however, produce lactic acid as a major by-product of energy production (lactic).

The anaerobic lactic system is used in moderately intense activity lasting from 10 seconds to 2–3 minutes. It is used when oxygen is in short supply or when there is a complete lack of oxygen.

The AEROBIC energy system takes in, transports and uses oxygen. It requires the presence of oxygen to function. It comes into play after about 2 minutes of intense exercise and is the main source of energy after 3–4 minutes.

The aerobic energy system is used for moderately intensive exercise and is developed and maintained through cardiovascular exercise, such as cycling, running, swimming, kayaking and rowing. Cardiovascular exercise stimulates the cardiovascular system (heart and blood vessels) and is any exercise that increases heart rate. It is also called cardiorespiratory exercise because it improves the ability of the heart and lungs to deliver oxygen to the working muscles. Why do you need to know this? Because your training intensities are built around them!

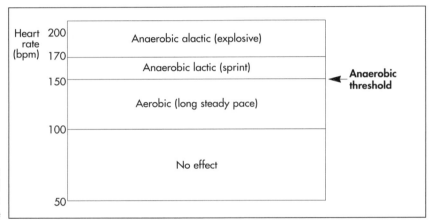

FIGURE 10.1:
Anaerobic and aerobic zones in relation to heart rate

TRAINING INTENSITIES AND HEART RATE

When someone asks you, 'How much are you training?' they usually want to know how far or how often you train each week. Seldom does anyone ask, 'How hard are you training?'

Yet understanding the 'hardness' or intensity of your training is the key to understanding how a progressive, balanced training programme is put together. While novice and élite athletes may be poles apart when it comes to how fast they train and race, the intensity (not speed) of the work each group does in each phase of their training is the same.

Training intensities have traditionally been categorised in many different ways, but they can easily be broken down into three basic types. Starting with the lowest intensity and moving up to the highest, these intensities are:

1. Low intensity: easy–medium.
2. Submaximal intensity: medium–hard.
3. High intensity: hard–very hard.

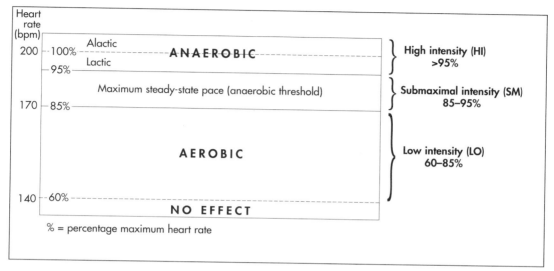

Low-intensity (LO) training is aerobic exercise (with oxygen) which can be performed for long periods of time. High-intensity (HI) training is anaerobic (without oxygen). High-intensity exercise (basically sprinting) can only be performed for brief periods before complete temporary fatigue occurs and you have to rest. Submaximal-intensity (SM) training occurs at what some regard as the threshold or crossover between LO and HI training. This is the maximum steady-state pace, or anaerobic threshold pace, you can hold (20 minutes–1 hour).

TRAINING INTENSITIES

Let's now take a look at training intensities in detail. As described earlier, training intensities are divided into three types: low, submaximal and high. Let's take a look at the least intense of these, low intensity.

LOW-INTENSITY (LO) TRAINING

Easy to Medium (60–85% Heart Rate Max)

LO training gives you basic aerobic fitness and muscular conditioning and it will improve your ability to metabolise (use) fat as an energy source. LO training, which can also be used to aid recovery, can be broken down into three types. These too have an order of intensity:

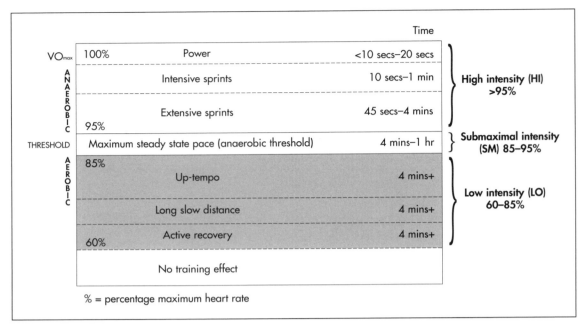

		Time	
VO$_{max}$	100%	Power	<10 secs–20 secs
A N A E R O B I C		Intensive sprints	10 secs–1 min
		Extensive sprints	45 secs–4 mins
	95%		
THRESHOLD		Maximum steady state pace (anaerobic threshold)	4 mins–1 hr
A E R O B I C	85%	Up-tempo	4 mins+
		Long slow distance	4 mins+
	60%	Active recovery	4 mins+
		No training effect	

High intensity (HI) >95%

Submaximal intensity (SM) 85–95%

Low intensity (LO) 60–85%

% = percentage maximum heart rate

FIGURE 10.3:
Low-intensity
training

1. Active recovery (AR).

2. Long slow distance (LSD).

3. Up-tempo (UT).

Active recovery occurs at the easy end of the LO training range, while up-tempo occurs just below submaximal intensity (SM) training. LO training is performed at approximately 60–85 percent of your HR^{max}.

Most athletes will work at the middle to low end of this range (AR, LSD) most of the time until up-tempo training begins in preparation for speedwork.

If you do not have access to a heart rate monitor or you don't wish to use heart rates as a guide to training intensity, LO pace can be described as an easy to medium effort (if you can't comfortably hold a conversation at this pace, i.e. you're gasping, then you're going too fast!).

Active recovery

Active recovery is performed at approximately 60 percent of HR^{max}, at the lowest end of the low-intensity training heart rate range. It is only used in training to assist recovery, for example by removing waste products from the muscles, or when you feel tired.

AR should be used on those days when you feel too tired to do your intended workout. But if after 10 – 15 minutes of training you still feel tired, go home and

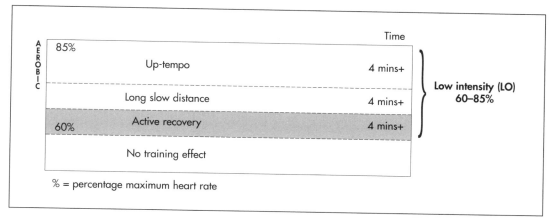

have a rest! Further training on that day will do more harm than good.

If you feel you need a day off altogether — take it (and forget about training until tomorrow).

Long slow distance

Long slow distance is performed at approximately 60–75 percent of HR^{max}. LSD is the most used training zone. Most of your training will be in this zone. It is often called the 'mileage zone' — the zone where you do most of your mileage, aerobic conditioning training.

This zone improves endurance, familiarises your body with training, improves efficiency, assists in weight control and improves strength or muscular endurance. This is not a very specific intensity, just an easy pace at which to hold a conversation. The pace will improve as you get fitter.

FIGURE 10.5:
Long slow distance

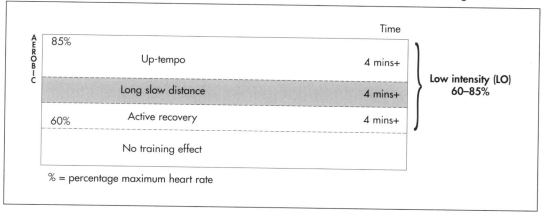

Up-tempo training

Up-tempo is performed at approximately 75–85 percent of HR^{max}, and is an intermediate intensity that bridges the gap between LO and higher intensity training. It's the start of aerobic (endurance) speed work. It conditions the body to the beginnings of 'going faster'.

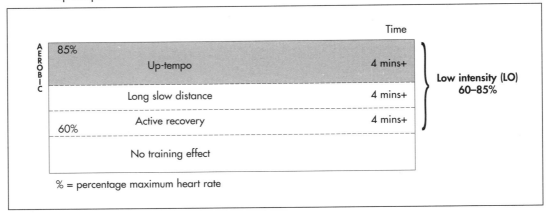

% = percentage maximum heart rate

The effects of low-intensity training

This intensity improves basic aerobic and muscular conditioning (including muscular endurance), speeds recovery and increases your tolerance to training. These training adaptations enable you to cope with the speedwork to come and condition you for the more intense, more specific work to come.

Low-intensity training also improves your ability to metabolise or use fat as a source of energy. This means you are better able to race over long distances with less likelihood of 'bonking' on the bike or 'hitting the wall'. That is valuable for endurance athletes and assists in fat loss.

SUBMAXIMAL INTENSITY (SM) TRAINING

Medium to Hard (85–95% Heart Rate Max)

SM training occurs at maximum steady-state/anaerobic threshold (approximately 85–95 percent of HR^{max}). It raises your maximum steady-state pace (often called 'anaerobic threshold pace') or race pace.

These days, 'anaerobic threshold' is a term frowned upon by sports scientists. This is because there is no absolute threshold but rather a 'grey area' where your body moves from functioning at a mainly aerobic level (where most of your energy needs are being met by oxygen) to functioning at a mainly anaerobic level (you can't take in enough oxygen to sustain your current level of exercise intensity). Therefore, the term 'submaximal intensity' is used to describe training

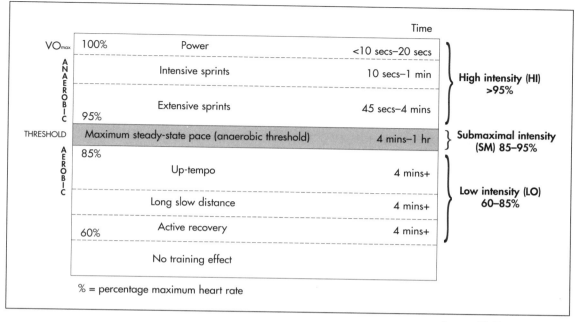

			Time	
VO$_{max}$ 100%	Power		<10 secs–20 secs	} High intensity (HI) >95%
A N A E R O B I C	Intensive sprints		10 secs–1 min	
	Extensive sprints		45 secs–4 mins	
95%				
THRESHOLD	Maximum steady-state pace (anaerobic threshold)		4 mins–1 hr	} Submaximal intensity (SM) 85–95%
A E R O B I C 85%	Up-tempo		4 mins+	} Low intensity (LO) 60–85%
	Long slow distance		4 mins+	
60%	Active recovery		4 mins+	
	No training effect			

% = percentage maximum heart rate

FIGURE 10.7:
Submaximal
training

that corresponds with that 'grey area' where you are exercising enough to go into oxygen debt, start puffing heavily or start sprinting. SM training is usually about 85–95 percent of HR^{max}, although these percentages vary a lot depending on your conditioning and the phase of training you are in.

In simple terms, SM training pace is medium to hard. You should find it difficult to converse at this pace.

The effects of submaximal intensity training

Various types of SM training will improve steady-state racing and playing speed and muscle endurance.

Submaximal intensity training is the cornerstone of your racing/playing speed in most sports.

HIGH-INTENSITY (HI) TRAINING

Hard to Very Hard (95–100% Heart Rate Max)

HI training is anaerobic, and performed at approximately 95–100 percent of HR^{max}. It bears some similarity to SM training, but it also improves your ability to cope with sprinting (acceleration, top speed and speed endurance), sprint recovery (oxygen debt), and high levels of exertion.

High-intensity training can be broken down into:

1. Sprinting (extensive) — ES.

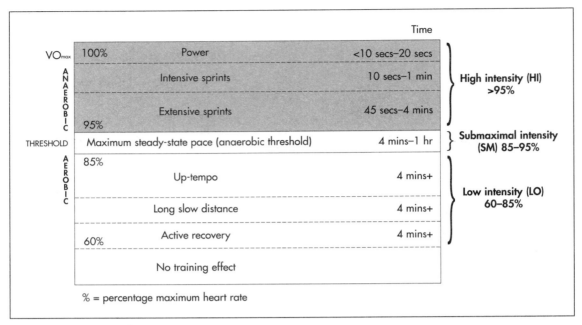

		Time	
VO_max 100%	Power	<10 secs–20 secs	} High intensity (HI) >95%
	Intensive sprints	10 secs–1 min	
	Extensive sprints	45 secs–4 mins	
95%			
THRESHOLD	Maximum steady-state pace (anaerobic threshold)	4 mins–1 hr	} Submaximal intensity (SM) 85–95%
85%	Up-tempo	4 mins+	} Low intensity (LO) 60–85%
	Long slow distance	4 mins+	
60%	Active recovery	4 mins+	
	No training effect		

% = percentage maximum heart rate

FIGURE 10.8:
High-intensity training

2. Sprinting (intensive) — IS.

3. Power (acceleration) — PWR.

To exercise at above 95 percent of your HR^max means sprinting. It is the only time in training when you should let all the brakes off and go for it. To some extent, it is hard to define and monitor exact heart rate levels at this intensity. If you are using a heart rate monitor, it is assumed that heart rates must be above 95 percent HR^max to have the desired effect. But it is better to use the duration of the sprint to control intensity. Why? Because in very short sprints your heart rate will not reach a constant, meaningful level.

HI training pace can be described as hard to very hard. You should not be able to talk. Actually, even thinking should be difficult!

What makes up high-intensity (HI) training?

Extensive sprints
Extensive sprints involve a 90–95 percent effort, and last between 45 seconds and 4 minutes.

These are long sprints, which are used to condition your body to extended sprinting (speed endurance). They are used for cycle racing, any multisport races that involve some aspect of cycle racing in a bunch (peloton), mountain bike starts, and many field and court sports.

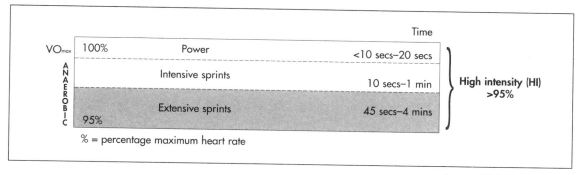

FIGURE 10.9:
Extensive sprints

Intensive sprints

Intensive sprints are short, lasting between 10 seconds and 1 minute, but they involve 100 percent effort. They are used to improve your top sprinting speed and speed endurance.

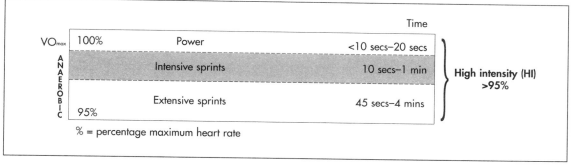

FIGURE 10.10:
Intensive sprints

Power sprints

Power sprints involve 100 percent effort, and last no more than 10–20 seconds. They are used to develop explosive ability (efforts generally lasting less than 10 seconds) and acceleration.

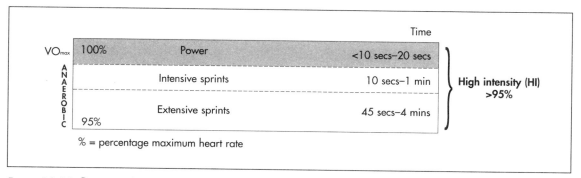

FIGURE 10.11: Power sprints

The value of high-intensity training

High-intensity training improves your recovery from oxygen debt and your ability to sustain pace in oxygen debt (lactate tolerance). It is good for fast starts and finishes, as well as explosive acceleration and sprinting.

Acceleration, top speed and speed endurance can be developed separately or in combination, generally progressing from ES to IS and finally to PW. Overspeed (an aspect of HI: lighter load and a muscle contraction slightly higher than race pace) can also be used in some sports. Overspeed is not an intensity as it is more to improve muscle contraction speed (biomechanical) than to improve cardiorespiratory function (physiological).

PUTTING IT ALL TOGETHER

DESCRIPTIONS OF TRAINING INTENSITIES
High intensity (anaerobic)

Power
Explosive exercise of less than 10 seconds' duration, e.g. jumps and starts
Jumps; acceleration

Intensive sprints
100% sprints at maximum effort (10 secs–1 min); e.g. full sprint
(top speed — speed endurance)
Sprints

Extensive sprints
Long or extended sprints (1–4 mins)
Intervals

Submaximal intensity (threshold)

Anaerobic threshold
Maximum steady-state race pace (4 mins–1 hour). The fastest you can go without sprinting
Intervals; time trials; races

Low intensity (aerobic)

Up-tempo
Tempo training, bridging intensity between long slow distance and higher speedwork intensities
Very long intervals; time trials; races

Long slow distance
Mileage duration training
Long; slow/continuous

Active recovery
Light recovery training
Short; easy/continuous

TRAINING INTENSITIES AND CONVERSION TABLE

Training intensities have not been standardised, consequently there are currently many different terminologies for the same intensities. This table is provided to bring many of the terminologies together to clarify training zones. Knowing the name of the intensity is not nearly as important as knowing what it does. Learn what your intensities mean.

Key:

1. Bompa   2. Hare (AIS cycling)   3. Brick   4. Polar(Sally Edwards)
5. Sleamkaer/Janssen   6. Rowing   7. Swimming

1	2	3	4	5	6	7			
6	–	MAXIMAL	–	–	AN	KI (SN)	100%	Power (Acceleration)	(HI) 95%
5	E4		REDLINE	V	AN	SN (SB)		Intensive sprints (Short sprints)	
5	E4			V	TR	K2	95%	Extensive sprints (Long sprints/spd end)	
4	E3	AT	AT	IV	AT	EB (ET)		Maximum steady-state pace	(SM) 85–95%
3	E2	Steady-state (Med)	AER	III	UI	G2	85%	Up-tempo (Tempo)	(LO) 60–85%
2	E1	AER (Con)	Wght	II	U2 (SE)	G1 (K3)		Long slow distance (Easy/continuous)	
1	RE	V. Easy	Mod ACT	I	U3	KB	60%	Active recovery (Recovery)	
								No training effect	

% = percentage maximum heart rate

CHAPTER 11

MANIPULATING TRAINING INTENSITIES

It's all very well to know your training intensities but how do they apply to your sport? To know this you need to know:

♥ Which intensities do you use?

♥ How much do you use?

♥ When do you use them?

WHICH INTENSITIES DO YOU USE?

The following table describes which intensities you should use for various sports (and to some extent, how much).

	LO			SM	HI			
	AR	LSD	UT	AT	ES	IS	PWR	O/S
Cycling								
Criterium	✓	✓✓✓	✓✓	✓✓✓	✓	✓✓	✓	✓
Road/Tour	✓	✓✓✓	✓✓✓	✓✓	✓	✓✓	✓	✓
Time Trial	✓	✓✓✓	✓✓✓	✓✓✓	✓	–	–	–
Duathlon								
Standard	✓	✓✓✓	✓✓	✓✓✓	✓	–	–	–
Long	✓	✓✓✓	✓✓✓	✓✓	–	–	–	–
Triathlon								
Standard	✓	✓✓✓	✓✓	✓✓✓	✓	–	–	–
Long	✓	✓✓✓	✓✓✓	✓✓	–	–	–	–
Multisport								
Standard	✓	✓✓✓	✓✓	✓✓✓	✓	–	–	–
Long	✓	✓✓✓	✓✓✓	✓✓	–	–	–	–

	AR	LO LSD	UT	SM AT	HI ES	IS	PWR	O/S
Running								
10–21 km	✓	✓✓✓	✓✓	✓✓✓	✓	–	–	–
Marathon/ Ultrathon	✓	✓✓✓	✓✓✓	✓✓	–	–	–	–
Rowing	✓	✓✓✓	✓✓	✓✓✓	✓✓	✓	✓	–
Mountain Bike	✓	✓✓✓	✓✓✓	✓✓	✓✓	–	–	–
Swimming	✓	✓✓	✓	✓✓✓	✓✓	✓✓	✓✓	✓
Rugby	✓	✓✓	✓	✓✓	✓	✓✓✓	✓✓✓	✓✓
Soccer	✓	✓✓	✓	✓✓	✓	✓✓✓	✓✓✓	✓✓
Basketball	✓	✓✓✓	✓	✓✓	✓	✓✓✓	✓✓✓	✓
Netball	✓	✓✓	✓	✓	✓✓	✓✓✓	✓✓✓	✓
Tennis/ Squash	✓	✓✓✓	✓	✓	✓✓	✓✓✓	✓✓✓	✓
General Fitness	✓	✓✓✓	✓✓✓	✓✓	–	–	–	–

More ✓s = More Important

HOW MUCH DO YOU USE?

In general different athletes and players will proportionately spend their time at lower training intensities. Here are approximate percentages.

	AR	LSD	LO UT	SM AT	HI ES	IS	PWR	O/S
Cycling								
Criterium	N/A	80	4	10	1	2	2	1
Road/Tour	N/A	84	6	4	2	1	1	–
Time Trial	N/A	80	8	10	2	–	–	–
Duathlon								
Standard	N/A	85	4	10	1	–	–	–
Long	N/A	86	10	4	–	–	–	–

		LO		SM			HI	
	AR	LSD	UT	AT	ES	IS	PWR	O/S
Triathlon								
Standard	N/A	85	4	10	1	–	–	–
Long	N/A	86	10	4	–	–	–	–
Multisport								
Standard	N/A	85	4	10	1	–	–	–
Long	N/A	86	10	4	–	–	–	–
Running								
10–21 km	N/A	85	7	7	1	–	–	–
Marathon/ Ultrathon	N/A	88	8	4	–	–	–	–
Rowing	N/A	77	4	10	4	3	2	–
Mountain Bike	N/A	85	4	10	1	–	–	–
Swimming	N/A	60	6	15	6	9	2	2
Rugby	N/A	75	4	10	3	4	4	2
Soccer	N/A	75	4	10	3	3	4	2
Basketball	N/A	77	4	10	4	3	2	–
Netball	N/A	60	6	15	6	9	2	2
Tennis/ Squash	N/A	77	4	10	4	3	2	–
General Fitness	N/A	90	5	5	–	–	–	–

These are general and will vary between individuals and positions. A loose forward in rugby will spend more time on endurance (LSD, UT, AT) training than a first-five. A striker in soccer will spend more time on sprinting (ES, IS, PWR) than a midfielder.

WHEN DO YOU USE THEM?

1. Adaptation
Adaptation allows you gradually and progressively to adapt to higher and higher training intensities so that you don't get injured, ill or overtrained. Because you are better conditioned it improves the quality of your workouts.

2. Timing

The higher the intensity, the shorter time you will be able to hold top form. So your highest intensities are always emphasised last.

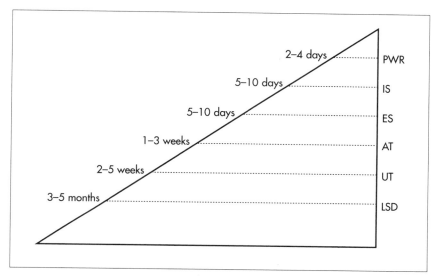

FIGURE 11.1: Approximate time peak held at a particular intensity

3. Training intensities

Intensities always progress from easy to hard or low to high during your programme build-up.

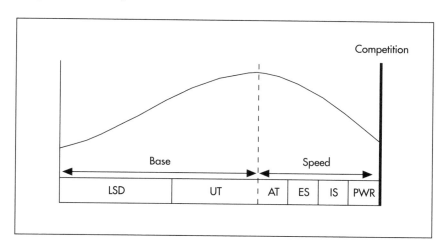

FIGURE 11.2: Progress of intensities from lowest to highest

PUTTING IT ALL TOGETHER

To use your training intensities you need to know:

♥ Which intensities do you use — the intensities that are used in your sport.

♥ How much do you use — most of the training is at low intensities.

♥ When do you use them — progress from lower to higher intensities as you move through your programme.

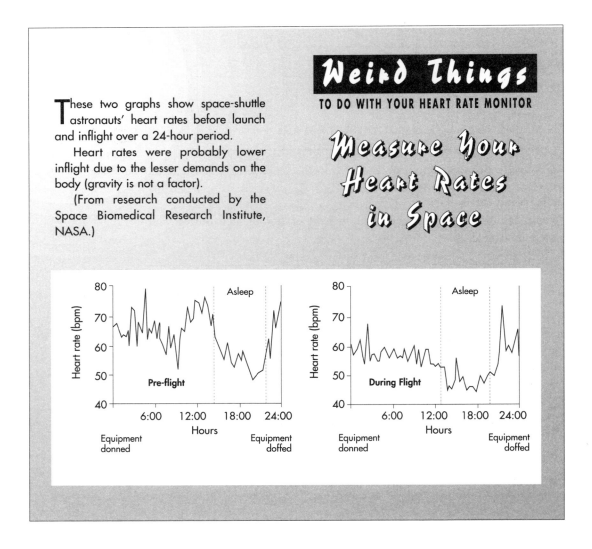

These two graphs show space-shuttle astronauts' heart rates before launch and inflight over a 24-hour period.

Heart rates were probably lower inflight due to the lesser demands on the body (gravity is not a factor).

(From research conducted by the Space Biomedical Research Institute, NASA.)

Weird Things
TO DO WITH YOUR HEART RATE MONITOR

Measure Your Heart Rates in Space

CALCULATING TRAINING HEART RATES

CALCULATING TRAINING INTENSITIES

Now that you know *what* your training intensities mean, we now need to discuss how to calculate them to suit you.

There are three ways to do this — the easiest but least accurate is to look up your training intensities in the tables. The second method is by assessing resting heart rate and calculating your maximum heart rate and your training intensities. The third and most accurate method is by assessing your resting and maximum heart rates and doing an anaerobic threshold test. Assess which method you should use in the table below:

Recommendations/Type	Method
Novice/General Fitness	1
Beginner Sports	2
Semi-Competitive	2 or 3
Competitive	3
Elite	3

Note: If your heart rates don't feel right, you
probably are different from the normal — use method 3.

Once you have worked out your training heart rates write them in the spaces provided at the end of this chapter and in the specific programme section of the book (pages 190–281). Either design your own programme using the instructions provided in *The Power to Perform*, or use the programmes in the back of this book.

If you are using the latter, you will find that next to each workout volume (distance or duration) there will be a number (e.g. 2). Look this number up in the subphases and detailed descriptions section and you will find an explanation of the workout. If you are using a programme from another source (from another book, magazine, coach or of your own design), you will need to read the subphases carefully and either incorporate the heart rates and training specifics, or translate the training terminology and adapt it for the programme.

METHOD 1: ASSESSING TRAINING INTENSITIES THROUGH TABLES — VERY EASY METHOD
(For novice and general fitness)

Look up your heart rates based on age and sex.

Male

| AGE | AR | LD | | SM | | HI | | | *HR max |
		LSD	UT	AT	ES	IS	PWR		
15–20	<140	140–170	170–180	180–190	190+	N/A	N/A		200
21–25	<135	135–165	165–175	175–185	185+	N/A	N/A		195
26–30	<130	130–160	160–170	170–180	180+	N/A	N/A		190
31–35	<125	125–155	155–165	165–175	175+	N/A	N/A		185
36–40	<120	120–150	150–160	160–170	170+	N/A	N/A		180
41–45	<113	115–145	145–155	155–165	165+	N/A	N/A		175
46–50	<110	110–140	140–150	150–160	160+	N/A	N/A		170
51–55	<105	105–135	135–145	145–155	155+	N/A	N/A		165
56–60	<100	100–130	130–140	140–150	150+	N/A	N/A		160
61–65	<95	95–125	125–135	135–145	145+	N/A	N/A		155
66–70	<90	90–120	120–130	130–140	140+	N/A	N/A		150
71–75	<85	85–115	115–125	125–135	135+	N/A	N/A		145
76–80	<80	80–110	110–130	120–130	130+	N/A	N/A		140
81–85	<75	75–105	105–115	115–125	125+	N/A	N/A		135
86–90	<70	70–100	100–110	110–120	120+	N/A	N/A		130

* Through prediction.

Female

| AGE | AR | LD | | SM | | HI | | | *HR max |
		LSD	UT	AT	ES	IS	PWR		
15–20	<145	145–175	175–185	185–195	195+	N/A	N/A		211
21–25	<140	140–170	170–180	180–190	190+	N/A	N/A		206
26–30	<135	135–165	165–175	175–185	185+	N/A	N/A		201

31–35	<130	130–160	160–170	170–180	180+	N/A	N/A	196
36–40	<125	125–155	155–165	165–175	175+	N/A	N/A	191
41–45	<120	120–150	150–160	160–170	170+	N/A	N/A	186
46–50	<115	115–145	145–155	155–165	165+	N/A	N/A	181
51–55	<110	110–140	140–150	150–160	160+	N/A	N/A	176
56–60	<105	105–135	135–145	145–155	155+	N/A	N/A	171
61–65	<100	100–130	130–140	140–150	150+	N/A	N/A	166
66–70	<95	95–125	125–135	135–145	145+	N/A	N/A	161
71–75	<90	90–120	120–130	130–140	140+	N/A	N/A	156
76–80	<85	85–115	115–125	125–135	135+	N/A	N/A	151
81–85	<80	80–110	110–130	120–130	130+	N/A	N/A	146
86–90	<75	75–105	105–115	115–125	125+	N/A	N/A	141

* Through prediction (male is 220 - age, female is 226 - age).

Note: These are estimated, not individualised. They may not feel like the descriptions stated. If so, they are not correct; to reassess use method 2.

Heart rates calculated on: HI heart rate is above AT. 85–95% of HR^{max} to get AT, UT is a 10-beat range below AT and LSD is 30 beats below.

Your Training Intensities

Sports		1	2	3	4	e.g. 43 year-old male
HI	ES/IS/PWR					165+
SM	AT					155-165
	UT					145-155
LD	LSD					115-145
	AR					<113

Note: If doing more than one sport use the 'sport converter' on page 113 basing these heart rates on run heart rates. Put the heart rates in the 'Putting it all together' section at the end of this chapter (pages 124–6).

METHOD 2: ASSESSING TRAINING INTENSITIES THROUGH CALCULATION — EASY METHOD

(For beginners and semi-competitive athletes)

To calculate training heart rates you first need to assess your resting heart rate, and then calculate maximum heart rate.

ASSESSING RESTING HEART RATE

By assessing your heart rate each morning for a week or two, you will be able to establish your average resting heart rate.

Take your heart rate in bed, lying down, upon waking. If you wake to an alarm, this can raise your heart rate slightly, so rest for two to three minutes before taking it. Make allowances if you have a busy day ahead (anxiety) or if you need to urinate, as both may elevate heart rate slightly. This is particularly important during a 'test' week.

Here's an example of how to assess resting heart rate:

	M	T	W	T	F	S	S
Heart rate	56	54	55	56	54	56	57

Total heart rates = 388, divided by seven days = 55.4. This gives you an average heart rate for the week of 55.

Note your resting heart rate: [   ]   e.g. [55]

Note: if you do not want to take the time to take your resting heart rate, here is a guide to approximate resting heart rates at various ages. But remember, heart rates vary greatly between individuals, so it is much better to take your own resting heart rate.

Resting heart rate (bpm)—Guide

Age (years)	Fit	Unfit
16–30	45–50	60–65
31–45	50–55	65–70
46–60	55–60	70–75
60+	55–65	70–90

CALCULATING MAXIMUM HEART RATE

To calculate theoretical maximum heart rates, you use a simple formula:

Men: 220 – age;

Women: 226 – age.

For example, a 30-year-old male will have a theoretical maximum heart rate of 220 – 30 = 190 bpm. A 45-year-old female will have a theoretical maximum heart rate of 226 – 45 = 181 bpm.

You can use the table to assess if you don't want to calculate.

Maximum Heart Rate Table

Age	Male	Female
15–20	200	206
21–25	195	201
26–30	190	196
31–35	185	191
36–40	180	186
41–45	175	181
46–50	170	176
51–55	165	171
56–60	160	166
61–65	155	161
66–70	150	156
71–75	145	151
76–80	140	146
81–85	135	141
86–90	130	136

Maximum heart rate calculated: 220/226 – age =

	e.g. 55-year-old female	171

KARVONEN HEART RATE CALCULATION

You can now use the Karvonen formula to calculate your heart rates for various training intensities. These intensities are usually expressed as a percentage of maximum heart rate.

Karvonen formula: $(HR^{max} - HR^{rest}) \times \%$ exercise intensity $+ HR^{rest}$.

For instance, submaximal (SM) intensity is considered to be an 85–95 percent effort (0.85 to 0.95 for multiplication purposes). Thus, if your maximum heart rate (HR^{max}) is 196 and your resting heart rate (HR^{rest}) is 55, then your submaximal intensity range is worked out like this:

$$196 \ (HR^{max}) - 55 \ (HR^{rest}) = 141$$

$$141 \times 0.85 \ (85\%) = 120$$

$$120 + 55 \ (HR^{rest}) = 175$$

The figure 175 is therefore the low end of your submaximal range. Repeat the calculation using 95 percent and you get 189. This gives you a submaximal heart rate intensity range of 175–189.

When you begin training at your submaximal intensity, you will start off at the lower end of the range, in this case, 175–180. As training progresses and you get stronger, you will train more often at the higher end of the range, e.g. 180–189.

This formula is very effective as it takes into account heart size and changing levels of fitness.

Maximum Heart Rate [ ]   **Resting heart rate** [ ]

For HI (196–55) = 141
    141 x 95% = 134
    134 + 55 = 189

For SM (196–55) = 141
    141 x 85% = 120
    120 + 55 = 175

For UT (196–55) = 141
    141 x 75% = 106
    106 + 55 = 161

For LSD (196–55) = 141
    141 x 60% = 85
    85 + 55 = 140

HI	189+	SM	175–189	UT	161–175
LSD	140–161	AR	<140		

Percentages to be used for calculations:

		Range
HI	ES IS PWR	95% +
SM	AT	85–95%
LO	UT	75–85%
	LSD	60–75%
	AR	<60%

		1	2	3	4	e.g. Running	Swimming
HI	ES/IS/PWR					189+	169+
SM	AT					175-189	155-169
	UT					161-175	141-155
LD	LSD					140-161	120-141
	AR					<140	<120

These heart rates are set up for running. To calculate heart rates for other sports quickly (without testing) if you are a multisport athlete, use the following.

Sport Converter

		\multicolumn{4}{c}{Convert to:}			
		C	S	R	K
	C	0	-10	+10	-15
	S	+10	0	+20	-5
Tested	R	-10	-20	0	-25
Sport	K	+15	+5	+25	0

Key:
C = Cycling
S = Swimming
R = Running
K = Kayaking
e.g. Tested sport is running (R)
Convert to swimming (S)
Result = -20 (all swimming rates will be 20 beats lower than corresponding running heart rates)

Put heart rates in the 'Putting it all together' section at the end of this chapter (pages 124–6).

Method 3: Assessing training intensities through calculation and testing— advanced method

(For experienced athletes)

You need to assess three areas (you can leave out the maximum heart rate test if you like). These are resting heart rate, maximum heart rate, and anaerobic threshold (Conconi test).

Assessing resting heart rate

By assessing your heart rate each morning for a week or two, you will be able to establish your average resting heart rate.

Take your heart rate in bed, lying down, upon waking. If you wake to an alarm, this can raise your heart rate slightly, so rest for two to three minutes before taking it. Make allowances if you have a busy day ahead (anxiety) or if you need to urinate, as both may elevate heart rate slightly. This is particularly important during a 'test' week.

Here's an example of how to assess resting heart rate:

	M	T	W	T	F	S	S
Heart rate	56	54	55	56	54	56	57

Total heart rates = 388, divided by seven days = 55.4. This gives you an average heart rate for the week of 55.

Note your resting heart rate:

Note: if you do not want to take the time to take your resting heart rate, go to the guide to approximate resting heart rates at various ages (bottom of page 110). But remember, heart rates vary greatly between individuals, so it is much better to take your own resting heart rate.

Assessing maximum heart rate

Maximum heart rate (HR^{max}) is the highest heart rate that you can achieve. This obviously occurs at maximum intensity or effort. Maximum heart rates can vary from 130–220 beats per minute, depending on the athlete.

Taking your heart rate to maximum is completely safe unless you have a heart abnormality. If you do have a heart abnormality, be warned: a maximum heart rate test can result in death! If you are simply unfit, a maximum heart rate test can still make you feel very unwell (dizzy or nauseous).

If possible, then, acquire some cardiovascular fitness before undergoing this test. If you do this, you will find that a maximum heart rate test is not anywhere near as bad as it sounds. A fit athlete can 'hit' maximum heart rate without any damaging effects — it just doesn't feel very comfortable. The American College of Sports Medicine has this to say about maximum heart rate tests:

> *At or above 35 years of age, it is necessary for individuals to have a medical examination and a maximal exercise test before beginning a vigorous exercise programme. At any age, the information gathered from an exercise test may be useful to establish an effective and safe exercise prescription. Maximal testing done for men at age 40 or above, and women at age 50 or above, even when no symptoms or risk factors are present, should be performed with physician supervision.*

The safest way to assess maximum heart rate is to get a doctor or sports physiologist to do a stress test and conduct a health appraisal. The test can be conducted accurately, safely and precisely to indicate maximum heart rate.

The test will also provide other interesting information:

♥ Resting heart function (ECG).

♥ Exercise and maximum heart function (ECG).

♥ Rest/exercise blood pressures.

♥ Anaerobic threshold (LT or VE).

♥ Aerobic threshold.

♥ Projected approximate training and racing speeds.

These tests cost between $50 and $200 and are available through most exercise testing labs.

The other way to go is to do a self-administered maximum heart rate test. But consider getting a testing lab to determine your maximum heart rate if:

♥ You are over 35 years of age.

♥ You have been sedentary (inactive) for over 12 months.

♥ You have never had a maximum heart rate test before, or have not exercised close to maximal exertion in the last 12 months.

♥ You are in poor physical condition (use the Borg scale, page 315, initially).

If you are in poor physical condition, have a complete physical check-up by a doctor and don't exercise until your doctor has cleared you to do so.

If none of the above apply, you are almost ready to do a self-administered maximum heart rate test.

PREPARATION FOR HR^{MAX} TESTS

Do not eat for 2–3 hours before a HR^{max} test. If you do, you may feel nauseous or have stomach cramps during or after the test. Always warm up and warm down for your tests.

SAFETY

If, during the test, you feel either dizzy or nauseous, want to stop, have chest pain or numbness down your left arm, have difficulty breathing, or your heart rate monitor gives unusually high or fluctuating readings, reduce intensity immediately (below 100 beats per minute) and stop the test.

Keep pedalling (or jogging) lightly, however, so you don't get dizzy and pass out. Consult a doctor as soon as possible. If during the test your heart rate goes above the age-adjusted formula (220 minus your age for men; 226 minus your age for women) be a little cautious. Do not do the test if you have a cold or other illness.

SELF-ADMINISTERED MAXIMUM HEART RATE TESTS

You need to find out your maximum tested heart rate for each discipline you are training in — cycling, kayaking, running, swimming, and so on. These heart rates must be worked out when you are not tired from training, so you need to have a couple of easy days before each test.

To find your maximum heart rate, warm up for 10–15 minutes. Once warmed up, exercise as hard you can for 4–8 minutes, with the last 1–2 minutes at maximum effort, until you 'blow'! (Hint: for running and cycling, sprinting up a steep hill is not very effective, as leg muscle fatigue may occur before you reach maximum heart rate, but a small incline is useful.)

Repeat this procedure for each sport (if you do more than one sport), making sure you are fully recovered between tests (allow a few days); otherwise the tests won't be valid and you won't be able to calculate your correct training intensities.

Your maximum heart rate is the highest reliable heart rate reached during testing — your 'high score'. This is best worked out using a heart rate monitor, but you can work it out manually as long as you manage to take your heart rate immediately after the test.

And remember, a maximum heart rate test can be dangerous, so if you are in any doubt about whether you can physically cope with it, see your doctor first.

Trouble-shooting maximum heart rate tests

You cannot achieve what you would regard as maximum heart rate if:

♥ You have a large heart, which means you won't achieve your theoretical maximum heart rate (see pages 22–5).

♥ Your legs/arms are too tired. Try again when you are fresher. Hint: never try to repeat the test on the same day because this can make you feel very sick.

♥ You were overgeared (e.g. too big a gear on your bike).

♥ Unfit or tired athletes may not reach true HR^{max} (which is very difficult), so add 5–10 bpm if you have seen a higher heart rate in training or racing.

As a simple check, calculate maximum theoretical heart rate by using the formula 220 minus age for men or 226 minus age for women.

ASSESSING BASIC ANAEROBIC THRESHOLD — CONCONI TEST

This test is very strenuous! Get medical clearance if you are unsure about your ability to cope with it, particularly if you are over the age of 35.

The advantage of the Conconi test is that it is very simple, does not require a lot of expensive testing equipment and, with the help of a couple of assistants, you can conduct it yourself. You will need:
- an accurate heart rate monitor;
- an assistant to record heart rates/lap splits;
- a bike equipped with a computer to measure speed and cadence for cycling: a stop-watch for running;
- a velodrome (choose a windless day) or a stationary cycle trainer for cycling or a track for running.

The test

Warm up for 10–20 minutes. Each lap should be between 300 and 450 m for cycling. Running should involve 200-m laps (two making a 400-m circuit of a running track). If you use a wind-trainer, use an appropriate time interval (30–60 seconds between speed increases).

Ride or run and maintain constant pace during each lap. Increase your speed by 1 or 2 kph on your bike or 1–2 seconds running for each lap (use the same increase each lap) until your legs are too tired to continue. At the end of each lap call out your heart rate so that it can be recorded by your assistant. (See page 303 for Conconi testing using heart rate monitors with a built-in test.)

How to calculate anaerobic threshold

Calculate your speed (running or cycling) per section of lap (see page 119). Plot your results on the graph on page 120, charting your recorded heart rates on the vertical axis and your speed on the horizontal axis. If your test has gone as planned, your graph should show an evenly sloping upward line until the point where your heart rate was unable to increase at the same rate as speed (heart rate plateau).

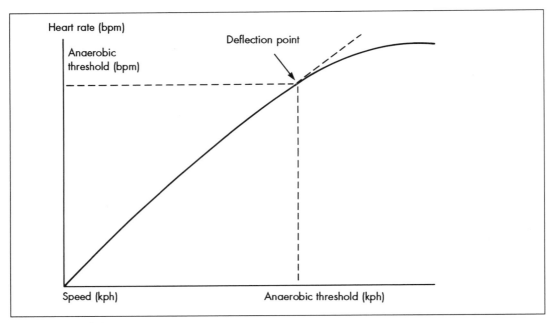

How often do you need to test?

Anaerobic threshold can move, so you need to test it regularly. AT should improve (get higher) during speedwork.

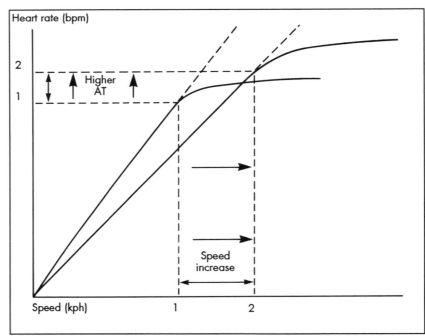

Figure 12.2:
Change in
anaerobic threshold
(heart rate and
speed) at the start of
speedwork (1) and
after peak (2)

Test every 2–8 weeks, towards the end of an easy week, in your mesocycles (mesocycles will be explained soon!). Rest for 18–24 hours before the test to freshen up. Test every two weeks in the Speed phase and every eight weeks in the Base phase (see chapter 16). Try to keep test conditions identical so that you get accurate results.

This test is useful but a lot of controversy does surround it (there is even controversy over whether anaerobic threshold exists at all). With extensive research being carried out in this area, exercise physiologists will produce further advances. In the meantime, this test is easy to conduct, inexpensive and relatively accurate for assessing heart rates.

CONCONI TEST RECORD SHEET

Name: Date:

Lap	Heart rate	Time (secs/lap)	Speed	
1.	....	....	....	*Speed calculations*
2.	....	....	....	*(in min/km):*
3.	....	....	....	Lap time (secs) ÷ 60
4.	....	....	....	= lap time (mins)
5.	....	....	....	Lap distance (m) ÷ 1000
6.	....	....	....	= lap distance (km)
7.	....	....	....	Lap time (mins) ÷ lap distance (km) = speed (mins/km)
8.	....	....	....	
9.	....	....	....	*In kph:*
10.	....	....	....	As above for lap time and lap distance
11.	....	....	....	
12.	....	....	....	Lap distance (km) ÷ lap time (mins) x 60 = speed (kph)
13.	....	....	....	
14.	....	....	....	
15.	....	....	....	
16.	....	....	....	
17.	....	....	....	
18.	....	....	....	
19.	....	....	....	
20.	....	....	....	

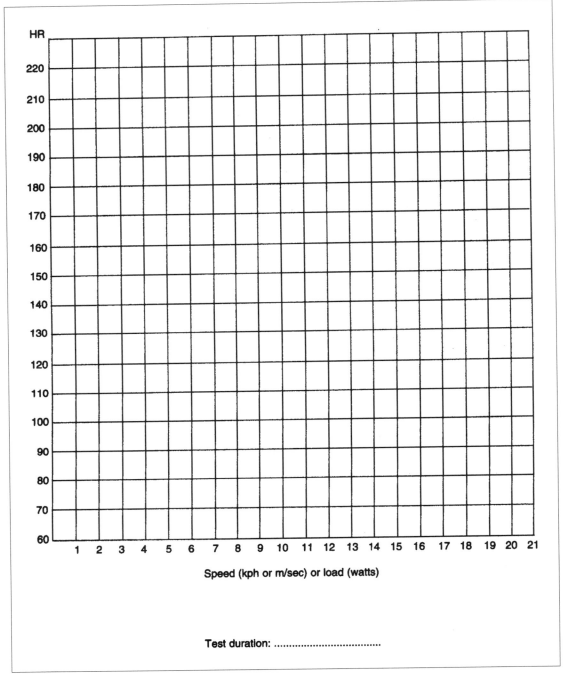

FIGURE 12.3: Anaerobic/aerobic threshold assessment sheet

Conconi test trouble-shooting

1. Good result — deflection achieved.

2. Deflects upwards instead of flattening:
   - indicates that the athlete went 'all out' towards the end of the test rather than controlling the stepped increase in effort. Adrenalin produced in an all-out effort causes heart rate to increase suddenly rather than flattening.

3. Heart rate does not increase in a straight line in relation to load:
   - uneven control of speed increase;
   - for cycling, cadence was not close to constant; athlete is probably inexperienced and is not controlling gear changing well. To improve this, reschedule the test in a few days and do the test using the big chain ring only. This will give better control as the gear change between the chain rings is what causes most of the trouble.

4. Heart rate increases in a straight line in relation to load but no deflection occurs:
   - athlete has poor muscle endurance in their sport-specific (e.g. cycling) muscles;
   - athlete has not recovered from previous training and is too tired to do an adequate test. Reschedule the test when the athlete is fully recovered.

5. Heart rate is lower for the same loads. You are fitter!

Assessment of muscular economy (strength endurance) and technique

Exercise economy

Exercise economy is determined by the length of time the athlete can last during the test. It is a basic measure of the efficiency and fitness of the athlete. An efficient athlete will last longer than an inefficient athlete, and a fitter athlete will last longer as well.

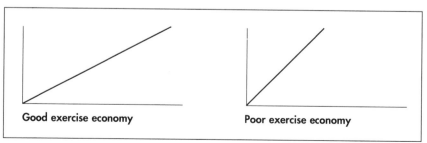

Figure 12.4: Good vs poor exercise economy

TECHNIQUE

The better their technique the longer the athlete will last and the more 'linear' (straighter) the line will be initially.

FIGURE 12.5:
Good vs poor technique/pace control

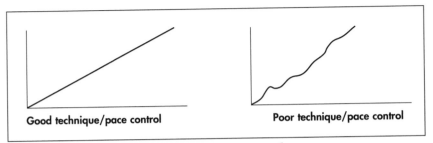

Good technique/pace control   Poor technique/pace control

STRENGTH/MUSCLE ENDURANCE

The longer the athlete can continue after the deflection or the fact that the athlete can achieve deflection indicates good strength endurance.

FIGURE 12.6:
Good vs poor strength endurance

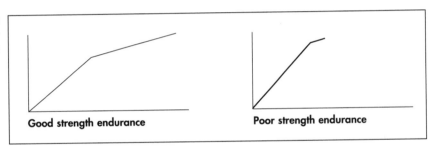

Good strength endurance   Poor strength endurance

For multiple discipline sports like duathlon (running and cycling):

You can either test each sport or if you can't be bothered, use the HR/sport converter below.

| | | Change to: | | | |
		C	S	R	K
	C	0	-10	+10	-15
	S	+10	0	+20	-5
Tested Sport	R	-10	-20	0	-25
	K	+15	+5	+25	0

Key:
C = Cycling
S = Swimming
R = Running
K = Kayaking

e.g. Cycle = 150   Swim = 140
     Run = 160   Kayak = 135

Anaerobic threshold heart rate

Sport	1	2	3	4
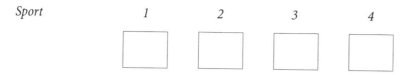				

To calculate training heart rates:

1. Take your AT heart rate and round it to the nearest 5 beats:
   e.g. 183 = 185.

2. Subtract and add 5 beats to give a range:
   e.g. 180–190.

3. Subtract 10 beats from the bottom of your SM range to give the bottom of your UT range:
   e.g. 180 - 10 = 170; UT = 170–180

4. Use the Karvonen formula at 60% to get the bottom of your LSD range:
   e.g. (204 - 45) x 60% + 45 = 140

5. The top of your AT heart rate to maximum heart rate is HI:
   e.g. 190–204

6. AR is the bottom of the LSD range or less (e.g. <140).

Put rates in the tables provided in the 'Putting it all together' section at the end of this chapter (pages 124–6).

HEART RATE MONITORS AND LISTENING TO YOUR BODY

When heart rate monitors first came out, athletes and players thought they were great — you go out training, your heart rate monitor shows a whole bunch of numbers, and you are kept interested watching it for hours. Unfortunately, this didn't achieve much.

Sports people then learnt about different training zones and the heart rates that go with them. They became very rigid about using them and they stuck to their prescribed heart rates like glue, ignoring the body's messages in the process. This didn't achieve much, either.

No matter what technological innovations appear, listening to your body is the most important indicator of how you feel in training. Other indicators (heart rate monitor, split times, speed) provide extra information that enable you to make the best decisions.

It's a bit like driving a car: you always listen to the sound of the motor to find out what's going on, and then you look at the rev counter. The same applies to the human body. Listen to your body first, then look at the other information.

In other words, a heart rate monitor should be considered a tool, not a dictator. You can't spend your entire training session in a training zone — so don't try. For example, if you ride up a hill on your bike in training and your heart rate rises above your training zone, don't get off your bike and walk up the hill (believe me, people do this!). Instead, accept the fact that you can't always be in your training zone, and get back in your zone when you are over the top of the hill.

Also, if you feel like a bit of a blast or a race with friends while training — go for it! There's nothing wrong with this. The aim is to spend *most* of your time in the training zone.

I've even heard of athletes who have incorrectly worked out their racing heart rate and raced at that rate even when they felt — their body told them — that the intensity was too low.

The moral of the story is: always listen to your body first. You can then use your heart rate monitor to provide you with any extra information you need to make the correct decisions about training and competition.

Putting it all together

♥ Put all your heart rates in.

Karvonen formula
$(HR^{max} - HR^{rest})$ x (% exercise intensity) + HR^{rest}

HR^{max} = maximum heart rate; HR^{rest} = resting heart rate.
Maximum heart rate:
(assessed either by physical test or 220 – age [males]; 226 – age [females])

Sport	1	2*	3*	4*

Threshold heart rate:
(by test or ignore)

Sport	1	2*	3*	4*

Only use 2, 3, and 4 if you are doing more than 1 sport.

Resting heart rate:
(taken lying down in bed on waking)

Sport   *1*

☐

High intensity (anaerobic)

Intensity	*Duration*	*%HR^{max}*
Power	Less than 10 sec	N/A
Intensive sprints	10 sec–1 min	N/A
Extensive sprints	1–4 min	95–100%

Sport   *1*   *2**   *3**   *4**

☐   ☐   ☐   ☐   (HI)

Submaximal intensity (threshold)

Intensity	*Duration*	*%HR^{max}*
Maximum steady-state pace	4 min–1 hr	N/A
Anaerobic threshold	1 hr	85–95%

Sport   *1*   *2**   *3**   *4**

☐   ☐   ☐   ☐   (AT)

Low intensity (aerobic)

Intensity	*Duration*	*%HR^{max}*
Up-tempo	4 min+	75–85%

Sport   *1*   *2**   *3**   *4**

☐   ☐   ☐   ☐   (UT)

Long Slow distance		4 min+	60–75%		
Sport	*1*	*2**	*3**	*4**	
					(LSD)

Active recovery		4 min+	<60%		
Sport	*1*	*2**	*3**	*4**	
					(AR)

* Only use 2, 3, and 4 if you are doing more than 1 sport.

Note: For calculated heart rates rather than assessed, it is impossible to obtain absolutely accurate training heart rate ranges. These percentages are designed to give you an approximate level to train in, and using the training intensity descriptions you should be able to establish your training levels accurately by heart rate and by feel.

In short intervals it is difficult to use heart rates as they may not react fast enough. For high-intensity workouts it is recommended that you use the specified durations.

CHAPTER 13

CHOOSING YOUR WEAPON

Deciding which heart rate monitor to use should be based on the programme to be undertaken (with the major considerations in this order).

1. How much can you afford?

2. What features do you need?

3. Are you a 'Gadget Freak'?

Here is a table of recommendations.

Features	Beginner	Cardiac rehab	Dieter	Athlete (rec)	Semi-Comp	Competitive	Élite
Time of day	✓	✓	✓	✓	✓	✓	✓
Stopwatch	•	✓	✓	•	✓	✓	✓
Target zone	•	✓	✓	•	✓	✓	✓
Water resistant	•	✓	✓	•	✓	✓	✓
Sample HR record	•	•	•	•	•	✓	✓
Continuous HR record	•	•	•	•	•	•	✓
Lap times	•	•	•	•	•	✓	✓
Computer software/ PC interface	•	•	•	•	•	✓	✓
Relaxation rate	•	✓	•	•	•	•	✓
Tests	•	•	•	•	•	•	✓
Coded transmission	•	•	•	•	✓	✓	✓
Backlight	•	•	•	•	✓	✓	✓
Recovery HR	•	✓	•	•	✓	✓	✓
Average HR	•	✓	•	•	✓	✓	✓
Cals consumed	•	•	✓	•	•	•	•
Countdown timer	•	•	•	•	✓	✓	✓

FIGURE 13.1: Recommended features and functions of heart rate monitors for athletes at various levels

EXPLANATION OF FEATURES

Water Resistant: Can swim in it and wear it in heavy rain.

Target Zones: Set training heart rate zones and heart rate monitor will either visually or audibly indicate if you are outside the zones.

Stop Watch: Able to time your workout, also lap times.

Time of Day: Chronograph standard watch functions.

Timers: Interval times that 'beep' at set points. Good for target times and fluid or nutritional strategies.

Alarm: Standard watch alarm.

Rotating Face: Watch face can be rotated to see better.

Back Light: Illuminates screen. Good for training at night.

Cycle Mount: Can mount onto a bicycle.

Relaxation Rate: Measures stress — mental stress, physical fatigue.

Time in Zone: Gives indication of the time in, above and below target training zone. Indicates quality of workout.

Sample Heart Rate Record (Computer Interface): Can record heart rate at a particular point in time, like 'lap times'.

Continuous Heart Rate Record: Records heart rate continuously to be reviewed manually later or downloaded into a computer for review.

Recovery Heart Rate: Measures recovery rate — the time that heart rate takes to drop to a set heart rate point or what heart rate drops to in a certain set time.

Average Heart Rate: Average heart rate over entire workout. Good measure of the intensity/effort of a workout.

Calories Consumed: Estimates amount of energy used during exercise or number of calories consumed.

Tests: Able to perform tests for anaerobic threshold and fitness (Conconi, UKK, walking test and interval test).

Battery Change: You can change the battery in the transmitter belt without having to replace it.

Coded Transmission: Contains 30 frequencies that can be altered so that 30 athletes can train in close proximity to each other without what is called 'cross talk' — when your heart rate's transmission signal is interfered with by the transmission from your training partner's watch, giving you erroneous readings.

Bike Computer: Has cycle computer functions.

Possibilities with bike computers include speed, cadence, altitude and power (watts).

More detailed information on heart rate monitor capabilities, features and functions is in Appendix 5 (page 295).

What does your heart do in the course of a day? Once again, I'm the brave individual that wore my heart rate monitor all day to see what would happen.

It's not very comfortable. The test started at 12:00 p.m. on a 'slothful' Sunday and concluded at 12:00 p.m. on an 'earn a living' Monday. I had 8 hours sleep and went for a 30-minute run on Monday. My average heart rate for the 24 hours was 61 (30% of HR^{MAX}) with a maximum heart rate during my 'up-tempo' run of 175–180. My heart beat 87,840 times in the day.

Weird Things
TO DO WITH YOUR HEART RATE MONITOR

A Day in the Life — 24 Hours

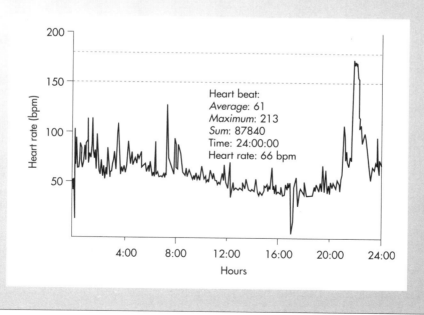

Heart beat:
Average: 61
Maximum: 213
Sum: 87840
Time: 24:00:00
Heart rate: 66 bpm

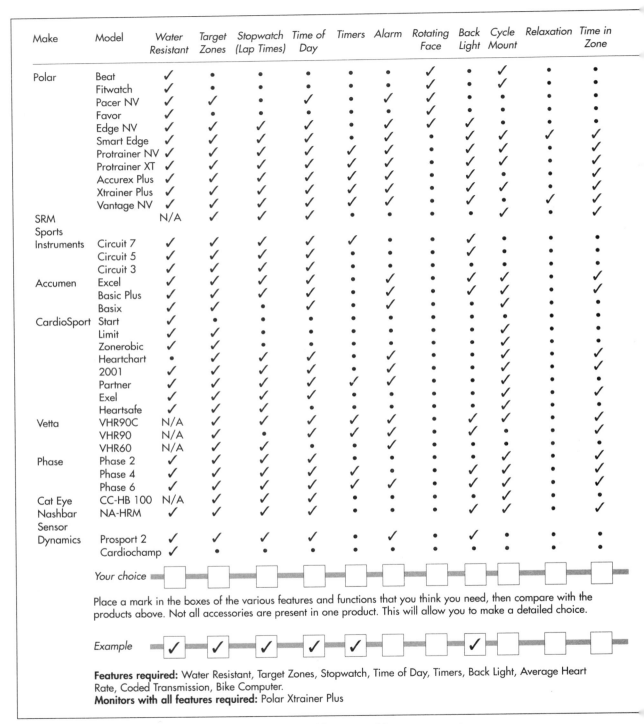

Make	Model	Water Resistant	Target Zones	Stopwatch (Lap Times)	Time of Day	Timers	Alarm	Rotating Face	Back Light	Cycle Mount	Relaxation	Time in Zone
Polar	Beat	✓	•	•	•	•	•	✓	•	✓	•	•
	Fitwatch	✓	•	•	•	•	•	✓	•	✓	•	•
	Pacer NV	✓	✓	•	✓	•	•	✓	•	•	•	•
	Favor	✓	•	•	•	•	•	✓	•	•	•	•
	Edge NV	✓	✓	✓	✓	•	✓	✓	✓	✓	•	✓
	Smart Edge	✓	✓	✓	✓	•	✓	✓	✓	✓	✓	✓
	Protrainer NV	✓	✓	✓	✓	✓	✓	✓	✓	•	•	✓
	Protrainer XT	✓	✓	✓	✓	✓	✓	✓	✓	•	•	✓
	Accurex Plus	✓	✓	✓	✓	✓	✓	✓	✓	•	•	✓
	Xtrainer Plus	✓	✓	✓	✓	✓	✓	✓	✓	•	•	✓
	Vantage NV	✓	✓	✓	✓	✓	✓	•	✓	•	✓	✓
SRM		N/A	✓	✓	✓	•	•	•	•	✓	•	•
Sports Instruments	Circuit 7	✓	✓	✓	✓	✓	•	•	✓	•	•	•
	Circuit 5	✓	✓	✓	✓	•	•	•	✓	•	•	•
	Circuit 3	✓	✓	✓	✓	•	•	•	•	•	•	✓
Accumen	Excel	✓	✓	✓	✓	•	✓	•	✓	•	•	✓
	Basic Plus	✓	✓	✓	✓	•	✓	•	✓	•	•	•
	Basix	✓	✓	•	✓	•	✓	•	✓	•	•	•
CardioSport	Start	✓	•	•	•	•	•	•	✓	•	•	•
	Limit	✓	✓	•	•	•	•	•	✓	•	•	•
	Zonerobic	✓	✓	•	•	•	•	•	✓	•	•	•
	Heartchart	•	✓	✓	✓	•	✓	•	✓	•	•	✓
	2001	✓	✓	✓	✓	•	✓	•	✓	•	•	✓
	Partner	✓	✓	✓	✓	✓	•	•	✓	•	•	✓
	Exel	✓	✓	✓	✓	•	•	•	•	•	•	✓
	Heartsafe	✓	✓	✓	✓	•	•	•	•	•	•	✓
Vetta	VHR90C	N/A	✓	✓	✓	✓	✓	•	✓	✓	•	✓
	VHR90	N/A	✓	•	✓	✓	✓	•	•	✓	•	✓
	VHR60	N/A	✓	•	✓	•	✓	•	•	✓	•	✓
Phase	Phase 2	✓	✓	✓	✓	•	•	•	✓	✓	•	✓
	Phase 4	✓	✓	✓	✓	✓	•	•	✓	✓	•	✓
	Phase 6	✓	✓	✓	✓	✓	✓	•	✓	✓	•	✓
Cat Eye	CC-HB 100	N/A	✓	✓	✓	•	•	•	•	✓	•	•
Nashbar	NA-HRM	✓	✓	✓	✓	•	•	•	✓	✓	•	✓
Sensor Dynamics	Prosport 2	✓	✓	✓	✓	•	✓	•	✓	•	•	•
	Cardiochamp	✓	•	•	•	•	•	•	•	•	•	•

Your choice ☐ ☐ ☐ ☐ ☐ ☐ ☐ ☐ ☐ ☐ ☐

Place a mark in the boxes of the various features and functions that you think you need, then compare with the products above. Not all accessories are present in one product. This will allow you to make a detailed choice.

Example ☑ ☑ ☑ ☑ ☑ ☐ ☐ ☑ ☐ ☐ ☐

Features required: Water Resistant, Target Zones, Stopwatch, Time of Day, Timers, Back Light, Average Heart Rate, Coded Transmission, Bike Computer.
Monitors with all features required: Polar Xtrainer Plus

FIGURE 13.2: Features and functions of heart rate monitors

Model	Sample Heart Rate	Computer Interface	Recovery Heart Rate	Average Heart Rate	Calories Consumed	Tests	Battery Change	Coded Transmission	Bike Computer	Special Notes
Beat	•	•	•	•	•	•	•	•	•	Buttonless
Fitwatch	•	•	•	•	•	•	•	•	•	Buttonless
Pacer NV	•	•	•	•	•	•	•	•	•	
Favor	•	•	•	•	•	•	•	•	•	
Edge NV	•	•	•	•	•	•	•	•	•	
Smart Edge	•	•	•	•	✓	•	•	•	•	
Protrainer NV	✓	✓	✓	✓	•	•	•	✓	•	Ownzone
Protrainer XT	✓	✓	✓	✓	•	•	•	✓	•	
Accurex Plus	✓	•	✓	✓	•	•	•	✓	✓	
Xtrainer	✓	✓	✓	✓	•	✓	•	✓	✓	Altitude Kit
Vantage NV	✓	✓	✓	•	•	✓	•	✓	•	
	•	✓	•	✓	✓	✓	•	•	✓	Records Watts
Circuit 7	✓	•	✓	✓	•	•	✓	•	•	Memory & Recall
Circuit 5	✓	•	•	✓	•	•	✓	•	•	Memory & Recall
Circuit 3	•	•	•	•	•	•	✓	•	•	
Excel	•	•	✓	•	•	•	✓	•	•	
Basic Plus	•	•	•	•	✓	•	✓	•	•	Buttonless
Basix	•	•	•	•	•	•	✓	•	•	Buttonless
Start	•	•	•	•	•	•	✓	•	•	Buttonless
Limit	•	•	•	•	•	•	✓	•	•	Buttonless
Zonerobic	•	•	•	•	•	•	✓	•	•	Buttonless
Heartchart	✓	✓	✓	•	✓	•	✓	•	•	
2001	✓	✓	✓	✓	✓	•	✓	•	•	
Partner	•	✓	•	•	✓	•	✓	•	•	
Excel	✓	•	•	•	•	•	✓	•	•	
Heartsafe	✓	•	•	•	•	•	✓	•	•	
VHR90C	•	•	•	•	✓	•	•	•	•	
VHR90	•	•	•	•	✓	•	•	•	✓	Temperature
VHR60	•	•	•	•	•	•	•	•	•	
Phase 2	•	•	•	✓	•	•	✓	•	•	
Phase 4	•	•	•	✓	✓	•	✓	•	•	
Phase 6	•	•	✓	✓	✓	✓	✓	•	•	
CC-HB100	•	•	•	✓	•	•	•	•	✓	
NA-HRM	•	•	•	•	•	•	•	•	•	
Prosport 2	•	•	•	•	•	•	✓	•	•	
Cardiochamp	•	•	•	•	•	•	✓	•	•	
Your choice	☐	☐	☐	☐	☐	☐	☐	☐	☐	
Example	☐	☐	☐	✓	☐	☐	☐	✓	✓	

PART
two

THE BASICS OF TRAINING

THE PRINCIPLES OF TRAINING

To discuss 'training intensities' without discussing 'training' is like having bacon without eggs or fish without chips. You can't use a heart rate monitor effectively without knowing how to train. So, let's discuss training.

The simplest way to describe training is:

Training is showing your body what will happen in competition.

In other words, as you move through a build-up, you try to get a closer and closer match between training and what you want to do on competition day.

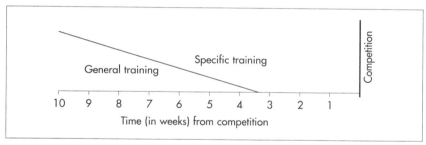

FIGURE 14.1: Movement over time from general to specific training

If you arrive at competition day and you have already shown your body what will happen, then you are ready. If, however, you arrive at competition day not having shown your body everything that is going to happen, then during competition your body will be screaming at you, 'What are you doing, you didn't show me this; how am I supposed to perform if I have never experienced this before?'

In my experience, this is almost always the reason why athletes fail to perform as well as they had hoped — they didn't prepare for one tiny aspect of the race, they didn't tick all the boxes.

Training, therefore, is about breaking a competition down into its various parts, practising them, and then gradually putting the parts back together until you can virtually do the whole competition at the right intensity.

Early in training, each part of the competition or race is trained for and refined separately. Then the parts are gradually joined together into bigger 'chunks' and these are coordinated, trained and refined. Eventually these chunks get so big that you are able to complete nearly the entire competition in training. Finally, you can complete the whole competition or very large chunks of it under competition conditions and pressure.

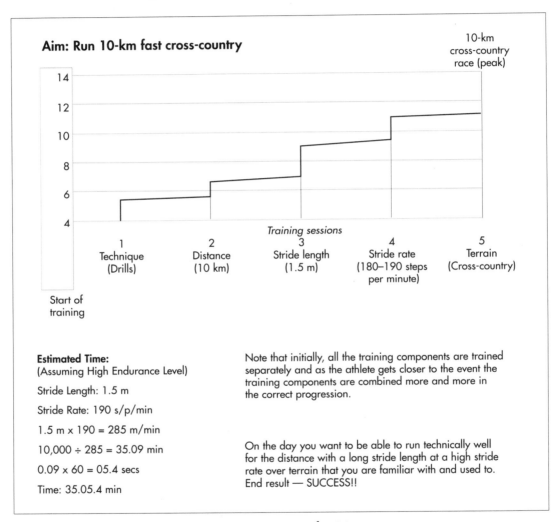

Aim: Run 10-km fast cross-country

10-km cross-country race (peak)

Training sessions

| 1 | 2 | 3 | 4 | 5 |
| Technique (Drills) | Distance (10 km) | Stride length (1.5 m) | Stride rate (180–190 steps per minute) | Terrain (Cross-country) |

Start of training

Estimated Time:
(Assuming High Endurance Level)

Stride Length: 1.5 m

Stride Rate: 190 s/p/min

1.5 m x 190 = 285 m/min

10,000 ÷ 285 = 35.09 min

0.09 x 60 = 05.4 secs

Time: 35.05.4 min

Note that initially, all the training components are trained separately and as the athlete gets closer to the event the training components are combined more and more in the correct progression.

On the day you want to be able to run technically well for the distance with a long stride length at a high stride rate over terrain that you are familiar with and used to. End result — SUCCESS!!

Figure 14.2: Separate components of training progressively combining as competition approaches

Basic training progression — 'The big three'

Developing performance

There are three major parts to training:

- ♥ Volume: the amount of training (measured in time or distance).

- ♥ Intensity: the energy or effort required for a specific form of training (measured objectively by heart rate, or subjectively by perceived effort).

- ♥ Performance: level of ability (measured in outcome, time, distance or placing).

Generally, volume comes before intensity. Changes in volume and intensity (and types of training) change performance.

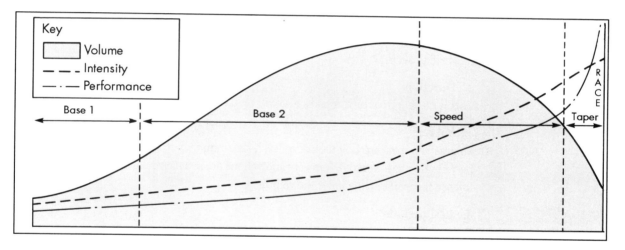

VOLUME + INTENSITY = PERFORMANCE

FIGURE 14.3:
Volume vs intensity vs performance

In most training programmes, volume moves progressively up, then progressively down, as intensity builds. On the other hand, intensity generally moves progressively up. Performance, if everything goes according to plan, moves up and peaks at competition (see figure 14.3).

FIGURE 14.4:
Schematic diagram
of how volume and
intensity proportions
change as a sports
person builds closer
and closer to
competition

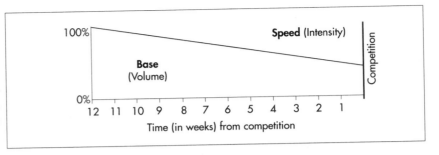

THE COMPONENTS OF TRAINING

By understanding and controlling the following training components you will train and compete more effectively.

1. Intensity

Intensity is the effort or energy required for a particular form of training. The intensity of the workout must be sufficiently stressful to allow adaptation to overload to occur.

2. Duration

This is the length of time it takes to complete a workout.

3. Volume

Volume is a measure (kilometres/miles, hours/minutes) of how much work you perform during a workout. Intensity and volume are inversely related — the more intense the workout, the lower the volume.

4. Rest periods

Rest periods are the length of time between periods of training; for example, between intervals or sprints or workouts. The length of the rest period depends on the relationship between the intensity/volume of the workout and the athlete's tolerance to training.

5. Repetitions

Repetitions (reps) are the number of times a specific form of training is completed during a workout; for example, 3 x 1 km. Repetitions, generally associated with speedwork and shorter intervals, are usually grouped into sets.

These can be combined in one workout (see figure 14.5)

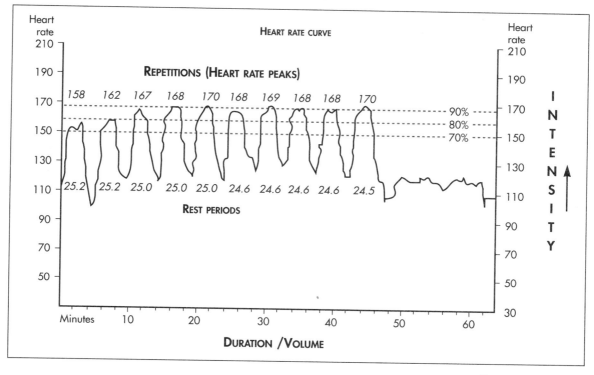

HEART RATE CURVE

REPETITIONS (HEART RATE PEAKS)

158 162 167 168 170 168 169 168 168 170

90%
80%
70%

25.2 25.2 25.0 25.0 25.0 24.6 24.6 24.6 24.6 24.5

REST PERIODS

Minutes 10 20 30 40 50 60

DURATION / VOLUME

Heart rate / 210 190 170 150 130 110 90 70 50

I N T E N S I T Y

FIGURE 14.5:
The components of
training together
in one workout

6. Planning

Training and perfomance is all about planning. As they say, 'Fail to plan, plan to fail'. To perform well or peak on the day or competition you have to *control* your training. The two main areas that you have to control are:

What you do: *correct training.*

When you do it: *correct timing.*

CORRECT TRAINING + CORRECT TIMING = PEAKING

PUTTING IT ALL TOGETHER

Training build-up to peak

	1st half of training	2nd half of training
Volume	Up	Down
Intensity	Up	Up
Performance	Up	Up

139

- ♥ Volume + Intensity = Performance.
- ♥ Training is showing your body what will happen in competition.
- ♥ To train, break your competition/race down into manageable 'chunks' (you can't go out and do the race every day) and show your body each 'chunk' (e.g. technique, distance, stride length, stride rate). As you get closer to competition, gradually bring the 'chunks' together to condition your body more specifically . Training is most specific ('chunks' combined) closest to the competition and least specific ('chunks' training separately) further away from competition.
- ♥ Performance is planning.
- ♥ Correct training + correct timing = peaking.

CHAPTER 15

PERIODISATION — THE SEASONS

We've discussed the basics, now let's go through how you plan your training — how you write a programme for yourself. We'll start with the biggest 'blocks' of training and gradually break the programme/plan down into smaller and smaller 'blocks', down to the 'nitty gritty'. We start at seasons and end up at specific workouts. This is so you can see the 'big picture'. It's like taking a jigsaw puzzle and putting all the pieces in place so you can see the picture only you can't understand and see the whole picture until every piece of the jigsaw is in place.

We'll start with seasons, then break the seasons into periods, the periods into subphases, the subphases into recovery cycles, and finally end up with a training programme where you completely understand the three major questions in a training programme:

1. How far/long do you go?

2. What do you do when you get out there?

3. How hard do you go?

Let's start with seasons — the off-season, pre-season and in-season that make up a training year.

OFF-SEASON

This is the transition or active recovery phase. It usually lasts between 2–12 weeks, although it can last for as long as 10 months.

Training during this phase should be recreational in nature, i.e. fun! The number of workouts should be greatly reduced during the off-season, or even limited to when the sports person wants to train. A good rule of thumb is 20–30 percent of the biggest training volume week from your last build-up. Recreational training will rest the body and mind while retaining performance potential for the build-up that follows.

The off-season is essentially a balancing act between recovery and main-taining fitness. The best way to achieve this is to do 'fun' workouts, or incorporate

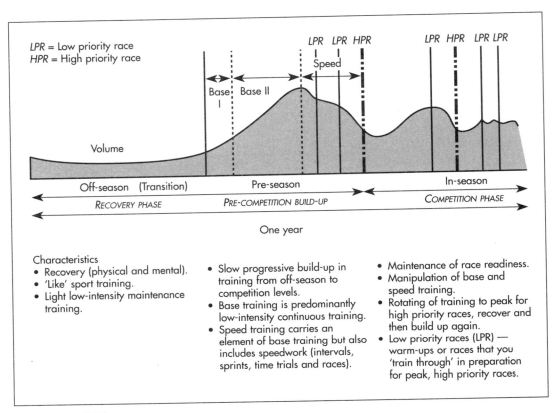

LPR = Low priority race
HPR = High priority race

LPR LPR HPR   LPR HPR   LPR LPR

Speed

Base Base II
I

Volume

Off-season (Transition)   Pre-season   In-season

RECOVERY PHASE   PRE-COMPETITION BUILD-UP   COMPETITION PHASE

One year

Characteristics
- Recovery (physical and mental).
- 'Like' sport training.
- Light low-intensity maintenance training.

- Slow progressive build-up in training from off-season to competition levels.
- Base training is predominantly low-intensity continuous training.
- Speed training carries an element of base training but also includes speedwork (intervals, sprints, time trials and races).

- Maintenance of race readiness.
- Manipulation of base and speed training.
- Rotating of training to peak for high priority races, recover and then build up again.
- Low priority races (LPR) — warm-ups or races that you 'train through' in preparation for peak, high priority races.

FIGURE 15.1:
Training seasons

training into things you like to do (e.g. cycle to a café). You can also do 'like' sport training — for example, mountain biking is very good for maintaining your road cycling form. Stopping training altogether during the off-season is not advised, as your base fitness will be greatly eroded. This will result in a smaller performance gain the following year. In other words: if you don't use it, you lose it!

The key is to recover mentally. Most athletes/players can recover physically in a very short space of time, but to recover mentally — to be enthusiastic to train

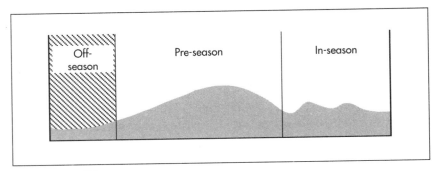

Off-season   Pre-season   In-season

FIGURE 15.2: Off-season

'full on' again — takes a little longer. You need to remove everything that reminds you of the structure, effort and process of training. Don't train in the same way, on the same courses, at the same times — do something different!

Pre-season

This is the preparatory phase, or build-up, and it usually lasts between 10–20

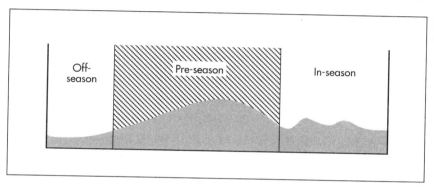

FIGURE 15.3:
Pre-season

weeks. It is the time to prepare and train, to build up from the off-season to high performance for your major competition(s).

Pre-season is broken into two major training periods: Base and Speed. These are discussed in more detail in Chapter 16.

In-season

This is the competition or racing phase. It can last between 1–6 months; the norm is 8–12 weeks. This is when you begin to compete seriously.

In-season may consist of a single peak for a specific high-priority, goal event (e.g. provincial, national or world champs), or it may involve several peaks (e.g. a mountain bike race series, a rugby or soccer season) that require a cycle of peaking, dropping form, and peaking again.

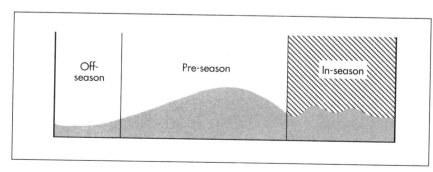

FIGURE 15.4:
In-season

Many athletes/players think they can peak for a whole competing season. This is, unfortunately, impossible, so training must be based around up to six goal events per year. For example, 1–4 short races (e.g. standard course triathlon, road races, mountain bike races) are tolerable for most athletes. For long distance races (e.g. Ironman, Coast to Coast, tours, mountain bike series) the number of races drops to 1–2. You may still do many more low-priority races, but they are not races you aim to peak in. Field team players (rugby, soccer, etc.) may be able to come up for around 6 major competitions and play the rest of their games at a high level, but not peak.

SINGLE, DOUBLE AND TRIPLE PERIODISATIONS

A periodisation is a single build-up (pre-season, in-season, and off-season) —

FIGURE 15.5:
Single periodisation: novice or junior or very recreational athlete/player

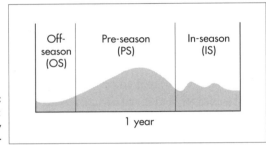

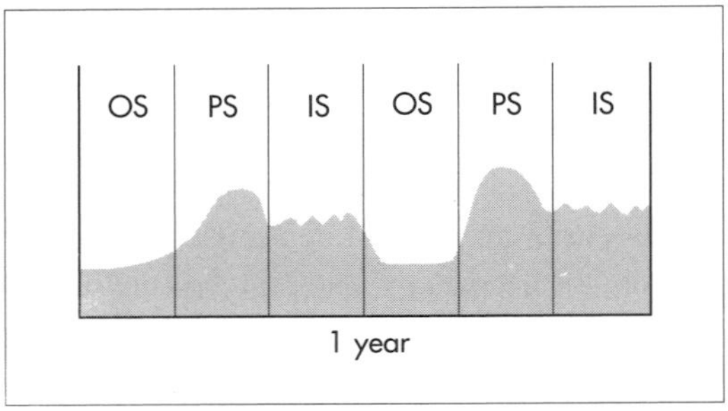

FIGURE 15.6:
Double periodisation experienced recreational, semi-competitive or competitive athlete/player

FIGURE 15.7:
Triple periodisation: very competitive, élite or pro athlete/player

More periodisations can be done but this is generally unwise and rare.

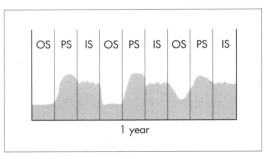

depending on the experience of the athlete/player in the sport, they may be able to do more than one periodisation (build-up) per year.

Two build-ups in a year is known as a double periodisation and three build-ups is known as a triple periodisation.

PUTTING IT ALL TOGETHER

♥ The diagram below shows how training is broken down in a year. The year breaks down into seasons:

> Off-season.
> Pre-season.
> In-season.

♥ You can do more than one periodisation (build-up) in a year depending on your experience in the sport.

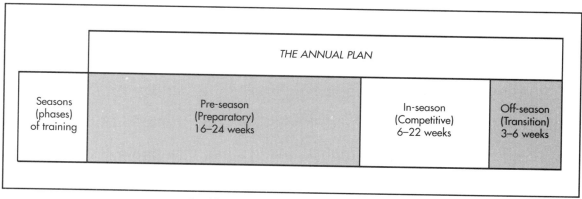

FIGURE 15.8: The 'blocks' of seasons within a year

CHAPTER 16

PERIODISATION — THE FOUNDATION OF A TRAINING PROGRAMME

PRE-SEASON IN DETAIL — TRAINING PERIODS

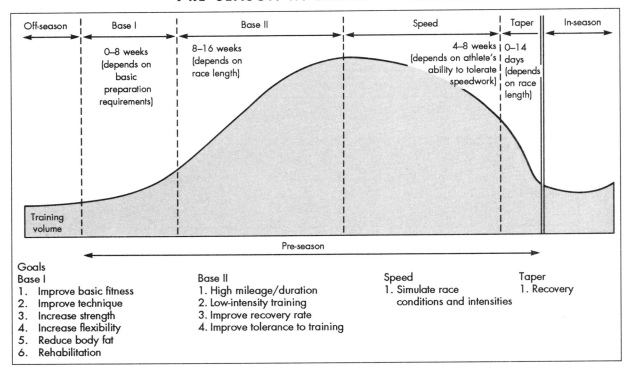

FIGURE 16.1: Training periods

As we've seen, pre-season is divided into two training periods, Base and Speed. Base is the mileage phase and Speed is competition-specific conditioning.

Base aims to build 'fitness', recovery and tolerance to training, to allow the athlete/player to do effective speedwork (the 'go fast' part). This results in a maximum potential performance. It is also used to show the athlete the distance or duration of the competition. If you look closely at training, Base is further broken down into endurance and strength endurance while Speed is, as it states, speed.

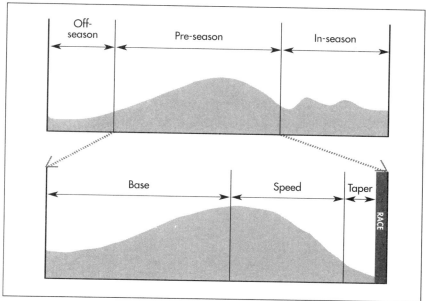

FIGURE 16.2:
Pre-season — Base
and Speed phases

BASE

Technique/endurance (Base 1)

Endurance is designed to get the athlete/player conditioned to training. It takes account of initial fitness and allows time to address weaker factors in the training. Once endurance training has been carried out the athlete/player will be 'fit' enough to cope with further, more strenuous types of training. Endurance enables the athlete to complete the race distance, or begin to, for longer races. Establishing good technique is vital during this phase. Strength training would involve conditioning or the 'hypertrophy/endurance phase' (high repetitions and sets and medium weight); the emphasis is on volume and technique.

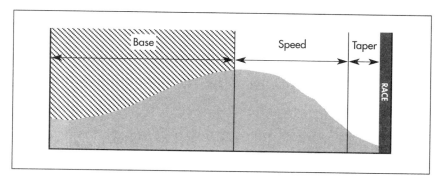

FIGURE 16.3:
Pre-season —
Base phase

Strength endurance (Base 2)

Strength endurance can now be trained. If endurance allows you to complete the race, strength endurance gives you the ability to apply more 'grunt' (strength, power, force). An example of this in cycling could be that endurance training is pedalling easily up to or above race distance; strength endurance is riding the same distance in a big gear (low cadence — uphill and flat).

Strength endurance moves from slowly increasing the muscular effort of the activity to maintaining the muscular effort and applying speed. Strength training would involve pure strength training in the 'strength phase' (medium reps and sets and high weight); the emphasis is on greater strength. Muscle endurance may be phased in towards the end for some sports (high reps, lower competition specific weights.)

SPEED

Speed is the time to simulate competition conditions and intensities. The athlete/player's body responds by adapting to this training, and their performance therefore goes up. If training is showing your body what will happen on race day so that it can adapt to it, speed makes this more and more specific to the race as it draws nearer.

Speed generally moves from longer, slower training to shorter, faster training — from tempo training to anaerobic threshold/maximum steady-state pace to long sprints, short sprints, power and overspeed, in that order. (We'll deal with these in detail later.)

Strength training involves moving the resistance at competition specific speeds in the 'power' phase as opposed to the slower speeds used in the earlier phases. (Reps, sets and weights variable — as close to competition requirements as possible.)

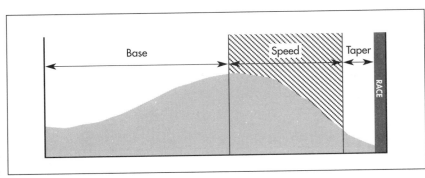

FIGURE 16.4:
Pre-season —
Speed phase

TAPER

The taper is actually part of the Speed phase as speedwork is still performed during the taper.

A taper is a gradual reduction in training volume to allow the athlete/player to recover fully before the race/competition, so that they are capable of maximum performance on race/competition day. Too long a taper and the athlete/player's form begins to drop, too short a taper and recovery is incomplete and the athlete/player will compete tired.

Taper occurs before every competition, the length depending on how high a priority it is. More important competitions require longer tapers so the athlete/player is fully ready to compete at maximum potential. Less important competitions are used as training for the main event; a trade-off is therefore made between recovery, so that the athlete/player performs well, and not missing too much training; the result is a shorter taper.

A taper is a very personal part of training, as what suits one competitor will not suit another. Tapers generally last between 2–14 days, depending on the competition. The longer the duration of the event, the longer the taper.

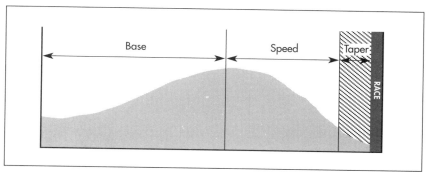

FIGURE 16.5:
Pre-season —
Taper phase

PUTTING IT ALL TOGETHER

♥ The diagram on the next page shows how training is broken down in a year. The year breaks down into seasons:

> Off-season.
> Pre-season.
> In-season.

♥ The pre-season further breaks down into periods:

> Base 1.
> Base 2.
> Speed (with taper).

	THE ANNUAL PLAN				
Seasons (phases) of training	Pre-season (Preparatory) 16–24 weeks			In-season (Competitive) 6–22 weeks	Off-season (Transition) 3–6 weeks
Periods of training	Base 1 (General prep)	Base 2 (Specific prep)	Speed (Pre comp)	Competitive racing	Transition to next build-up

FIGURE 16.6: The 'blocks' of training periods within seasons

TYPES OF TRAINING — COMBINING THE BIG THREE

TECHNIQUE, ENDURANCE, STRENGTH ENDURANCE AND SPEED

We've looked at seasons and periods, now we look at what we do in the Base and Speed periods.

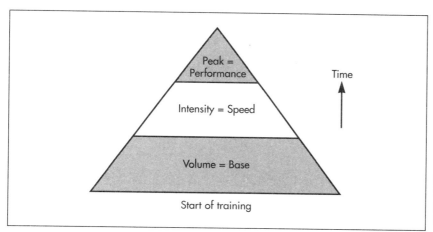

FIGURE 17.1: Progression of training from volume to speed to peak.

SUBPHASES: TYPES OF TRAINING

Intensity and volume are combined to give different types of training! Here is how the types of training progress through the programme to peak.

The first thing you need to be able to do is perform the action properly. That's what correct **technique** is all about. Then you need to perform the action properly for a long time. That's **endurance**. You need to get 'fit' doing the technique.

Then you need to perform the action properly for a long time with 'grunt'. There's no point in being technically good and fit if you can't apply the power.

151

That's **strength/strength endurance**. Finally, you add pace — you need to perform the action properly for a long time with 'grunt' and pace. This is **speed**.

In other words, development occurs through the progression from technique to endurance to strength/strength endurance to speed (see figure 17.2).

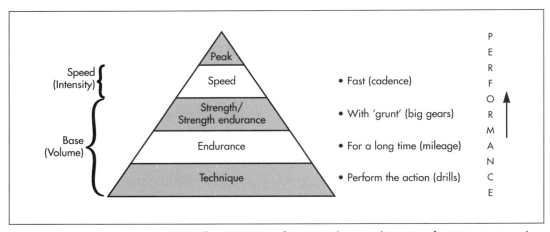

FIGURE 17.2: Full progression of training showing the types of training in Base that progress through to other types of training during speedwork to peak

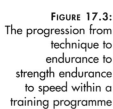

FIGURE 17.3:
The progression from technique to endurance to strength endurance to speed within a training programme

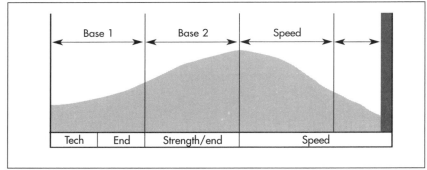

This is how performance is developed. Intensity and volume must be combined sequentially into types of training to improve performance.

Training history also affects performance and peak. The longer you have been doing the sport, the more you can cope with. The more you can cope with, the more speedwork you can do. And the more speedwork you can do, the faster you will go in competition.

Training history affects how much technique you can do, which affects how much endurance you can do, which affects how much strength/strength endurance you can do, which affects how much speed you can do, which determines how high you can peak (see fig 17.4).

Top performance (peak potential) does not happen overnight — it takes somewhere between 3–5 years on average (and sometimes 6–15 years if you start as a junior). An Olympic gold medal winner was once asked what it was like to be an 'overnight success'. He replied, 'It took me many years to become an "overnight success".'

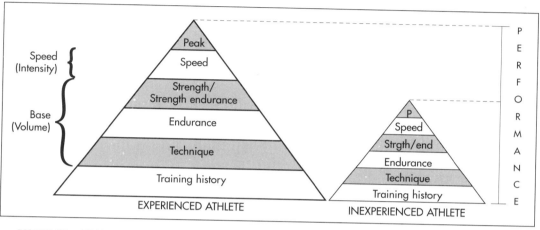

VOLUME + INTENSITY + TRAINING HISTORY = PERFORMANCE
(IN TYPES OF TRAINING)

FIGURE 17.4: How training history affects the amount of other training athletes can do and how high they can peak

To sum up, training initially involves various aspects of a competition, taken separately. These aspects are progressively brought together as the event gets closer. If all aspects of the competition were trained together from the start of the programme, the athlete would become overtrained. Break the competition down into its parts, train for them, and then progressively put them back together.

Weeks left	Time (weeks)					
0	Race			40-km cycle time trial		
2	2				fluid requirements	
6	4		speed			
7	1				aero position	
11	4		gears used			
15	4				distance 40-km	
17	2		pedal cadence 85–95 rpm			
18	1			technique		

FIGURE 17.5: Example showing the various aspects required to complete a 40-km cycle time trial and how each is brought in progressively and trained. Each aspect is trained separately then trained together, building performance.

PUTTING IT ALL TOGETHER

Figure 17.6 shows you how training is broken down over a year.

♥ The year breaks down into seasons — pre-season, in-season, off-season.

♥ The pre-season breaks down into periods — Base and Speed.

♥ The periods break down into subphases — they can be referred to as technique, endurance, strength endurance and speed.

Figure 17.8 shows the career of an athlete. Training through an athlete/player's career follows the same training fundamentals. Training moves from emphasis on technique as a novice, through emphasis on endurance, to strength endurance and finally to emphasis on speed.

THE ANNUAL PLAN						
Seasons (phases) of training	Pre-season (Preparatory) 16–24 weeks				In-season (Competitive) 6–22 weeks	Off-season (Transition) 3–6 weeks
Periods of training	Base 1 (General prep)	Base 2 (Specific prep)		Speed (Pre-comp)	Competitive racing (maintenance)	Transition to next build-up
Sub-phases	Technique	Endurance	Strength/ Endurance	Speed	High maintenance	Low maintenance

FIGURE 17.6: Subphases within periods and seasons in a year

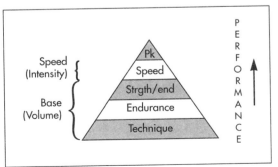

The performance triangle shows that you must teach your body to perform the action:
• correctly
• for a long time
• with 'grunt'
• fast.

FIGURE 17.7: The performance triangle

Applying the Big Three to an athletic career:

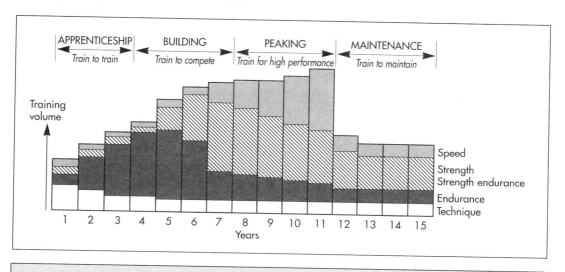

PHASES OF CAREER AND REQUIREMENTS

Apprenticeship

TRAIN TO TRAIN

FOCUS = ENDURANCE

- Have fun
- Learn technique
- Learn to train
- General training
- 1 build-up/year
- Duration 1–5 years
- Test/start/peak

Building

TRAIN TO COMPETE

FOCUS = STRENGTH/
STRENGTH ENDURANCE

- Build performance
- Refine technique
- Maintenance
- Specialised training
- 2 build-ups/year
- Duration 1–5 years
- Start/base-speed/peak

Peaking

TRAIN TO WIN/
MAX POTENTIAL
FOCUS = SPEED

- Peak performance
- Maintain technique
- Maintenance
- Individualised training
- Multiple build-ups
- Duration of peak ability
- End of each mesocycle

Maintenance

TRAIN TO MAINTAIN

FOCUS = MAINTENANCE

- Health/competition
- Coach
- Maintenance
- Individualised
- 2 build-ups/year
- Rest of life
- Fit/health check-ups

FIGURE 17.8: The career of an athlete/player: training follows the same
fundamentals throughout an athlete/player's career, moving from an emphasis on
technique to an emphasis on endurance, strength endurance and finally speed.

CHAPTER 18

RECOVERY

The more you train the better you perform! That's what a lot of people think. Is it true?

In some cases the more you train the more fatigued you get and the worse you perform. There is a limiting factor — improvements will only occur if you train as much as you can recover from. No recovery, no improvement! Why?

First you need to know how training works, and to understand the principle of **overload**. I know that's how you feel at work, but this is a little different. Overload works like this (see figure 18.1):

1. You train (e.g. a 1-hour bike ride). Your body gets fatigued.

2. You finish and over a period of time you recover from the workout.

3. As you recover your body reacts to the workout by adapting to a higher performance level so that it can cope with it better next time.

Bottom line: your performance goes up!

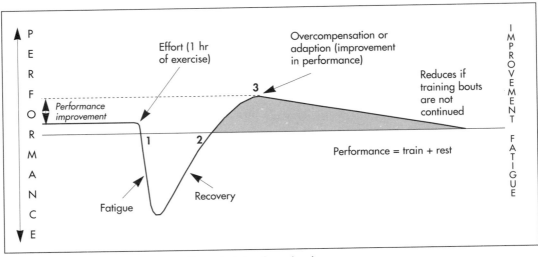

FIGURE 18.1: The principle of overload

This is the mechanism that improves performance. You slightly overload your body with training, your body adapts, modifying its training tolerance, and you get fitter. That's how the principle of overload works.

Now let's take an interesting situation and see what happens. Here's the plan:

Workout 1	Rest	Workout 2	Rest	Workout 3	Rest	Workout 4
2 hours	20 mins	2 hours	20 mins	2 hours	20 mins	2 hours
Result:						
TIRED		VERY TIRED		EXHAUSTED		SHATTERED (HOSPITALISED)

This may seem obvious but it illustrates an interesting point: you did eight hours' training and got worse!!!

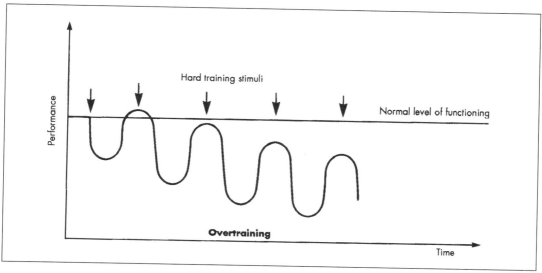

FIGURE 18.2: The effect of overtraining on performance

Training alone does not improve performance — recovery from training does! (See figure 18.2.) Training makes you worse! Recovery from training makes you better!

NO RECOVERY, NO IMPROVEMENT!

An athlete friend of mine and I were training for the Ironman. We had both finished neck and neck in a half-Ironman two months earlier. My friend went on to do up to 30-hour training weeks. The biggest I did was 15–16 hours. On

Ironman day I beat him by two hours. This goes to prove in a very anecdotal way that it doesn't matter how much you do, it matters how much you can recover from. If you don't recover, you end up doing lots of wasted training.

Training does not make you perform better if you haven't recovered from the previous workout. If you recover you are fresh enough to train correctly each time and performance goes up (see figure 18.3).

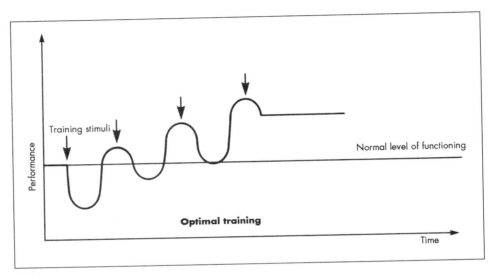

FIGURE 18.3:
The effect of
correct training
on performance

What we are talking about therefore is **absorption of training**. It's not how much training you do that counts, it's how much training your body can absorb. Your body will only absorb training if it is recovered.

It's a bit like studying a text book. If you are very tired (not mentally recovered) you will absorb (comprehend) very little of what you are reading. If you are not tired you will absorb a lot more.

The key point here is that recovery affects how much training you can absorb, which affects how much you can improve by doing the training.

If you can't recover from it, don't do it!! You'll just get progressively more overtired and end up performing worse.

TRAINING + RECOVERY = PERFORMANCE IMPROVEMENT

RECOVERY STRATEGIES

Recovery is as important as training. Therefore, you should not only plan your training, but you should also plan your recovery. There is no such thing as just a good training programme. It must be a good training and recovery programme.

So before you write the training in a programme you have to write the recovery. How do you do this? Three strategies are used:

- microcycles.
- mesocycles.
- macrocycles.

MICROCYCLES — DAY-TO-DAY RECOVERY

On a day-to-day basis, the aim is to allow recovery from training while at the same time slowly increasing mileage and/or speedwork. A good way to achieve this is to use the hard/easy/hard/easy principle. This means that easy days are used to recover from hard workouts, which progressively increase in intensity, duration or mileage (see table 1).

TABLE 1: The hard/easy/hard/easy principle for sport.

M	T	W	T	F	S	S
Easy	Speed/hills	Easy	Med-long	Day off	Speed/hills	Long
Easy	**Hard**	**Easy**	**Hard**	**Easy**	**Hard**	**Hard**

In multisport-type events, different sports should generally be performed on alternate days in order to allow the muscles used in the previous workout to be rested while you exercise in another sport. Keep workouts apart (e.g. bikes away from bikes, runs away from runs; see table 2).

TABLE 2: Keeping workouts apart to allow recovery.

M	T	W	T	F	S	S
S/K		S/K		Day Off	S/K	
	B		B			B
R		R			R	

Key: B = Bike, R = Run, S/K = Swim or Kayak

You will notice that no two of the same workout occur in a row. Similarly, like workouts in different sports (e.g. speedwork in running and cycling) should be set as far apart as possible each week. For example, speedwork for running might be on Monday, with speedwork for cycling on Thursday (see table 3, 4 and 5).

Therefore, the two rules of day-to-day recovery are:

♥ Hard day/easy day/hard day/easy day.

♥ Keep 'like' workouts apart (e.g. keep long workouts away from long workouts; see table 3), and keep the sports apart (e.g. keep swim sessions away from swim sessions; see table 4).

TABLE 3: Examples of training sequences for cycling/mountain biking, allowing time for recovery

M	T	W	T	F	S	S
Easy	Speed/hill	Easy	Med-long	Day off	Speed/hill	Long
Easy	**Hard**	**Easy**	**Hard**	**Easy**	**Hard**	**Hard**

TABLE 4: Examples of training sequences for triathlon/multisport/duathlon, allowing time for recovery (remove swims for duathlons)

M	T	W	T	F	S	S
S/K		S/K		Day Off	S/K	
	Bike (HILLS)		Bike (SPEED)	Day Off		Bike (LONG)
Run (SPEED)		Run (LONG)			Run (HILLS)	

TABLE 5: Rugby — In-season and pre-season

IN-SEASON

M	T	W	T	F	S	S
Easy	Strength	Speed	Strength	Easy	Game	Endurance
Easy	**Hard**	**Hard**	**Hard**	**Easy**	**Hard**	**Hard**

PRE-SEASON

M	T	W	T	F	S	S
Day off	Speed/ Strength	Speed	Endurance/ Strength	Easy	Speed/ Strength	Endurance/ Strength
Easy	**Hard**	**Easy**	**Hard**	**Easy**	**Hard**	**Hard**

Microcycles generally operate on 3-day, 4-day, 5-day, 7-day, 14-day or 21-day cycles, depending on the programme.

MESOCYCLES — WEEK-TO-WEEK RECOVERY

To increase training volume systematically also requires recovery on a week-to-week basis. Continually increasing mileage each week will not allow recovery from the cumulative effect of several weeks of training. Nor will it allow ongoing

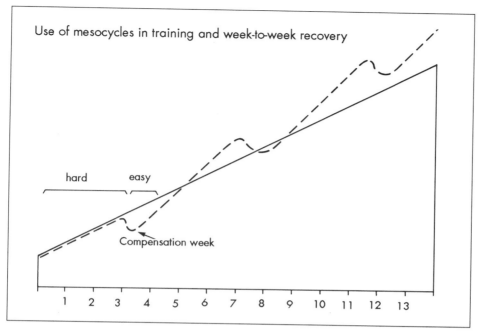

Use of mesocycles in training and week-to-week recovery

hard   easy

Compensation week

1 2 3 4 5 6 7 8 9 10 11 12 13

improvement. Build-up, therefore, also requires hard weeks and easy weeks.

Mesocycles allow for a compensation (easy) week every second, third, fourth, sixth or eighth week to allow recovery from previous training weeks (see fig 18.4).

Every compensation week gives a super-compensation effect that boosts training improvements more significantly than a 'continuous build-up' format.

FIGURE 18.4: Mesocycles — week-to-week recovery

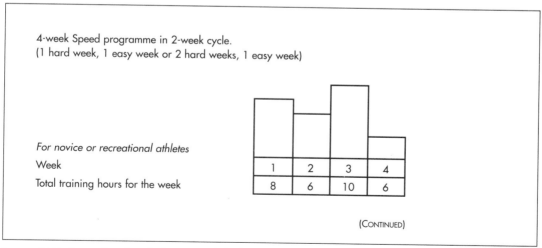

4-week Speed programme in 2-week cycle.
(1 hard week, 1 easy week or 2 hard weeks, 1 easy week)

For novice or recreational athletes

Week	1	2	3	4
Total training hours for the week	8	6	10	6

(CONTINUED)

FIGURE 18.5: Examples of cycle/mountain bike/triathlon/duathlon/multisport programmes for athletes at various levels.

(FIGURE 18.5 CONTINUED)

6-week Speed programme in 3-week cycle.
(2 hard weeks, 1 easy week or 3 hard weeks, 1 easy week)

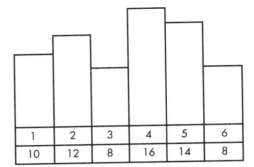

For semi-competitive athletes

Week	1	2	3	4	5	6
Total training hours for the week	10	12	8	16	14	8

8-week Speed programme in 4-week cycle (3 hard weeks, 1 easy week).

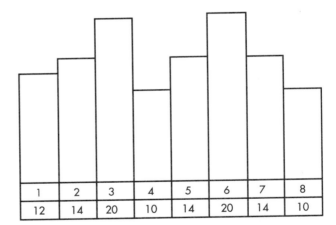

For competitive athletes,
3 hard weeks, 1 easy week

Week	1	2	3	4	5	6	7	8
Total training hours for the week	12	14	20	10	14	20	14	10

Compare the graphs in figures 18.6 and 18.7 in relation to recovery/fatigue and performance based on various training plans.

Figure 18.6 shows a mesocyclic plan where you train two hard weeks in a row, followed by an easy week. In the three hard weeks, you become progressively more tired. In the easy week, performance improves.

This graph illustrates two interesting points:

1. If you don't recover, you don't improve.

2. Performance does not increase at a constant rate.

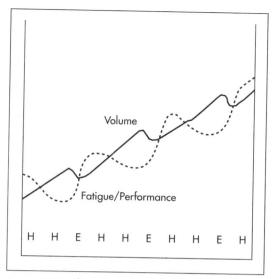

FIGURE 18.6: The effect of weekly training and recovery

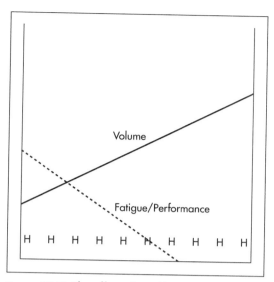

FIGURE 18.7: The effect of weekly training with no recovery

Figure 18.7 shows a constant increase in the volume of training every week. Without recovery, the athlete progressively gets more tired and performance starts to deteriorate. The rule of week-to-week recovery is:

Have several hard weeks to train.

Then have an easy week to recover and absorb the training.

MACROCYCLES — YEAR-TO-YEAR RECOVERY

Lastly, recovery should occur from year to year (from build-up to build-up). An off-season should be implemented to allow for recovery from base mileage, speedwork and competition (i.e. there should be hard parts of the year and easy parts of the year). If you train full on, all year round, with no recovery part of the year, your performance will start to drop and/or you'll get overtrained. If a very reduced amount of training (in your sport or in a similar type of sport) is done during the off-season, so you can recover, your previous year's work is, to some extent, maintained. This allows you to recover and achieve much greater performance gains in the following year.

The rule of year-to-year recovery is:

Have hard parts of the year to train and improve.

Have easy parts of the year to recover and maintain.

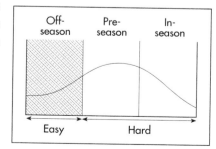

FIGURE 18.8: Year-to-year training and recovery

PUTTING IT ALL TOGETHER

♥ The yearly macrocycle breaks down into seasons — off-season, pre-season and in-season.

♥ The pre-season breaks down into periods — Base and Speed.

♥ The periods break down into subphases — technique, endurance, strength/endurance and speed.

♥ The subphases are made up of mesocycles.

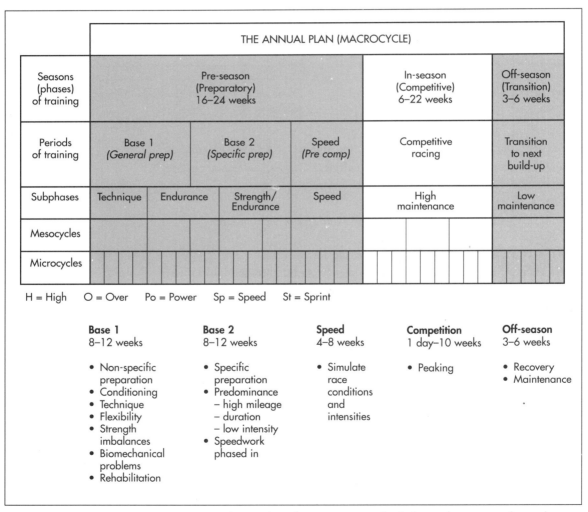

FIGURE 18.9: Integration of recovery strategies (microcycles, mesocycles and macrocycles) into the total structure of training.

- ♥ The mesocycles are made up of microcycles.

- ♥ Macrocycles form the cycle of training and resting on a yearly basis.

- ♥ Mesocycles (week-to-week, month-to-month recovery) occur within the macrocycle and have a cycle of training and resting over a 2–6-week (usually 3-week) period.

- ♥ Microcycles within each mesocycle form the stress-plus-rest strategy on a day-to-day basis.

- ♥ Macrocycles are used to plan the broad aspects of a training programme. These would include high-priority and low-priority races, training goals and periodisation.

- ♥ Mesocycles have more specific performance goals.

- ♥ Microcycles are used to determine daily/weekly training. Figure 18.9 illustrates how everything fits together neatly .

- ♥ When planning training you need to remember: *Training + Recovery = Performance*. This immediately suggests that to plan a programme that enhances performance you must not only plan training, but you must also plan recovery from training.

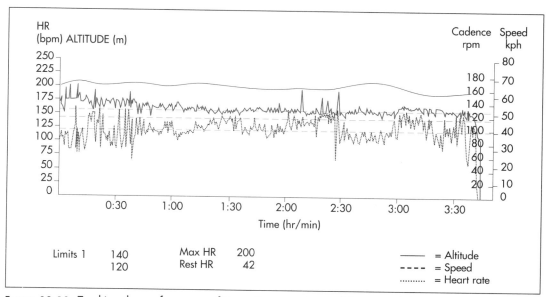

FIGURE 18.10: Tracking the performance of Scott Guyton, winner of the 'Round The Mountain' race in record time.

CHAPTER 19

PERIODISATION — THE SPECIFICS OF YOUR DAILY TRAINING WORKOUTS

DAILY WORKOUTS

Now that the general phases of training (seasons, periods, subphases and recovery cycles) have been covered, we need to cover the specifics, the 'nitty gritty' of training. This explains what types of training you do during a workout. You will hopefully find a programme that suits you in the 'training programmes' chapter immediately after this chapter.

We have discussed seasons (and macrocycles), training periods (Base and Speed) within the seasons, subphases within the training periods, then mesocycles within the subphases, and microcycles within the mesocycles.

We are now at the point of discussing daily workouts, telling you what types of training you do on a specific workout day.

This finally brings together your programme as the three main questions:

How far/long to go? (Mins/kms/reps)
What do I do? (Subphase 1, 2, 3, 4, 5, 6, 7, 8 or 9)
How hard do I go? (Heart rate)

This chapter contains a general overview of subphases and then descriptions of each subphase.

SUBPHASES

Base and Speed can be further broken down into subphases. These are small 'chunks' of training (usually around 3–4 weeks long) where specific forms of training are emphasised. These may be aspects of technique, endurance, strength endurance or speed.

The following table represents a breakdown of the pre-season into Base and Speed periods, and then into subphases. Note that there is a logical progression from the preparation phase, through to sport-specific strength endurance training, and finally to speed training. Training also moves from less competition-specific to more competition-specific.

SUBPHASES	PERIODS	
1. Preparation (easy)	Endurance (conditioning)	} Base 1
2. Load 3. High load 4. Load/speed	Strength/endurance	} *BASE PHASE* Base 2
5. Low-speed work 6. High-speed work 7. Sprints 8. Power 9. Overspeed	Speed (if needed) (if needed) (if needed)	} *SPEED PHASE*

The following pages provide a more detailed explanation of subphases 1–9 so that you can apply these easily to your daily workouts.

BASE PHASE

1. PREPARATION (EASY)
Easy training/Getting fit

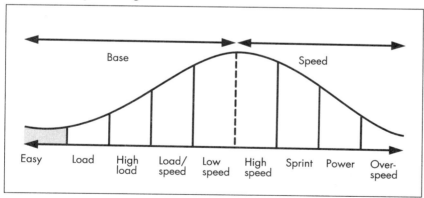

FIGURE 19.1: Preparation subphase

This involves easy conditioning, starting back into a more structured training programme from your off-season and getting your body ready for the training that lies ahead. All problems (muscle and strength imbalances, injuries and rehabilitation) are dealt with before the training load increases. This phase can be avoided if you are already well conditioned, or could take many weeks if several problems need to be resolved. Technique particularly should be concentrated on. You have initially shown your body how to perform the action correctly for a relatively long time (see fig 19.1).

SPECIFICS: Light/easy conditioning (aerobic)

EFFORT: Easy conversation pace (50–60% effort)

TRAINING HEART RATES: Long slow distance(60–75% HR^{max})

2. LOAD
Getting stronger

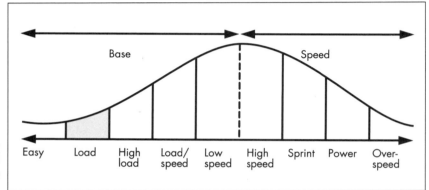

FIGURE 19.2: Load subphase

Load is the beginning of strength endurance. At this point the athlete/player is fit and conditioned enough to start to increase the training effort without fear of injury and to get the most out of it. You have, through your training, reached a point where you have shown your body how to perform the action for a long time with a moderate degree of grunt!

Load is emphasised in early Base, and would occur progressively from once to twice per week. This phase could last from 2–8 weeks (generally 4).

SPECIFICS: Strength endurance training

EFFORT: Easy conversation pace (60–70% effort; effort will obviously be slightly higher under load — 70–80%, no higher)

TRAINING HEART RATE: During — N/A
Between — 60–75% HR^{max}

3. HIGH LOAD
Getting stronger

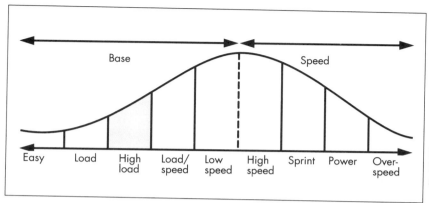

FIGURE 19.3: High-load subphase

This is an extension of strength endurance training. As the athlete/player becomes conditioned to load training the load is further increased and the resistance is increased.

Runners may move from hill running to stride outs up a hill. Cyclists may move from hill training to riding hills in a big gear.

Be very careful when doing this training as it is easy to become injured. Younger athletes/players should skip this subphase.

Also be careful that this form of training does not affect your form as technique can deteriorate if you don't remain vigilant.

This further 'strengthens' the athlete and prepares them for the upcoming speedwork (in the subsequent subphase). You have, through your training, reached a point where you have shown your body how to perform the action for a long time, with grunt!

This phase is emphasised in the middle of Base. It should be applied at incidences from not at all to 1–2 times per week over a 2- to 8-week period (generally 4 weeks).

SPECIFICS: High strength endurance

EFFORT: Easy conversation pace (60–75% effort; during high load 75–85% effort)

TRAINING HEART RATE: During — N/A
Between — LSD (60–75% HR^{max})

4. LOAD/SPEED
Applying strength (grunt, power) to speed

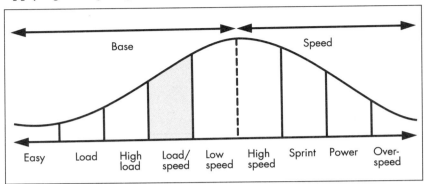

FIGURE 19.4:
Load/speed
subphase

Load/speed is the transition form of training that ties strength endurance training to speed training. It's often called conversion or transfer training. So far the athlete/player has been conditioned through endurance training and has then progressed to strength endurance training, with load increased to higher and higher levels. You can't just go immediately from high load, low speed to high speed, so load/speed is used to begin speed but maintain an aspect of strength. This allows a gradual progression to speed (your body hates anything sudden) and allows the strength to be applied to speed.

You have, through your training, reached a point where you have shown your body how to perform the action, for a long time, with grunt and the beginnings of going fast.

This would occur from not at all to once or twice a week over a 2- to 8-week period (usually 2–4 weeks). This is emphasised at the end of Base.

SPECIFICS: Strength endurance moving to speed endurance

EFFORT: Easy conversation pace (60–75% effort)

TRAINING HEART RATE: During — N/A
Between — LSD (60–75% HR^{max})

SPEED PHASE

You are now ready for the Speed phase. You have conditioned your body, dealt with any problems and improved your strength, so you can now begin to increase the tempo of your training. This is when the real work starts. Everything up until now has been necessary but the final weeks of the Speed phase 'make or break' your chances of a top performance.

The following subphases are progressively combined into between 1–3 speed sessions per week (1 = novice, 3 = elite) over the last 4–8 weeks of the Speed phase. Racing and competition is often a better form of speed training (more specific) and therefore can be substituted for a speed session.

Speedwork is very intense and demanding. Too much speedwork can quickly overfatigue an athlete/player and destroy a build-up. Be careful, it is a fine line between too much and too little. As a rule of thumb, 10 percent of your training in your biggest speedwork week can be at high speed work (6–9) or higher, or 20 percent low speed work (5–8) or higher; 80 percent easy (1), load (2), high load (3) and load/speed (4). Each of the following phases is initiated progressively each week during the Speed phase.

5. LOW-SPEED WORK
The beginnings of speed conditioning

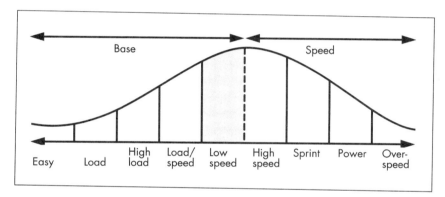

FIGURE 19.5:
Low-speed
subphase

Up-tempo is the beginning of conditioning for speed. This form of training is faster than easy conversation pace but not as fast as 10- to 60-minute race pace. You should be training fast at about 70–75 percent effort, feeling comfortable, strong, in control and not 'hammering'. Because this form of training is only moderately intense, the interval periods can be quite long (10–20 mins).

This would occur once or twice a week and would be gradually phased in over a period of 2–4 weeks (usually 2). The emphasis is at the end of Base for competitions under four hours and at the start of Speed for competitions over four hours.

You have, through your training, reached a point where you have shown your body how to perform the action for a long time with grunt, fast.

SPECIFICS: Long intervals at tempo pace (Ironman race pace)
                   should feel fast and strong

6. High-speed work

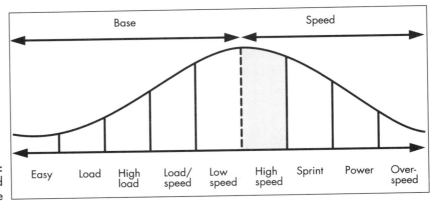

Figure 19.6:
High-speed
subphase

Base   Speed

Easy   Load   High   Load/   Low   High   Sprint   Power   Over-
              load   speed speed speed   speed

Getting fast in terms of endurance (high aerobic speed)

Anaerobic threshold: anaerobic threshold is defined as the highest intensity that an athlete/player can hold for approximately one hour. This equates to around 40-km time trial pace on your bike or 16-km run pace.

Anaerobic threshold training can be conducted as time trials or as less psychologically demanding intervals (frequently between 4–10 minutes). This improves your anaerobic threshold pace. It also allows your race/playing pace to come up, or improves high steady-state race/playing pace. This improves your high aerobic ability to sustain a high continuous pace (more than 20 minutes; e.g. ability to get to the ball fast for a loose forward in rugby, for a full 80 minutes of the game; ability for a midfielder in soccer to maintain a high playing pace, as with a centre in netball).

This subphase lasts between 2–8 weeks (usually 1–4 weeks). It is emphasised at the start of Speed for competitions of less than four hours, and in the middle of Speed for competitions over four hours.

Specifics: Short intervals (16-km run or 40-km bike time trial
                      pace); you should feel like you are hammering (anaerobic
                      threshold)

Effort: Difficult to converse (75–85% effort)

Training heart rate: During — AT (85–95% HR^{max})
                      Between — LSD (60–75% HR^{max})

7. SPRINTS (EXTENSIVE/INTENSIVE SPRINTS) — LONG AND SHORT
Getting fast in terms of long and short sprinting
(Low and high anaerobic speed)

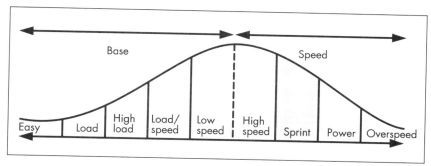

FIGURE 19.7: Sprint subphase

Sprints improve your anaerobic speed — your ability to hold very high speeds for very short distances. Sprints break down into two parts.

Extensive sprints: long sprints (between 45 seconds and 4 minutes is typical) are used to improve the ability to sustain sprint speed at the start or end of a race, to bridge gaps, to break away from the peloton close to the finish or to initiate breakaways. In sports like rugby, this is once again effective to help loose forwards to get to the ball very fast.

Intensive sprints: short sprints (usually between 10 seconds and 1 minute) are used to improve ability at top sprinting speed. Intensive sprints can be broken into uphill (5–50 m), crest (5–30 m uphill/5–30 m over the top) and on the flat (200–400 m) for running and cycling. Uphill sprints occur during the load and high-load phase, crest occurs in the load/speed phase, and flat occurs in speed. This would help a striker in soccer or a wing in rugby.

These types of training occur once or twice a week over a 1–4-week period (usually 2 weeks). This is emphasised in the middle to end of Speed.

SPECIFICS: Extensive sprints (long sprints) are 2–4-min sprints.
Intensive sprints (short sprints) are 10 sec to 1 min 30 sec
Sprints (anaerobic lactic and alactic)

EFFORT: Very difficult to converse (90–100% effort)

TRAINING HEART RATE: During — N/A (above 95% HR^{max})
Between — LSD (60–75% HR^{max})

8. POWER (ACCELERATION)
Getting fast in terms of explosive speed
(Very high anaerobic speed)

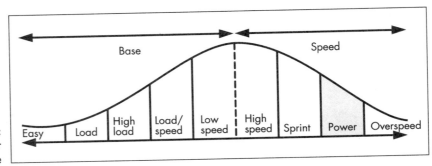

Power training improves explosive ability. Power training is used to improve the ability in cycling to attack a rider or the peloton in an initial 'jump'. Power training can be conducted using plyometrics (for rugby, soccer and netball) or big gear wind-outs, or by using a dip in the road to gain speed down a hill in a big gear, then sprinting using the same gear up a short climb on the other side of the dip and stopping when you are not 'on top of the gear' (for cycling).

Power training for rowing usually involves weight training but may also involve training in the boat. You should feel strong as you do these forms of training (i.e. you should not labour to turn the gear over in cycling).

In rugby, soccer and netball this is the principal requirement to play well. Excellent accceleration in the first 1–10 metres provides space from your competition for passing and receiving.

This subphase can occur once or twice a week over a 1–4-week period. The subphase is emphasised towards the end of Speed.

SPECIFICS: Explosive acceleration (anaerobic alactic)

EFFORT: 100% effort

TRAINING HEART RATE: During — N/A
Between — (60–75% HR^{max})

9. OVERSPEED

Getting you fast in terms of speed of movement
(Top-end biomechanics speed — over pace movement of limbs)

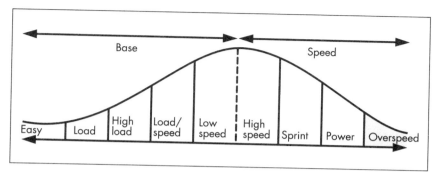

FIGURE 19.9:
Overspeed subphase

Overspeed training involves increasing muscular contraction speed, which is the final aspect of speedwork. Downhill spinning sprints in cycling (sprinting downhill in a small gear at a high cadence) and motor pacing (high-cadence training drafting behind a vehicle to decrease the effects of wind resistance) are useful forms of overspeed (for cycling). Running and most team sports can use a form of overspeed; for example, running down a slight hill (3 percent or less) to gain extra speed as you run onto the flat.

SPECIFICS: Short downhill sprint intervals or motor pacing
(drafting behind a motor vehicle) at above race pace
speed to enhance muscle contraction speed

EFFORT: Moderate/low load and high speed

TRAINING HEART RATE: During — N/A
Between — (60–75% HR^{max})

In most cases, once you start to use a training intensity you don't stop. It may be slowly initiated and progressively increased between 1–3 weeks before you focus on a specific training subphase, and will reach its peak emphasis and then be maintained as other training phases are initiated.

PUTTING THE SUBPHASES TOGETHER

So there it is: those are all the ingredients. But training is like cooking — it's not the ingredients that count, it's how they are put together.

To put the ingredients together successfully you first need an experienced athlete or coach to advise you. They can use their experience to take the guesswork out of your training and will save you having to learn the hard way. Be specific about what you require in training for your event. You may not use every subphase as you may not have enough time, or may not require some of the intensities (e.g. sprint training will not greatly improve your time-trial ability), or you may want to spend more time on a specific phase that is your weakness.

MAINTAIN THE GAIN — PRESERVING PERFORMANCE

Your body operates on a 'use it or lose it' principle. You train for a while, you perform better; you stop for a long time, you perform worse.

It takes a lot of work to build performance but surprisingly little to maintain it (20–30 percent of your biggest volumes to hold most of your performance for 4–8 weeks). It's like building a house: it takes a lot of work to build and not nearly as much to maintain.

So when you start a build-up, you emphasise each form of training as you go through and then maintain it — you don't stop doing it.

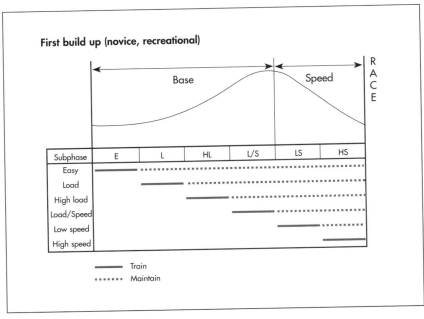

FIGURE 19.10:
Maintain the gain

After you've done your first build-up, you need to maintain everything all of the time.

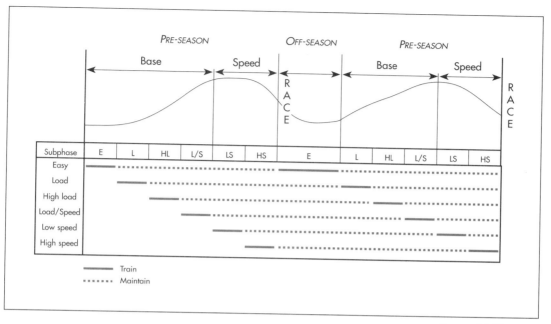

Subphase	E	L	HL	L/S	LS	HS	E	L	HL	L/S	LS	HS
Easy												
Load												
High load												
Load/Speed												
Low speed												
High speed												

Train
Maintain

IF YOU DON'T USE IT, YOU LOSE IT!

FIGURE 19.11:
Maintain the gain

CHANGING THE SUBPHASE PERIOD

Subphases vary in terms of the time when they are initiated depending on the length and type of the race. See the graphs below.

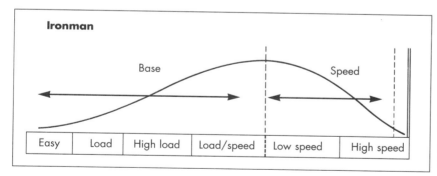

Ironman

Base   Speed

Easy	Load	High load	Load/speed	Low speed	High speed

FIGURE 19.12:
The timing of subphases for an Ironman race

FIGURE 19.13:
The timing of
subphases for a
40-km cycle race

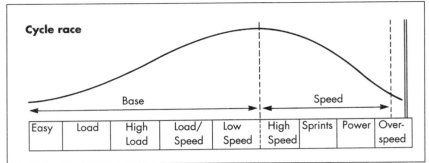

FIGURE 19.14:
Examples of changes
in subphase location
for different distance
events

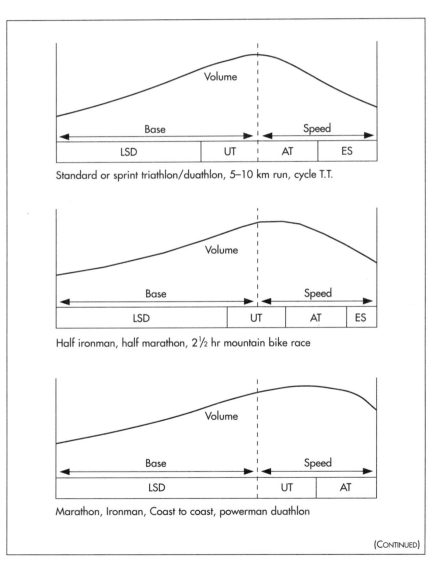

Standard or sprint triathlon/duathlon, 5–10 km run, cycle T.T.

Half ironman, half marathon, 2½ hr mountain bike race

Marathon, Ironman, Coast to coast, powerman duathlon

(CONTINUED)

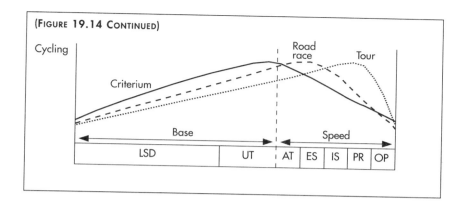

(FIGURE 19.14 CONTINUED)

TRAINING ORDER — WHAT DO I DO FIRST IN MY WORKOUT?

1. In most cases, try to keep training types apart — keep endurance away from strength endurance away from speed. This goes back to the principle of microcyclic training (see pages 159–60), where 'like' modes of training are kept as far apart as possible within a week to facilitate recovery and absorption of training. There are some situations where you may deliberately combine different training types (e.g. triathlon — you might do strength endurance hills on the bike followed by speed on the run to get used to running tired) but in most cases they are best kept apart.

2. If you are doing more than one training type in the same workout, in general use the order shown in the following example of cycling. (Note: these types of training are not normally combined in one session.)

Warm-up:	10 mins
Technique:	20 mins
Speed(sprints):	2 x 1 min (+10 mins rest between)
Speed(up-tempo and anaerobic threshold):	3 x 5 mins (+5 mins rest between)
Strength endurance:	20 mins flat, big gear
Endurance:	60 mins
Warm-down:	10 mins

Total: 157 mins cycling for workout

The reason for this order is that you should be freshest to do technique and train adequately at the highest intensities ('got to go fast, to go fast'). This also has relevance in terms of recovery between workouts. Speed and technique training require the longest recovery, whereas endurance requires the least recovery.

MISSING WORKOUTS

In almost every build-up you will miss workouts and training days due to overtiredness or lack of time. Athletes/players generally miss up to four days/workouts per month, over and above prescribed days off. This obviously varies depending on the individual, but missing workouts is a fact of training life and nothing to get concerned about.

If you miss a day unexpectedly, never try to catch up the missed mileage the following day or do extra on your day off. If a workout is missed, it is gone! It is better to look at a missed day in a positive way — it is both a physical and a mental day off. It is a day when your body rests, recovers and improves.

Trying to catch up mileage destroys the balance (exercise versus recovery) of the programme and may lead to excessive fatigue and extended negative effects on your training programme. Listen to your body. If you feel tired, adjust your training accordingly. Trying to do prescribed mileage in a fatigued state is of no benefit whatsoever.

Put another way, resting for a day because of fatigue may mean only one day of training is affected. However, trying to do the workout despite fatigue may affect several days or even weeks of training, increasing the likelihood of overtraining.

Think about it: which would you rather have? One day off or one week off? Now, that's a 'no-brainer'!

If you miss three or four days in a row through tiredness or lack of enthusiasm for training, then it is likely that total mileage or speedwork is too excessive. If it is not quickly reduced or adjusted, overtraining may occur.

Monitoring your fatigue levels is always the most important guide to training. Listen to your body first, then listen to your coach or follow your programme.

PUTTING IT ALL TOGETHER

♥ The year breaks down into seasons — off-season, pre-season, in-season.

♥ The pre-season breaks down into periods — Base and Speed.

♥ The periods break down into subphases — easy, load, high load, load/speed, low speed, high speed, sprints, power and overspeed. These are the specifics of technique, endurance, strength endurance and speed.

♥ Maintain the gain — use it or lose it.

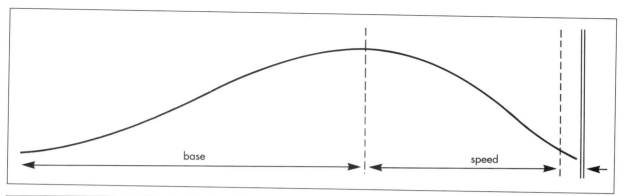

Subphase	1 easy	2 load	3 high load	4 load/speed	5 low speed	6 high speed	7 sprints	8 power	9 over speed
Triathlon	easy	hills/ pull buoy	hills, big gear hills, long stride paddles/band	flat, big gear stride outs (bound) pull buoys	up tempo	anaerobic threshold			
Duathlon	easy	hills	hills, big gear hills, long stride	flat, big gear stride outs (bound)	up tempo	anerobic threshold			
Multi-sport	easy	hills/ bungy	hills, big gear hills, long stride bungy	flat, big gear stride outs (bound) bungy	up tempo	anaerobic threshold			
Running	easy	hills	hills long stride	stride outs (bound)	up tempo	anaerobic threshold	extensive sprints		
Mountain biking	easy	hills	hills, big gear	flat, big gear	up tempo	anaerobic threshold	extensive sprints		
Row	easy	bungy rope tow	bungy rope tow	bungy rope tow	up tempo	anaerobic threshold	sprints	power	
Road cycle	easy	hills	hills big gear	flat big gear	up tempo	anaerobic threshold	sprints	power	over speed

Note: Subphases timing in a buildup can change depending on the duration of the race.

FIGURE 19.15: Examples of forms of training within subphases for specific sports

	THE ANNUAL PLAN (MACROCYCLE)										
Seasons (phases) of training	Pre-season (Preparatory) 16–24 weeks								In-season (Competitive) 6–22 weeks	Off-season (Transition) 3–6 weeks
Periods of training	Base 1 *(General prep)*		Base 2 *(Specific prep)*		Speed *(Pre-comp)*				Competitive racing (maintenance)	Transition to next build-up
Subphases	Easy	Load	High Load	Load/ Speed	Low Sp	H Sp	St	Po	O Sp	High maintenance	Low maintenance
Mesocycles											
Microcycles											

Low Sp = Low speed   H Sp = High speed   Po = Power   O Sp = Overspeed   St = Sprint

Base 1 8–12 weeks	**Base 2** 8–12 weeks	**Speed** 4–8 weeks	**Competition** 1 day–10 weeks	**Off-season** 3–6 weeks
• Non-specific preparation • Conditioning • Technique • Flexibility • Strength imbalances • Biomechanical problems • Rehabilitation	• Specific preparation • Predominance: – high mileage – duration – low intensity • Speedwork phased in	• Simulate race conditions and intensities	• Peaking	• Recovery • Maintenance

FIGURE 19.16: All the components of periodisation combine to produce high performance.

Summary Table

Subphases	Physical effort (%) (cardiovascular)	Muscular effort (%)	Heart Rate Intensity
Overspeed	0–25	0–55	N/A
Power	45–55	90–100	N/A
Sprint (in/ex)	85–100	85–100	HI
High speed	75–85	75–85	AT
Low speed	60–70	60–70	UT
Load/speed	45–55	75–85	N/A
High load	75–85	85–95	N/A
Load	60–70	75–85	N/A
Easy	30–45	30–55	LSD
Recovery	5–30	5–25	AR

Key: N/A = not applicable; HI = high intensity; AT = anaerobic threshold; UT = up-tempo; LSD = long slow distance; AR = active recovery. LSD is used between all forms of specific training.

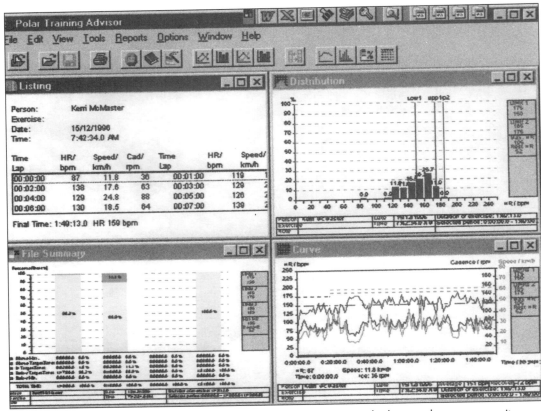

FIGURE 19.17: Cycling — Polar X Trainer: using the latest in heart rate monitors, heart rates, speeds and pedal cadences can be recorded during training and downloaded into a computer for analysis.

CHAPTER 20

TRAINING PROGRAMMES

Finally, we combine heart rates and training together into training programmes.

As discussed, we needed to answer three questions :

How far/long do I go ? (Mins/kms/reps)

What do I do ? (Subphase 1, 2, 3, 4, 5, 6, 7, 8 or 9)

How hard do I go ? (Heart rate)

Go through the programmes and find one that suits you. If you can't find one that seems appropriate, refer to *The Power to Perform*, where there are many examples and an explanation of how to design your own programme. The training programmes are set up in this book so that you have a choice of over 260 programmes across 27 different sports.

Bookmark the programmes for your sport now before we finish the explanation as you will need to look at them several times during this explanation.

DECIDING ON YOUR TRAINING LEVEL

The programmes have three different training levels (providing specific workout quantities within the detailed descriptions tables). You will need to select the level that best suits you.

Rec (Recreational)

You want to get the most out of your training on limited time. You are in your first year in the sport. You want to be involved, not competitive.

Semi (Semi-Competitive)

You are prepared to invest a moderate amount of time into the sport but having fun is more important than doing really well. You've been doing your sport for quite a while and are happy with your level of commitment.

Comp (Competitive)

You are serious. You are experienced (in the sport for 3–5 years). You want to do well.

Running Your Programme

1. For triathlon, duathlon, multisport, rowing, kayaking, road cycling, mountain biking, distance running, general fitness and fat loss.

Within each sport there is usually more than one programme. This takes into account the type and duration/distance of the race you are doing. (Check the title of the programme under 'race' in the top left-hand corner of each programme. The general fitness/fat loss programmes have the title at the top of each programme.) Select the programme most appropriate to you.

How far/long do I go ? (Mins/kms/reps)
You will see on the programmes that you have a training duration/distance for each day in minutes or kilometres. This is how long you should train for or how much distance you should cover.

What do I do ? (Subphase 1, 2, 3, 4, 5, 6, 7, 8 or 9)
Next to the duration/distance is a subtext number which indicates the type of training (subphase) you should do. You can look up this number in the Detailed Descriptions section following each programme. The subtext number that matches the Detailed Descriptions number gives you information on how to do the training in that workout. (If you are unsure what 'reps' means, see page 138.)

To summarise: you do the specified duration or distance set in the programme, and the subtext number beside it directs you to the Detailed Descriptions. All training that is not specific to making up the duration/distance is easy.

How hard do I go ? (Heart rate)
Transfer the training heart rates that you calculated on pages 124–6 (at the end of Chapter 12) to the heart rates column in the appropriate Detailed Descriptions. This gives you your training intensities for all the varieties of training in your programme.

2. For rugby union, rugby league, soccer, netball, basketball, hockey, skiing, surfing, golf, tennis, squash, cricket, softball, motor racing, sail boarding, volleyball and martial arts.

Each sport has two programmes: semi competitive/competitive and recreational. Select the programme that is most appropriate to you.

How far/long do I go ? (Mins/kms/reps)

What do I do ? (Subphase 1, 2, 3, 4, 5, 6, 7, 8 or 9)

Each programme has a weekly layout at the top of the page. Underneath you have the programme which sets out the workouts on a day-to-day basis over a 16-week period. Finally at the bottom of the page you have a guide to the periodisation of your strength training. Refer to page 323–5 for more detail.

To find out what training you need to do on a particular day, refer to the number set in the programme and then to the Detailed Descriptions for an explanation of what to do.

If the training number is in normal type, you aim gradually to increase the amount of that type of training as you do more of these workouts. If the number is in bold type, it means you are maintaining that form of training so you would do only the lowest volume (e.g. if you had 2–6 reps you would do only 2 reps).

That's the workout: it takes a bit of learning but once you get the idea, the programmes are very easy to follow.

How hard do I go ? (Heart rate)

Transfer the training heart rates that you calculated on pages 124–6 (at the end of Chapter 12) to the heart rates column in the appropriate Detailed Descriptions. This gives you your training intensities for all the varieties of training in your programme.

Your sport will not use heart rates as much as more continuous endurance sports.

If you want to write your own programme, consult *The Power to Perform*. The programmes are a blueprint for achieving your training goals. Discussing your training with a coach or an experienced athlete is very useful. It's hard to learn from your mistakes, but easier to learn from someone else's.

POINTS TO NOTE BEFORE STARTING YOUR PROGRAMME

♥ Some people mistakenly think that the closer you follow a programme, the better the chances of top performance. This is in fact not true. Listen to your body first, then look at the programme, and then decide how you will train for the day or week.

♥ Without recovery there is no improvement. Without improvement there are no increases in performance. Recovery is very important.

♥ Do not try to keep your log-book numbers straight. Your programme is a plan, reality is different. You should miss around 10% of the programme.

- ♥ Never try to catch up a missed workout. If it's gone, it's gone. You will destroy the balance of your programme if you try to catch up the workout.

- ♥ Learn as much as you can about how to train: the 'whys, whens and whats'. If you understand how to train you will get closer to training optimally.

- ♥ Cruise on your easy days so you can save up your energy for your harder (long, hills, speed) days. In Base, your long days have highest priority with hills being next: in Speed for longer distance events, long is still most important followed by speed, hills and finally easy. Speed phases for shorter distance events have speed as the highest priority, with hills next and finally long. Always think in your workouts, 'Am I going to be fresh enough for my next key session?' You may even cut your workout short on an easy day to ensure that you are ready for your high-priority session.

- ♥ Keep a log-book. Log-books ensure that you have a record of training. If your training went optimally, you have a record of how you did it. You can use this again with some refinements for your next build-up. This way you are learning what forms of training work and which are ineffective. This allows far greater improvements in training from one build-up to the next. Also, if you are having problems in training with increasing your performance, a log-book will act as a guide to discovering what your training errors are. This can then be rectified.

- ♥ Don't stick to your heart rates like 'glue' — they are designed to give you a general intensity or 'average' intensity. Try to spend most of your time at the training heart rates but not all the time. There is nothing wrong with your heart rate going up because you went up a hill or you raced someone for 5–15 minutes. If your training heart rates seem wrong, particularly if they are not calculated from a test, use a more advanced method for assessing heart rates.

- ♥ Be patient. While this programme will help your performance it generally takes two to three build-ups to get everything running really smoothly.

WARM-UPS/WARM-DOWNS AND STRETCHING

See pages 46–9 for information on warm-ups and warm-downs. Use appropriate stretches below.

FIGURE 20.1:
Stretches suitable
for various sports

T
R
I
A
T
H
L
O
N

Race: Triathlon (sprint/Olympic)
Race date: 20 April
Training starts: 30 December

Maximum distance for the 100% week
Swim: 4 km
Bike: 100 kms
Run: 16 km

Mileage profile

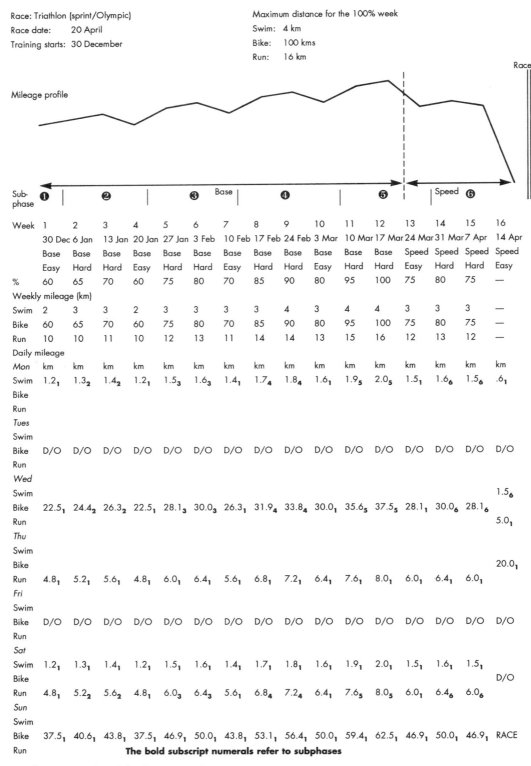

Race

Sub-phase: ① ② ③ Base ④ ⑤ Speed ⑥

	Week 1	2	3	4	5	6	7	8	9	10	11	12	13	14	15	16
	30 Dec	6 Jan	13 Jan	20 Jan	27 Jan	3 Feb	10 Feb	17 Feb	24 Feb	3 Mar	10 Mar	17 Mar	24 Mar	31 Mar	7 Apr	14 Apr
	Base	Base	Base	Base	Base	Base	Base	Base	Base	Base	Base	Base	Speed	Speed	Speed	Speed
	Easy	Hard	Hard	Easy	Hard	Hard	Easy	Hard	Hard	Easy	Hard	Hard	Easy	Hard	Hard	Easy
%	60	65	70	60	75	80	70	85	90	80	95	100	75	80	75	—
Weekly mileage (km)																
Swim	2	3	3	2	3	3	3	3	4	3	4	4	3	3	3	—
Bike	60	65	70	60	75	80	70	85	90	80	95	100	75	80	75	—
Run	10	10	11	10	12	13	11	14	14	13	15	16	12	13	12	—
Daily mileage																
Mon	km	km	km	km	km	km	km	km	km	km	km	km	km	km	km	km
Swim	1.2_1	1.3_2	1.4_2	1.2_1	1.5_3	1.6_3	1.4_1	1.7_4	1.8_4	1.6_1	1.9_5	2.0_5	1.5_1	1.6_6	1.5_6	$.6_1$
Bike																
Run																
Tues																
Swim																
Bike	D/O	D/O	D/O	D/O	D/O	D/O	D/O	D/O	D/O	D/O	D/O	D/O	D/O	D/O	D/O	D/O
Run																
Wed																
Swim																1.5_6
Bike	22.5_1	24.4_2	26.3_2	22.5_1	28.1_3	30.0_3	26.3_1	31.9_4	33.8_4	30.0_1	35.6_5	37.5_5	28.1_1	30.0_6	28.1_6	
Run																5.0_1
Thu																
Swim																
Bike																20.0_1
Run	4.8_1	5.2_1	5.6_1	4.8_1	6.0_1	6.4_1	5.6_1	6.8_1	7.2_1	6.4_1	7.6_1	8.0_1	6.0_1	6.4_1	6.0_1	
Fri																
Swim																
Bike	D/O	D/O	D/O	D/O	D/O	D/O	D/O	D/O	D/O	D/O	D/O	D/O	D/O	D/O	D/O	D/O
Run																
Sat																
Swim	1.2_1	1.3_1	1.4_1	1.2_1	1.5_1	1.6_1	1.4_1	1.7_1	1.8_1	1.6_1	1.9_1	2.0_1	1.5_1	1.6_1	1.5_1	
Bike																D/O
Run	4.8_1	5.2_2	5.6_2	4.8_1	6.0_3	6.4_3	5.6_1	6.8_4	7.2_4	6.4_1	7.6_5	8.0_5	6.0_1	6.4_6	6.0_6	
Sun																
Swim																
Bike	37.5_1	40.6_1	43.8_1	37.5_1	46.9_1	50.0_1	43.8_1	53.1_1	56.4_1	50.0_1	59.4_1	62.5_1	46.9_1	50.0_1	46.9_1	RACE
Run																

The bold subscript numerals refer to subphases

Read pages 185–8 before starting.

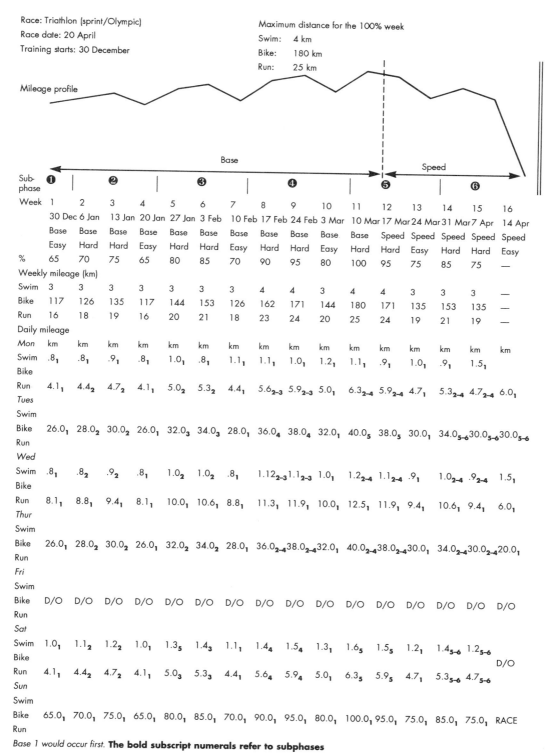

Race: Triathlon (sprint/Olympic)
Race date: 20 April
Training starts: 30 December

Maximum distance for the 100% week
Swim: 4 km
Bike: 180 km
Run: 25 km

Mileage profile

Base ←———————————————————→ | Speed ←————→

Sub-phase	❶		❷		❸		❹		❺		❻				
Week	1	2	3	4	5	6	7	8	9	10	11	12	13	14	15	16
	30 Dec	6 Jan	13 Jan	20 Jan	27 Jan	3 Feb	10 Feb	17 Feb	24 Feb	3 Mar	10 Mar	17 Mar	24 Mar	31 Mar	7 Apr	14 Apr
	Base	Base	Base	Base	Base	Base	Base	Base	Base	Base	Base	Speed	Speed	Speed	Speed	Speed
	Easy	Hard	Hard	Easy	Hard	Hard	Easy	Hard	Hard	Easy	Hard	Hard	Easy	Hard	Hard	Easy
%	65	70	75	65	80	85	70	90	95	80	100	95	75	85	75	—

Weekly mileage (km)

	1	2	3	4	5	6	7	8	9	10	11	12	13	14	15	16
Swim	3	3	3	3	3	3	3	4	4	3	4	4	3	3	3	—
Bike	117	126	135	117	144	153	126	162	171	144	180	171	135	153	135	—
Run	16	18	19	16	20	21	18	23	24	20	25	24	19	21	19	—

Daily mileage

Mon	km	km	km	km	km	km	km	km	km	km	km	km	km	km	km	km
Swim	$.8_1$	$.8_1$	$.9_1$	$.8_1$	1.0_1	$.8_1$	1.1_1	1.1_1	1.0_1	1.2_1	1.1_1	$.9_1$	1.0_1	$.9_1$	1.5_1	
Bike																
Run	4.1_1	4.4_2	4.7_2	4.1_1	5.0_2	5.3_2	4.4_1	5.6_{2-3}	5.9_{2-3}	5.0_1	6.3_{2-4}	5.9_{2-4}	4.7_1	5.3_{2-4}	4.7_{2-4}	6.0_1

Tues	1	2	3	4	5	6	7	8	9	10	11	12	13	14	15	16
Swim																
Bike	26.0_1	28.0_2	30.0_2	26.0_1	32.0_3	34.0_3	28.0_1	36.0_4	38.0_4	32.0_1	40.0_5	38.0_5	30.0_1	34.0_{5-6}	30.0_{5-6}	30.0_{5-6}
Run																

Wed	1	2	3	4	5	6	7	8	9	10	11	12	13	14	15	16
Swim	$.8_1$	$.8_2$	$.9_2$	$.8_1$	1.0_2	1.0_2	$.8_1$	1.12_{2-3}	1.1_{2-3}	1.0_1	1.2_{2-4}	1.1_{2-4}	$.9_1$	1.0_{2-4}	$.9_{2-4}$	1.5_1
Bike																
Run	8.1_1	8.8_1	9.4_1	8.1_1	10.0_1	10.6_1	8.8_1	11.3_1	11.9_1	10.0_1	12.5_1	11.9_1	9.4_1	10.6_1	9.4_1	6.0_1

Thur	1	2	3	4	5	6	7	8	9	10	11	12	13	14	15	16
Swim																
Bike	26.0_1	28.0_2	30.0_2	26.0_1	32.0_2	34.0_2	28.0_1	36.0_{2-4}	38.0_{2-4}	32.0_1	40.0_{2-4}	38.0_{2-4}	30.0_1	34.0_{2-4}	30.0_{2-4}	20.0_1
Run																

Fri	1	2	3	4	5	6	7	8	9	10	11	12	13	14	15	16
Swim																
Bike	D/O	D/O	D/O	D/O	D/O	D/O	D/O	D/O	D/O	D/O	D/O	D/O	D/O	D/O	D/O	D/O
Run																

Sat	1	2	3	4	5	6	7	8	9	10	11	12	13	14	15	16
Swim	1.0_1	1.1_2	1.2_2	1.0_1	1.3_5	1.4_3	1.1_1	1.4_4	1.5_4	1.3_1	1.6_5	1.5_5	1.2_1	1.4_{5-6}	1.2_{5-6}	
Bike																D/O
Run	4.1_1	4.4_2	4.7_2	4.1_1	5.0_3	5.3_3	4.4_1	5.6_4	5.9_4	5.0_1	6.3_5	5.9_5	4.7_1	5.3_{5-6}	4.7_{5-6}	

Sun	1	2	3	4	5	6	7	8	9	10	11	12	13	14	15	16
Swim																
Bike	65.0_1	70.0_1	75.0_1	65.0_1	80.0_1	85.0_1	70.0_1	90.0_1	95.0_1	80.0_1	100.0_1	95.0_1	75.0_1	85.0_1	75.0_1	RACE
Run																

Base 1 would occur first. **The bold subscript numerals refer to subphases**

Read pages 185–8 before starting.

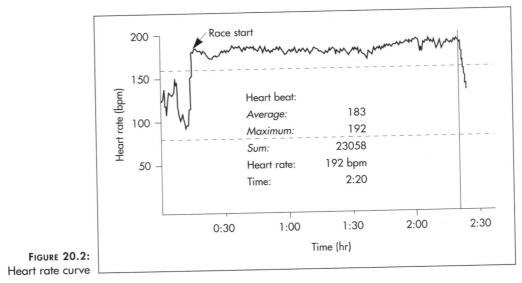

FIGURE 20.2:
Heart rate curve

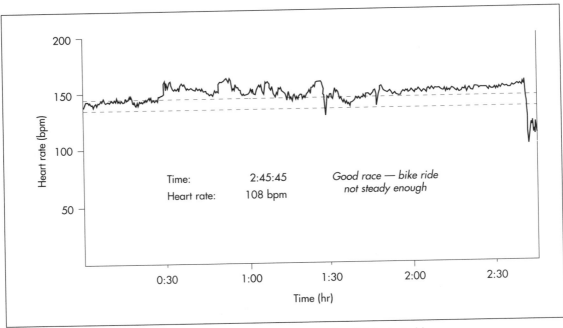

FIGURE 20.3: Standard distance (1.5/40/10 km) triathlon

Race: Triathlon (Olympic/half-Ironman)
Race date: 20 April
Training starts: 30 December

Maximum distance for the 100% week
Swim: 12 km
Bike: 240 km
Run: 50 km

Mileage profile

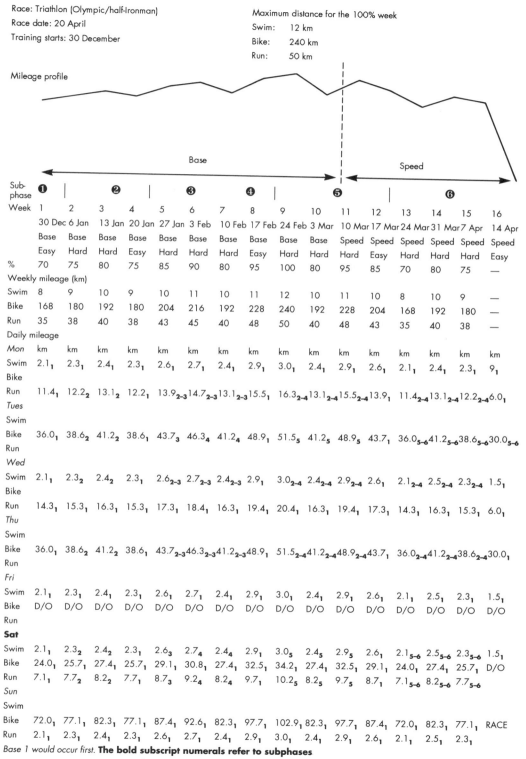

Base — Speed

Sub-phase	❶		❷		❸		❹			❺			❻			
Week	1	2	3	4	5	6	7	8	9	10	11	12	13	14	15	16
	30 Dec	6 Jan	13 Jan	20 Jan	27 Jan	3 Feb	10 Feb	17 Feb	24 Feb	3 Mar	10 Mar	17 Mar	24 Mar	31 Mar	7 Apr	14 Apr
	Base	Base	Base	Base	Base	Base	Base	Base	Base	Base	Speed	Speed	Speed	Speed	Speed	Speed
	Easy	Hard	Hard	Easy	Hard	Hard	Hard	Easy	Hard	Hard	Hard	Easy	Hard	Hard	Hard	Easy
%	70	75	80	75	85	90	80	95	100	80	95	85	70	80	75	—
Weekly mileage (km)																
Swim	8	9	10	9	10	11	10	11	12	10	11	10	8	10	9	—
Bike	168	180	192	180	204	216	192	228	240	192	228	204	168	192	180	—
Run	35	38	40	38	43	45	40	48	50	40	48	43	35	40	38	—

Daily mileage (all values in km)

Day	1	2	3	4	5	6	7	8	9	10	11	12	13	14	15	16
Mon Swim	2.1_1	2.3_1	2.4_1	2.3_1	2.6_1	2.7_1	2.4_1	2.9_1	3.0_1	2.4_1	2.9_1	2.6_1	2.1_1	2.4_1	2.3_1	9_1
Bike																
Run	11.4_1	12.2_2	13.1_2	12.2_1	13.9_{2-3}	14.7_{2-3}	13.1_{2-3}	15.5_1	16.3_{2-4}	13.1_{2-4}	15.5_{2-4}	13.9_1	11.4_{2-4}	13.1_{2-4}	12.2_{2-4}	6.0_1
Tues Swim																
Bike	36.0_1	38.6_2	41.2_2	38.6_1	43.7_3	46.3_4	41.2_4	48.9_1	51.5_5	41.2_5	48.9_5	43.7_1	36.0_{5-6}	41.2_{5-6}	38.6_{5-6}	30.0_{5-6}
Run																
Wed Swim	2.1_1	2.3_2	2.4_2	2.3_1	2.6_{2-3}	2.7_{2-3}	2.4_{2-3}	2.9_1	3.0_{2-4}	2.4_{2-4}	2.9_{2-4}	2.6_1	2.1_{2-4}	2.5_{2-4}	2.3_{2-4}	1.5_1
Bike																
Run	14.3_1	15.3_1	16.3_1	15.3_1	17.3_1	18.4_1	16.3_1	19.4_1	20.4_1	16.3_1	19.4_1	17.3_1	14.3_1	16.3_1	15.3_1	6.0_1
Thu Swim																
Bike	36.0_1	38.6_2	41.2_2	38.6_1	43.7_{2-3}	46.3_{2-3}	41.2_{2-3}	48.9_1	51.5_{2-4}	41.2_{2-4}	48.9_{2-4}	43.7_1	36.0_{2-4}	41.2_{2-4}	38.6_{2-4}	30.0_1
Run																
Fri Swim	2.1_1	2.3_1	2.4_1	2.3_1	2.6_1	2.7_1	2.4_1	2.9_1	3.0_1	2.4_1	2.9_1	2.6_1	2.1_1	2.5_1	2.3_1	1.5_1
Bike	D/O	D/O	D/O	D/O	D/O	D/O	D/O	D/O	D/O	D/O	D/O	D/O	D/O	D/O	D/O	D/O
Run																
Sat Swim	2.1_1	2.3_2	2.4_2	2.3_1	2.6_3	2.7_4	2.4_4	2.9_1	3.0_5	2.4_5	2.9_5	2.6_1	2.1_{5-6}	2.5_{5-6}	2.3_{5-6}	1.5_1
Bike	24.0_1	25.7_1	27.4_1	25.7_1	29.1_1	30.8_1	27.4_1	32.5_1	34.2_1	27.4_1	32.5_1	29.1_1	24.0_1	27.4_1	25.7_1	D/O
Run	7.1_1	7.7_2	8.2_2	7.7_1	8.7_3	9.2_4	8.2_4	9.7_1	10.2_5	8.2_5	9.7_5	8.7_1	7.1_{5-6}	8.2_{5-6}	7.7_{5-6}	
Sun Swim																
Bike	72.0_1	77.1_1	82.3_1	77.1_1	87.4_1	92.6_1	82.3_1	97.7_1	102.9_1	82.3_1	97.7_1	87.4_1	72.0_1	82.3_1	77.1_1	RACE
Run	2.1_1	2.3_1	2.4_1	2.3_1	2.6_1	2.7_1	2.4_1	2.9_1	3.0_1	2.4_1	2.9_1	2.6_1	2.1_1	2.5_1	2.3_1	

Base 1 would occur first. **The bold subscript numerals refer to subphases**

Read pages 185–8 before starting.

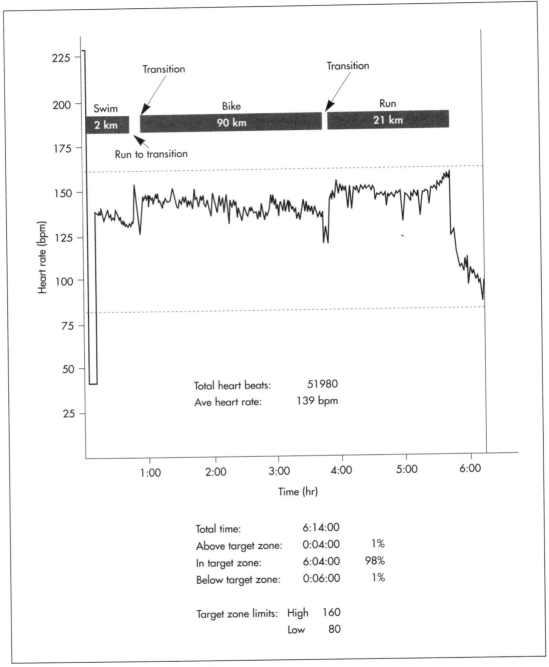

Total heart beats: 51980
Ave heart rate: 139 bpm

Total time: 6:14:00
Above target zone: 0:04:00   1%
In target zone: 6:04:00   98%
Below target zone: 0:06:00   1%

Target zone limits: High   160
                  Low   80

FIGURE 20.4: Half-Ironman

Race: Ironman
Race date: 20 April
Training starts: 30 December

Maximum distance for the 100% week
Swim: 9 km
Bike: 280 km
Run: 60 km

Mileage profile

		Base										Speed					
Subphase	❶		❷		❸		❹			❺			❻				
Week	1	2	3	4	5	6	7	8	9	10	11	12	13	14	15	16
	30 Dec	6 Jan	13 Jan	20 Jan	27 Jan	3 Feb	10 Feb	17 Feb	24 Feb	3 Mar	10 Mar	17 Mar	24 Mar	31 Mar	7 Apr	14 Apr
	Base	Base	Base	Base	Base	Base	Base	Base	Base	Base	Speed	Speed	Speed	Speed	Speed	Speed
	Easy	Hard	Hard	Easy	Hard	Hard	Easy	Hard	Hard	Easy	Hard	Hard	Easy	Hard	Hard	Easy
%	58	72	79	65	86	93	72	93	100	79	93	100	72	86	72	—
Weekly mileage (km)																
Swim	5	6	7	6	8	8	6	8	9	7	8	9	6	8	6	—
Bike	162	202	221	182	241	260	202	260	280	221	260	280	202	241	172	—
Run	35	43	47	39	52	56	43	56	60	47	56	60	43	52	43	—

Daily mileage (km)

	W1	W2	W3	W4	W5	W6	W7	W8	W9	W10	W11	W12	W13	W14	W15	W16
Mon																
Swim	1.6_1	1.9_1	2.1_1	1.8_1	2.3_1	2.5_1	1.9_1	2.5_1	2.7_1	2.1_1	2.5_1	2.7_1	1.9_1	2.3_1	1.9_1	$.8_1$
Bike																
Run	10.5_1	13.1_2	14.4_2	11.8_1	15.6_2	16.9_2	13.1_1	16.9_{2-3}	18.2_{2-3}	14.4_1	16.9_{2-4}	18.2_{2-4}	13.1_1	15.6_{2-4}	13.1_{2-4}	6.0_1
Tues																
Swim																
Bike	34.8_1	43.2_2	47.4_2	39.0_1	51.6_3	55.8_3	43.2_1	55.8_4	60.0_4	47.4_1	55.8_5	60.0_5	43.2_1	51.6_{5-6}	43.2_{5-6}	30.0_{5-6}
Run																
Wed																
Swim	1.6_1	1.9_2	2.1_2	1.8_1	2.3_2	2.5_2	1.9_1	2.5_{2-3}	2.7_{2-3}	2.1_1	2.5_{2-4}	2.7_{2-4}	1.9_1	2.3_{2-4}	1.9_{2-4}	1.5_1
Bike																
Run	15.8_1	19.6_1	21.5_1	17.7_1	23.5_1	25.4_1	19.6_1	25.4_1	27.3_1	21.5_1	25.4_1	27.3_1	19.6_1	23.5_1	19.6_1	6.0_1
Thu																
Swim																
Bike	23.2_1	28.8_2	31.6_2	26.0_1	34.4_2	37.2_2	28.8_1	37.2_{2-3}	40.0_{2-3}	31.6_1	37.2_{2-4}	40.0_{2-4}	28.8_1	34.4_{2-4}	28.8_{2-4}	20.0_1
Run																
Fri																
Swim																
Bike	D/O	D/O	D/O	D/O	D/O	D/O	D/O	D/O	D/O	D/O	D/O	D/O	D/O	D/O	D/O	D/O
Run																
Sat																
Swim	2.1_1	2.6_2	2.8_2	2.3_1	3.1_3	3.3_3	2.6_1	3.3_4	3.6_4	2.8_1	3.3_5	3.6_5	2.6_1	3.1_{5-6}	2.6_{5-6}	
Bike																D/O
Run	8.4_1	10.5_2	11.5_2	9.5_1	12.5_3	13.5_3	10.5_1	13.5_4	14.5_4	11.5_1	13.5_5	14.5_5	10.5_1	12.5_{5-6}	10.5_{5-6}	
Sun																
Swim																
Bike	104.4_1	129.6_1	142.2_1	117.0_1	154.8_1	167.4_1	129.6_1	167.4_1	180.0_1	142.2_1	167.4_1	180.0_1	129.6_1	154.8_1	100.0_1	RACE
Run																

Note: mileages would be set based on this guide. In Ironman training more 180 km bike rides may be trained. Base 1 would occur first.
The bold subscript numerals refer to subphases.

Read pages 185–8 before starting.

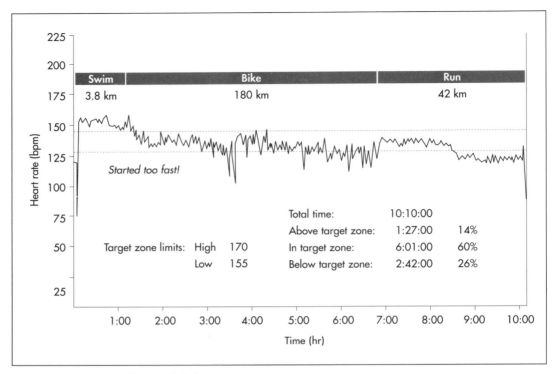

FIGURE 20.5: Ironman

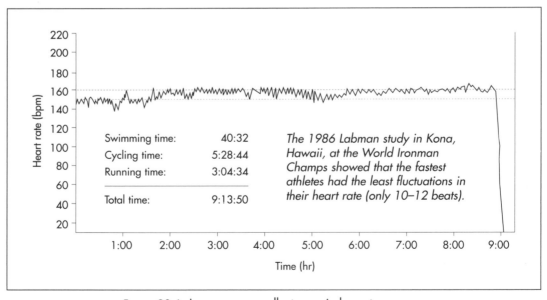

FIGURE 20.6: Ironman — excellent pace judgment

Detailed descriptions

Bike heart rates	Subphase	Sport		Run heart rates
		BIKE	**RUN**	
.... (LSD)	EASY 1	EASY: easy rolling **aim:** establish base fitness **easy gears:** 42 x 15–18 **speed:** 25–28 kph **cadence:** 85–105 rpm **reps:** whole workout	EASY: easy jogging **aim:** establish base fitness **speed:** 5–7 min/km **reps:** whole workout	(LSD)
During N/A Between .... (LSD)	LOAD 2 HILLS	HILLS: roll over hills in a small gear. Number & length of hills is important NOT how hard you do them. So the aim is easy climbing. **aim:** prep for strength endurance training **easy gears:** 42 x 18–21 on hills **speed:** 12–20 kph on hills **cadence:** 40–70 rpm on hills **reps:** whole workout	HILLS HILLS: Easy jogging up hills. Number & length of hills is important NOT how hard you do them so the aim is easy climbing. **aim:** prep for strength endurance training. **speed:** 6–9 min/km on hills **reps:** whole workout	During N/A Between .... (LSD)
During N/A Between .... (LSD)	HIGH LOAD 3 H (BG)	HILLS BIG GEAR: climbing short hills of moderate gradient in a bigger gear than normal (i.e. 43 x 14) should be hard muscularly but not too hard. **aim:** strength endurance **gears:** 42 x 13–17 on hills **speed:** 12–20 kph on hills **cadence:** 30–60 rpm on hills **distance:** 200–700 m **80% seated, 20% standing** **reps:** rec = 0–2 semi = 2–4 comp = 4–6	H(LS) HILLS LONG STRIDE: jog along the flat towards a hill and with 2–5 m to go, extend your stride out and raise the tempo of your running so that you stride out up the hill using your racing stride length to strengthen the full length of your stride. As soon as you feel 'bogged' down as you run up the hill (stride length or stride rate drops or you start to puff) pull out and jog back down to the bottom of the hill and jog/rest to recovery before the next one. Repeat. **speed:** 4–7 min/km **distance:** 30-200 m (20 s-1 min) **gradient:** shallow/moderate: the hill cannot be so steep that you cannot use a stride and action that replicates a racing running action on the flat. **reps:** rec = 0–4 semi = 4–10 comp = 10–20	During N/A Betweeen .... (LSD)
During N/A Between .... (LSD)	LOAD/ SPEED 4 F(BG)	FLAT BIG GEAR: 'roll' a big gear (i.e. 52 x 16) but don't 'push' it. It should not feel hard till you have been going for at least 20 mins. **aim:** conversion of strength endurance to speed. **gears:** 52 x 12–16 **speed:** 27–32 kph **cadence:** 40–70 rpm **reps:** rec = 0–1 x 20 mins semi = 1–4 x 20 mins comp = 2–10 x 20 mins	F(LS) FLAT LONG STRIDE: during your run at frequent intervals pick up the tempo slightly and extend your stride length out to a racing stride length for 100–200 m. Pull out before you get 'bogged' down (ie. stride length or rate drops or you start to puff) **speed:** 3.5–5 min/km **reps:** rec = 0–4 semi = 4–8 comp = 8–15	During N/A Between .... (LSD) (CONTINUED)

Bike heart rates	Subphase	Sport		Run heart rates
		BIKE	**RUN**	

During
 	
.... (UT)
 	
Between
 	
.... (LSD)
	LOW SPEED 5
	
	UT
		UP-TEMPO: you should feel fast, strong, comfortable and in control. This is an effort at 3 hr max. race pace — NO HARDER! It is only slightly faster than cruising.
		aim: prep for speed
		gears: 52 x 17–21
		speed: 30–36 kph
		cadence: 85–105 rpm
		reps: rec = 1–2 x 10 mins
		     semi = 1–3 x 10 mins
		     comp = 1–6 x 10 mins
			UP-TEMPO: as for bike speed: 3.5–5 min/km
			reps: rec = 1–2 x 10 mins
			     semi = 1–3 x 10 mins
			     comp = 1–6 x 10 mins
			
			UT
				During
				
				.... (UT)
				
				Between
				
				.... (LSD)

During
 	
.... (AT)
 	
Between
 	
.... (LSD)
	HIGH SPEED 6
	
	AT
		ANAEROBIC THRESHOLD: Max steady state pace or 20 min–1 hr race pace — NO HARDER. This is hard but not hell.
		aim: increase AT & race pace
		gears: 52 x 14–16
		speed: 36–46 kph
		cadence: 85–105 rpm
		reps: rec = 1–2 x 5 mins
		     semi = 1–3 x 5 mins
		     comp = 1–6 x 5 mins
			ANAEROBIC THRESHOLD: as for bike
			
			speed: 3-5 min/km
			reps: rec = 1–2 x 5 mins
			     semi = 1–3 x 5 mins
			     comp = 1–6 x 5 mins
			
			AT
				During
				
				.... (AT)
				
				Between
				
				.... (LSD)

Note: The best action to take for swimming is to join a swim squad.

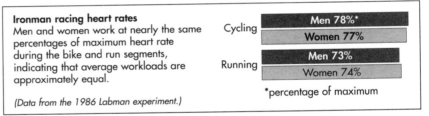

Ironman racing heart rates
Men and women work at nearly the same percentages of maximum heart rate during the bike and run segments, indicating that average workloads are approximately equal.

(*Data from the 1986 Labman experiment.*)

Cycling — Men 78%*
Cycling — Women 77%
Running — Men 73%
Running — Women 74%

*percentage of maximum

Types of training used for triathlon, when initiated and effects.

Type	When initiated (intensity)	Effect	Example	Race use
Power	—	—	—	—
Intensive	—	—	—	—
Extensive sprints	—	—	—	—
Submaximal	Speed phase	Improves max steady state race pace	4–6 x 6–8 min 4–1 min rest btwn or 20–30 min TT	Standard, sprint, half-Ironman
Up-tempo	Late base, early speed, speed	Transition from base to speedwork or long dist race pace — Ironman speedwork recover rate	1–2 x 10–30 min rest 10–20– min btwn	Standard, sprint, half-Ironman, Ironman
Long slow distance	Base/speed	Improves ability to do mileage, builds training tolerance and improves recovery rate	Continuous	All
Active recovery	Base/speed	Assists recovery (only if needed)	Continuous	All

Key: min = minutes; btwn = between; TT = time trial; dist = distance

Race: Duathlon 4 km/20/ km/ 4 km
Race date: 20 April
Training starts: 30 December

Maximum distance for the 100% week
Run: 38 km
Bike: 160 km

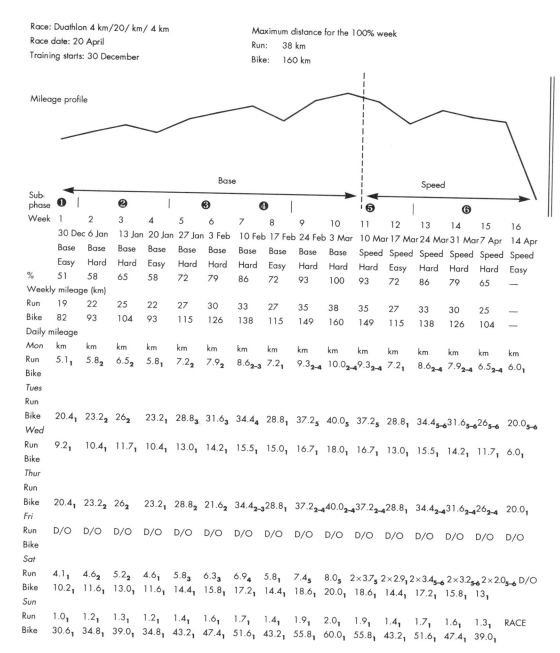

Mileage profile

Base · Speed

The bold subscript numerals refer to subphases

Sub-phase	❶		❷		❸		❹			❺		❻			
Week	1	2	3	4	5	6	7	8	9	10	11	12	13	14	15	16
	30 Dec	6 Jan	13 Jan	20 Jan	27 Jan	3 Feb	10 Feb	17 Feb	24 Feb	3 Mar	10 Mar	17 Mar	24 Mar	31 Mar	7 Apr	14 Apr
	Base	Base	Base	Base	Base	Base	Base	Base	Base	Base	Speed	Speed	Speed	Speed	Speed	Speed
	Easy	Hard	Hard	Easy	Hard	Hard	Hard	Easy	Hard	Hard	Hard	Easy	Hard	Hard	Hard	Easy
%	51	58	65	58	72	79	86	72	93	100	93	72	86	79	65	—
Weekly mileage (km)																
Run	19	22	25	22	27	30	33	27	35	38	35	27	33	30	25	—
Bike	82	93	104	93	115	126	138	115	149	160	149	115	138	126	104	—
Daily mileage																
Mon	km	km	km	km	km	km	km	km	km	km	km	km	km	km	km	km
Run	5.1_1	5.8_2	6.5_2	5.8_1	7.2_2	7.9_2	8.6_{2-3}	7.2_1	9.3_{2-4}	10.0_{2-4}	9.3_{2-4}	7.2_1	8.6_{2-4}	7.9_{2-4}	6.5_{2-4}	6.0_1
Bike																
Tues																
Run																
Bike	20.4_1	23.2_2	26_2	23.2_1	28.8_3	31.6_3	34.4_4	28.8_1	37.2_5	40.0_5	37.2_5	28.8_1	34.4_{5-6}	31.6_{5-6}	26_{5-6}	20.0_{5-6}
Wed																
Run	9.2_1	10.4_1	11.7_1	10.4_1	13.0_1	14.2_1	15.5_1	15.0_1	16.7_1	18.0_1	16.7_1	13.0_1	15.5_1	14.2_1	11.7_1	6.0_1
Bike																
Thur																
Run																
Bike	20.4_1	23.2_2	26_2	23.2_1	28.8_2	21.6_2	34.4_{2-3}	28.8_1	37.2_{2-4}	40.0_{2-4}	37.2_{2-4}	28.8_1	34.4_{2-4}	31.6_{2-4}	26_{2-4}	20.0_1
Fri																
Run	D/O	D/O	D/O	D/O	D/O	D/O	D/O	D/O	D/O	D/O	D/O	D/O	D/O	D/O	D/O	D/O
Bike																
Sat																
Run	4.1_1	4.6_2	5.2_2	4.6_1	5.8_3	6.3_3	6.9_4	5.8_1	7.4_5	8.0_5	$2\times3.7_5$	$2\times2.9_1$	$2\times3.4_{5-6}$	$2\times3.2_{5-6}$	$2\times2.0_{5-6}$	D/O
Bike	10.2_1	11.6_2	13.0_1	11.6_1	14.4_1	15.8_1	17.2_1	14.4_1	18.6_1	20.0_1	18.6_1	14.4_1	17.2_1	15.8_1	13_1	
Sun																
Run	1.0_1	1.2_1	1.3_1	1.2_1	1.4_1	1.6_1	1.7_1	1.4_1	1.9_1	2.0_1	1.9_1	1.4_1	1.7_1	1.6_1	1.3_1	RACE
Bike	30.6_1	34.8_1	39.0_1	34.8_1	43.2_1	47.4_1	51.6_1	43.2_1	55.8_1	60.0_1	55.8_1	43.2_1	51.6_1	47.4_1	39.0_1	

The bold subscript numerals refer to subphases

Read pages 185–8 before starting.

Race: Duathlon 10 km/60 km/10 km
Race date: 20 April
Training starts: 30 December

Maximum distance for the 100% week
Run: 69 km
Bike: 320 km

Mileage profile

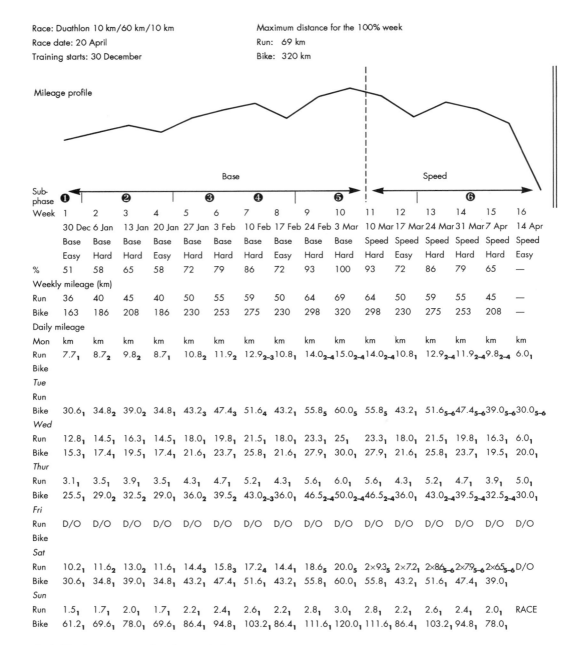

		Base										Speed					
Sub-phase	❶		❷		❸		❹		❺		❻					
Week		1	2	3	4	5	6	7	8	9	10	11	12	13	14	15	16
		30 Dec	6 Jan	13 Jan	20 Jan	27 Jan	3 Feb	10 Feb	17 Feb	24 Feb	3 Mar	10 Mar	17 Mar	24 Mar	31 Mar	7 Apr	14 Apr
		Base	Base	Base	Base	Base	Base	Base	Base	Base	Base	Speed	Speed	Speed	Speed	Speed	Speed
		Easy	Hard	Hard	Easy	Hard	Hard	Hard	Easy	Hard	Hard	Hard	Easy	Hard	Hard	Hard	Easy
%		51	58	65	58	72	79	86	72	93	100	93	72	86	79	65	—
Weekly mileage (km)																	
Run		36	40	45	40	50	55	59	50	64	69	64	50	59	55	45	—
Bike		163	186	208	186	230	253	275	230	298	320	298	230	275	253	208	—
Daily mileage																	
Mon		km	km	km	km	km	km	km	km	km	km	km	km	km	km	km	km
Run		7.7_1	8.7_2	9.8_2	8.7_1	10.8_2	11.9_2	12.9_{2-3}	10.8_1	14.0_{2-4}	15.0_{2-4}	14.0_{2-4}	10.8_1	12.9_{2-4}	11.9_{2-4}	9.8_{2-4}	6.0_1
Bike																	
Tue																	
Run																	
Bike		30.6_1	34.8_2	39.0_2	34.8_1	43.2_3	47.4_3	51.6_4	43.2_1	55.8_5	60.0_5	55.8_5	43.2_1	51.6_{5-6}	47.4_{5-6}	39.0_{5-6}	30.0_{5-6}
Wed																	
Run		12.8_1	14.5_1	16.3_1	14.5_1	18.0_1	19.8_1	21.5_1	18.0_1	23.3_1	25_1	23.3_1	18.0_1	21.5_1	19.8_1	16.3_1	6.0_1
Bike		15.3_1	17.4_1	19.5_1	17.4_1	21.6_1	23.7_1	25.8_1	21.6_1	27.9_1	30.0_1	27.9_1	21.6_1	25.8_1	23.7_1	19.5_1	20.0_1
Thur																	
Run		3.1_1	3.5_1	3.9_1	3.5_1	4.3_1	4.7_1	5.2_1	4.3_1	5.6_1	6.0_1	5.6_1	4.3_1	5.2_1	4.7_1	3.9_1	5.0_1
Bike		25.5_1	29.0_2	32.5_2	29.0_1	36.0_2	39.5_2	43.0_{2-3}	36.0_1	46.5_{2-4}	50.0_{2-4}	46.5_{2-4}	36.0_1	43.0_{2-4}	39.5_{2-4}	32.5_{2-4}	30.0_1
Fri																	
Run		D/O	D/O	D/O	D/O	D/O	D/O	D/O	D/O	D/O	D/O	D/O	D/O	D/O	D/O	D/O	D/O
Bike																	
Sat																	
Run		10.2_1	11.6_2	13.0_2	11.6_1	14.4_3	15.8_3	17.2_4	14.4_1	18.6_5	20.0_5	$2{\times}9.3_5$	$2{\times}7.2_1$	$2{\times}8_{5-6}$	$2{\times}79_{5-6}$	$2{\times}65_{5-6}$	D/O
Bike		30.6_1	34.8_1	39.0_1	34.8_1	43.2_1	47.4_1	51.6_1	43.2_1	55.8_1	60.0_1	55.8_1	43.2_1	51.6_1	47.4_1	39.0_1	
Sun																	
Run		1.5_1	1.7_1	2.0_1	1.7_1	2.2_1	2.4_1	2.6_1	2.2_1	2.8_1	3.0_1	2.8_1	2.2_1	2.6_1	2.4_1	2.0_1	RACE
Bike		61.2_1	69.6_1	78.0_1	69.6_1	86.4_1	94.8_1	103.2_1	86.4_1	111.6_1	120.0_1	111.6_1	86.4_1	103.2_1	94.8_1	78.0_1	

The bold subscript numerals refer to subphases

To adjust from standard Powerman distances to Zolfingen Powerman distances, use the Ironman programmes on pages 243-4.

Read pages 185–8 before starting.

Detailed descriptions

Bike heart rates	*Subphase*	*Sport*			*Run heart rates*
		BIKE		**RUN**	
.... (LSD)	EASY 1	EASY: easy rolling **aim:** establish base fitness **easy gears:** 42 x 15–18 **speed:** 25–28 kph **cadence:** 85–105 rpm **reps:** whole workout		EASY: easy jogging **aim**: establish base fitness **speed:** 5–7min/km **reps:** whole workout	.... (LSD)
During N/A Between .... (LSD)	LOAD 2 HILLS	HILLS: roll over hills in a small gear. Number & length of hills is important NOT how hard you do them. So the aim is easy climbing. **aim:** prep for strength endurance training **easy gears**: 42 x 18–21 on hills **speed:** 12–20 kph on hills **cadence:** 40–70 rpm on hills **reps:** whole workout	HILLS	HILLS: Easy jogging up hills. Number & length of hills is important NOT how hard you do them so the aim is easy climbing. **aim:** prep for strength endurance training. **speed:** 6–9 min/km on hills **reps:** whole workout	During N/A Between .... (LSD)
During N/A Between .... (LSD)	HIGH LOAD 3 H (BG)	HILLS BIG GEAR: climbing short hills of moderate gradient in a bigger gear than normal (i.e. 43 x 14) it should be hard muscularly but not too hard. **aim:** strength endurance **gears:** 42 x 13–17on hills **speed:** 12–20 kph on hills **cadence:** 30–60 rpm on hills **distance:** 200–700 m **80% seated, 20% standing** **reps:** rec = 0–2 semi = 2–4 comp = 4–6	H(LS)	HILLS LONG STRIDE: jog along the flat towards a hill and with 2–5 m to go, extend your stride out and raise the tempo of your running so that you stride out up the hill using your racing stride length to strengthen the full length of your stride. As soon as you feel 'bogged' down as you run up the hill (stride length or stride rate drops or you start to puff) pull out and jog back down to the bottom of the hill and jog/rest to recovery before the next one. Repeat. **speed:** 4–7 min/km **distance:** 30–200 m (20 s–1 min) **gradient:** shallow/moderate: the hill cannot be so steep that you cannot use a stride and action that replicates a racing running action on the flat. **reps:** rec = 0–4 semi = 4–10 comp = 10–20	During N/A Betweeen .... (LSD)
During N/A Between .... (LSD)	LOAD/ SPEED 4 F(BG)	FLAT BIG GEAR: 'roll' a big gear (i.e. 52 x 16) but don't 'push' it. It should not feel hard till you have been going for at least 20 mins. **aim:** conversion of strength endurance to speed. **gears:** 52 x 12–16 **speed:** 27–32 kph **cadence:** 40–70 rpm **reps:** rec = 0–1 x 20 mins semi = 1–4 x 20 mins comp = 2–10 x 20 mins	F(LS)	FLAT LONG STRIDE: during your run at frequent intervals pick up the tempo slightly and extend your stride length out to a racing stride length for 100–200 m. Pull out before you get 'bogged' down (i.e. stride length or rate drops or you start to puff) **speed:** 3.5–5 min/km **reps:** rec = 0–4 semi = 4–8 comp = 8–15	During N/A Between .... (LSD)

(Continued)

Bike heart rates	Subphase	Sport		Run heart rates
		BIKE	**RUN**	
During .... (UT) Between .... (LSD)	LOW SPEED 5 UT	UP-TEMPO: you should feel fast, strong, comfortable and in control. This is a effort at 3 hr max. race pace — NO HARDER! It is only slightly faster than cruising. **aim:** prep for speed **gears:** 52 x 17–21 **speed:** 30–36 kph **cadence:** 85–105 rpm **reps:** rec = 1–2 x 10 mins semi = 1–3 x 10 mins comp = 1–6 x 10 mins	UP-TEMPO: as for bike speed: 3.5 - 5 min/km **reps:** rec = 1–2 x 10 mins semi = 1–3 x 10 mins comp = 1–6 x 10 mins UT	During .... (UT) Between .... (LSD)
During .... (AT) Between .... (LSD)	HIGH SPEED 6 AT	ANAEROBIC THRESHOLD: Max steady-state pace or 20 min–1 hr race pace — NO HARDER. This is hard but not hell. **aim:** increase AT & race pace **gears:** 52 x 14–16 **speed:** 36–46 kph **cadence:** 85–105 rpm **reps:** rec = 1–2 x 5 mins semi = 1–3 x 5 mins comp = 1–6 x 5 mins	ANAEROBIC THRESHOLD: as for bike **speed:** 3-5min/km **reps:** rec = 1–2 x 5 mins semi = 1–3 x 5 mins comp = 1–6 x 5 mins AT	During .... (AT) Between .... (LSD)

Types of training used for duathlon, when initiated and effects.

Type	When initiated (intensity)	Effect	Example	Race use
Power	—	—	—	—
Intensive	—	—	—	—
Extensive sprints	—	—	—	—
Submaximal	Speed phase	Improves max steady-state race pace	4–6 x 6–8 min 4–1 min rest btwn or 20–30 min TT	Duathlon
Up-tempo	Late base, early speed,	Transition from base to speedwork	1–2 x 10–30 min rest 10–20– min btwn	Duathlon, long-dist duathlon (4 hrs+)
Long slow distance	Base/speed	Improves ability to do mileage, builds training tolerance, improves recovery rate	Continuous	All
Active recovery	Base/speed	Assists recovery (only if needed)	Continuous	All

PROPORTIONS:
1. Base: 100% long slow distance and active recovery; some speedwork may be used.
2. Speed: approx. 85–90% long slow distance and active recovery;
   approx. 10–15% up-tempo and submaximal intensity.

Key: min = minutes; btwn = between; TT = time trial; dist = distance

Note: Training intensity proportions change continually and the right proportion for one week will not be right for the next. These are approximations to provide a guide only. Higher training intensities may also be used only very rarely.

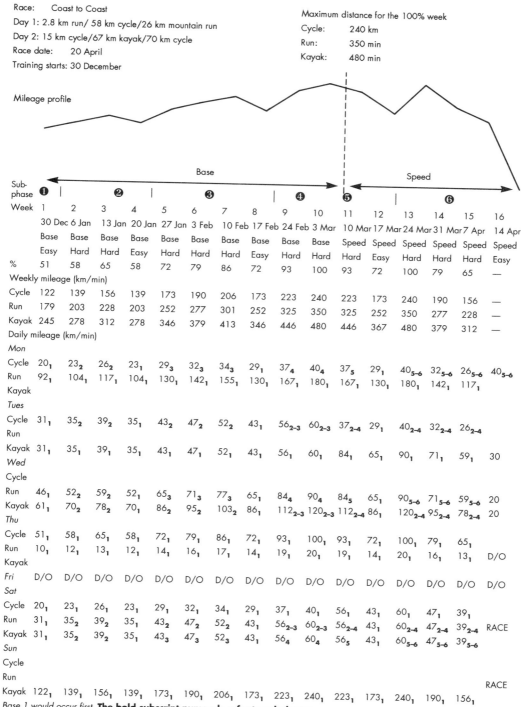

Race: Coast to Coast
Day 1: 2.8 km run/ 58 km cycle/26 km mountain run
Day 2: 15 km cycle/67 km kayak/70 km cycle
Race date: 20 April
Training starts: 30 December

Maximum distance for the 100% week
Cycle: 240 km
Run: 350 min
Kayak: 480 min

Mileage profile

Base ⟶ | Speed ⟶

Subphase: ❶ ❷ ❸ ❹ ❺ ❻

Week	1	2	3	4	5	6	7	8	9	10	11	12	13	14	15	16
	30 Dec	6 Jan	13 Jan	20 Jan	27 Jan	3 Feb	10 Feb	17 Feb	24 Feb	3 Mar	10 Mar	17 Mar	24 Mar	31 Mar	7 Apr	14 Apr
	Base	Base	Base	Base	Base	Base	Base	Base	Base	Base	Speed	Speed	Speed	Speed	Speed	Speed
	Easy	Hard	Hard	Easy	Hard	Hard	Hard	Easy	Hard	Hard	Hard	Easy	Hard	Hard	Hard	Easy
%	51	58	65	58	72	79	86	72	93	100	93	72	100	79	65	—
Weekly mileage (km/min)																
Cycle	122	139	156	139	173	190	206	173	223	240	223	173	240	190	156	—
Run	179	203	228	203	252	277	301	252	325	350	325	252	350	277	228	—
Kayak	245	278	312	278	346	379	413	346	446	480	446	367	480	379	312	—
Daily mileage (km/min)																
Mon																
Cycle	20_1	23_2	26_2	23_1	29_3	32_3	34_3	29_1	37_4	40_4	37_5	29_1	40_{5-6}	32_{5-6}	26_{5-6}	40_{5-6}
Run	92_1	104_1	117_1	104_1	130_1	142_1	155_1	130_1	167_1	180_1	167_1	130_1	180_1	142_1	117_1	
Kayak																
Tues																
Cycle	31_1	35_2	39_2	35_1	43_2	47_2	52_2	43_1	56_{2-3}	60_{2-3}	37_{2-4}	29_1	40_{2-4}	32_{2-4}	26_{2-4}	
Run																
Kayak	31_1	35_1	39_1	35_1	43_1	47_1	52_1	43_1	56_1	60_1	84_1	65_1	90_1	71_1	59_1	30
Wed																
Cycle																
Run	46_1	52_2	59_2	52_1	65_3	71_3	77_3	65_1	84_4	90_4	84_5	65_1	90_{5-6}	71_{5-6}	59_{5-6}	20
Kayak	61_1	70_2	78_2	70_1	86_2	95_2	103_2	86_1	112_{2-3}	120_{2-3}	112_{2-4}	86_1	120_{2-4}	95_{2-4}	78_{2-4}	20
Thu																
Cycle	51_1	58_1	65_1	58_1	72_1	79_1	86_1	72_1	93_1	100_1	93_1	72_1	100_1	79_1	65_1	
Run	10_1	12_1	13_1	12_1	14_1	16_1	17_1	14_1	19_1	20_1	19_1	14_1	20_1	16_1	13_1	D/O
Kayak																
Fri	D/O	D/O	D/O	D/O	D/O	D/O	D/O	D/O	D/O	D/O	D/O	D/O	D/O	D/O	D/O	D/O
Sat																
Cycle	20_1	23_1	26_1	23_1	29_1	32_1	34_1	29_1	37_1	40_1	56_1	43_1	60_1	47_1	39_1	
Run	31_1	35_2	39_2	35_1	43_2	47_2	52_2	43_1	56_{2-3}	60_{2-3}	56_{2-4}	43_1	60_{2-4}	47_{2-4}	39_{2-4}	RACE
Kayak	31_1	35_2	39_2	35_1	43_3	47_3	52_3	43_1	56_4	60_4	56_5	43_1	60_{5-6}	47_{5-6}	39_{5-6}	
Sun																
Cycle																
Run																RACE
Kayak	122_1	139_1	156_1	139_1	173_1	190_1	206_1	173_1	223_1	240_1	223_1	173_1	240_1	190_1	156_1	

Base 1 would occur first. **The bold subscript numerals refer to subphases**

Cycle volumes are displayed in kilometres; kayak and running volumes are in minutes.

'Longest day' is the 1-day version of the original Coast to Coast. Training volumes need not alter much (up 5–10% if you're keen), but longer multidiscipline workouts would be needed (in the 3rd and 5th, or 3rd, 5th and 7th weeks back from the race).

Read pages 185–8 before starting.

DETAILED DESCRIPTIONS

Bike heart rates	Subphase	Sport		Run heart rates
		BIKE	**RUN**	
.... (LSD)	EASY 1	EASY: easy rolling **aim:** establish base fitness **easy gears:** 42 x 15–18 **speed:** 25–28 kph **cadence:** 85–105 rpm **reps:** whole workout	EASY: easy jogging **aim:** establish base fitness **speed:** 5–7 min/km **reps:** whole workout	(LSD)
During N/A Between .... (LSD)	LOAD 2 HILLS	HILLS: roll over hills in a small gear. Number & length of hills is important NOT how hard you do them. So the aim is easy climbing. **aim:** prep for strength endurance training **easy gears:** 42 x 18–21 on hills **speed:** 12–20 kph **cadence:** 40–70 rpm on hills **reps:** whole workout	*HILLS* HILLS: Easy jogging up hills. Number & length of hills is important NOT how hard you do them so the aim is easy climbing. **aim:** prep for strength endurance training. **speed:** 6–9min/km on hills **reps:** whole workout	During N/A Between .... (LSD)

During N/A Between
 	
.... (LSD)
	HIGH LOAD 3
	
	H (BG)
		HILLS BIG GEAR: climbing short hills of moderate gradient in a bigger gear than normal (i.e. 43 x 14) should be hard muscularly but not too hard.
		aim: strength endurance
		gears: 42 x 13–17 on hills
		speed: 12–20 kph
		cadence: 30–60 rpm on hills
		distance: 200–700 m
		80% seated, 20% standing
		reps: rec = 0–2
		    semi = 2–4
		    comp = 4–6
			H(LS) HILLS LONG STRIDE: jog along the flat towards a hill and with 2–5 m to go, extend your stride out and raise the tempo of your running so that you stride out up the hill using your racing stride length to strengthen the full length of your stride. As soon as you feel 'bogged' down as you run up the hill (stride length or stride rate drops or you start to puff) pull out and jog back down to the bottom of the hill and jog/rest to recovery before the next one. Repeat.
			speed: 4–7 min/km
			distance: 30-200 m (20 s–1 min)
			gradient: shallow/moderate — the hill cannot be so steep that you cannot use a stride and action that replicates a racing running action on the flat.
			reps: rec = 0–4
			    semi = 4–10
			    comp = 10–20
				During N/A Betweeen
				
				.... (LSD)

During N/A Between
 	
.... (LSD)
	LOAD/ SPEED 4
	
	F(BG)
		FLAT BIG GEAR: 'roll' a big gear (i.e. 52 x 16) but don't 'push' it. It should not feel hard till you have been going for at least 20 mins.
		aim: conversion of strength endurance to speed.
		gears: 52 x 12–16
		speed: 27–32 kph
		cadence: 40–70 rpm
		reps: rec = 0–1 x 20 mins
		    semi = 1–4 x 20 mins
		    comp = 2–10 x 20 mins
			F(LS) FLAT LONG STRIDE: during your run at frequent intervals pick up the tempo slightly and extend your stride length out to a racing stride length for 100–200m. Pull out before you get 'bogged' down (i.e. stride length or rate drops or you start to puff)
			speed: 3.5–5 min/km
			reps: rec = 0–4
			    semi = 4–8
			    comp = 8–15
				During N/A Between
				
				.... (LSD)
				
				(CONTINUED)

204

Bike heart rates	Subphase	Sport		Run heart rates
		BIKE	**RUN**	
During .... (UT) Between .... (LSD)	LOW SPEED 5 UT	UP-TEMPO: you should feel fast, strong, comfortable and in control. This is an effort at 3 hr max. race pace — NO HARDER! It is only slightly faster than cruising. **aim:** prep for speed **gears:** 52 x 17–21 **speed:** 30–36 kph **cadence:** 85–105 rpm **reps:** rec = 1–2 x 10 mins semi = 1–3 x 10 mins comp = 1–6 x 10 mins	UT UP-TEMPO: as for bike speed: 3.5 - 5 min/km **reps:** rec = 1–2 x 10 mins semi = 1–3 x 10 mins comp = 1–6 x 10 mins	During .... (UT) Between .... (LSD)
During .... (AT) Between .... (LSD)	HIGH SPEED 6 AT	ANAEROBIC THRESHOLD: Max steady state pace or 20 mins–1 hr race pace — NO HARDER. This is hard but not hell. **aim:** increase AT & race pace **gears:** 52 x 14–16 **speed:** 36–46 kph **cadence:** 85–105 rpm **reps:** rec = 1–2 x 5 mins semi-comp = 1–3 x 5 mins comp = 1–6 x 5 mins	AT ANAEROBIC THRESHOLD: as for bike **speed:** 3-5 min/km **reps:** rec = 1–2 x 5 mins semi-comp = 1–3 x 5 mins comp = 1–6 x 5 mins	During .... (AT) Between .... (LSD)

Kayak heart rates			
		KAYAK	
During N/A Between .... (LSD) During .... (UT) Between .... (LSD)	EASY LOAD 2 LOAD 3 LOAD 4	**aim:** easy paddling BUNGY TRAINING: attach a bungy cord around the hull of your kayak. This creates a resistance. **aim:** develop more strength endurance. Try to keep your technique 'long' and as much like your ideal racing stroke as possible. **cadence:** 20–40 strokes per minute lower than race cadence H/M/E or REPS X 20 MINS	**reps:** whole workout **reps:** rec = 0–1 x 20 mins semi = 1–4 x 20 mins comp = 2–10 x 20 mins **reps:** rec = 1–2 x 20 mins
During .... (AT) Between .... (LSD)	LOW- SPEED 5	UP-TEMPO: as for bike and run, should feel fast, strong, comfortable and in control. This is an effort at your 3-hour max race pace — no harder.	semi = 1–3 x 10 mins comp = 1–6 x 10 mins
	HIGH- SPEED 6	ANAEROBIC THRESHOLD: As for bike and run max steady-state pace or 20–60 min race pace.	**reps:** rec = 1–2 x 5 mins semi = 1–3 x 5 mins comp = 1–6 x 5 mins

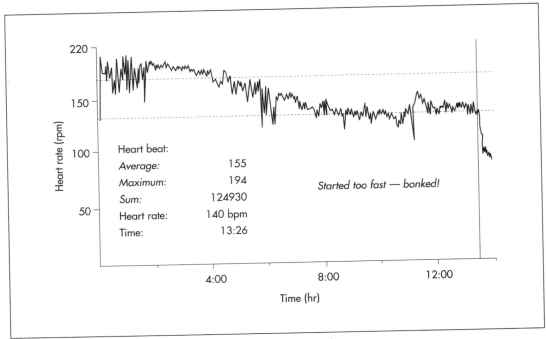

FIGURE 20.7: Coast to Coast — longest day

Types of training used for multisport, when initiated and effects.

Type	When initiated (intensity)	Effect	Example	Race use
Power	—	—	—	—
Intensive sprints	—	—	—	—
Extensive sprints	Late Speed phase	Improves extended sprint	4–6 x 1–3 m rest to recovery, bike race, initial race	Coast to Coast bike ride Initial run
Submaximal	Speed phase	Improves max steady-state race pace	4–6 x 6–8 min 4–1 min rest btwn or 20–30 min TT	All Small amount if in 4 hr+ races
Up-tempo	Late base, early speed,	Transition from base to speedwork	1–2 x 10–30 min rest 10–20– min btwn	
Long slow distance	Base/speed	Improves ability do mileage, builds training tolerance, improves recovery rate	Continuous	All
Active recovery	Base/speed	Assists recovery (only if needed)	Continuous	All

PROPORTIONS:
1. Base: 100% long slow distance and active recovery; some speedwork may be used.
2. Speed: approx. 85–90% long slow distance and active recovery;
   approx. 10–15% up-tempo and submaximal intensity.

Key: min = minutes; btwn = between; TT = time trial

Note: Training intensity proportions change continually and the right proportion for one week will not be right for the next. These are approximations to provide a guide only. Higher training intensities may also be used very rarely.

Race: Rowing (novice/semi-competitive) coxed 4 / kayaking
Race date: 20 April
Training starts: 30 December

Maximum distance for the 100% week
Row: 5 hr 50 min

Mileage profile

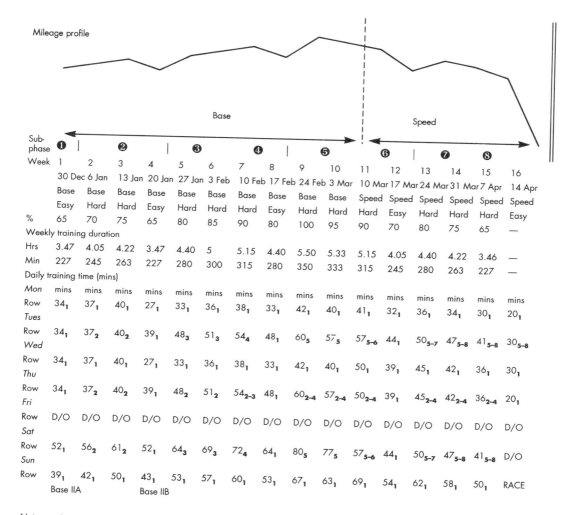

Base | Speed

Sub-phase	❶		❷		❸		❹		❺		❻		❼	❽	
Week	1	2	3	4	5	6	7	8	9	10	11	12	13	14	15	16
	30 Dec	6 Jan	13 Jan	20 Jan	27 Jan	3 Feb	10 Feb	17 Feb	24 Feb	3 Mar	10 Mar	17 Mar	24 Mar	31 Mar	7 Apr	14 Apr
	Base	Base	Base	Base	Base	Base	Base	Base	Base	Base	Speed	Speed	Speed	Speed	Speed	Speed
	Easy	Hard	Hard	Easy	Hard	Hard	Hard	Easy	Hard	Hard	Hard	Easy	Hard	Hard	Hard	Easy
%	65	70	75	65	80	85	90	80	100	95	90	70	80	75	65	—
Weekly training duration																
Hrs	3.47	4.05	4.22	3.47	4.40	5	5.15	4.40	5.50	5.33	5.15	4.05	4.40	4.22	3.46	—
Min	227	245	263	227	280	300	315	280	350	333	315	245	280	263	227	—
Daily training time (mins)																
Mon Row	34_1	37_1	40_1	27_1	33_1	36_1	38_1	33_1	42_1	40_1	41_1	32_1	36_1	34_1	30_1	20_1
Tues Row	34_1	37_2	40_2	39_1	48_3	51_3	54_4	48_1	60_5	57_5	57_{5-6}	44_1	50_{5-7}	47_{5-8}	41_{5-8}	30_{5-8}
Wed Row	34_1	37_1	40_1	27_1	33_1	36_1	38_1	33_1	42_1	40_1	50_1	39_1	45_1	42_1	36_1	30_1
Thu Row	34_1	37_2	40_2	39_1	48_2	51_2	54_{2-3}	48_1	60_{2-4}	57_{2-4}	50_{2-4}	39_1	45_{2-4}	42_{2-4}	36_{2-4}	20_1
Fri Row	D/O	D/O	D/O	D/O	D/O	D/O	D/O	D/O	D/O	D/O	D/O	D/O	D/O	D/O	D/O	D/O
Sat Row	52_1	56_2	61_2	52_1	64_3	69_3	72_4	64_1	80_5	77_5	57_{5-6}	44_1	50_{5-7}	47_{5-8}	41_{5-8}	D/O
Sun Row	39_1	42_1	50_1	43_1	53_1	57_1	60_1	53_1	67_1	63_1	69_1	54_1	62_1	58_1	50_1	RACE
	Base IIA			Base IIB												

Note: times given are actual rowing times, not training times. Base I would occur first.

The bold subscript numerals refer to subphases

Read pages 185–8 before starting.

Race: Rowing (senior) coxed 4 / kayaking
Race date: 20 April
Training starts: 30 December

Maximum distance for the 100% week
Row: 100 km

Mileage profile

Base   Speed

Sub-phase	❶		❷		❸	❹		❺		❻		❼	❽	
Week	1	2	3	4	5	6	7	8	9	10	11	12	13	14	15	16
	30 Dec	6 Jan	13 Jan	20 Jan	27 Jan	3 Feb	10 Feb	17 Feb	24 Feb	3 Mar	10 Mar	17 Mar	24 Mar	31 Mar	7 Apr	14 Apr
	Base	Base	Base	Base	Base	Base	Base	Base	Base	Base	Speed	Speed	Speed	Speed	Speed	Speed
	Easy	Hard	Hard	Easy	Hard	Hard	Hard	Easy	Hard	Hard	Hard	Easy	Hard	Hard	Hard	Easy
%	65	70	75	65	80	85	90	80	100	95	90	70	80	75	65	—
Weekly km Row	65	70	75	65	80	85	90	80	100	95	90	70	80	75	65	—
Daily training	km	km	km	km	km	km	km	km	km	km	km	km	km	km	km	km
Mon Row	9.8_1	10.5_1	11.3_1	7.8_1	9.6_1	10.2_1	10.8_1	9.6_1	12_1	11.4_1	11.7_1	9.1_1	10.4_1	9.8_1	8.5_1	6_1
Tues Row	9.8_1	10.5_2	11.3_2	11.1_1	13.6_3	14.5_3	15.3_4	13.6_1	17_5	16.2_5	16.2_{5-6}	12.6_1	14.4_{5-7}	13.5_{5-8}	11.7_{5-8}	10_1
Wed Row	9.8_1	10.5_1	11.3_1	7.8_1	9.6_1	10.2_1	10.8_1	9.6_1	12_1	11.4_1	14.4_1	11.2_1	12.8_1	12_1	10.4_1	8_1
Thur Row	9.8_1	10.5_2	11.3_2	11.1_1	13.6_2	14.5_2	15.3_{2-3}	13.6_1	17_{2-4}	16.2_{2-4}	14.4_{2-4}	11.2_1	12.8_{2-4}	12_{2-4}	10.4_{2-4}	6_1
Fri Row	D/O	D/O	D/O	D/O	D/O	D/O	D/O	D/O	D/O	D/O	D/O	D/O	D/O	D/O	D/O	D/O
Sat Row	15_1	16.1_2	17.3_2	15_1	18.4_3	19.6_3	20.7_4	18.4_1	23_5	21.9_5	16.2_{5-6}	12.6_1	14.4_{5-7}	15.5_{5-8}	11.7_{5-8}	D/O
Sun Row	11.1_1	11.9_1	12.8_1	12.4_1	15.2_1	16.2_1	17.1_1	15.2_1	19_1	18.1_1	19.8_1	15.4_1	17.6_1	16.5_1	14.3_1	RACE
	Base IIA			Base IIB												

Note: Base IA and Base IB would occur first.

The bold subscript numerals refer to subphases

Read pages 185–8 before starting.

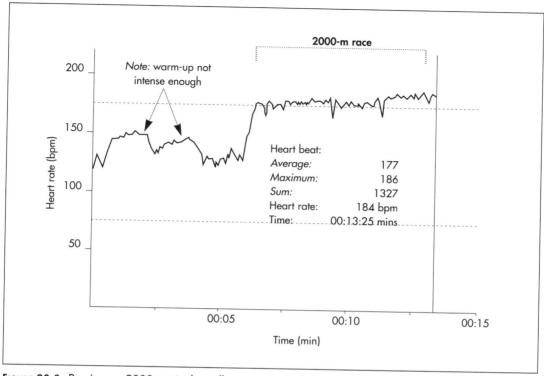

FIGURE 20.8: Rowing — 2000-m single sculls

DETAILED DESCRIPTIONS

Subphase	Training theme	Rowing	Kayaking	Heart rate
EASY 1	General fitness and technique	EASY ROWING (U2) TECHNIQUE: time on slide; body position; blade entry and exit; low resistance/low rating, 18–22 st/p/min **reps:** whole workout	EASY KAYAKING TECHNIQUE: **reps:** whole workout	During .... (LSD)
LOAD 2	Strength/strength endurance and basic skills	STRENGTH ENDURANCE: small bungy around hull creates slight resistance; shouldn't be tiring for at least 10–15 mins initially; watch deterioration in technique; easy to injure yourself, halfway between easy and race stroke resistance; medium resistance/low rating, 18–22 st/p/min rec : 1–2 x 10–15 mins semi : 1–3 x 10–15 mins comp: 1–6 x 10–15 mins	STRENGTH ENDURANCE: small bungy around hull creates slight resistance; shouldn't be tiring for at least 10–15 mins initially; watch deterioration in technique; easy to injure yourself halfway between easy and race stroke resistance; medium resistance/low stroke rate rec : 1–2 x 10–15 mins semi : 1–3 x 10–15 mins comp: 1–6 x 10–15 mins	During N/A Between .... (LSD) (CONTINUED)

Subphase	Training theme	Rowing	Kayaking	Heart rate
HIGH LOAD 3	Strength/strength endurance	STRENGTH ENDURANCE: big bungy around hull or rope tow; high resistance at or slightly above race-stroke resistance; aim to do race stroke (e.g. 220 strokes in race — start 10 x 20 strokes; then 5 x 50 strokes, 2 x 100 strokes, 1 x 220 strokes); watch deterioration in technique; easy to injure yourself; high resistance/low rating, 18–22 st/p/min rec: N/A semi: 10–5 x 20–50 strokes comp: 10–1 x 20–220 strokes	STRENGTH ENDURANCE: big bungy around hull or rope tow; high resistance at or slightly above race-stroke resistance; aim to do race stroke (e.g. 220 strokes in race — start 10 x 20 strokes; then 5 x 50 strokes, 2 x 100 strokes, 1 x 220 strokes); watch deterioration in technique; easy to injure yourself; high resistance/low stroke rate rec: N/A semi: 10–5 x 20–50 strokes comp: 10–1 x 20–220 strokes	During N/A Between .... (LSD)
LOAD/ SPEED 4	Begin to 'transfer' strength/strength endurance to speed	UP-TEMPO (U1): tempo rowing rec: 1–2 x 2–10 min semi: 2–3 x 2–10 min comp: 2–4 x 2–10 min generally best to break up into pyramids, etc (max steady-state pace for 1 hour+); medium resistance; med/high rating 22–26 st/p/min	UP-TEMPO (U1): tempo paddling rec: 1–2 x 2–10 min semi: 2–3 x 2–10 min comp: 2–4 x 2–10 min generally best to break up into pyramids, etc (max steady-state pace for 1 hour+); medium resistance; med/high stroke rate	During N/A Between .... (LSD)
LOW SPEED 5	The beginnings of speed	ANAEROBIC THRESHOLD: max steady-state for 20 mins (AT) rec: 1–3 x 1–5 mins semi: 1–4 x 1–5 mins comp: 1–8 x 1–5 mins generally best to break up into pyramids, etc; med/high resistance; high rating, 26–30 st/p/min	ANAEROBIC THRESHOLD: max steady-state for 20 mins (AT) rec: 1–3 x 1–5 mins semi: 1–4 x 1–5 mins comp: 1–8 x 1–5 mins generally best to break up into pyramids, etc; med/high resistance; high stroke rate	During .... (UT) Between .... (LSD)
HIGH SPEED 6	High aerobic speed	RACE PACE (TR): competition simulation and racing rec: 1–2 x 500–1000 m semi: 1–2 x 500–1000 m comp: 2–4 x 500–2000 m or racing high resistance; high rating 30–34 st/p/min	RACE PACE: competition simulation and racing rec: 1–2 x ¼–½ race distance semi: 1–2 x ¼–½ race distance comp: 2–4 x ¼–full race distance or racing high resistance; high stroke rate	During .... (AT) Between .... (LSD)
SPRINT 7	Anaerobic speed	SPRINTS AND POWER STROKES: moves and starts at high resistance; sprints (moves) 40 strokes rec: 1–2 semi: 1–3 comp: 1–6 power strokes: 10–30 strokes race start stroke with little bungy rec: 1–2 semi: 1–3 comp: 2–6 above race resistance race stroke rate 34+ st/p/min	SPRINTS AND POWER STROKES: moves and starts at high resistance; sprints (moves) 40 strokes rec: 1–2 semi: 1–3 comp: 1–6 power strokes: 10–30 strokes race start stroke with little bungy rec: 1–2 semi: 1–3 comp: 2–6 above race resistance race stroke rate	During N/A Between .... (LSD) (CONTINUED)

Subphase	Training theme	Rowing	Kayaking	Heart rate
POWER 8	Competition simulation	STARTS: 10–30 strokes rec: 1–4 semi: 2–6 comp: 2–8 race resistance; race stroke rate 34+ st/p/min	STARTS: 10–30 strokes rec: 1–4 semi: 2–6 comp: 2–8 race resistance; race stroke rate	During N/A Between ....(LSD)
OVER-SPEED 9	Competition simulation and competition pressure	MAX PREDICTED RATING: low resistance; max race rating training 37–40 st/p/min rec: 1–2 x 1–2 mins @ 37–40 semi: 1–2 x 1–3 mins @ 37–40 comp: 1–4 x 1–4 mins @ 37–40	MAX PREDICTED STROKE RATE: low resistance; max race stroke rate training rec: 1–2 x 1–2 mins semi: 1–2 x 1–3 mins comp: 1–4 x 1–4 mins	During N/A Between ....(LSD)

Types of training used for rowing/kayaking

Type	When initiated (intensity)	Effect	Example
Power	Late speed phase	Faster, more powerful stroke	Starts rest to recovery
Intensive sprints	Late speed phase	Improves starts and finishes	Extended starts 20–30 strokes
Extensive sprints	Speed phase	Improves extended starts and finishes	4–6 x 1–3 min rest to recovery
Submaximal	Early speed phase	Improves max steady-state race pace	4–6 x 2–8 min 4–1 min rest btwn
Up-tempo	Late base, early speed	Transition from base to speedwork	20–40 min pieces rest to recovery btwn
Long slow distance	Base/speed	Improves ability to do mileage, builds training tolerance and improves recovery rate	Continuous
Active	Base/speed	Assists recovery	Continuous

PROPORTIONS:
1. Base: 100% long slow distance and active recovery; some speedwork may be used.
2. Speed: approx. 85–90% long slow distance and active recovery;
      approx. 10–15% up-tempo and submaximal intensity.

Key: min = minutes; btwn = between

Note: Training intensity proportions change continually and what is right for one week will not be right for the next. These are approximations to provide a guide only.

Race: Cycle (40 km)
Race date: 20 April
Training starts: 30 December

Maximum distance for the 100% week
Cycle: 160 km

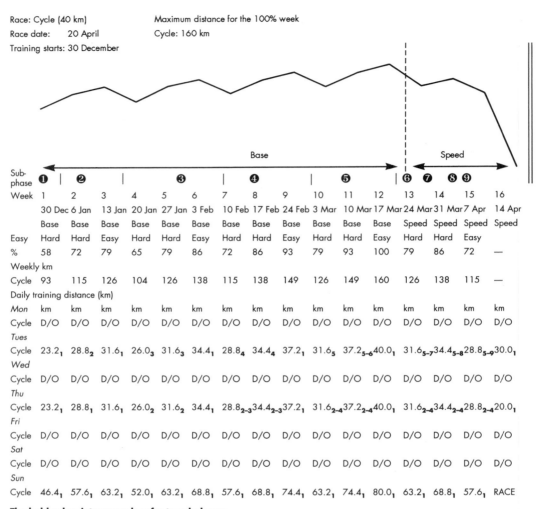

Sub-phase	❶	❷		❸		❹		❺		❻ ❼	❽❾			
Week	1	2	3	4	5	6	7	8	9	10	11	12	13	14	15	16
	30 Dec	6 Jan	13 Jan	20 Jan	27 Jan	3 Feb	10 Feb	17 Feb	24 Feb	3 Mar	10 Mar	17 Mar	24 Mar	31 Mar	7 Apr	14 Apr
	Base	Base	Base	Base	Base	Base	Base	Base	Base	Base	Base	Base	Speed	Speed	Speed	Speed
	Easy	Hard	Hard	Easy	Hard	Hard	Easy	Hard	Hard	Easy	Hard	Hard	Easy	Hard	Hard	Easy
%	58	72	79	65	79	86	72	86	93	79	93	100	79	86	72	—
Weekly km Cycle	93	115	126	104	126	138	115	138	149	126	149	160	126	138	115	—
Daily training distance (km)																
Mon Cycle	D/O	D/O	D/O	D/O	D/O	D/O	D/O	D/O	D/O	D/O	D/O	D/O	D/O	D/O	D/O	D/O
Tues Cycle	23.2_1	28.8_2	31.6_1	26.0_3	31.6_3	34.4_1	28.8_4	34.4_4	37.2_1	31.6_5	37.2_{5-6}	40.0_1	31.6_{5-7}	34.4_{5-8}	28.8_{5-9}	30.0_1
Wed Cycle	D/O	D/O	D/O	D/O	D/O	D/O	D/O	D/O	D/O	D/O	D/O	D/O	D/O	D/O	D/O	D/O
Thu Cycle	23.2_1	28.8_1	31.6_1	26.0_2	31.6_2	34.4_1	28.8_{2-3}	34.4_{2-3}	37.2_1	31.6_{2-4}	37.2_{2-4}	40.0_1	31.6_{2-4}	34.4_{2-4}	28.8_{2-4}	20.0_1
Fri Cycle	D/O	D/O	D/O	D/O	D/O	D/O	D/O	D/O	D/O	D/O	D/O	D/O	D/O	D/O	D/O	D/O
Sat Cycle	D/O	D/O	D/O	D/O	D/O	D/O	D/O	D/O	D/O	D/O	D/O	D/O	D/O	D/O	D/O	D/O
Sun Cycle	46.4_1	57.6_1	63.2_1	52.0_1	63.2_1	68.8_1	57.6_1	68.8_1	74.4_1	63.2_1	74.4_1	80.0_1	63.2_1	68.8_1	57.6_1	RACE

The bold subscript numerals refer to subphases

Read pages 185–8 before starting.

Race: Cycle (100 km)
Race date: 20 April
Training starts: 30 December

Maximum distance for the 100% week
Cycle: 500 km

Mileage profile

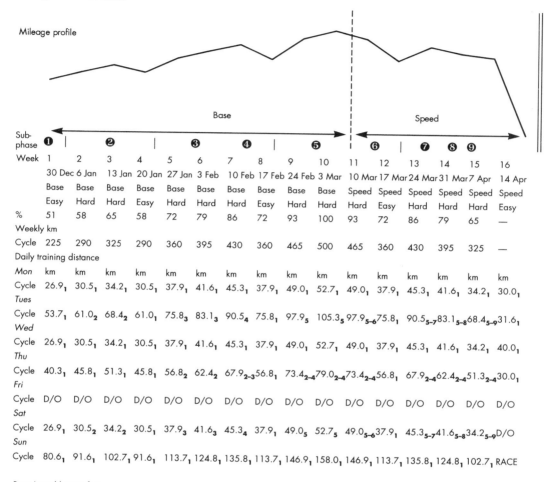

Sub-phase	❶	❷	❸	❹	❺	❻	❼	❽	❾
	Base →					Speed →			
Week	1	2	3	4	5	6	7	8	9	10	11	12	13	14	15	16
	30 Dec	6 Jan	13 Jan	20 Jan	27 Jan	3 Feb	10 Feb	17 Feb	24 Feb	3 Mar	10 Mar	17 Mar	24 Mar	31 Mar	7 Apr	14 Apr
	Base	Base	Base	Base	Base	Base	Base	Base	Base	Base	Speed	Speed	Speed	Speed	Speed	Speed
	Easy	Hard	Hard	Easy	Hard	Hard	Hard	Easy	Hard	Hard	Hard	Easy	Hard	Hard	Hard	Easy
%	51	58	65	58	72	79	86	72	93	100	93	72	86	79	65	—
Weekly km Cycle	225	290	325	290	360	395	430	360	465	500	465	360	430	395	325	—

Daily training distance

	Week 1	2	3	4	5	6	7	8	9	10	11	12	13	14	15	16
Mon	km	km	km	km	km	km	km	km	km	km	km	km	km	km	km	km
Cycle	26.9_1	30.5_1	34.2_1	30.5_1	37.9_1	41.6_1	45.3_1	37.9_1	49.0_1	52.7_1	49.0_1	37.9_1	45.3_1	41.6_1	34.2_1	30.0_1
Tues Cycle	53.7_1	61.0_2	68.4_2	61.0_1	75.8_3	83.1_3	90.5_4	75.8_1	97.9_5	105.3_5	97.9_{5-6}	75.8_1	90.5_{5-7}	83.1_{5-8}	68.4_{5-9}	31.6_1
Wed Cycle	26.9_1	30.5_1	34.2_1	30.5_1	37.9_1	41.6_1	45.3_1	37.9_1	49.0_1	52.7_1	49.0_1	37.9_1	45.3_1	41.6_1	34.2_1	40.0_1
Thu Cycle	40.3_1	45.8_1	51.3_1	45.8_1	56.8_2	62.4_2	67.9_{2-3}	56.8_1	73.4_{2-4}	79.0_{2-4}	73.4_{2-4}	56.8_1	67.9_{2-4}	62.4_{2-4}	51.3_{2-4}	30.0_1
Fri Cycle	D/O	D/O	D/O	D/O	D/O	D/O	D/O	D/O	D/O	D/O	D/O	D/O	D/O	D/O	D/O	D/O
Sat Cycle	26.9_1	30.5_2	34.2_2	30.5_1	37.9_3	41.6_3	45.3_4	37.9_1	49.0_5	52.7_5	49.0_{5-6}	37.9_1	45.3_{5-7}	41.6_{5-8}	34.2_{5-9}	D/O
Sun Cycle	80.6_1	91.6_1	102.7_1	91.6_1	113.7_1	124.8_1	135.8_1	113.7_1	146.9_1	158.0_1	146.9_1	113.7_1	135.8_1	124.8_1	102.7_1	RACE

Base I would occur first.
The bold subscript numerals refer to subphases

Read pages 185–8 before starting.

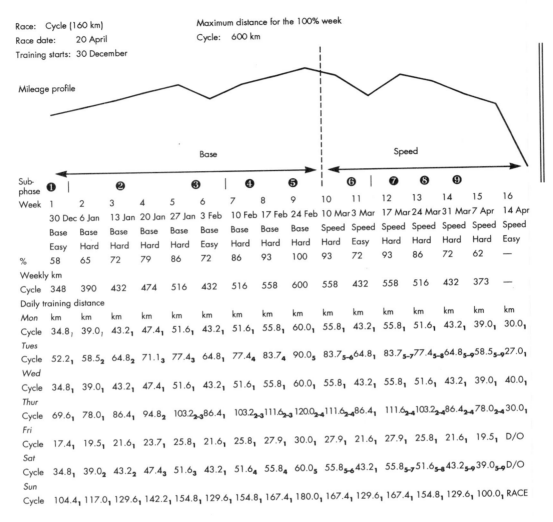

Race: Cycle (160 km)
Race date: 20 April
Training starts: 30 December

Maximum distance for the 100% week
Cycle: 600 km

Mileage profile

Base — Speed

Subphase	❶		❷		❸		❹		❺		❻	❼	❽	❾		
Week	1	2	3	4	5	6	7	8	9	10	11	12	13	14	15	16
	30 Dec	6 Jan	13 Jan	20 Jan	27 Jan	3 Feb	10 Feb	17 Feb	24 Feb	10 Mar	3 Mar	17 Mar	24 Mar	31 Mar	7 Apr	14 Apr
	Base	Base	Base	Base	Base	Base	Base	Base	Base	Speed	Speed	Speed	Speed	Speed	Speed	Speed
	Easy	Hard	Hard	Hard	Hard	Easy	Hard	Hard	Hard	Hard	Easy	Hard	Hard	Hard	Hard	Easy
%	58	65	72	79	86	72	86	93	100	93	72	93	86	72	62	—
Weekly km Cycle	348	390	432	474	516	432	516	558	600	558	432	558	516	432	373	—

Daily training distance (km)

	1	2	3	4	5	6	7	8	9	10	11	12	13	14	15	16
Mon Cycle	34.8_1	39.0_1	43.2_1	47.4_1	51.6_1	43.2_1	51.6_1	55.8_1	60.0_1	55.8_1	43.2_1	55.8_1	51.6_1	43.2_1	39.0_1	30.0_1
Tues Cycle	52.2_1	58.5_2	64.8_2	71.1_3	77.4_3	64.8_1	77.4_4	83.7_4	90.0_5	$83.7_{5\text{-}6}$	64.8_1	$83.7_{5\text{-}7}$	$77.4_{5\text{-}8}$	$64.8_{5\text{-}9}$	$58.5_{5\text{-}9}$	27.0_1
Wed Cycle	34.8_1	39.0_1	43.2_1	47.4_1	51.6_1	43.2_1	51.6_1	55.8_1	60.0_1	55.8_1	43.2_1	55.8_1	51.6_1	43.2_1	39.0_1	40.0_1
Thur Cycle	69.6_1	78.0_1	86.4_1	94.8_2	$103.2_{2\text{-}3}$	86.4_1	$103.2_{2\text{-}3}$	$111.6_{2\text{-}3}$	$120.0_{2\text{-}4}$	$111.6_{2\text{-}4}$	86.4_1	$111.6_{2\text{-}4}$	$103.2_{2\text{-}4}$	$86.4_{2\text{-}4}$	$78.0_{2\text{-}4}$	30.0_1
Fri Cycle	17.4_1	19.5_1	21.6_1	23.7_1	25.8_1	21.6_1	25.8_1	27.9_1	30.0_1	27.9_1	21.6_1	27.9_1	25.8_1	21.6_1	19.5_1	D/O
Sat Cycle	34.8_1	39.0_2	43.2_2	47.4_3	51.6_3	43.2_1	51.6_4	55.8_4	60.0_5	$55.8_{5\text{-}6}$	43.2_1	$55.8_{5\text{-}7}$	$51.6_{5\text{-}8}$	$43.2_{5\text{-}9}$	$39.0_{5\text{-}9}$	D/O
Sun Cycle	104.4_1	117.0_1	129.6_1	142.2_1	154.8_1	129.6_1	154.8_1	167.4_1	180.0_1	167.4_1	129.6_1	167.4_1	154.8_1	129.6_1	100.0_1	RACE

Base I would occur first.
The bold subscript numerals refer to subphases

Read pages 185–8 before starting.

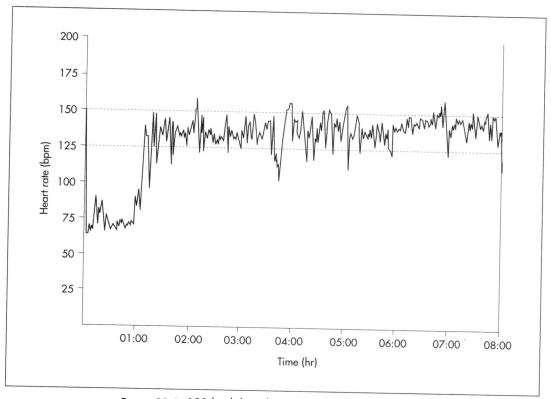

FIGURE 20.9: 180-km bike ride

Race: Tour (700 km)
Race date: 20 April
Training starts: 30 December

Maximum distance for the 100% week
Cycle: 800 km

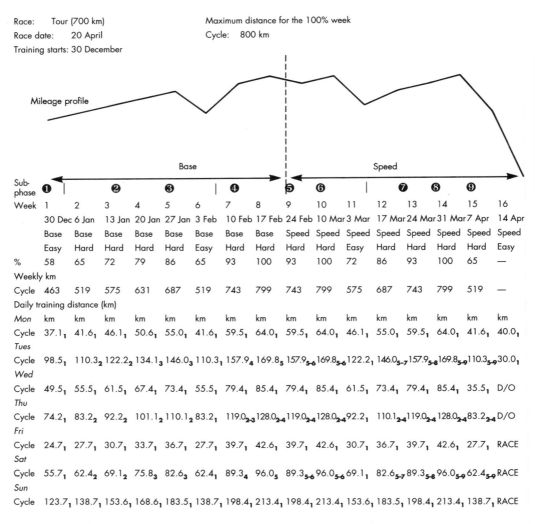

Mileage profile

	Base								Speed							
Sub-phase	❶	❷		❸		❹	❺	❻		❼		❽	❾			
Week	1	2	3	4	5	6	7	8	9	10	11	12	13	14	15	16
	30 Dec	6 Jan	13 Jan	20 Jan	27 Jan	3 Feb	10 Feb	17 Feb	24 Feb	10 Mar	3 Mar	17 Mar	24 Mar	31 Mar	7 Apr	14 Apr
	Base	Base	Base	Base	Base	Base	Base	Base	Speed	Speed	Speed	Speed	Speed	Speed	Speed	Speed
	Easy	Hard	Hard	Hard	Hard	Easy	Hard	Hard	Hard	Hard	Easy	Hard	Hard	Hard	Hard	Easy
%	58	65	72	79	86	65	93	100	93	100	72	86	93	100	65	—
Weekly km Cycle	463	519	575	631	687	519	743	799	743	799	575	687	743	799	519	—

Daily training distance (km)

	Mon km	km	km	km	km	km	km	km	km	km	km	km	km	km	km	km
Mon Cycle	37.1_1	41.6_1	46.1_1	50.6_1	55.0_1	41.6_1	59.5_1	64.0_1	59.5_1	64.0_1	46.1_1	55.0_1	59.5_1	64.0_1	41.6_1	40.0_1
Tues Cycle	98.5_1	110.3_2	122.2_2	134.1_3	146.0_3	110.3_1	157.9_4	169.8_5	157.9_{5-6}	169.8_{5-6}	122.2_1	146.0_{5-7}	157.9_{5-8}	169.8_{5-9}	110.3_{5-9}	30.0_1
Wed Cycle	49.5_1	55.5_1	61.5_1	67.4_1	73.4_1	55.5_1	79.4_1	85.4_1	79.4_1	85.4_1	61.5_1	73.4_1	79.4_1	85.4_1	35.5_1	D/O
Thu Cycle	74.2_1	83.2_2	92.2_2	101.1_1	110.1_1	83.2_1	119.0_{2-3}	128.0_{2-4}	119.0_{2-4}	128.0_{2-4}	92.2_1	110.1_{2-4}	119.0_{2-4}	128.0_{2-4}	83.2_{2-4}	D/O
Fri Cycle	24.7_1	27.7_1	30.7_1	33.7_1	36.7_1	27.7_1	39.7_1	42.6_1	39.7_1	42.6_1	30.7_1	36.7_1	39.7_1	42.6_1	27.7_1	RACE
Sat Cycle	55.7_1	62.4_2	69.1_2	75.8_3	82.6_3	62.4_1	89.3_4	96.0_5	89.3_{5-6}	96.0_{5-6}	69.1_1	82.6_{5-7}	89.3_{5-8}	96.0_{5-9}	62.4_{5-9}	RACE
Sun Cycle	123.7_1	138.7_1	153.6_1	168.6_1	183.5_1	138.7_1	198.4_1	213.4_1	198.4_1	213.4_1	153.6_1	183.5_1	198.4_1	213.4_1	138.7_1	RACE

Base I would occur first.

The bold subscript numerals refer to subphases

Read pages 185–8 before starting.

Four sessions per week

M	T	W	T	F	S	S
Day off	Bike (Hills)	Day off	Bike (Speed)	Day off	Bike (Easy)	Bike (Long)

Five sessions per week

M	T	W	T	F	S	S
Day off	Bike (Hills)	Bike (Easy)	Bike (Speed)	Day off	Bike (Easy)	Bike (Long)

Types of training used in road cycling

Type	When initiated (intensity)	Effect	Example
Power	Late speed phase	Improves jump accels	4–6 x 10–15 sec rest to recovery
Intensive sprints	Late speed phase	Improves full sprint phase	6–10 sec x 30 sec– 1 min rest to recovery or short rest < 1 min
Extensive sprint	Speed phase	Improves long sprint bridging gaps	4–6 x 1–3 min rest to recovery or 1–2 min btwn
Submaximal	Speed phase	Improves max steady-state pace in TTs, peloton and breaks	4–6 x 6–8 min 4–1 min rest btwn or 20–30 min TT
Up-tempo	Late base, early speed	Transition from base to speedwork	1–2 x 5–10 km rest 5 km btwn
Long slow distance	Base/speed	Improves ability to do mileage, builds training tolerance and improves recovery rate	Continuous
Active recovery	Base/speed	Assists recovery	Continuous

PROPORTIONS:
1. Base: 100% long slow distance and active recovery; some speedwork may be used.
2. Speed: approx. 85–90% long slow distance and active recovery;
    approx. 10–15% up-tempo and submaximal intensity.

Key: min = minutes; sec = seconds; btwn = between; km = kilometres; TT = time trial;
    accels = accelerations

Note: Training intensity proportions change continually and what is right for one week will not be right for the next. These are approximations to provide a guide only.

DETAILED DESCRIPTIONS

	Subphase	Sport	Heart rates	Type
	EASY 1	**BIKE** EASY: easy rolling **aim:** establish base fitness **easy gears:** 42 x 15–18 **speed:** 25–28 kph **cadence:** 85–105 rpm	During: .... (LSD)	Whole workout
HILLS	LOAD 2	HILLS: Roll over hills in a small gear. Number and length of hills is important NOT how hard you do them. So the aim is easy climbing. **aim:** prep for strength endurance training **easy gears:** 42 x 18–21 on the hills **speed:** 12–20 kph **cadence:** 40–70 rpm on hills	During: N/A Between: .... (LSD)	Whole workout
H(BG)	HIGH LOAD 3	HILLS BIG GEAR: Climbing short hills of moderate gradient in a bigger gear than normal (i.e. 42 x 14). It should be hard muscularly but not too hard. **aim:** strength endurance **gears:** 42 x 13–17 on hills **speed:** 12–20 kph on hills **cadence:** 30–60 rpm on hills **distance:** 200–700 m 80% Seated, 20% Standing	During: N/A Between: .... (LSD)	Reps rec = 0–3 semi = 2–4 comp = 4–6
F(BG)	LOAD/SPEED 4	FLAT BIG GEAR 'Roll' a big gear (i.e. 52 x 16) but don't 'push' it. It should not feel hard till you have been going for at least 20 mins. **aim:** conversion of strength endurance to speed. **gears:** 52 x 12–16 **speed:** 27–32 kph **cadence:** 40–70 rpm	During: N/A Between: .... (LSD)	Reps rec = 0–1x 20 mins semi = 0–3 x 10 mins comp = 2–10 x 20 mins
UT	LOW SPEED 5	UP TEMPO: You should feel fast, strong, comfortable and in control. This is an effort at 3-hr max. race pace — NO HARDER! It is only slightly faster than cruising. **aim:** prep for speed **gears:** 52 x 17–21 **speed:** 30–36 kph **cadence:** 85–105 rpm	During: .... (UT) Between: .... (LSD)	Reps x 10 mins (10 min intervals at 3-hr max pace not 10-min max pace) rec = 1–2 x 10 mins semi = 1–3 x 10 mins comp = 1–6 x 10 mins
AT	HIGH SPEED 6	ANAEROBIC THRESHOLD: Max steady-state pace or 20 min–1 hour race pace — NO HARDER. This is hard but not hell. **aim:** increase AT & race pace **gears:** 52 x 14–16 **speed:** 36–46 kph **cadence:** 85–105 rpm	During: .... (AT) Between: .... (LSD)	Reps x 5 mins (5-min intervals at 1-hr max pace not 5-min max pace) rec = 1–2 x 5 mins semi = 1–3 x 5 mins comp = 1–6 x 5 mins (CONTINUED)

	Subphase	Sport	Heart rates	Type
ES	SPRINT 7	EXTENSIVE SPRINTS (Long Sprint): Nearly full effort extended sprint like launching a lone attack 1–2 km from the finish of a road race or bridging a gap. Don't get 'bogged down' or 'buried' by it, pull out of the effort before this happens. **aim:** improve extended sprint speed **gears:** 52 x 13–14 **speed:** 40–50 kph **cadence:** 85–105 rpm	During: N/A Between: .... (LSD)	Reps 30 s–4 min rec = 1–2 semi = 1–3 comp = 1–4
IS	SPRINT 7	INTENSIVE SPRINTS (Short Sprint): full effort sprint that you might do at the finish of a road race. Don't get 'bogged down' or 'buried' by it, pull out of the effort before this happens. *Format:* flat — 100–300 m on flat crest — 30 m up and 20 m over uphill — 50 m up **aim:** improve sprint speed **gears:** 52 x 13–14 **speed:** 40–50 kph **cadence:** 85–105 rpm	During: N/A Between: .... (LSD)	Reps 50–300 m rec = 1–4 semi = 3–8 comp = 2–6 (between types)
PWR	POWER 8	EXPLOSIVE ACCELERATION: Explosive accelerations such as you would use when attacking at lower speeds or 'jumping'. Don't get 'bogged down' or 'buried' by it, pull out of the effort before this happens. *Format:* A — Big gear windout from rolling (5–20 kph/50–200 m) PC — Power Climb: come down a hill in a big gear at high rpm, roll up the other side of the hill and accelerate in the big gear (50–200 m after rolling start). **aim:** Improve explosive speed and acceleration **gears:** 52 x 12–14 **speed:** up to 40–70 kph **cadence:** up to 85–105 rpm	During: N/A Between: .... (LSD)	Reps rec = 1–2 semi = 2–4 comp = 2–6 (between types)
O/SPD	OVERSPEED 9	DOWNHILL SPINNING SPRINT: Little gear windout or sustained high cadence. *Format:* Downhill spinning sprint — accelerating down a hill in a small gear at a high cadence and trying to maintain a smooth pedal action by learning to contract and RELAX the muscles quickly. (50–200 m) **aim:** 'leg speed' **gears:** 42 x 16–18 **speed:** 40–70 kph **cadence:** 100–170 rpm	During: N/A Between: .... (LSD)	Reps rec = 2–4 semi = 2–6 comp = 2–8

MOUNTAIN BIKING

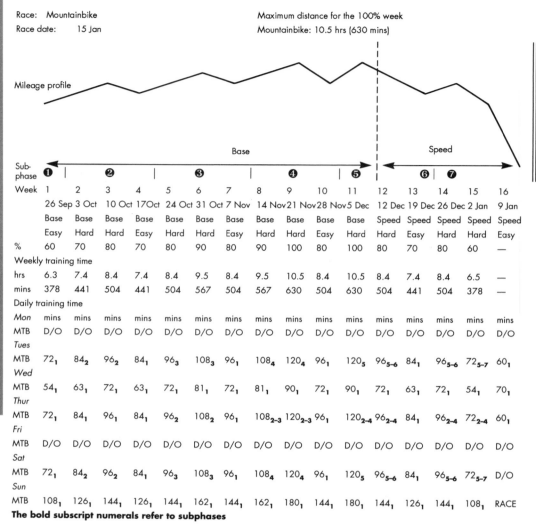

Race: Mountainbike
Race date: 15 Jan

Maximum distance for the 100% week
Mountainbike: 10.5 hrs (630 mins)

Mileage profile

Base | Speed

Sub-phase	❶		❷		❸		❹		❺		❻	❼		
Week	1	2	3	4	5	6	7	8	9	10	11	12	13	14	15	16
	26 Sep	3 Oct	10 Oct	17Oct	24 Oct	31 Oct	7 Nov	14 Nov	21 Nov	28 Nov	5 Dec	12 Dec	19 Dec	26 Dec	2 Jan	9 Jan
	Base	Base	Base	Base	Base	Base	Base	Base	Base	Base	Base	Speed	Speed	Speed	Speed	Speed
	Easy	Hard	Hard	Easy	Hard	Hard	Easy	Hard	Hard	Easy	Hard	Hard	Easy	Hard	Hard	Easy
%	60	70	80	70	80	90	80	90	100	80	100	80	70	80	60	—
Weekly training time																
hrs	6.3	7.4	8.4	7.4	8.4	9.5	8.4	9.5	10.5	8.4	10.5	8.4	7.4	8.4	6.5	—
mins	378	441	504	441	504	567	504	567	630	504	630	504	441	504	378	—
Daily training time																
Mon	mins	mins	mins	mins	mins	mins	mins	mins	mins	mins	mins	mins	mins	mins	mins	mins
MTB	D/O	D/O	D/O	D/O	D/O	D/O	D/O	D/O	D/O	D/O	D/O	D/O	D/O	D/O	D/O	D/O
Tues MTB	72_1	84_2	96_2	84_1	96_3	108_3	96_1	108_4	120_4	96_1	120_5	96_{5-6}	84_1	96_{5-6}	72_{5-7}	60_1
Wed MTB	54_1	63_1	72_1	63_1	72_1	81_1	72_1	81_1	90_1	72_1	90_1	72_1	63_1	72_1	54_1	70_1
Thur MTB	72_1	84_1	96_1	84_1	96_2	108_2	96_1	108_{2-3}	120_{2-3}	96_1	120_{2-4}	96_{2-4}	84_1	96_{2-4}	72_{2-4}	60_1
Fri MTB	D/O	D/O	D/O	D/O	D/O	D/O	D/O	D/O	D/O	D/O	D/O	D/O	D/O	D/O	D/O	D/O
Sat MTB	72_1	84_2	96_2	84_1	96_3	108_3	96_1	108_4	120_4	96_1	120_5	96_{5-6}	84_1	96_{5-6}	72_{5-7}	D/O
Sun MTB	108_1	126_1	144_1	126_1	144_1	162_1	144_1	162_1	180_1	144_1	180_1	144_1	126_1	144_1	108_1	RACE

The bold subscript numerals refer to subphases

Read pages 185–8 before starting.
Detailed Descriptions: as for Road Cycling, pages 218–9.

Race Mountainbike 2.5 hrs advanced
Race date 15 Jan

Maximum distance for 100% week
Mountain bike 16 hrs (960 mins)

Mileage profile

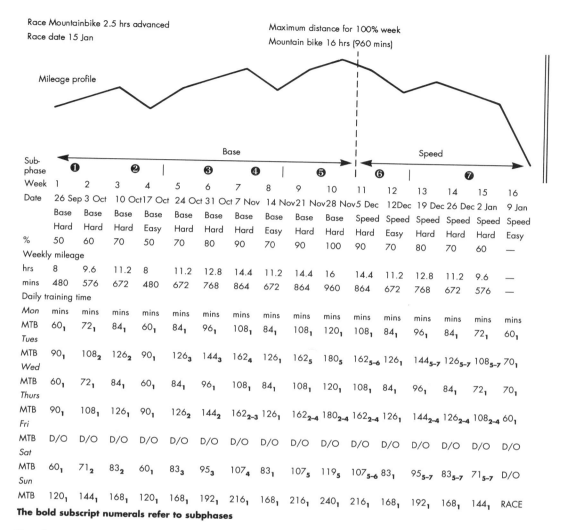

	Base										Speed					
Sub-phase	❶		❷		❸		❹		❺		❻		❼			
Week	1	2	3	4	5	6	7	8	9	10	11	12	13	14	15	16
Date	26 Sep	3 Oct	10 Oct	17 Oct	24 Oct	31 Oct	7 Nov	14 Nov	21 Nov	28 Nov	5 Dec	12 Dec	19 Dec	26 Dec	2 Jan	9 Jan
	Base Hard	Base Hard	Base Hard	Base Easy	Base Hard	Base Hard	Base Hard	Base Easy	Base Hard	Base Hard	Speed Hard	Speed Easy	Speed Hard	Speed Hard	Speed Hard	Speed Easy
%	50	60	70	50	70	80	90	70	90	100	90	70	80	70	60	—
Weekly mileage																
hrs	8	9.6	11.2	8	11.2	12.8	14.4	11.2	14.4	16	14.4	11.2	12.8	11.2	9.6	—
mins	480	576	672	480	672	768	864	672	864	960	864	672	768	672	576	—
Daily training time																
Mon	mins	mins	mins	mins	mins	mins	mins	mins	mins	mins	mins	mins	mins	mins	mins	mins
MTB	60_1	72_1	84_1	60_1	84_1	96_1	108_1	84_1	108_1	120_1	108_1	84_1	96_1	84_1	72_1	60_1
Tues																
MTB	90_1	108_2	126_2	90_1	126_3	144_3	162_4	126_1	162_5	180_5	162_{5-6}	126_1	144_{5-7}	126_{5-7}	108_{5-7}	70_1
Wed																
MTB	60_1	72_1	84_1	60_1	84_1	96_1	108_1	84_1	108_1	120_1	108_1	84_1	96_1	84_1	72_1	70_1
Thurs																
MTB	90_1	108_1	126_1	90_1	126_2	144_2	162_{2-3}	126_1	162_{2-4}	180_{2-4}	162_{2-4}	126_1	144_{2-4}	126_{2-4}	108_{2-4}	60_1
Fri																
MTB	D/O	D/O	D/O	D/O	D/O	D/O	D/O	D/O	D/O	D/O	D/O	D/O	D/O	D/O	D/O	D/O
Sat																
MTB	60_1	71_2	83_2	60_1	83_3	95_3	107_4	83_1	107_5	119_5	107_{5-6}	83_1	95_{5-7}	83_{5-7}	71_{5-7}	D/O
Sun																
MTB	120_1	144_1	168_1	120_1	168_1	192_1	216_1	168_1	216_1	240_1	216_1	168_1	192_1	168_1	144_1	RACE

The bold subscript numerals refer to subphases.

Read pages 185–8 before starting.

Detailed Descriptions: as for Road Cycling, pages 218–9.

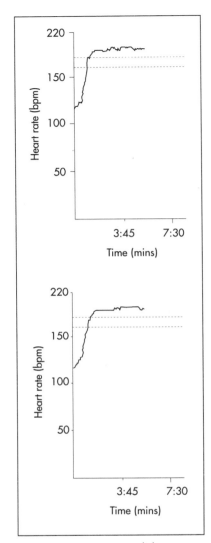

Figure 20.10: Mountain bike, downhill

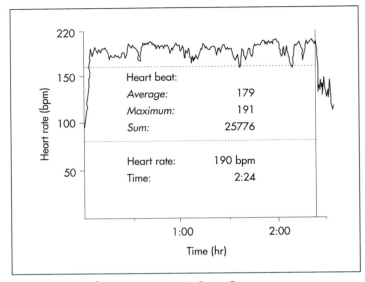

Figure 20.11: John Hume, Karapoti Cross Country, 1st, course record

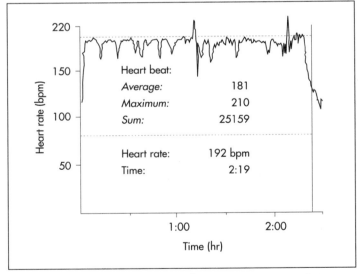

Figure 20.12: John Hume, Dome Valley Cross Country, 2nd

Speedwork

Intervals (1) on Wednesday
Uphill run/push/carry/run (sub-maximal) hilly

First 2–4 weeks: ride 4–6 mins at SM uphill followed by a racing dismount to run either pushing or carrying your mountain bike for 1–2 min. This is followed by a racing mount to ride a further 4–6 min at SM uphill. Do this 2–4 times. Rest with 10–20 min easy pedalling between.
Second 2–4 weeks: off-road rides, time trials and long intervals (6–8 min); do this 2–4 times at SM.

Intervals (2) on Tuesday
80% SM and 20% HI
80% (SM) = 2–6 reps of 4–8 min at SM. Rest for 8–10 min between.
20% (HI) = 2–4 reps of 2–3 min at HI. Variable rest periods; rest to recovery to less than 30 s rest.

Move Wednesday's speedwork to Thursday if you are not racing or find two speed workouts in a row too much. Alternatively, remove Wednesday's speedwork altogether and have a day off or an easy day.

Types of training used in mountain biking

Type	When initiated (intensity)	Effect	Example
Power	—	—	—
Intensive sprints	—	—	—
Extensive sprint	Speed phase	Improves short hill climbs and starts	4–6 x 1–3 min rest to recovery or 1–2 min btwn
Submaximal	Speed phase	Improves max steady-state pace for racing	4–6 x 6–8 min 4–1 min rest btwn or 20–30 min TT
Up-tempo	Late base, early speed	Transition from base to speedwork	1–2 x 5–10 km rest 5 km btwn
Long slow distance	Base/speed	Improves ability to do mileage, builds training tolerance and improves recovery rate	Continuous
Active recovery	Base/speed	Assists recovery	Continuous

Key: min = minutes; btwn = between; TT = time trial

Race: 10 km
Race date: 20 April
Training starts: 30 December

Maximum distance for the 100% week
Run: 70 km

Mileage profile

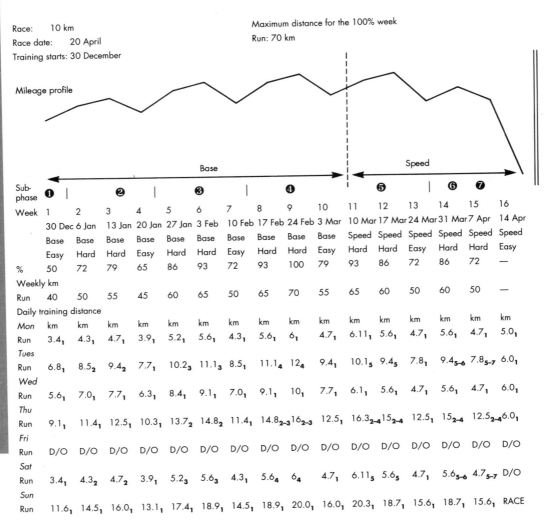

Base | Speed

Sub-phase	❶		❷		❸		❹			❺		❻	❼		
Week	1	2	3	4	5	6	7	8	9	10	11	12	13	14	15	16
	30 Dec	6 Jan	13 Jan	20 Jan	27 Jan	3 Feb	10 Feb	17 Feb	24 Feb	3 Mar	10 Mar	17 Mar	24 Mar	31 Mar	7 Apr	14 Apr
	Base	Base	Base	Base	Base	Base	Base	Base	Base	Base	Speed	Speed	Speed	Speed	Speed	Speed
	Easy	Hard	Hard	Easy	Hard	Hard	Easy	Hard	Hard	Easy	Hard	Hard	Easy	Hard	Hard	Easy
%	50	72	79	65	86	93	72	93	100	79	93	86	72	86	72	—
Weekly km Run	40	50	55	45	60	65	50	65	70	55	65	60	50	60	50	—

Daily training distance

	km	km	km	km	km	km	km	km	km	km	km	km	km	km	km	km
Mon Run	3.4_1	4.3_1	4.7_1	3.9_1	5.2_1	5.6_1	4.3_1	5.6_1	6_1	4.7_1	6.11_1	5.6_1	4.7_1	5.6_1	4.7_1	5.0_1
Tues Run	6.8_1	8.5_2	9.4_2	7.7_1	10.2_3	11.1_3	8.5_1	11.1_4	12_4	9.4_1	10.1_5	9.4_5	7.8_1	9.4_{5-6}	7.8_{5-7}	6.0_1
Wed Run	5.6_1	7.0_1	7.7_1	6.3_1	8.4_1	9.1_1	7.0_1	9.1_1	10_1	7.7_1	6.1_1	5.6_1	4.7_1	5.6_1	4.7_1	6.0_1
Thu Run	9.1_1	11.4_1	12.5_1	10.3_1	13.7_2	14.8_2	11.4_1	14.8_{2-3}	16_{2-3}	12.5_1	16.3_{2-4}	15_{2-4}	12.5_1	15_{2-4}	12.5_{2-4}	6.0_1
Fri Run	D/O	D/O	D/O	D/O	D/O	D/O	D/O	D/O	D/O	D/O	D/O	D/O	D/O	D/O	D/O	D/O
Sat Run	3.4_1	4.3_2	4.7_2	3.9_1	5.2_3	5.6_3	4.3_1	5.6_4	6_4	4.7_1	6.11_5	5.6_5	4.7_1	5.6_{5-6}	4.7_{5-7}	D/O
Sun Run	11.6_1	14.5_1	16.0_1	13.1_1	17.4_1	18.9_1	14.5_1	18.9_1	20.0_1	16.0_1	20.3_1	18.7_1	15.6_1	18.7_1	15.6_1	RACE

Base I would occur first.

The bold subscript numerals refer to subphases

Read pages 185–8 before starting.

Race: Half-marathon (novice)
Race date: 20 April
Training starts: 30 December

Maximum distance for the 100% week
Run: 53 km

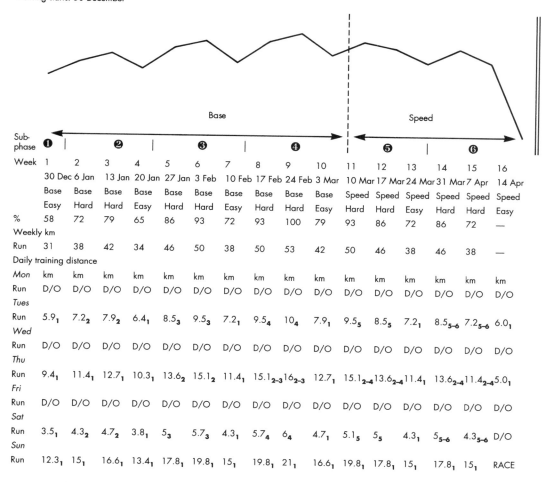

Sub-phase	❶		❷		❸		❹			❺		❻		
Week	1	2	3	4	5	6	7	8	9	10	11	12	13	14	15	16
	30 Dec	6 Jan	13 Jan	20 Jan	27 Jan	3 Feb	10 Feb	17 Feb	24 Feb	3 Mar	10 Mar	17 Mar	24 Mar	31 Mar	7 Apr	14 Apr
	Base	Base	Base	Base	Base	Base	Base	Base	Base	Base	Speed	Speed	Speed	Speed	Speed	Speed
	Easy	Hard	Hard	Easy	Hard	Hard	Easy	Hard	Hard	Easy	Hard	Hard	Easy	Hard	Hard	Easy
%	58	72	79	65	86	93	72	93	100	79	93	86	72	86	72	—
Weekly km Run	31	38	42	34	46	50	38	50	53	42	50	46	38	46	38	—
Daily training distance Mon km Run	D/O	D/O	D/O	D/O	D/O	D/O	D/O	D/O	D/O	D/O	D/O	D/O	D/O	D/O	D/O	D/O
Tues Run	5.9_1	7.2_2	7.9_2	6.4_1	8.5_3	9.5_3	7.2_1	9.5_4	10_4	7.9_1	9.5_5	8.5_5	7.2_1	8.5_{5-6}	7.2_{5-6}	6.0_1
Wed Run	D/O	D/O	D/O	D/O	D/O	D/O	D/O	D/O	D/O	D/O	D/O	D/O	D/O	D/O	D/O	D/O
Thu Run	9.4_1	11.4_1	12.7_1	10.3_1	13.6_2	15.1_2	11.4_1	15.1_{2-3}	16_{2-3}	12.7_1	15.1_{2-4}	13.6_{2-4}	11.4_1	13.6_{2-4}	11.4_{2-4}	5.0_1
Fri Run	D/O	D/O	D/O	D/O	D/O	D/O	D/O	D/O	D/O	D/O	D/O	D/O	D/O	D/O	D/O	D/O
Sat Run	3.5_1	4.3_2	4.7_2	3.8_1	5_3	5.7_3	4.3_1	5.7_4	6_4	4.7_1	5.1_5	5_5	4.3_1	5_{5-6}	4.3_{5-6}	D/O
Sun Run	12.3_1	15_1	16.6_1	13.4_1	17.8_1	19.8_1	15_1	19.8_1	21_1	16.6_1	19.8_1	17.8_1	15_1	17.8_1	15_1	RACE

Base I occurs first.

The bold subscript numerals refer to subphases

Read pages 185–8 before starting.

Race: Marathon
Race date: 20 April
Training starts: 30 December

Maximum distance for the 100% week
Run: 84 km

Mileage profile

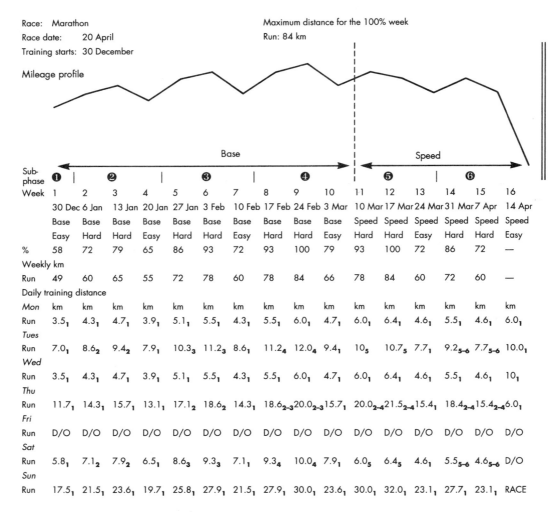

Sub-phase	❶		❷		❸			❹			❺		❻			
	Base										Speed					
Week	1	2	3	4	5	6	7	8	9	10	11	12	13	14	15	16
	30 Dec	6 Jan	13 Jan	20 Jan	27 Jan	3 Feb	10 Feb	17 Feb	24 Feb	3 Mar	10 Mar	17 Mar	24 Mar	31 Mar	7 Apr	14 Apr
	Base	Base	Base	Base	Base	Base	Base	Base	Base	Base	Speed	Speed	Speed	Speed	Speed	Speed
	Easy	Hard	Hard	Easy	Hard	Hard	Easy	Hard	Hard	Easy	Hard	Hard	Easy	Hard	Hard	Easy
%	58	72	79	65	86	93	72	93	100	79	93	100	72	86	72	—
Weekly km Run	49	60	65	55	72	78	60	78	84	66	78	84	60	72	60	—

Daily training distance

	km	km	km	km	km	km	km	km	km	km	km	km	km	km	km	km
Mon Run	3.5_1	4.3_1	4.7_1	3.9_1	5.1_1	5.5_1	4.3_1	5.5_1	6.0_1	4.7_1	6.0_1	6.4_1	4.6_1	5.5_1	4.6_1	6.0_1
Tues Run	7.0_1	8.6_2	9.4_2	7.9_1	10.3_3	11.2_3	8.6_1	11.2_4	12.0_4	9.4_1	10_5	10.7_5	7.7_1	9.2_{5-6}	7.7_{5-6}	10.0_1
Wed Run	3.5_1	4.3_1	4.7_1	3.9_1	5.1_1	5.5_1	4.3_1	5.5_1	6.0_1	4.7_1	6.0_1	6.4_1	4.6_1	5.5_1	4.6_1	10_1
Thu Run	11.7_1	14.3_1	15.7_1	13.1_1	17.1_2	18.6_2	14.3_1	18.6_{2-3}	20.0_{2-3}	15.7_1	20.0_{2-4}	21.5_{2-4}	15.4_1	18.4_{2-4}	15.4_{2-4}	6.0_1
Fri Run	D/O	D/O	D/O	D/O	D/O	D/O	D/O	D/O	D/O	D/O	D/O	D/O	D/O	D/O	D/O	D/O
Sat Run	5.8_1	7.1_2	7.9_2	6.5_1	8.6_3	9.3_3	7.1_1	9.3_4	10.0_4	7.9_1	6.0_5	6.4_5	4.6_1	5.5_{5-6}	4.6_{5-6}	D/O
Sun Run	17.5_1	21.5_1	23.6_1	19.7_1	25.8_1	27.9_1	21.5_1	27.9_1	30.0_1	23.6_1	30.0_1	32.0_1	23.1_1	27.7_1	23.1_1	RACE

Base I would occur first.
The bold subscript numerals refer to subphases

Read pages 185–8 before starting.

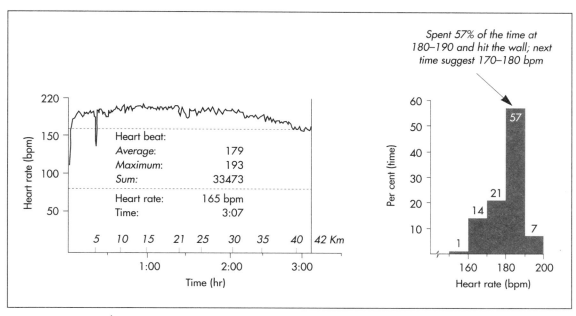

FIGURE 20.13: Marathon

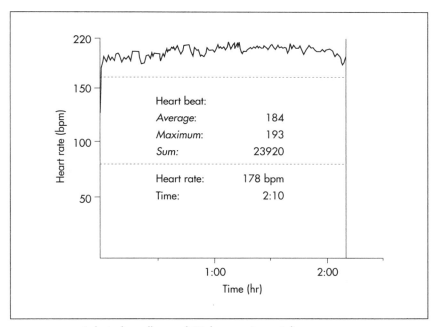

FIGURE 20.14: Relatively well-paced 30-km run time trial

DETAILED DESCRIPTIONS

Subphase		Sport	Heart rates	Type
EASY 1		**RUN** EASY: easy jogging to establish base fitness **speed:** 5–7 min/km	.... (LSD)	Whole workout
LOAD 2	**HILLS**	HILLS: Easy jogging up hills. Number and length of hills is important NOT how hard you do them so the aim is easy climbing. **aim:** prep for strength endurance training **speed:** 6–9 min/km on hills	During: N/A Between: .... (LSD)	Whole workout
HIGH LOAD 3	**H(LS)**	HILLS LONG STRIDE: Jog along the flat towards a hill and with 2–5 km to go, extend your stride out up the hill using your racing stride. As soon as you feel 'bogged' down as you run up the hill (stride rate drops or you start to puff) pull out and jog back down to the bottom of the hill and jog/rest to recovery before the next one. Repeat. **speed:** 4–7 min/km **distance:** 30–200 m (20 s –1 min) **gradient:** shallow/moderate — the hill cannot be so steep that you cannot use a stride and action that replicates a racing action on the flat.	During: N/A Between: .... (LSD)	Reps rec = 0–4 semi = 4–10 comp = 10–20
LOAD/ SPEED 4	**F(LS)**	FLAT LONG STRIDE: During your run at frequent intervals pick up the tempo slightly and extend your stride length out to a racing stride length for 100–200 m. Pull out before you get 'bogged' down (i.e. stride length or rate drops, or you start to puff) **speed:** 3–5 min/km	During: N/A Between: .... (LSD)	Rep rec = 0–4 semi = 4–10 comp = 10–20
LOW SPEED 5	**UT**	UP-TEMPO: You should feel fast, strong, comfortable and in control. This is an effort at 3-hr max race pace — NO HARDER! It is only slightly faster than cruising. **speed:** 3.5–5 min/km	During: .... (UT) Between: .... (LSD)	Reps x 10 mins (10-min intervals at 3-hr max pace) rec = 1–2 x 10 mins semi = 1–3 x 10 mins comp = 1–6 x 10 mins
HIGH SPEED 6	**AT**	ANAEROBIC THRESHOLD: Max steady-state pace or 20 min–1 hour race pace — NO HARDER. This is hard but not hell. **speed:** 3–5 min/km	During: .... (AT) Between: .... (LSD)	Reps x 5 mins (5-min intervals at 1-hr max pace not 5-min max pace) rec = 1–2 x 5 mins semi = 1–3 x 5 mins comp = 1–6 x 5 mins

Semi-competitive and competitive

Weekly layout:

	Mon	Tues	Wed	Thu	Fri	Sat	Sun
Training week	Day off	Speed or practice Gym	Endurance	Strength endurance or practice Gym	Easy	Speed or game Gym	Long strength endurance Gym
Playing week	Day off	Strength endurance or practice Gym	Endurance	Speed or practice Gym	Easy	Game	Long strength endurance

Training volume profile:

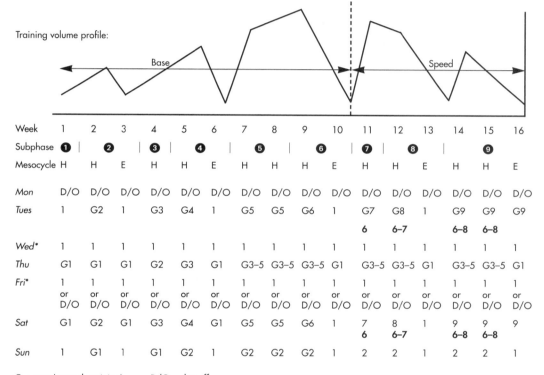

Week	1	2	3	4	5	6	7	8	9	10	11	12	13	14	15	16
Subphase	❶		❷	❸		❹		❺		❻	❼	❽			❾	
Mesocycle	H	H	E	H	H	E	H	H	H	E	H	H	E	H	H	E
Mon	D/O	D/O	D/O	D/O	D/O	D/O	D/O	D/O	D/O	D/O	D/O	D/O	D/O	D/O	D/O	D/O
Tues	1	G2	1	G3	G4	1	G5	G5	G6	1	G7	G8	1	G9	G9	G9
											6	**6–7**		**6–8**	**6–8**	
Wed*	1	1	1	1	1	1	1	1	1	1	1	1	1	1	1	1
Thu	G1	G1	G1	G2	G3	G1	G3–5	G3–5	G3–5	G1	G3–5	G3–5	G1	G3–5	G3–5	G1
Fri*	1 or D/O	1 or D/O	1 or D/O	1 or D/O	1 or D/O	1 or D/O	1 or D/O	1 or D/O	1 or D/O	1 or D/O	1 or D/O	1 or D/O	1 or D/O	1 or D/O	1 or D/O	1 or D/O
Sat	G1	G2	G1	G3	G4	G1	G5	G5	G6	1	7	8	1	9	9	9
											6	**6–7**		**6–8**	**6–8**	
Sun	1	G1	1	G1	G2	1	G2	G2	G2	1	2	2	1	2	2	1

G = gym (strength training)   D/O = day off

Numbers 1–9 in the daily workout part of the programme refer to different types of workouts which are explained in the 'Detailed Descriptions' on pages 231–3. Background information is provided in Chapter 19.

* Wed and Fri = Running technique and ball-handling drills

Bold type = workout maintenance (maintain at lowest reps)

Regular type = workout emphasis (work up to max reps)

Strength Training:

HYPERTROPHY	STRENGTH	POWER	PEAK

See pages 323–5 for information.

Read pages 185–8 before starting.

Rugby Union — recreational

Weekly layout:

	Mon	Tues	Wed	Thu	Fri	Sat	Sun
Training week	Day off	Speed or practice Gym?	Endurance	Strength endurance or practice Gym?	Day off	Easy or game Gym?	Long strength endurance Gym
Playing week	Day off	Strength endurance or practice Gym?	Endurance	Speed or practice Gym?	Day off	Game	Long strength endurance

Training volume profile:

Base — Speed

Week	1	2	3	4	5	6	7	8	9	10	11	12	13	14	15	16
Subphase	❶		❷		❸		❹		❺		❻			❼			❽		❾	
Mesocycle	H	E	H	E	H	H	E	H	H	E	H	H	E	H	H	E
Mon	D/O	D/O	D/O	D/O	D/O	D/O	D/O	D/O	D/O	D/O	D/O	D/O	D/O	D/O	D/O	D/O
Tues	1	1	2	1	3	4	1	5	6	1	7 **6**	7 **6**	1	8 **6–7**	9 **6–8**	9
Wed*	1	1	1	1	1	1	1	1	1	1	1	1	1	1	1	1
Thu	1	1	2	1	2	3	1	3–4	3–5	1	3–5	3–5	1	3–5	3–5	1
Fri	D/O	D/O	D/O	D/O	D/O	D/O	D/O	D/O	D/O	D/O	D/O	D/O	D/O	D/O	D/O	D/O
Sat*	1 or D/O	1 or D/O	1 or D/O	1 or D/O	1 or D/O	1 or D/O	1 or D/O	1 or D/O	1 or D/O	1 or D/O	1 or D/O	1 or D/O	1 or D/O	1 or D/O	1 or D/O	1 or D/O
Sun	1	1	1	1	1	2	1	2	2	1	2	2	1	2	2	1

Note: gym (strength) training can be used on the days allotted on the weekly layout above, if you like.
G = gym (strength training)   D/O = day off
Numbers 1–9 in the daily workout part of the programme refer to different types of workouts which are explained in the 'Detailed Descriptions' on pages 231–3. Background information is provided in Chapter 19.
* Wed and Sat = Running technique and ball handling drills
Bold type = workout maintenance (maintain at lowest reps)
Regular type = workout emphasis (work up to max reps)

Strength Training:

HYPERTROPHY	STRENGTH	POWER	PEAK

See pages 323–5 for information.
Read pages 185–8 before starting.

DETAILED DESCRIPTIONS

(For information on exercises marked in italics, see 'Extra Information', pages 282–6.)

Sub-phase	Team	Positions				Heart rates
		Tight 5 (Hooker, Props, Locks)	Loose Forwards and Half-Back	Inside Backs (1st and 2nd 5/8)	Outside Backs (Centre, Wing and Fullback)	
EASY 1	general fitness, ball-handling skills, technique, teamwork	*easy running* 20–40 min (may do 30–50% on a bike) *rugby drills* ball-handling drills (see coach re drills)	*easy running* 20–60 min *rugby drills* ball-handling drills (see coach re drills) sprint drills	*easy running* 20–40 min *rugby drills* ball-handling drills (see coach re drills) sprint drills	*easy running* 20–40 min *rugby drills* ball-handling drills (see coach re drills) sprint drills	(LSD)
LOAD 2	work on strength and basic game skills	*cross-country rolling hill running* 25–35 min *hills long stride* (10–80 m) rec: 1–2 semi: 2–4 comp: 3–6 rest to recovery btwn	*cross-country rolling hill running* 20–40 min *hills long stride* (10–100 m) rec: 1–4 semi: 2–6 comp: 3–10 rest to recovery btwn	*cross-country rolling hill running* 20–30 min *hills long stride* (10–40 m) rec: 1–4 semi: 2–6 comp: 3–10 rest to recovery btwn	*cross-country rolling hill running* 20–35 min *hills long stride* (10–60 m) rec: 1–4 semi: 2–6 comp: 3–10 rest to recovery btwn	During : N/A Between : (LSD)
HIGH LOAD 3	work on strength develop new 'moves' practice 'moves' with accuracy	N/A stay on previous sub	N/A stay on previous sub	*stadium/box bounding* + 20–30 min easy run (10–20 m) rec: 1–2 semi: 2–4 comp: 2–6 rest to recovery btwn	*stadium/box bounding* + 20–30 min easy run (10–20 m) rec: 1–2 semi: 2–4 comp: 2–6 rest to recovery btwn	During : N/A Between : (LSD)
LOAD/ SPEED 4	begin to 'transfer' strength to speed together with accuracy	*flat long stride and hill sprints during a 20–30 min easy run flat long stride* (30–60 m) rest to recovery btwn rec: 1–3 semi: 2–4 comp: 3–6 *hill sprints* (10–20 m) rec: 1–2 semi: 1–3 comp: 1–4 rest to recovery btwn	*flat long stride and hill sprints during a 20–30 min easy run flat long stride* (30–60 m) rest to recovery btwn rec: 2–4 semi: 4–6 comp: 4–8 *hill sprints* (10–20 m) rec: 1–3 semi: 2–4 comp: 2–5 rest to recovery btwn	*flat long stride and hill sprints during a 20–30 min easy run flat long stride* (30–60 m) rest to recovery btwn rec: 2–4 semi: 4–6 comp: 4–8 *hill sprints* (10–20 m) rec: 2–5 semi: 3–6 comp: 3–7 rest to recovery btwn	*flat long stride and hill sprints during a 20–30 min easy run flat long stride* (30–60 m) rest to recovery btwn rec: 4–6 semi: 6–8 comp: 4–12 *hill sprints* (10–20 m) rec: 2–4 semi: 3–5 comp: 3–6 rest to recovery btwn	During: N/A Between: (LSD)

(CONTINUED)

Sub-phase	Team	Positions				Heart rates
		Tight 5 (Hooker, Props, Locks)	Loose Forwards and Half-Back	Inside Backs (1st and 2nd 5/8)	Outside Backs (Centre, Wing and Fullback)	
LOW SPEED 5	the beginnings of speed multiple 'plays' put together with speed and accuracy	**accelerations during a 20–30 min *easy run*** 10–20 m accelerations to top sprint speed and 20–40 m accelerations to max steady-state playing pace (multi-directional) **accelerations** (10–20 m): rec: 1–2 semi: 2–4 comp: 4–6 vary recovery btwn **accelerations** (30–40 m): rec: 3–4 semi: 3–6 comp: 4–8 vary recovery btwn	**accelerations during a 20–30 min *easy run*** 10–20 m accelerations to top sprint speed and 50–100 m accelerations to max steady-state playing pace (multi-directional) **accelerations** (10–20 m): rec: 1–2 semi: 2–4 comp: 4–6 vary recovery btwn **accelerations** (30–40 m): rec: 3–6 semi: 3–8 comp: 4–10 vary recovery btwn	**accelerations during a 20–30 min *easy run*** 10–20 m & 30–40 m accelerations to top speed (multi-directional) **accelerations** (10–20 m): rec: 2–4 semi: 4–6 comp: 4–8 vary recovery btwn **accelerations** (30–40m): rec: 1–2 semi: 1–2 comp: 1–2 vary recovery btwn	**accelerations during a 20–30 min *easy run*** 10–20 m & 30–60 m accelerations to top speed (multi-directional) **accelerations** (10–20 m): rec: 2–4 semi: 4–6 comp: 4–8 vary recovery btwn **accelerations** (30–60 m): rec: 1–2 semi: 1–2 comp: 1–2 vary recovery btwn	During: N/A Between: ...... (LSD)
HIGH SPEED 6	high aerobic speed, putting multiple 'plays' together at high speed with accuracy	**AT intervals +20 min *easy run*** 150–200 m (multi-directional) break up into 10–30 m blocks rec: 1–2 semi: 2–4 comp: 4–6 rest to recovery btwn	**AT intervals +20 min *easy run*** 150–200 m (multi-directional) break up into 10–30 m blocks rec: 1–2 semi: 2–4 comp: 4–6 rest to recovery btwn	N/A stay on previous sub	N/A stay on previous sub	During: ...... (AT) Between: ...... (LSD) (CONTINUED)

| | | Positions | | | | Heart rates |
Sub-phase	Team	Tight 5 (Hooker, Props, Locks)	Loose Forwards and Half-Back	Inside Backs (1st and 2nd 5/8)	Outside Backs (Centre, Wing and Fullback)	
SPRINT 7	competition simulation with high aerobic/ anaerobic speed and accuracy w/up, w/down - 10 min easy run	**long and short sprints** **long sprints**: 20–30 m (multi-directional) rec: 1–2 semi: 1–2 comp: 2–4 **short sprints: 10–20 m** rec: 2–4 semi: 2–4 comp: 4–6 vary recovery bwn - long for speed - short for speed endurance w/up, w/down - 10 min easy run	**long and short sprints** **long sprints**: 30–60 m (multi-directional) rec: 1–2 semi: 1–2 comp: 2–4 **short sprints: 10–20 m** rec: 2–4 semi: 2–4 comp: 4–6 vary recovery bwn - long for speed - short for speed endurance w/up, w/down - 10 min easy run	**long and short sprints** **long sprints**: 20–30 m (multi-directional) rec: 1–2 semi: 1–2 comp: 2–4 **short sprints: 10–20 m** rec: 2–4 semi: 2–4 comp: 4–6 vary recovery bwn - long for speed - short for speed endurance w/up, w/down - 10 min easy run	**long and short sprints** **long sprints**: 30–60 m (multi-directional) rec: 1–2 semi: 1–2 comp: 2–4 **short sprints: 10–20 m** rec: 2–4 semi: 2–4 comp: 4–6 vary recovery bwn - long for speed - short for speed endurance	During: N/A Between: .... (LSD)
POWER 8	competition simulation with speed and accuracy under full competition pressure	**plyometrics:** see pages 316–22 rec: 4–6 semi: 6–10 comp: 10–20 (straight line then multidirectional) rest to recovery bwn	**plyometrics:** see pages 316–22 rec: 4–6 semi: 6–10 comp: 10–20 (straight line then multidirectional) rest to recovery bwn	**plyometrics:** see pages 316–22 rec: 4–6 semi: 6–10 comp: 10–20 (straight line then multidirectional)	**plyometrics:** see pages 316–22 rec: 4–6 semi: 6–10 comp: 10–20 (straight line then multidirectional)	During: N/A Between: .... (LSD)
OVER-SPEED 9	competition simulation with speed and accuracy under full competition pressure aiming at fast reactions	N/A stay on previous sub	N/A stay on previous sub	**overspeed sprints** rec: 2–4 semi: 4–6 comp: 6–8 rest to recovery bwn	**overspeed sprints** rec: 2–4 semi: 4–6 comp: 6–8 rest to recovery bwn	During: N/A Between: .... (LSD)

Key: rec = recreational (club); semi = semi competitive (serious club — provincial); comp = competitive (provincial — international)

Note: Start at the bottom of the rep ranges in each subphase and gradually move the number of reps or duration as you progress through the subphase and as you feel fitter specific to that form of training. As you move from one subphase to the next maintain a little of all previously trained subphases to hold your form. This is already written into your programme. All reps are included in training volumes.

Semi-competitive and competitive

Weekly layout:

	Mon	Tues	Wed	Thu	Fri	Sat	Sun
Training week	Day off	Speed or practice Gym	Endurance	Strength endurance or practice Gym	Easy	Speed or game Gym	Long strength endurance Gym
Playing week	Day off	Strength endurance or practice Gym	Endurance	Speed or practice Gym	Easy	Game	Long strength endurance

Training volume profile:

Week	1	2	3	4	5	6	7	8	9	10	11	12	13	14	15	16
Subphase	❶		❷		❸		❹		❺		❻		❼	❽			❾
Mesocycle	H	H	E	H	H	E	H	H	H	E	H	H	E	H	H	E
Mon	D/O	D/O	D/O	D/O	D/O	D/O	D/O	D/O	D/O	D/O	D/O	D/O	D/O	D/O	D/O	D/O
Tues	1	G2	1	G3	G4	1	G5	G5	G6	1	G7 **6**	G8 **6–7**	1	G9 **6–8**	G9 **6–8**	G9
Wed*	1	1	1	1	1	1	1	1	1	1	1	1	1	1	1	1
Thu	G1	G1	G1	G2	G3	G1	G3–5	G3–5	G3–5	G1	G3–5	G3–5	G1	G3–5	G3–5	G1
Fri*	1 or D/O	1 or D/O	1 or D/O	1 or D/O	1 or D/O	1 or D/O	1 or D/O	1 or D/O	1 or D/O	1 or D/O	1 or D/O	1 or D/O	1 or D/O	1 or D/O	1 or D/O	1 or D/O
Sat	G1	G2	G1	G3	G4	G1	G5	G5	G6	1	7 **6**	8 **6–7**	1	9 **6–8**	9 **6–8**	9G
Sun	G1	G1	1	G1	G2	1	G2	G2	G2	1	2	2	1	2	2	1

G = gym (strength training)   D/O = day off
Numbers 1–9 in the daily workout part of the programme refer to different types of workouts which are explained in the 'Detailed Descriptions' on pages 236–8. Background information is provided in Chapter 19.
* Wed and Fri = Running technique and ball-handling drills
Bold type = workout maintenance (maintain at lowest reps)
Regular type = workout emphasis (work up to max reps)

Strength training:

HYPERTROPHY	STRENGTH	POWER	PEAK

See pages 323–5 for information.
Read pages 185–8 before starting.

Rugby League — recreational

Weekly layout:

	Mon	Tues	Wed	Thu	Fri	Sat	Sun
Training week	Day off	Speed or practice Gym	Endurance	Strength endurance or practice Gym	Day off	Easy or game Gym	Long strength endurance Gym
Playing week	Day off	Strength endurance or practice Gym	Endurance	Speed or practice Gym	Day off	Game	Long strength endurance

Training volume profile:

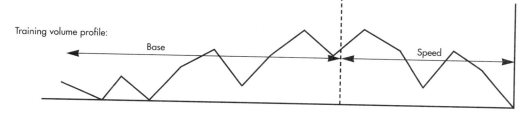

	1	2	3	4	5	6	7	8	9	10	11	12	13	14	15	16
Week	1	2	3	4	5	6	7	8	9	10	11	12	13	14	15	16
Subphase	❶		❷		❸		❹		❺		❻		❼		❽	❾
Mesocycle	H	E	H	E	H	H	E	H	H	E	H	H	E	H	H	E
Mon	D/O	D/O	D/O	D/O	D/O	D/O	D/O	D/O	D/O	D/O	D/O	D/O	D/O	D/O	D/O	D/O
Tues	1	1	2	1	3	4	1	5	6	1	7	7	1	8	9	9
											6	**6**		**6-7**	**6-8**	
Wed*	1	1	1	1	1	1	1	1	1	1	1	1	1	1	1	1
Thu	1	1	2	1	2	3	1	3-4	3-5	1	3-5	3-5	1	3-5	3-5	1
Fri	D/O	D/O	D/O	D/O	D/O	D/O	D/O	D/O	D/O	D/O	D/O	D/O	D/O	D/O	D/O	D/O
Sat*	1 or D/O	1 or D/O	1 or D/O	1 or D/O	1 or D/O	1 or D/O	1 or D/O	1 or D/O	1 or D/O	1 or D/O	1 or D/O	1 or D/O	1 or D/O	1 or D/O	1 or D/O	1 or D/O
Sun	1	1	1	1	1	2	1	2	2	1	2	2	1	2	2	1

G = gym (strength training)   D/O = day off
Numbers 1–9 in the daily workout part of the programme refer to different types of workouts which are explained in the 'Detailed Descriptions' on pages 236–8. Background information is provided in Chapter 19.
Note: gym (strength) training can be used on the days allotted on the weekly layout above, if you like.
* Wed and Sat = Running technique and ball handling drills
Bold type = workout maintenance (maintain at lowest reps)
Regular type = workout emphasis (work up to max reps)

Strength Training:

HYPERTROPHY	STRENGTH	POWER	PEAK

See pages 323–5 for information.

Read pages 185–8 before starting.

Detailed Descriptions

(For information on exercises marked in italics, see 'Extra Information', pages 282–6.)

Sub-phase	Team	Positions				Heart rates
		Forwards	Loose Forwards	Inside Backs	Outside Backs	
EASY 1	general fitness, ball-handling skills, technique, teamwork	*easy running* 20–40 min (may do 30–50% on a bike) *rugby drills* ball-handling drills (see coach for drills)	*easy running* 20–60 min *rugby drills* ball-handling drills (see coach for drills) *sprint drills*	*easy running* 20–40 min *rugby drills* ball-handling drills (see coach for drills) *sprint drills*	*easy running* 20–40 min *rugby drills* ball-handling drills (see coach for drills) *sprint drills*	
LOAD 2	work on strength and basic game skills	*cross-country rolling* hill running 25–35 min *hills long stride* (10–30 m) rec: 1–2 semi: 2–4 comp: 3–6 rest to recovery btwn	*cross-country rolling* hill running 20–40 min *hills long stride* (10–50 m) rec: 1–4 semi: 2–6 comp: 3–10 rest to recovery btwn	*cross-country rolling* hill running 20–30 min *hills long stride* (10–40 m) rec: 1–4 semi: 2–6 comp: 3–10 rest to recovery btwn	*cross-country rolling* hill running 20–35 min *hills long stride* (10–60 m) rec: 1–4 semi: 2–6 comp: 3–10 rest to recovery btwn	During : N/A Between : .... (LSD)
HIGH LOAD 3	work on strength develop new 'moves' practice 'moves' with accuracy	N/A stay on previous sub	N/A stay on previous sub	*stadium/box bounding* + 20–30 min *easy run* (10–20 m) rec: 1–2 semi: 2–4 comp: 2–6 rest to recovery btwn	*stadium/box bounding* +20–30 min *easy run* (10–20 m) rec: 1–2 semi: 2–4 comp: 2–6 rest to recovery btwn	During : N/A Between : .... (LSD)
LOAD/ SPEED 4	begin to 'transfer' strength to speed. together with accuracy	*flat long stride and hill sprints during 20– 30 min easy run* *flat long stride* (20–30 m) rec: 1–3 semi: 2–4 comp: 3–6 rest to recovery *hill sprints* (10–20 m) rec: 1–2 semi: 1–3 comp: 1–4 rest to recovery btwn	*flat long stride and hill sprints during 20– 30 min easy run* *flat long stride* (20–40 m) rec: 2–4 semi: 4–6 comp: 4–8 rest to recovery *hill sprints* (10–20 m) rec: 1–3 semi: 2–4 comp: 2–5 rest to recovery btwn	*flat long stride and hill sprints during 20– 30 min easy run* *flat long stride* (30–60 m) rec: 2–4 semi: 4–6 comp: 4–8 rest to recovery *hill sprints* (10–20 m) rec: 2–5 semi: 3–6 comp: 3–7 rest to recovery btwn	*flat long stride and hill sprints during 20– 30 min easy run* *flat long stride* (30–60 m) rec: 4–6 semi: 6–8 comp: 4–12 rest to recovery *hill sprints* (10–20 m) rec: 2–4 semi: 3–5 comp: 3–6 rest to recovery btwn	During: N/A Between : .... (LSD)

(CONTINUED)

Sub-phase	Team	Positions				Heart rates
		Forwards	Loose Forwards	Inside Backs	Outside Backs	
LOW SPEED 5	the beginings of speed multiple 'plays' put together with speed and accuracy	**accelerations and fartlek during 20-30 min easy run** 10-20 m accelerations to top sprint speed and 20-40 m accelerations to max steady-state playing pace (multi-directional) **accelerations (10-20 m):** rec: 1-2 semi: 2-4 comp: 4-6 vary recovery btwn **accelerations (20-40 m):** rec: 3-6 semi: 3-8 comp: 4-10 vary recovery btwn	**accelerations and fartlek during 20-30 min easy run** 10-20 m accelerations to top sprint speed and 20-40 m accelerations to max steady-state playing pace (multi-directional) **accelerations (10-20 m):** rec: 1-2 semi: 2-4 comp: 4-6 vary recovery btwn **accelerations (50-100 m):** rec: 3-6 semi: 3-8 comp: 4-10 vary recovery btwn	**accelerations and fartlek during 20-30 min easy run** 10-20 m & 30-40 m accelerations to top speed (multi-directional) **accelerations (10-20 m):** rec: 2-4 semi: 4-6 comp: 4-8 vary recovery btwn **accelerations (30-40 m):** rec: 1-2 semi: 1-2 comp: 1-2 vary recovery btwn	**accelerations and fartlek during 20-30 min easy run** 10-20 m & 30-60 m accelerations to top speed (multi-directional) **accelerations (10-20 m):** rec: 2-4 semi: 4-6 comp: 4-8 vary recovery btwn **accelerations (30-60 m):** rec: 1-2 semi: 1-2 comp: 1-2 vary recovery btwn	During: N/A Between: .... (LSD)
HIGH SPEED 6	high aerobic speed, putting multiple 'plays' together with high speed with accuracy	**AT intervals +20-30 easy run** 150-200 m (multi-directional) break up into varied 10-30 m blocks rec: 1-2 semi: 2-4 comp: 4-6 rest to recovery btwn	**AT intervals +20-30 easy run** 150-200 m (multi-directional) break up into varied 10-30 m blocks rec: 1-2 semi: 2-4 comp: 4-6 rest to recovery btwn	N/A stay on previous sub	N/A stay on previous sub	During: .... (AT) Between: .... (LSD)

(CONTINUED)

Sub-phase	Team	Positions				Heart rates
		Forwards	Loose Forwards	Inside Backs	Outside Backs	
SPRINT 7	competition simulation with high aerobic/anaerobic speed and accuracy	**long and short sprints** **long sprints: 20–30 m** (multi-directional) rec: 1–2 semi: 1–2 comp: 2–4 **short sprints: 10–20 m** rec: 2–4 semi: 2–4 comp: 4–6 vary recovery btwn - long for speed - short for speed endurance w/up, w/down - 10 min easy run	**long and short sprints** **long sprints: 30–60 m** (multi-directional) rec: 1–2 semi: 1–2 comp: 2–4 **short sprints: 10–20 m** rec: 2–4 semi: 2–4 comp: 4–6 vary recovery btwn - long for speed - short for speed endurance w/up, w/down - 10 min easy run	**long and short sprints** **long sprints: 20–30 m** (multi-directional) rec: 1–2 semi: 1–2 comp: 2–4 **short sprints: 10–20 m** rec: 2–4 semi: 2–4 comp: 4–6 vary recovery btwn - long for speed - short for speed endurance w/up, w/down - 10 min easy run	**long and short sprints** **long sprints: 30–60 m** (multi-directional) rec: 1–2 semi: 1–2 comp: 2–4 **short sprints: 10–20 m** rec: 2–4 semi: 2–4 comp: 4–6 vary recovery btwn - long for speed - short for speed endurance w/up, w/down - 10 min easy run	During: N/A Between: .... (LSD)
POWER 8	competition simulation with speed and accuracy under full competition pressure	**plyometrics:** see pages 316–22 rec: 4–6 semi: 6–10 comp: 10–20 (straight line then multidirectional) rest to recovery btwn	**plyometrics:** see pages 316–22 rec: 4–6 semi: 6–10 comp: 10–20 (straight line then multidirectional) rest to recovery btwn	**plyometrics:** see pages 316–22 rec: 4–6 semi: 6–10 comp: 10–20 (straight line then multidirectional) rest to recovery btwn	**plyometrics:** see pages 316–22 rec: 4–6 semi: 6–10 comp: 10–20 (straight line then multidirectional) rest to recovery btwn	During: N/A Between: .... (LSD)
OVER-SPEED 9	competition simulation with speed and accuracy under full competition pressure aiming at fast reactions	N/A stay on previous sub	N/A stay on previous sub	**overspeed sprints** rec: 2–4 **semi:** 4–6 **comp:** 6–8 rest to recovery	**overspeed sprints** rec: 2–4 **semi:** 4–6 **comp:** 6–8 rest to recovery	During: N/A Between: .... (LSD)

Key: rec = recreational (club); semi = semi competitive (serious club — provincial); comp = competitive (provincial — international)

Note: Start at the bottom of the rep ranges in each subphase and gradually move the number of reps or duration as you progress through the subphase and as you feel fitter specific to that form of training. As you move from one subphase to the next maintain a little of all previously trained subphases to hold your form. This is already written into your programme. All reps are included in training volumes.

Semi-competitive and competitive

Weekly layout:

	Mon	Tues	Wed	Thu	Fri	Sat	Sun
Training week	Day off	Speed or practice Gym	Endurance	Strength endurance or practice Gym	Easy	Speed or game Gym	Long strength endurance Gym
Playing week	Day off	Strength endurance or practice Gym	Endurance	Speed or practice Gym	Easy	Game	Long strength endurance

Training volume profile:

Base — Speed

Week	1	2	3	4	5	6	7	8	9	10	11	12	13	14	15	16
Subphase	❶	❷		❸	❹		❺			❻	❼	❽		❾		
Mesocycle	H	H	E	H	H	E	H	H	H	E	H	H	E	H	H	E
Mon	D/O	D/O	D/O	D/O	D/O	D/O	D/O	D/O	D/O	D/O	D/O	D/O	D/O	D/O	D/O	D/O
Tues	1	G2	1	G3	G4	1	G5	G5	G6	1	G7 **6**	G8 **6–7**	1	G9 **6–8**	G9 **6–8**	G9
Wed*	1	1	1	1	1	1	1	1	1	1	1	1	1	1	1	1
Thu	G1	G1	G1	G2	G3	G1	G3–5	G3–5	G3–5	G1	G3–5	G3–5	G1	G3–5	G3–5	G1
Fri*	1 or D/O	1 or D/O	1 or D/O	1 or D/O	1 or D/O	1 or D/O	1 or D/O	1 or D/O	1 or D/O	1 or D/O	1 or D/O	1 or D/O	1 or D/O	1 or D/O	1 or D/O	1 or D/O
Sat	G1	G2	G1	G3	G4	G1	G5	G5	G6	1	7 **6**	8 **6–7**	1	9 **6–8**	9 **6–8**	9
Sun	G1	G1	G1	G1	G2	1	G2	G2	G2	1	2	2	1	2	2	1

G = gym (strength training)   D/O = day off

Numbers 1–9 in the daily workout part of the programme refer to different types of workouts which are explained in the 'Detailed Descriptions' on pages 241–3. Background information is provided in Chapter 19.

* Wed and Fri = Running technique and ball-handling drills

Bold type = workout maintenance (maintain at lowest reps)

Regular type = workout emphasis (work up to max reps)

Strength training:

HYPERTROPHY	STRENGTH	POWER	PEAK

See pages 323–5 for information.

Read pages 185–8 before starting.

Soccer — recreational

Weekly layout:

	Mon	Tues	Wed	Thu	Fri	Sat	Sun
Training week	Day off	Speed or practice Gym?	Endurance	Strength endurance or practice Gym?	Day off	Easy or game Gym?	Long strength endurance Gym?
Playing week	Day off	Strength endurance or practice Gym?	Endurance	Speed or practice Gym?	Day off	Game	Long strength endurance

Training volume profile:

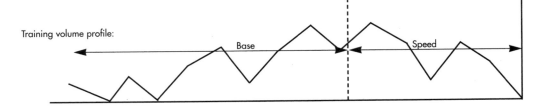

Base Speed

Week	1	2	3	4	5	6	7	8	9	10	11	12	13	14	15	16
Subphase		❶		❷	❸		❹		❺		❻		❼		❽	❾
Mesocycle	H	E	H	E	H	H	E	H	H	E	H	H	E	H	H	E
Mon	D/O	D/O	D/O	D/O	D/O	D/O	D/O	D/O	D/O	D/O	D/O	D/O	D/O	D/O	D/O	D/O
Tues	1	1	2	1	3	4	1	5	6	1	7 **6**	7 **6**	1	8 **6–7**	9 **6–8**	9
Wed*	1	1	1	1	1	1	1	1	1	1	1	1	1	1	1	1
Thu	1	1	2	1	2	3	1	3–4	3–5	1	3–5	3–5	1	3–5	3–5	1
Fri	D/O	D/O	D/O	D/O	D/O	D/O	D/O	D/O	D/O	D/O	D/O	D/O	D/O	D/O	D/O	D/O
Sat*	1 or D/O	1 or D/O	1 or D/O	1 or D/O	1 or D/O	1 or D/O	1 or D/O	1 or D/O	1 or D/O	1 or D/O	1 or D/O	1 or D/O	1 or D/O	1 or D/O	1 or D/O	1 or D/O
Sun	1	1	1	1	1	2	1	2	2	1	2	2	1	2	2	1

Note: gym (strength) training can be used on the days allotted on the weekly layout above, if you like.

G = gym (strength training)   D/O = day off

Numbers 1–9 in the daily workout part of the programme refer to different types of workouts which are explained in the 'Detailed Descriptions' on pages 241–3. Background information is provided in Chapter 19.

* Wed and Sat = Running technique and ball control drills

Bold type = workout maintenance (maintain at lowest reps)

Regular type = workout emphasis (work up to max reps)

Strength training:

HYPERTROPHY	STRENGTH	POWER	PEAK

See pages 323–5 for information.

Read pages 185–8 before starting.

(For information on exercises marked in italics, see 'Extra Information', pages 282–6.)

Sub-phase	Team	Positions				Heart rates
		Goalkeeper	Midfield	Central forwards and backs	Outside forwards and backs	
EASY 1	general fitness, ball handling skills, technique, teamwork	*easy running* 20–30 mins **soccer drills** ball-handling drills (see coach for drills) analyse top goal-keepers' technique (video?)	*easy running* 20–60 mins **soccer drills** ball-handling drills (see coach for drills) sprint drills	*easy running* 20–40 mins **soccer drills** ball-handling drills (see coach for drills) sprint drills	*easy running* 20–40 mins **soccer drills** ball-handling drills (see coach for drills) sprint drills	(LSD)
LOAD 2	work on strength and basic game skills	*cross-country rolling* hill running 20–30 mins **goal mouth drills + shuttles** (see coach for drills) 10–20 mins	*cross-country rolling* hill running 20–40 mins **hills long stride** (10–100 m) rec: 1–4 semi: 2–6 comp: 3–10 rest to recovery btwn	*cross-country rolling* hill running 20–30 mins **hills long stride** (10–40 m) rec: 1–4 semi: 2–6 comp: 3–10 rest to recovery btwn	*cross-country rolling* hill running 20–35 mins **hills long stride** (10–80 m) rec: 1–4 semi: 2–6 comp: 3–10 rest to recovery btwn	During: N/A Between: (LSD)
HIGH LOAD 3	work on strength develop new 'moves' practice 'moves' with accuracy	**goal mouth drills and shuttles** with the ball **stadium/box bounding** (5–10 m) rec: 2–4 semi: 4–6 comp: 4–10 rest to recovery btwn	**stadium/box bounding** (10–20 m) rec: 1–2 semi: 2–4 comp: 2–4 rest to recovery btwn	**stadium/box bounding** (10–20 m) rec: 1–2 semi: 2–4 comp: 2–6 rest to recovery btwn	**stadium/box bounding** (10–20 m) rec: 1–2 semi: 2–4 comp: 2–6 rest to recovery btwn	During: N/A Between: (LSD)
LOAD/SPEED 4	begin to 'transfer' strength to speed. Put multiple 'plays' together with accuracy	**goal mouth drills and shuttles** with the ball (high volume) and **hill sprints** *shuttles* (20–30 mins medium effort) *hill sprints* (5–10 m) rec: 1–2 semi: 1–3 comp: 1–4 rest to recovery btwn	*flat long stride and hill sprints during 20–30 min easy run* *flat long stride* (30–60 m) rec: 2–4 semi: 4–6 comp: 4–8 rest to recovery btwn *hill sprints* (10–20 m) rec: 1–3 semi: 2–4 comp: 2–5 rest to recovery btwn	*flat long stride and hill sprints during 20–30 min easy run* *flat long stride* (30–60 m) rec: 2–4 semi: 4–6 comp: 4–8 rest to recovery btwn *hill sprints* (10–20 m) rec: 2–5 semi: 3–6 comp: 3–7 rest to recovery btwn	*flat long stride and hill sprints during 20–30 min easy run* *flat long stride* (30–80 m) rec: 4–6 semi: 6–8 comp: 4–12 rest to recovery btwn *hill sprints* (10–20 m) rec: 2–4 semi: 3–5 comp: 3–6 rest to recovery btwn	During: N/A Between: (LSD)

(CONTINUED)

Sub-phase	Team	Positions				Heart rates
		Goalkeeper	Midfield	Central forwards and backs	Outside forwards and backs	
LOW SPEED 5	the beginings of speed puting multiple 'plays' together with speed and accuracy	**accelerations/shuttles** 5–10 m accelerations competition simulation (high volume) **shuttles:** 20–30 mins game pace accelerations to max steady-state playing pace **accelerations** (5–20 m): rec: 1–2 semi: 2–4 comp: 4–6 vary recovery btwn	**accelerations/shuttles and fartlek** (multi-directional) 10–20 m accelerations to top sprint speed and 50–100 m **shuttles on run** (20–30 mins) **accelerations** (10–20 m): rec: 1–2 semi: 2–4 comp: 4–6 vary recovery btwn **accelerations** (50–100 m): rec: 1–2 semi: 1–2 comp: 1–2 vary recovery btwn	**accelerations/shuttles and fartlek** (multi-directional) 10–20 m and 30–40 m accelerations to top speed **shuttles on run** (20–30 mins) **accelerations** (10–20 m): rec: 2–4 semi: 4–6 comp: 4–8 vary recovery btwn **accelerations** (30–40 m): rec: 1–2 semi: 1–2 comp: 1–2 vary recovery btwn	**accelerations/shuttles and fartlek** (multi-directional) 10–20 m and 30–60 m accelerations to top speed **shuttles on run** (20–30 mins) **accelerations** (10–20 m): rec: 2–4 semi: 4–6 comp: 4–8 vary recovery btwn **accelerations** (30–60 m): rec: 1–2 semi: 1–2 comp: 1–2 vary recovery btwn	During: N/A Between: ....(LSD)
HIGH SPEED 6	high aerobic speed, putting multiple 'plays' together at high speed with accuracy	**competition simulation and speed (low volume) general plyometrics** 0–10 m see pages 316–22 rec: 4–6 semi: 6–10 comp: 10–20 rest to recovery btwn **competition simulation shuttles** (20–30 mins) competition pace	**AT intervals and 20-min easy run** 1 50–200 m break up into varied 10–40 m blocks rec: 1–2 semi: 2–4 comp: 4–6 rest to recovery btwn	N/A move to next sub	N/A move to next sub	During: ....(AT) Between: ....(LSD) Plyometrics N/A

(CONTINUED)

Sub-phase	Team	Goalkeeper	Midfield	Central forwards and backs	Outside forwards and backs	Heart rates
			Positions			
SPRINT 7	competition simulation with aerobic/anaerobic speed and accuracy	**sprints and game-specific plyometrics** (multi-directional) 0–10 m rec: 4–6 semi: 6–10 comp: 10–20 **short sprints:** 10–20 m rec: 2–4 semi: 2–4 comp: 4–6 **competition simulation** shuttles (20–30 mins) competition pace w/up, w/down - 10 min easy run	**long and short sprints** **long sprints:** 30–60 m (multi-directional) rec: 1–2 semi: 1–2 comp: 2–4 **short sprints:** 10–20 m rec: 2–4 semi: 2–4 comp: 4–6 vary recovery bhwn - long for speed - short for speed **endurance** w/up, w/down - 10 min easy run	**long and short sprints** **long sprints:** 20–30 m (multi-directional) rec: 1–2 semi: 1–2 comp: 2–4 **short sprints:** 10–20 m rec: 2–4 semi: 2–4 comp: 4–6 vary recovery bhwn - long for speed - short for speed **endurance** w/up. w/down - 10 min easy run	**long and short sprints** **long sprints:** 30–60 m (multi-directional) rec: 1–2 semi: 1–2 comp: 2–4 **short sprints:** 20–30 m rec: 2–4 semi: 2–4 comp: 4–6 vary recovery bhwn - long for speed - short for speed **endurance** w/up, w/down - 10 min easy run	During: N/A Between: .... (LSD)
POWER 8	competition simulation with speed and accuracy under full competition pressure	**plyometrics:** (multi-directional) see pages 316–22 rec: 4–6 semi: 6–10 comp: 10–20 rest to recovery bhwn **competition simulation shuttles** and game pressure with fast reactions (20–30 mins)	**plyometrics:** (multi-directional) see pages 316–22 rec: 4–6 semi: 6–10 comp: 10–20 straight line then multi-directional rest to recovery bhwn	**plyometrics:** (multi-directional) see pages 316–22 rec: 4–6 semi: 6–10 comp: 10–20 straight line then multi-directional rest to recovery bhwn	**plyometrics:** (multi-directional) see pages 316–22 rec: 4–6 semi: 6–10 comp: 10–20 straight line then multi-directional rest to recovery bhwn	During: N/A Between: .... (LSD)
OVER-SPEED 9	competition simulation with speed and accuracy under full competition pressure aiming at fast reactions	N/A stay on previous sub	**overspeed sprints** rec: 2–4 semi: 4–6 comp: 6–8 rest to recovery bhwn	**overspeed sprints** rec: 2–4 semi: 4–6 comp: 6–8 rest to recovery bhwn	**overspeed sprints** rec: 2–4 semi: 4–6 comp: 6–8 rest to recovery bhwn	During: N/A Between: .... (LSD)

Key: rec = recreational (club); semi = semi competitive (serious club — provincial); comp = competitive (provincial — international)

Note: Start at the bottom of the rep ranges in each subphase and gradually move the number of reps or duration as you progress through the subphase and as you feel fitter specific to that form of training. When you move from one subphase to the next maintain a little of all previously trained subphases to hold your form. This is already written into your programme. All reps are included in training volumes.

Semi-competitive and competitive

Weekly layout:

	Mon	Tues	Wed	Thu	Fri	Sat	Sun
Training week	Day off	Speed or practice Gym	Endurance	Strength endurance or practice Gym	Easy	Speed or game Gym	Long strength endurance Gym
Playing week	Day off	Strength endurance or practice Gym	Endurance	Speed or practice Gym	Easy	Game	Long strength endurance

Training volume profile:

Week	1	2	3	4	5	6	7	8	9	10	11	12	13	14	15	16
Subphase	❶		❷		❸		❹	❺		❻		❼			❽	
Mesocycle	H	H	E	H	H	E	H	H	H	E	H	H	E	H	H	E
Mon	D/O	D/O	D/O	D/O	D/O	D/O	D/O	D/O	D/O	D/O	D/O	D/O	D/O	D/O	D/O	D/O
Tues	1	G2	1	G3	G3	1	G4	G5	G6	1	G7 **6**	G7 **6**	1	G8 **6–7**	G8 **6–7**	G8 **6–7**
Wed*	1	1	1	1	1	1	1	1	1	1	1	1	1	1	1	1
Thu	G1	G1	G1	G2	G2	G1	G3	G3–4	G3–5	G1	G3–5	G3–5	G1	G3–5	G3–5	G1
Fri*	1 or D/O	1 or D/O	1 or D/O	1 or D/O	1 or D/O	1 or D/O	1 or D/O	1 or D/O	1 or D/O	1 or D/O	1 or D/O	1 or D/O	1 or D/O	1 or D/O	1 or D/O	1 or D/O
Sat	G1	G2	G1	G3	G3	G1	G4	G5	G6	1	7 **6**	7 **6**	1	8 **6–7**	8 **6–7**	1
Sun	1	G1	1	G1	G1	1	G2	G2	G2	1	2	2	1	2	2	1

G = gym (strength training)   D/O = day off

Numbers 1–9 in the daily workout part of the programme refer to different types of workouts which are explained in the 'Detailed Descriptions' on pages 246–8. Background information is provided in Chapter 19.

* Wed and Fri = Ball skills

Bold type = workout maintenance (maintain at lowest reps)

Regular type = workout emphasis (work up to max reps)

Strength training:

HYPERTROPHY	STRENGTH	POWER	PEAK

See pages 323–5 for information.

Read pages 185–8 before starting.

Netball — recreational

Weekly layout:

	Mon	Tues	Wed	Thu	Fri	Sat	Sun
Training week	Day off	Speed or practice Gym?	Endurance	Strength endurance or practice Gym?	Day off	Speed or game Gym?	Long strength endurance Gym?
Playing week	Day off	Strength endurance or practice Gym?	Endurance	Speed or practice Gym?	Day off	Game	Long strength endurance

Training volume profile:

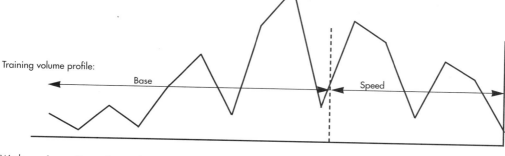

Base — Speed

Week	1	2	3	4	5	6	7	8	9	10	11	12	13	14	15	16
Subphase	❶		❷		❸		❹		❺		❻	❼			❽	
Mesocycle	H	E	H	E	H	H	E	H	H	E	H	H	E	H	H	E
Mon	D/O	D/O	D/O	D/O	D/O	D/O	D/O	D/O	D/O	D/O	D/O	D/O	D/O	D/O	D/O	D/O
Tues	1	1	2	1	3	4	1	5	6	1	7 **(6)**	7 **(6)**	1	8 (6–7)	8 (6–7)	8 (6–7)
Wed*	1 or D/O	1 or D/O	1 or D/O	1 or D/O	1 or D/O	1 or D/O	1 or D/O	1 or D/O	1 or D/O	1 or D/O	1 or D/O	1 or D/O	1 or D/O	1 or D/O	1 or D/O	1 or D/O
Thu	1	1	1	1	2	3	1	3–4	3–5	1	3–5	3–5	1	3–5	3–5	1
Fri	D/O	D/O	D/O	D/O	D/O	D/O	D/O	D/O	D/O	D/O	D/O	D/O	D/O	D/O	D/O	D/O
Sat*	1	1	1	1	1	1	1	1	1	1	1	1	1	1	1	1
Sun	1	1	1	1	1	2	1	2	2	1	2	2	1	2	2	1

Note: gym (strength) training can be used on the days allotted on the weekly layout above, if you like.
G = gym (strength training)   D/O = day off
Numbers 1–9 in the daily workout part of the programme refer to different types of workouts which are explained in the 'Detailed Descriptions' on pages 246–8. Background information is provided in Chapter 19.
* Wed and Sat = Ball skills
Bold type = workout maintenance (maintain at lowest reps)
Regular type = workout emphasis (work up to max reps)

Strength training:

HYPERTROPHY	STRENGTH	POWER	PEAK

See pages 323–5 for information.

Read pages 185–8 before starting.

DETAILED DESCRIPTIONS
(For information on exercises marked in italics, see 'Extra Information', pages 282–6.)

Sub-phase	Team	Positions				Heart rates
		Goal keep/shoot	Goal defence/attack	Wing attack/defence	Centre	
EASY 1	general fitness, ball-handling skills, technique, teamwork	*easy running* 20–30 min **netball drills** ball-handling drills (see coach for drills) technique (video?)	*easy running* 20–40 min **netball drills** ball-handling drills (see coach for drills) *sprint drills* see pg 316	*easy running* 20–30 min **netball drills** ball-handling drills (see coach for drills) *sprint drills* see pg 316	*easy running* 20–40 min **netball drills** ball-handling drills (see coach for drills) *sprint drills* see pg 316	.... (LSD)
LOAD 2	work on strength and basic game skills	*cross-country rolling hill running* 20–30 min drills and shuttles (see coach for drills)	*cross-country rolling hill running* 20–40 min **goal shooting/defence** (10–20 m) rec: 1–4 semi: 2–6 comp: 3–10 rest to recovery btwn goal shooting/defence drills (see coach)	*cross-country rolling hill running* 20–30 min **hills long stride** (10–20 m) rec: 1–4 semi: 2–6 comp: 3–10 rest to recovery btwn	*cross-country rolling hill running* 20–35 min **hills long stride** (10–20 m) rec: 1–4 semi: 2–6 comp: 3–10 rest to recovery btwn	During: N/A Between: .... (LSD)
HIGH LOAD 3	work on strength develop new 'moves' practice 'moves' with accuracy	**goal shooting/defence drills and shuttles** with the ball easy shuttles: 15–30 min(high vol) **stadium/box bounding** (0–5m) rec: 2–4 semi: 4–6 comp: 4–10 rest to recovery btwn	*court shuttles/drills* **stadium/box bounding** **court shuttles/drills** 15–30 min (high vol) **stadium/box bounding** (5–15 m) rec: 1–2 semi: 2–4 comp: 2–4 rest to recovery btwn goal shooting/defence drills (see coach)	*court shuttles/drills* **stadium/box bounding** **court shuttles/drills** 15–30 min (high vol) **stadium/box bounding** (5–15 m) rec: 1–2 semi: 2–4 comp: 2–6 rest to recovery btwn	*court shuttles/drills* **stadium/box bounding** **court shuttles/drills** 15–30 min (high vol) **stadium/box bounding** (5–20 m) rec: 1–2 semi: 2–4 comp: 2–6 rest to recovery btwn	During: N/A Between: .... (LSD)
LOAD/ SPEED 4	begin to 'transfer' strength to speed putting multiple 'plays' together with accuracy	**goal shoot/defence drills and shuttles** with the ball (high volume) and *hill sprints* goal shooting/defence drills (see coach)	*flat long stride and hill sprints* *flat long stride* (10–20 m) rec: 2–4 semi: 4–6 comp: 4–8 rest to recovery btwn goal shooting/defence drills (see coach)	*flat long stride and hill sprints* *flat long stride* (10–20 m) rec: 2–4 semi: 4–6 comp: 4–8 rest to recovery btwn	*flat long stride and hill sprints* *flat long stride* (10 –30 m) rec: 4–6 semi: 6–8 comp: 4–12 rest to recovery btwn	During: N/A Between: .... (LSD)

(CONTINUED)

Sub-phase	Team	Positions				Heart rates
		Goal keep/shoot	Goal defence/attack	Wing attack/defence	Centre	
		hill sprints (0–10 m) rec: 1–2 semi: 1–3 comp: 1–4 rest to recovery btwn **court shuttles/drills** rec/semi: 15–30 min (high vol) easy shuttles	**hill sprints** (5–15 m) rec: 1–3 semi: 2–4 comp: 2–5 rest to recovery btwn **court shuttles/drills** rec/semi: 15–30 min (high vol) easy shuttles	**hill sprints** (5–15 m) rec: 2–5 semi: 3–6 comp: 3–7 rest to recovery btwn **court shuttles/drills** rec/semi: 15–30 min (high vol) easy shuttles	**hill sprints** (5–20 m) rec: 2–4 semi: 3–5 comp: 3–6 rest to recovery bwn **court shuttles/drills** rec/semi: 15–30 min (high vol) easy shuttles	
LOW SPEED 5	the beginings of speed putting multiple 'plays' together with speed and accuracy	**accelerations/shuttles** 5–10 m accelerations competition simulation (high volume) multi-directional **court shuttles/drills** rec/semi: med easy shuttles 15–30 min (high vol) goal shooting/defence drills (see coach) **accelerations** (5–10 m) rec: 1–2 semi: 2–4 comp: 4–6 vary recovery btwn	**accelerations/shuttles and fartlek** 10–20 m accelerations to top sprint speed multi-directional **court shuttles/drills** rec/semi: med easy shuttles 15–30 min (high vol) goal shooting/defence drills (see coach) **accelerations** (10–20 m) rec: 1–2 semi: 2–4 comp: 4–6 vary recovery btwn	**accelerations/shuttles and fartlek** 10–20 m accelerations to top speed multi-directional **court shuttles/drills** rec/semi: med easy shuttles 15–30 min (high vol) **accelerations** (10–20 m) rec: 2–4 semi: 4–6 comp: 4–8 vary recovery btwn	**accelerations/shuttles and fartlek** 10–30 m accelerations to top speed multi-directional **court shuttles/drills** rec/semi: med easy shuttles 15–30 min (high vol) **accelerations** (10–30 m) rec: 2–4 semi: 4–6 comp: 4–8 vary recovery btwn	During: N/A Between: .... (LSD)
HIGH SPEED 6	high aerobic speed, putting multiple 'plays' together at high speed with accuracy	N/A move to next sub	N/A move to next sub	N/A move to next sub	**AT shuttles + 20 min easy run** (100–200 m) break up into 10–20 m blocks **rec: 2–4** **semi: 2–4** **comp: 4–6** vary recovery btwn	During: .... (AT) Between: .... (LSD)
SPRINT 7	competition simulation with aerobic/ anaerobic speed and accuracy	**sprints and general plyometrics:** 0–10 m (straight line) rec: 4–6: semi: 6–10 comp: 10–20	**multi-directional sprints:** 10–20 m rec: 2–4 semi: 2–4 comp: 4–6 vary recovery btwn	**multi-directional sprints:** 10–20 m rec: 2–4 semi: 2–4 comp: 4–6 vary recovery btwn	**multi-directional sprints:** 10–30 m rec: 2–4 semi: 2–4 comp: 4–6 vary recovery btwn	During: N/A Between: .... (LSD) (CONTINUED)

Sub-phase	Team	Positions				Heart rates
		Goal keep/shoot	Goal defence/attack	Wing attack/defence	Centre	
		rest to recovery btwn **sprints:** 0–10 m rec: 2–4 semi: 2–4 comp: 4–6 competiton simulation shuttles **court shuttles/drills** rec/semi/comp: (game speed) 15–30 min (high vol) goal shooting/defence drills	**court shuttles/drills** rec/semi: (game speed) 15–30 min (high vol) goal shooting/defence drills	**court shuttles/drills** rec/semi: (game speed) 15–30 min (high vol)	**court shuttles/drills** rec/semi: (game speed) 15–30 min (high vol)	
POWER 8	competition simulation with speed and accuracy under full competition pressure	**game-specific plyometrics:** concentrate on: GK = lateral jumps GS = lateral jumps **plyometrics:** see pages 316–22 **rec:** 4–6 **semi:** 6–10 **comp:** 10–20 rest to recovery btwn competition simulation shuttles and game pressure with fast reactions 20–30 mins	**game-specific plyometrics:** concentrate on: GD = back and high jumps GA = running jumps **plyometrics:** see pages 316–22 **rec:** 4–6 **semi:** 6–10 **comp:** 10–20 competition simulation shuttles and game pressure with fast reactions 20–30 mins	**game-specific plyometrics:** concentrate on: WA = running jumps WD = side and high jumps **plyometrics:** see pages 316–22 **rec:** 4–6 **semi:** 6–10 **comp:** 10–20 competition simulation shuttles and game pressure with easy reactions 20–30 mins	**game-specific plyometrics:** concentrate on: running jumps **plyometrics:** see pages 316–22 **rec:** 4–6 **semi:** 6–10 **comp:** 10–20 rest to recovery btwn competition simulation shuttles and game pressure with easy reactions 20–30 mins	During: N/A Between: .... (LSD)
OVER-SPEED 9	competition simulation with speed and accuracy under full competition pressure aiming at fast reactions	N/A stay on previous sub	N/A stay on previous sub	N/A stay on previous sub	N/A stay on previous sub	During: N/A Between:

Key: rec = recreational (club); semi = semi competitive (serious club — provincial); comp = competitive (provincial — international)

Note: Start at the bottom of the rep ranges in each subphase and gradually move the number of reps or duration as you progress through the subphase and as you feel fitter specific to that form of training. As you move from one subphase to the next maintain a little of all previously trained subphases to hold your form. This is already written into your programme.

PRECISION TRAINING

Semi-competitive and competitive

Weekly layout:

	Mon	Tues	Wed	Thu	Fri	Sat	Sun
Training week	Day off	Speed or practice Gym	Endurance	Strength endurance or practice Gym	Easy	Speed or game Gym	Long strength endurance Gym
Playing week	Day off	Strength endurance or practice Gym	Endurance	Speed or practice Gym	Easy	Game	Long strength endurance

Training volume profile:

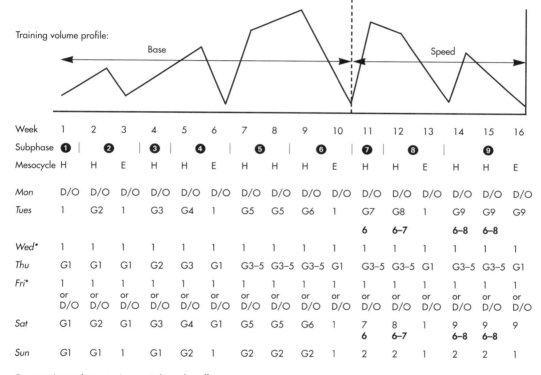

Base — Speed

Week	1	2	3	4	5	6	7	8	9	10	11	12	13	14	15	16
Subphase	❶	❷		❸		❹		❺		❻		❼	❽			❾
Mesocycle	H	H	E	H	H	E	H	H	H	E	H	H	E	H	H	E
Mon	D/O	D/O	D/O	D/O	D/O	D/O	D/O	D/O	D/O	D/O	D/O	D/O	D/O	D/O	D/O	D/O
Tues	1	G2	1	G3	G4	1	G5	G5	G6	1	G7	G8	1	G9	G9	G9
Tues (bold)											**6**	**6–7**		**6–8**	**6–8**	
Wed*	1	1	1	1	1	1	1	1	1	1	1	1	1	1	1	1
Thu	G1	G1	G1	G2	G3	G1	G3–5	G3–5	G3–5	G1	G3–5	G3–5	G1	G3–5	G3–5	G1
Fri*	1 or D/O	1 or D/O	1 or D/O	1 or D/O	1 or D/O	1 or D/O	1 or D/O	1 or D/O	1 or D/O	1 or D/O	1 or D/O	1 or D/O	1 or D/O	1 or D/O	1 or D/O	1 or D/O
Sat	G1	G2	G1	G3	G4	G1	G5	G5	G6	1	7	8	1	9	9	9
Sat (bold)											**6**	**6–7**		**6–8**	**6–8**	
Sun	G1	G1	1	G1	G2	1	G2	G2	G2	1	2	2	1	2	2	1

G = gym (strength training)   D/O = day off
Numbers 1–9 in the daily workout part of the programme refer to different types of workouts which are explained in the 'Detailed Descriptions' on pages 251–3. Background information is provided in Chapter 19.
* Wed and Fri = Running technique and ball-handling drills
Bold type = workout maintenance (maintain at lowest reps)
Regular type = workout emphasis (work up to max reps)

Strength training:

HYPERTROPHY	STRENGTH	POWER	PEAK

See pages 323–5 for information.

Read pages 185–8 before starting.

Basketball — recreational

Weekly layout:

	Mon	Tues	Wed	Thu	Fri	Sat	Sun
Training week	Day off	Speed or practice Gym?	Endurance	Strength endurance or practice Gym?	Day off	Easy or game Gym?	Long strength endurance Gym?
Playing week	Day off	Strength endurance or practice Gym?	Endurance	Speed or practice Gym?	Day off	Game	Long strength endurance

Training volume profile:

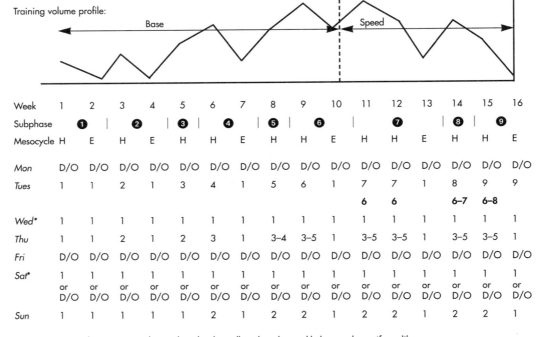

Week	1	2	3	4	5	6	7	8	9	10	11	12	13	14	15	16
Subphase	❶		❷		❸		❹		❺		❻		❼		❽	❾
Mesocycle	H	E	H	E	H	H	E	H	H	E	H	H	E	H	H	E
Mon	D/O	D/O	D/O	D/O	D/O	D/O	D/O	D/O	D/O	D/O	D/O	D/O	D/O	D/O	D/O	D/O
Tues	1	1	2	1	3	4	1	5	6	1	7 **6**	7 **6**	1	8 **6–7**	9 **6–8**	9
Wed*	1	1	1	1	1	1	1	1	1	1	1	1	1	1	1	1
Thu	1	1	2	1	2	3	1	3–4	3–5	1	3–5	3–5	1	3–5	3–5	1
Fri	D/O	D/O	D/O	D/O	D/O	D/O	D/O	D/O	D/O	D/O	D/O	D/O	D/O	D/O	D/O	D/O
Sat*	1 or D/O	1 or D/O	1 or D/O	1 or D/O	1 or D/O	1 or D/O	1 or D/O	1 or D/O	1 or D/O	1 or D/O	1 or D/O	1 or D/O	1 or D/O	1 or D/O	1 or D/O	1 or D/O
Sun	1	1	1	1	1	2	1	2	2	1	2	2	1	2	2	1

Note: gym (strength) training can be used on the days allotted on the weekly layout above, if you like.
G = gym (strength training)   D/O = day off
Numbers 1–9 in the daily workout part of the programme refer to different types of workouts which are explained in the 'Detailed Descriptions' on pages 251–3. Background information is provided in Chapter 19.
* Wed and Sat = Running technique and ball-handling drills
Bold type = workout maintenance (maintain at lowest reps)
Regular type = workout emphasis (work up to max reps)

Strength training:

HYPERTROPHY	STRENGTH	POWER	PEAK

See pages 323–5 for information.

Read pages 185–8 before starting.

DETAILED DESCRIPTIONS

(For information on exercises marked in italics, see 'Extra Information', pages 282–6.)

Sub-phase	Team	Positions Centre	Forwards	Guards (Point, Off)	Heart rates
EASY 1	general fitness, ball-handling skills, technique, teamwork	*easy running* 20–30 min **basketball drills** ball-handling drills shooting/defence (see coach) cycling 50% of time (if needed)	*easy running* 20–30 min **basketball drills** ball-handling drills shooting/defence (see coach) cycling 50% of time (if needed) *sprint drills*	*easy running* 20–40 min **basketball drills** ball-handling drills shooting/defence (see coach) cycling 50% of time (if needed) *sprint drills*	.... (LSD)
LOAD 2	work on strength and basic game skills	*easy running* with *cross-country rolling hill running* 20–30 min *hills long stride* (10–20 m) rec: 1–2 semi: 1–2 comp: 2–4 rest to recovery btwn **goal shooting/defence drills** 10–20 mins (see coach)	*easy running* with *cross-country rolling hill running* 20–30 min *hills long stride* (10–20 m) rec: 1–4 semi: 2–6 comp: 3–10 rest to recovery btwn **goal shooting/defence drills** 10–20 mins (see coach) smaller forward: hill run larger forward: easy plus hills	*cross-country rolling hill running* 20–35 min *hills long stride* (10–30 m) rec: 1–4 semi: 2–6 comp: 3–10 rest to recovery btwn **goal shooting/defence drills** 10–20 mins (see coach)	During: N/A Between: .... (LSD)
HIGH LOAD 3	work on strength develop new 'moves' practice 'moves' with accuracy	*court shuttles/drills* *hill/stadium tempo* reps rec: 1–2 semi: 2–4 comp: 2–6 rest to recovery btwn **goal shooting/defence drills** 10–20 mins **shuttles:** 15–30 mins easy	*court shuttles/drills* *stadium/box bounding* *court shuttles/drills* rec/semi/comp: 15–30 min (high vol) *stadium/box bounding* (5–15m) rec: 1–2 semi: 2–4 comp: 2–4 rest to recovery btwn **goal shooting/defence drills** larger forward: may want to do centre training smaller forward: more reps longer sprints	*court shuttles/drills* *stadium/box bounding* *court shuttles/drills* rec/semi/comp: 15–30 min (high vol) *stadium/box bounding* (5–20m) rec: 1–2 semi: 2–4 comp: 2–6 rest to recovery btwn **goal shooting/defence drills** 10–20 mins point guard: more reps longer sprints	During: N/A Between: .... (LSD) (CONTINUED)

Sub-phase	Team	Positions			Heart rates
		Centre	Forwards	Guards (Point, Off)	
LOAD/ SPEED 4	begin to 'transfer' strength to speed. putting multiple 'plays' together with accuracy	*flat long stride* and *hill sprints/shuttles* *flat long stride* (10–20 m) rec: 2–4 semi: 4–6 comp: 4–8 rest to recovery btwn *hill sprints* (5–10 m) rec: 1–3 semi: 2–4 comp: 2–5 rest to recovery btwn *court shuttles/drills* rec/semi/comp: 15–30 mins (high vol) *goal shooting/ defence drills* 10–20 mins	*flat long stride* and *hill sprints/shuttles* *flat long stride* (10–20 m) rec: 2–4 semi: 4–6 comp: 4–8 rest to recovery btwn *hill sprints* (5–15 m) rec: 2–5 semi: 3–6 comp: 3–7 rest to recovery btwn *court shuttles/drills* rec/semi/comp: 15–30 mins (high vol) *goal shooting/ defence drills* 10–20 mins larger forward: may want do centre training smaller forward: more reps longer sprints	*flat long stride* and *hill sprints/shuttles* *flat long stride* (10–30 m) rec: 4–6 semi: 6–8 comp: 4–12 rest to recovery btwn *hill sprints* (5–20 m) rec: 2–4 semi: 3–5 comp: 3–6 rest to recovery btwn *court shuttles/drills* rec/semi/comp: 15–30 mins (high vol) *goal shooting/ defence drills* 10–20 mins point guard: more reps longer sprints	During: N/A Between: .... (LSD)
LOW SPEED 5	the beginings of speed multiple 'plays' put together with speed and accuracy	*accelerations/shuttles* and *fartlek* (multi-directional) 5–10 m accelerations to top sprint speed *court shuttles/drills* rec/semi/comp: 15–30 mins (high vol) medium effort *goal shooting/ defence drills* 10–20 mins *accelerations* (5–10 m) rec: 1–2 semi: 2–4 comp: 4–6 vary recovery btwn	*accelerations/shuttles* and *fartlek* (multi-directional) 10–15 m accelerations to top speed *court shuttles/drills* rec/semi/comp: 15–30 mins (high vol) medium effort *goal shooting/ defence drills* (10–20 mins) *accelerations* (10–15 m) rec: 2–4 semi: 4–6 comp: 4–8 vary recovery btwn larger forward: centre training smaller forward: more reps longer sprints	*accelerations/shuttles* and *fartlek* (multi-directional) 10–20 m accelerations to top speed *court shuttles/drills* rec/semi/comp: 15–30 mins (high vol) medium effort *goal shooting/ defence drills* (10–20 mins) *accelerations* (10–20 m) rec: 2–4 semi: 4–6 comp: 4–8 vary recovery btwn point guard: more reps longer sprints	During: N/A Between: .... (LSD)
HIGH SPEED 6	high aerobic speed, putting multiple 'plays' together at high speed with accuracy	*AT shuttles* (100–200 m) + *easy run/bike* (10–15 mins) *AT intervals* break up into varied 10–20 m blocks rec: 2–4 semi: 2–4 comp: 4–6 rest to recovery btwn	*AT shuttles* (100–200 m) + *easy run/bike* (10–15 mins) *AT intervals* break up into varied 10–20 m blocks rec: 2–4 semi: 2–4 comp: 4–6 rest to recovery btwn smaller forward: more reps longer sprints	*AT shuttles* (100–200 m) + *easy run/bike* (10–15 mins) *AT intervals* break up into varied 10–20 m blocks rec: 2–4 semi: 2–4 comp: 4–6 rest to recovery btwn point guard: more reps longer sprints	During: .... (AT) Between .... (LSD) (Continued)

PRECISION TRAINING

Sub-phase	Team	Positions Centre	Positions Forwards	Guards (Point, Off)	Heart rates
SPRINT 7	competition simulation with aerobic/ anaerobic speed and accuracy	**sprints/general plyometrics** **sprints:** 5–10 m (multi-directional) rec: 1–2 semi: 2–4 comp: 2–4 rest to recovery btwn **court shuttles/drills** rec/semi/comp: 15–30 mins (high vol/comp pace) **goal shooting/ defence drills** (10–15 mins) **general plyometrics** rec: 4–6 semi: 4–10 comp: 10–15 rest to recovery btwn	**sprints/general plyometrics** **sprints:** 10–15 m (multi-directional) rec: 2–3 semi: 2–4 comp: 4–6 rest to recovery btwn **court shuttles/drills** rec/semi/comp: 15–30 mins (high vol/comp pace) **goal shooting/ defence drills** (10–15 mins) **general plyometrics** rec: 4–6 semi: 6–15 comp: 10–20 rest to recovery btwn smaller forward: more reps longer sprints	**sprints/general plyometrics** **sprints:** 10–20 m (multi-directional) rec: 2–4 semi: 2–6 comp: 4–8 rest to recovery btwn **court shuttles/drills** rec/semi/comp: 15–30 mins (high vol/comp pace) **goal shooting/ defence drills** (10–15 mins) **general plyometrics** rec: 4–6 semi: 10–15 comp: 10–30 rest to recovery btwn point guard: more reps longer sprints	During: N/A Between: .... (LSD)
POWER 8	competition simulation with speed and accuracy under full competition pressure	**game-specific (multi-directional) plyometrics** concentrate on: jumps: forward, side back and high **plyometrics** see pages 316–22 rec: 4–6 semi: 4–10 comp: 10–15 rest to recovery btwn incorporate passing and shooting competition simulation shuttles and game pressure with fast reactions or games	**game-specific (multi-directional) plyometrics** concentrate on: smaller = lateral, running jumps larger = forward, back, side and high jumps **plyometrics** see pages 316–22 rec: 4–6 semi: 10–15 comp: 10–30 rest to recovery btwn incorporate passing and shooting competition simulation shuttles and game pressure with fast reactions or games	**game-specific (multi-directional) plyometrics** concentrate on: lateral and running jumps **plyometrics** see pages 316–22 rec: 4–6 semi: 6–15 comp: 10–20 rest to recovery btwn incorporate passing and shooting competition simulation shuttles and game pressure with fast reactions or games	During: N/A Between: .... (LSD)
OVER-SPEED 9	competition simulation with speed and accuracy under full competition pressure aiming at fast reactions	N/A stay on previous sub	N/A stay on previous sub	N/A stay on previous sub	During: N/A Between: .... (LSD)

Key: rec = recreational (club); semi = semi competitive (serious club — provincial); comp = competitive (provincial — international)

Note: Start at the bottom of the rep ranges in each subphase and gradually move the number of reps or duration as you progress through the subphase and as you feel fitter specific to that form of training. As you move from one subphase to the next maintain a little of all previously trained subphases to hold your form. This is already written into your programme. All reps are included in training volumes.

Semi-competitive and competitive

Weekly layout:

	Mon	Tues	Wed	Thu	Fri	Sat	Sun
Training week	Day off	Speed or practice Gym	Endurance	Strength endurance or practice Gym	Easy	Speed or game Gym	Long strength endurance Gym
Playing week	Day off	Strength endurance or practice Gym	Endurance	Speed or practice Gym	Easy	Game	Long strength endurance

Training volume profile:

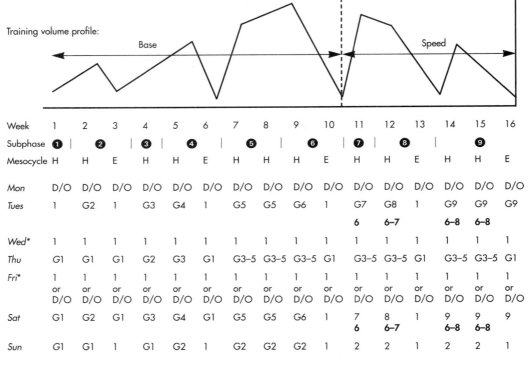

Base   Speed

Week	1	2	3	4	5	6	7	8	9	10	11	12	13	14	15	16
Subphase	❶	❷		❸		❹		❺		❻		❼	❽		❾	
Mesocycle	H	H	E	H	H	E	H	H	H	E	H	H	E	H	H	E
Mon	D/O	D/O	D/O	D/O	D/O	D/O	D/O	D/O	D/O	D/O	D/O	D/O	D/O	D/O	D/O	D/O
Tues	1	G2	1	G3	G4	1	G5	G5	G6	1	G7 **6**	G8 **6–7**	1	G9 **6–8**	G9 **6–8**	G9
Wed*	1	1	1	1	1	1	1	1	1	1	1	1	1	1	1	1
Thu	G1	G1	G1	G2	G3	G1	G3–5	G3–5	G3–5	G1	G3–5	G3–5	G1	G3–5	G3–5	G1
Fri*	1 or D/O	1 or D/O	1 or D/O	1 or D/O	1 or D/O	1 or D/O	1 or D/O	1 or D/O	1 or D/O	1 or D/O	1 or D/O	1 or D/O	1 or D/O	1 or D/O	1 or D/O	1 or D/O
Sat	G1	G2	G1	G3	G4	G1	G5	G5	G6	1	7 **6**	8 **6–7**	1	9 **6–8**	9 **6–8**	9
Sun	G1	G1	1	G1	G2	1	G2	G2	G2	1	2	2	1	2	2	1

G = gym (strength training)   D/O = day off

Numbers 1–9 in the daily workout part of the programme refer to different types of workouts which are explained in the 'Detailed Descriptions' on pages 256–8. Background information is provided in Chapter 19.

* Wed and Fri = Running technique and ball-control drills

Bold type = workout maintenance (maintain at lowest reps)

Regular type = workout emphasis (work up to max reps)

Strength training:

HYPERTROPHY	STRENGTH	POWER	PEAK

See pages 323–5 for information.

Read pages 185–8 before starting.

Hockey — recreational

Weekly layout:

	Mon	Tues	Wed	Thu	Fri	Sat	Sun
Training week	Day off	Speed or practice Gym?	Endurance	Strength endurance or practice Gym?	Day off	Easy or game Gym?	Long strength endurance Gym?
Playing week	Day off	Strength endurance or practice Gym?	Endurance	Speed or practice Gym?	Day off	Game	Long strength endurance

Training volume profile:

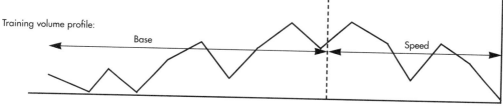

Base — Speed

Week	1	2	3	4	5	6	7	8	9	10	11	12	13	14	15	16
Subphase	❶		❷		❸	❹		❺		❻		❼		❽	❾	
Mesocycle	H	E	H	E	H	H	E	H	H	E	H	H	E	H	H	E
Mon	D/O	D/O	D/O	D/O	D/O	D/O	D/O	D/O	D/O	D/O	D/O	D/O	D/O	D/O	D/O	D/O
Tues	1	1	2	1	3	4	1	5	6	1	7 **6**	7 **6**	1	8 **6–7**	9 **6–8**	9
Wed*	1	1	1	1	1	1	1	1	1	1	1	1	1	1	1	1
Thu	1	1	2	1	2	3	1	3–4	3–5	1	3–5	3–5	1	3–5	3–5	1
Fri	D/O	D/O	D/O	D/O	D/O	D/O	D/O	D/O	D/O	D/O	D/O	D/O	D/O	D/O	D/O	D/O
Sat*	1 or D/O	1 or D/O	1 or D/O	1 or D/O	1 or D/O	1 or D/O	1 or D/O	1 or D/O	1 or D/O	1 or D/O	1 or D/O	1 or D/O	1 or D/O	1 or D/O	1 or D/O	1 or D/O
Sun	1	1	1	1	1	2	1	2	2	1	2	2	1	2	2	1

Note: gym (strength) training can be used on the days allotted on the weekly layout above, if you like.
G = gym (strength training)   D/O = day off
Numbers 1–9 in the daily workout part of the programme refer to different types of workouts which are explained in the 'Detailed Descriptions' on pages 256–8. Background information is provided in Chapter 19.
* Wed and Sat = Running technique and ball-control drills
Bold type = workout maintenance (maintain at lowest reps)
Regular type = workout emphasis (work up to max reps)

Strength training:

HYPERTROPHY	STRENGTH	POWER	PEAK

See pages 323–5 for information.
Read pages 185–8 before starting.

DETAILED DESCRIPTIONS

(For information on exercises marked in italics, see 'Extra Information', pages 282–6.)

Sub-phase	Team	Positions — Goalkeeper	Links	Backs/Forwards	Sweeper	Heart rates
EASY 1	general fitness, ball handling skills, technique, teamwork	*easy running* 20–30 min; **hockey drills**; ball-handling drills; analyse top goalkeepers' technique (video?)	*easy running* 20–60 min; **hockey drills**; ball-handling drills; (see coach); *sprint drills*	*easy running* 20–40 min; **hockey drills**; ball-handling drills; (see coach); *sprint drills*	*easy running* 20–40 min; **hockey drills**; ball-handling drills; (see coach); *sprint drills*	...........(LSD)
LOAD 2	work on strength and basic game skills	*cross-country rolling*; **hill running** 20–30 min; **goal mouth drills plus shuttles** (see coach)	*cross-country rolling*; **hill running** 20–40 min; **hills long stride** (10–60 m); rec: 1–4; semi: 2–6; comp: 3–10; rest to recovery btwn	*cross-country rolling*; **hill running** 20–30 min; **hills long stride** (10–40 m); rec: 1–4; semi: 2–6; comp: 3–10; rest to recovery btwn	*cross-country rolling*; **hill running** 20–35 min; **hills long stride** (10–60 m); rec: 1–4; semi: 2–6; comp: 3–10; rest to recovery btwn	During: N/A; Between: ....(LSD)
HIGH LOAD 3	work on strength; develop new 'moves'; practice 'moves' with accuracy	**goal mouth drills and shuttles with the ball** (20 mins easy); **stadium/box bounding** (5–10 m); rec: 2–4; semi: 4–6; comp: 4–10; rest to recovery btwn	**stadium/box bounding** (10–20 m); rec: 1–2; semi: 2–4; comp: 2–4; rest to recovery btwn; *easy run or shuttles* (20 mins)	**stadium/box bounding** (10–20 m); rec: 1–2; semi: 2–4; comp: 2–6; rest to recovery btwn; *easy run or shuttles* (20 mins)	**stadium/box bounding** (10–20 m); rec: 1–2; semi: 2–4; comp: 2–6; rest to recovery btwn; *easy run or shuttles* (20 mins)	During: N/A; Between:
LOAD/ SPEED 4	begin to 'transfer' strength to speed; putting multiple 'plays' together with accuracy	**goal mouth drills and shuttles with the ball** (high volume) and **hill sprints** (30–60 m); **shuttles:** 20 mins easy; *hill sprints* (5–10 m); rec: 1–2; semi: 1–3; comp: 1–4; rest to recovery btwn	*flat long stride and hill sprints during* 30–40 min easy run; *flat long stride* (30–60 m); rec: 2–4; semi: 4–6; comp: 4–8; rest to recovery btwn; *hill sprints* (10–20 m); rec: 1–3; semi: 2–4; comp: 2–5; rest to recovery btwn	*flat long stride and hill sprints during* 30–40 min easy run; *flat long stride* (30–60 m); rec: 2–4; semi: 4–6; comp: 4–8; rest to recovery btwn; *hill sprints* (10–20 m); rec: 2–5; semi: 3–6; comp: 3–7; rest to recovery btwn	*flat long stride and hill sprints* 30–40 min easy run; *flat long stride* (30–60 m); rec: 4–6; semi: 6–8; comp: 4–12; rest to recovery btwn; *hill sprints* (10–20 m); rec: 2–4; semi: 3–5; comp: 3–6; rest to recovery btwn	During: N/A; Between: ....(LSD)

(Continued)

Sub-phase	Team	Positions				Heart rates
		Goalkeeper	Links	Backs/Forwards	Sweeper	
LOW SPEED 5	the beginings of speed putting multiple plays together with and accuracy	*accelerations/shuttles* 5–15 m accelerations (multi-directional) competition simulation (high volume) *accelerations* (5–15m) rec: 1–2 semi: 2–4 comp: 4–6 vary recovery btwn *shuttles:* medium pace (20 mins)	*accelerations and fartlek* 10–20 m accelerations to top sprint speed and 30–60 m accelerations to max steady-state playing pace (multi-directional) & 20 min easy run *accelerations* (10–20 m) rec: 1–2 semi: 2–4 comp: 4–6 vary recovery btwn *accelerations* (30–60 m) rec: 1–2 semi: 1–2 comp: 1–2 vary recovery btwn w/up, w/down before and after	*accelerations and fartlek* 10–20 m and 30–40 m accelerations to top speed (multi-directional) & 20 min easy run *accelerations* rec: 2–4 semi: 4–6 comp: 4–8 vary recovery btwn *accelerations* (30–40 m): rec: 1–2 semi: 1–2 comp: 1–2 vary recovery btwn w/up, w/down before and after	*accelerations/shuttles and fartlek* 10–20m and 30–60 m accelerations to top speed (multi-directional) & 20 min easy run *accelerations* rec: 2–4 semi: 4–6 comp: 4–8 vary recovery btwn *accelerations* (30–60 m): rec: 1–2 semi: 1–2 comp: 1–2 vary recovery btwn w/up,w/down before and after	During: N/A Between: ....(LSD)
HIGH SPEED 6	high aerobic speed, putting multiple 'plays' together at high speed with accuracy	*competition simulation* and speed (low volume) *general plyometrics* 0–10 m (straight line) see pages 316–22 rec: 4–6 semi: 6–10 comp: 10–20 rest to recovery btwn *competition simulation shuttles* 20 min game pace	*AT intervals* + 20 min run 150–200 m break up into varied 10–30 m blocks rec: 1–2 semi: 2–4 comp: 4–6 rest to recovery btwn	N/A move to next sub	N/A move to next sub	During: ....(LSD) Between: ....(LSD) Plyometrics: N/A

(CONTINUED)

Sub-phase	Team	Positions				Heart rates
		Goalkeeper	Links	Backs/Forwards	Sweeper	
SPRINT 7	competition simulation with aerobic/anaerobic speed and accuracy	**sprints and game-specific plyometrics** (multi-directional) **plyometrics:** 0–10 m rec: 4–6 semi: 6–10 comp: 10–20 vary recovery btwn **short sprints:** 10–20 m rec: 2–4 semi: 2–4 comp: 4–6 vary recovery btwn **competition simulation shuttles** - game pace (20 mins)	**long and short sprints** **long sprints:** 30–60 m (multi-directional) rec: 1–2 semi: 1–2 comp: 2–4 vary recovery btwn **short sprints:** 10–20 m rec: 2–4 semi: 2–4 comp: 4–6 vary recovery btwn + 20 min easy run	**long and short sprints** **long sprints:** 20–30 m (multi-directional) rec: 1–2 semi: 1–2 comp: 2–4 vary recovery btwn **short sprints:** 10–20 m rec: 2–4 semi: 2–4 comp: 4–6 vary recovery btwn + 20 min easy run	**long and short sprints** **long sprints:** 30–60 m (multi-directional) rec: 1–2 semi: 1–2 comp: 2–4 vary recovery btwn **short sprints:** 20–30 m rec: 2–4 semi: 2–4 comp: 4–6 vary recovery btwn + 20 min easy run	During: N/A Between: .... (LSD)
POWER 8	competition simulation with speed and accuracy under full competition pressure	**game-specific plyometrics** (multi-directional) see pages 316–22 rec: 4–6 semi: 6–10 comp: 10–20 **competition simulation shuttles** and game pressure with fast reactions (20 mins)	**general & game-specific plyometrics** (multi-directional) see pages 316–22 rec: 4–6 semi: 6–10 comp: 10–20 **game simulation** and games	**general & game-specific plyometrics** (multi-directional) see pages 316–22 rec: 4–6 semi: 6–10 comp: 10–20 **game simulation** and games	**general & game-specific plyometrics** (multi-directional) see pages 316–22 rec: 4–6 semi: 6–10 comp: 10–20 **game simulation** and games	During: N/A Between: .... (LSD)
OVER SPEED 9	competition simulation with speed and accuracy under full competition pressure aiming at fast reactions	N/A stay on previous sub	N/A stay on previous sub	**overspeed sprints** rec: 2–4 semi: 4–6 comp: 6–8 rest to recovery btwn	**overspeed sprints** rec: 2–4 semi: 4–6 comp: 6–8 rest to recovery btwn	During: N/A Between: .... (LSD)

Key: rec = recreational (club); semi = semi competitive (serious club — provincial); comp = competitive (provincial — international)

Note: Start at the bottom of the rep ranges in each subphase and gradually move the number of reps or duration as you progress through the subphase and as you feel fitter specific to that form of training. As you move from one subphase to the next maintain a little of all previously trained subphases to hold your form. This is already written into your programme.

Semi-competitive and competitive

Weekly layout:

	Mon	Tues	Wed	Thu	Fri	Sat	Sun
Training week	Day off	Speed or practice Gym	Endurance	Strength endurance or practice Gym	Easy	Speed or game Gym	Long strength endurance Gym
Playing week	Day off	Strength endurance or practice Gym	Endurance	Speed or practice Gym	Easy	Game	Long strength endurance

Training volume profile:

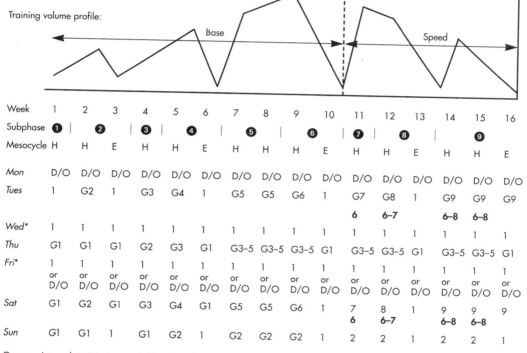

Base Speed

Week	1	2	3	4	5	6	7	8	9	10	11	12	13	14	15	16
Subphase	❶		❷		❸		❹		❺		❻		❼	❽		❾
Mesocycle	H	H	E	H	H	E	H	H	H	E	H	H	E	H	H	E
Mon	D/O	D/O	D/O	D/O	D/O	D/O	D/O	D/O	D/O	D/O	D/O	D/O	D/O	D/O	D/O	D/O
Tues	1	G2	1	G3	G4	1	G5	G5	G6	1	G7 **6**	G8 **6–7**	1	G9 **6–8**	G9 **6–8**	G9
Wed*	1	1	1	1	1	1	1	1	1	1	1	1	1	1	1	1
Thu	G1	G1	G1	G2	G3	G1	G3–5	G3–5	G3–5	G1	G3–5	G3–5	G1	G3–5	G3–5	G1
Fri*	1 or D/O	1 or D/O	1 or D/O	1 or D/O	1 or D/O	1 or D/O	1 or D/O	1 or D/O	1 or D/O	1 or D/O	1 or D/O	1 or D/O	1 or D/O	1 or D/O	1 or D/O	1 or D/O
Sat	G1	G2	G1	G3	G4	G1	G5	G5	G6	1	7 **6**	8 **6–7**	1	9 **6–8**	9 **6–8**	9
Sun	G1	G1	1	G1	G2	1	G2	G2	G2	1	2	2	1	2	2	1

G = gym (strength training) D/O = day off

Numbers 1–9 in the daily workout part of the programme refer to different types of workouts which are explained in the 'Detailed Descriptions' on pages 261–2. Background information is provided in Chapter 19.

Training primarily applies to skiing but may also be used for surfing and golf.

* Wed and Fri = Skills

Bold type = workout maintenance (maintain at lowest reps), Regular type = workout emphasis (work up to max reps)

Strength or condition training:

Skiing	HYPERTROPHY		STRENGTH		POWER	PEAK
Surfing	HYPERTROPHY		STRENGTH		POWER/MUSCLE ENDURANCE	
Golf	MUSCLE ENDURANCE					

See pages 323–5 for information.

Read pages 185–8 before starting.

Skiing, Surfing, Golf — recreational

Weekly layout:

	Mon	Tues	Wed	Thu	Fri	Sat	Sun
Training week	Day off	Speed or practice Gym?	Endurance	Strength endurance or practice Gym?	Day off	Easy or game Gym?	Long strength endurance Gym?
Playing week	Day off	Strength endurance or practice Gym?	Endurance	Speed or practice Gym?	Day off	Game	Long strength endurance

Training volume profile:

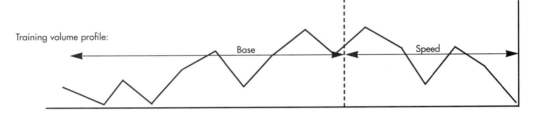

Week	1	2	3	4	5	6	7	8	9	10	11	12	13	14	15	16
Subphase	❶	|	❷	|	❸	|	❹	|	❺	|	❻	|	❼	|	❽	| ❾
Mesocycle	H	E	H	E	H	H	E	H	H	E	H	H	E	H	H	E
Mon	D/O	D/O	D/O	D/O	D/O	D/O	D/O	D/O	D/O	D/O	D/O	D/O	D/O	D/O	D/O	D/O
Tues	1	1	2	1	3	4	1	5	6	1	7 **6**	7 **6**	1	8 **6–7**	9 **6–8**	9
Wed*	1	1	1	1	1	1	1	1	1	1	1	1	1	1	1	1
Thu	1	1	2	1	2	3	1	3–4	3–5	1	3–5	3–5	1	3–5	3–5	1
Fri	D/O	D/O	D/O	D/O	D/O	D/O	D/O	D/O	D/O	D/O	D/O	D/O	D/O	D/O	D/O	D/O
Sat*	1 or D/O	1 or D/O	1 or D/O	1 or D/O	1 or D/O	1 or D/O	1 or D/O	1 or D/O	1 or D/O	1 or D/O	1 or D/O	1 or D/O	1 or D/O	1 or D/O	1 or D/O	1 or D/O
Sun	1	1	1	1	1	2	1	2	2	1	2	2	1	2	2	1

G = gym (strength training)   D/O = day off
Numbers 1–9 in the daily workout part of the programme refer to different types of workouts which are explained in the 'Detailed Descriptions' on pages 261–2. Background information is provided in Chapter 19.
* Wed and Sat =Skills

Bold type = workout maintenance (maintain at lowest reps)
Regular type = workout emphasis (work up to max reps)

Strength or condition training:

Skiing	HYPERTROPHY		STRENGTH		POWER	PEAK

Skiing	HYPERTROPHY	STRENGTH	POWER	PEAK
Surfing	HYPERTROPHY	STRENGTH	POWER/MUSCLE ENDURANCE	
Golf	MUSCLE ENDURANCE			

See pages 323–5 for information.
Read pages 185–8 before starting.

DETAILED DESCRIPTIONS

(For information on exercises marked in italics, see 'Extra Information', pages 282–6.)

Subphase	Training theme	Sport		Heart rates
		Skiing/Surfing	Golf	
EASY 1	general fitness and technique	*easy fitness* (run/cycle/ gym/swim) 20–40 mins (see general fitness prog- rammes, pages 275–9) general technique **surf**: prefer swim **ski**: prefer cycle or run general *proprioception training* easy surf and ski technique	*easy fitness* (run/cycle/ gym/swim) 20–40 mins (see general fitness prog- ramme, pages 275–9) driving and putting concentrate on technique	.... (LSD)
LOAD 2	work on strength/ strength endurance and basic skills	*specific fitness* **and** *muscle endurance* 30–60 mins aim at technique for long periods of time **surf**: swim with pullbuoys rec: 1–3 x 100–200 m semi: 1–6 x 100–200 m comp: 1–10 x 100–200 m rest to recovery btwn **ski**: see specific programme training (pg. 262) easy and lots of surfing and skiing	*specific fitness* 30–60 mins driving and putting: technique and accuracy	During: N/A Between: .... (LSD)
HIGH LOAD 3	work on strength/ strength endurance	*specific fitness* **and** *strength* **surf**: swim with *paddles* rec: 1–2 x 100 m semi: 1–4 x 100 m comp: 1–8 x 100 m rest to recovery btwn **ski**: repeat previous sub specific *proprioception training*, see pg. 262 high volume of surfing and skiing	high volume *easy fitness* training: pages 275–9 driving and putting: technique and accuracy (*specific muscle endurance*)	During: N/A Between: .... (LSD)
LOAD/ SPEED 4	begin to 'transfer' strength/strength endurance to speed	*easy tempo* **surf**: *paddle* on surfboard rec: 1–2 x 5–10 m and 1–2 x 200 m semi: 2–4 x 5–10 m and 1–2 x 200 m comp: 4–6 x 5–10 m and 1–2 x 200 m rest to recovery btwn *high resistance* bungy around board for more resistance, same reps and dist as above **ski**: see specific programme (pg. 262) or cycle-specific *proprioception training*	*easy fitness training* pages 275–9 driving and putting: (specific muscular endurance and power)	During: N/A Between: .... (LSD) (CONTINUED)

Subphase	Training theme	Sport Skiing/Surfing	Golf	Heart rates
LOW SPEED 5	the beginings of speed	N/A stay on previous sub	N/A repeat previous subphase	
HIGH SPEED 6	high aerobic speed	**surf: high resistance accelerations on board** small bungy around board to create drag rec: 1–2 x 5–10 m semi: 1–4 x 5–10 m comp: 1–8 x 5–10 m **ski:** repeat previous subphase specific proprioception training	N/A repeat previous subphase	During: .... (AT) Between: .... (LSD)
SPRINT 7	anaerobic speed	**surf: accelerations on board** (no bungy) rec: 1–2 x 5–10m semi: 1–4 x 5–10m comp: 1–8 x 5–10m rest to recovery btwn **ski:** repeat previous subphase specific proprioception training	N/A repeat previous subphase	During: N/A Between: .... (LSD)
POWER 8	competition simulation	**competition simulation** or competition	**competition simulation**	During: N/A Between: .... (LSD)
OVER- SPEED 9	competition simulation and competition pressure	**competition simulation** short/sharp bursts with pressure and fast reactions or competition	**competition simulation** under competition pressure	During: N/A Between: .... (LSD)

Key: rec = recreational (club); semi = semi competitive (serious club — provincial); comp = competitive (provincial — international)

Note: Start at the bottom of the rep ranges in each subphase and gradually move the number of reps or duration as you progress through the subphase and as you feel fitter specific to that form of training. As you move from one subphase to the next maintain a little of all previously trained subphases to hold your form. This is already written into your programme.

SPECIFIC SKI CONDITIONING PROGRAMME (Circuit: 1–3 times through)

Lunge jumps	20	
Step ups	10 each leg	Note: This can make your knees sore if you do
Bench dips	10	too much of it or if combined with too much skiing.
1/2 Squat jumps	10	In this case, substitute more cycling.
Side to side jumps	10 each side	

PROPRIOCEPTION TRAINING: To improve balance (2–10 x 10–20 seconds)
1. Stand on one leg   2. Stand on one leg, do 1/2 squats   3. Stand on one leg, 1/2 squats with eyes closed
4. Stand on one leg, 1/2 squat jump, eyes open   5. Stand on one leg, 1/2 squat jump with eyes closed
This is more effective on a rebounder or bed, or you can use a wobble board.

262

Semi-competitive and competitive

Weekly layout:

	Mon	Tues	Wed	Thu	Fri	Sat	Sun
Training week	Day off	Speed or practice Gym	Endurance	Strength endurance or practice Gym	Easy	Speed or game Gym	Long strength endurance Gym
Playing week	Day off	Strength endurance or practice Gym	Endurance	Speed or practice Gym	Easy	Game	Long strength endurance

Training volume profile:

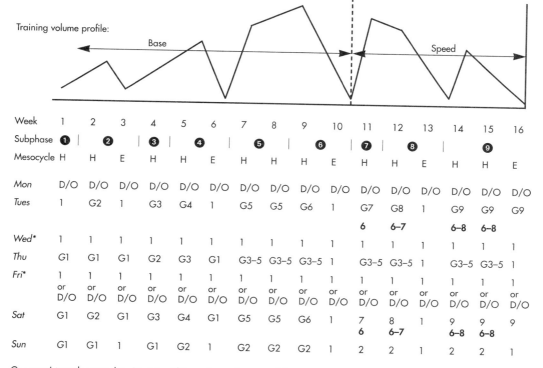

Week	1	2	3	4	5	6	7	8	9	10	11	12	13	14	15	16
Subphase	❶		❷	❸		❹		❺		❻	❼	❽			❾	
Mesocycle	H	H	E	H	H	E	H	H	H	E	H	H	E	H	H	E
Mon	D/O	D/O	D/O	D/O	D/O	D/O	D/O	D/O	D/O	D/O	D/O	D/O	D/O	D/O	D/O	D/O
Tues	1	G2	1	G3	G4	1	G5	G5	G6	1	G7 **6**	G8 **6–7**	1	G9	G9 **6–8**	G9 **6–8**
Wed*	1	1	1	1	1	1	1	1	1	1	1	1	1	1	1	1
Thu	G1	G1	G1	G2	G3	G1	G3–5	G3–5	G3–5	1	G3–5	G3–5	1	G3–5	G3–5	1
Fri*	1 or D/O	1 or D/O	1 or D/O	1 or D/O	1 or D/O	1 or D/O	1 or D/O	1 or D/O	1 or D/O	1 or D/O	1 or D/O	1 or D/O	1 or D/O	1 or D/O	1 or D/O	1 or D/O
Sat	G1	G2	G1	G3	G4	G1	G5	G5	G6	1	7 **6**	8 **6–7**	1	9	9 **6–8**	9 **6–8**
Sun	G1	G1	1	G1	G2	1	G2	G2	G2	1	2	2	1	2	2	1

Note: on Tues and Sat the bold second-line values (**6**, **6–7**, **6–8**) appear under weeks 11, 12, 14 and 15.

G = gym (strength or condition) training (this can be used as part of the programme or deleted)   D/O = day off
Numbers 1–9 in the daily workout part of the programme refer to different types of workouts which are explained in the 'Detailed Descriptions' on pages 265–8. Background information is provided in Chapter 19.
* Wed and Fri = Skills
Bold type = workout maintenance (maintain at lowest reps)
Regular type = workout emphasis (work up to max reps)

Strength or condition training:

Tennis/Squash	Hypertrophy	Strength	Power	Peak
Cricket	Hypertrophy	Strength	Power	Peak
Softball	Hypertrophy	Strength	Power	Peak

See pages 323–5 for information.

Read pages 185–8 before starting.

Tennis, Squash, Cricket, Softball — recreational

Weekly layout:

	Mon	Tues	Wed	Thu	Fri	Sat	Sun
Training week	Day off	Speed or practice Gym?	Endurance	Strength endurance or practice Gym?	Day off	Easy or game Gym?	Long strength endurance Gym?
Playing week	Day off	Strength endurance or practice Gym?	Endurance	Speed or practice Gym?	Day off	Game	Long strength endurance

Training volume profile:

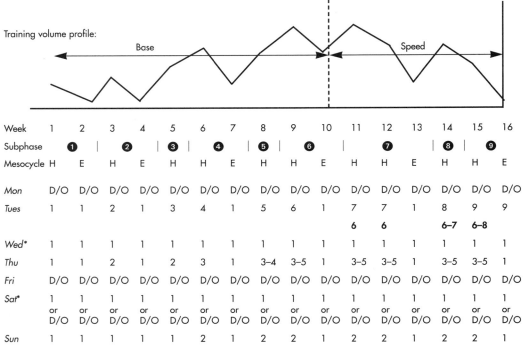

Week	1	2	3	4	5	6	7	8	9	10	11	12	13	14	15	16
Subphase	❶		❷		❸		❹		❺		❻		❼		❽	❾
Mesocycle	H	E	H	E	H	H	E	H	H	E	H	H	E	H	H	E
Mon	D/O	D/O	D/O	D/O	D/O	D/O	D/O	D/O	D/O	D/O	D/O	D/O	D/O	D/O	D/O	D/O
Tues	1	1	2	1	3	4	1	5	6	1	7	7	1	8	9	9
											6	**6**		**6–7**	**6–8**	
*Wed**	1	1	1	1	1	1	1	1	1	1	1	1	1	1	1	1
Thu	1	1	2	1	2	3	1	3–4	3–5	1	3–5	3–5	1	3–5	3–5	1
Fri	D/O	D/O	D/O	D/O	D/O	D/O	D/O	D/O	D/O	D/O	D/O	D/O	D/O	D/O	D/O	D/O
*Sat**	1 or D/O	1 or D/O	1 or D/O	1 or D/O	1 or D/O	1 or D/O	1 or D/O	1 or D/O	1 or D/O	1 or D/O	1 or D/O	1 or D/O	1 or D/O	1 or D/O	1 or D/O	1 or D/O
Sun	1	1	1	1	1	2	1	2	2	1	2	2	1	2	2	1

G = gym (strength training)   D/O = day off

Numbers 1–9 in the daily workout part of the programme refer to different types of workouts which are explained in the 'Detailed Descriptions' on pages 265–8. Background information is provided in Chapter 19.   * Wed and Sat = Skills

Note: gym (strength) training can be used on the days allotted on the weekly layout above, if you like.

Bold type = workout maintenance (maintain at lowest reps)

Regular type = workout emphasis (work up to max reps)

Strength or condition training:

Tennis/Squash				
	HYPERTROPHY	STRENGTH	POWER	PEAK
Cricket	HYPERTROPHY	STRENGTH	POWER	PEAK
Softball	HYPERTROPHY	STRENGTH	POWER	PEAK

See pages 323–5 for information.

Detailed Descriptions

(For information on exercises marked in italics, see 'Extra Information', pages 282–6.)

Sub-phase	General training theme	Softball	Cricket	Tennis	Squash	Heart rates
EASY 1	general fitness, ball-handling skills, technique, teamwork (if required)	*easy running* 20–30 min general softball drills batting/throwing catching/pitching technique and drills (see coach) *bat/pitch/throw/catch* practical technique and accuracy pitcher practise pitching with catcher (easy) in- and outfielders practise catching and throwing 10–15 mins	*easy running* 20–40 min general cricket drills batting/throwing catching/bowling technique and drills (see coach) *bat/bowl/throw/catch* practical technique and accuracy 10–15mins	*easy running* 20–60 min general tennis drills (see coach) technique for playing easy shuttles with racquet 10 min *easy games* practice shots: technique and accuracy	*easy running* 20–60 min general squash drills (see coach) technique for playing easy shuttles with racquet 10 min *easy games* practice shots: technique and accuracy	accuracy (LSD)
LOAD 2	work on strength and basic game skills	*shuttles and hill reps* 20–30 min general softball drills and easy *shuttles* – use diamond (20, 40, 60 and 80 m) mainly shorter (20–40 m) or run (20–30 m) *hill reps* (20–40 m) rec: 1–2 semi: 2–4 comp: 4–6 throw/bat/pitch specific resistance exercises 10–15 mins *bat/pitch/throw/catch* practical technique and accuracy many times (10–15 mins) pitcher practise with catcher in and outfielders practise together	*cross-country rolling hill running* 20–30 min *shuttles* 10–20 min use wicket simulation (11, 22 m and 30 m) mainly shorter rec: 1–4 semi: 2–6 comp: 3–10 *bat/pitch/throw/catch* practical technique and accuracy many times 10–15 mins bowlers, esp.fast bowlers do more reps wicketkeeper does shorter distances with more reps	*cross-country rolling hill running* (easy) 20–40 min shuttles on court use court (5, 10 and 20 m) 10–20 min mainly shorter distance rec: 1–2 min on 30 s off semi: 1–3 min on 30 s off comp: 1–4 min on 30 s off substitute long easy games sometimes practice shots: technique and accuracy many times 10–15 min	*cross-country rolling hill running* (easy) 20 min shuttles on court use court (3, 6 and 8 m) 10–20 min mainly shorter distance rec: 1–2 min on 30 s off semi: 1–3 min on 30 s off comp: 1–4 min on 30 s off substitute long easy games sometimes practice shots: technique and accuracy many times 10–15 min	During: N/A Between: (LSD)

(CONTINUED)

Sub-phase	General training theme	Softball	Cricket	Tennis	Squash	Heart rates
HIGH LOAD 3	work on strength develop new 'plays' practice 'plays' with accuracy	**easy shuttles/run** rec/semi/comp: 15–30 mins (high vol) **stadium/box bounding** (18 m) rec: 2–4 semi: 4–6 comp: 4–10 rest to recovery btwn throw/bat/pitch **specific resistance exercises** (10–15 mins) bat/pitch/throw/catch practical technique and accuracy with power (10–15 mins)	**easy shuttles/run and stadium/box bounding** **easy shuttles/drills** rec/semi/comp: 15–30 mins (high vol) **stadium/box bounding** (11 m) rec: 1–2 semi: 2–4 comp: 2–4 throw/bat/bowl **specific resistance exercises** (10–15 mins) bat/bowl/throw/catch practical technique and accuracy with power (10–15 mins)	**court shuttles/drills and hill bounding** **easy hill reps** **easy court shuttles/drills** rec/semi: 15–30 mins (high vol) **stadium/box bounding** (5–15 m) rec: 1–2 semi: 2–4 comp: 2–6 rest to recovery btwn substitute long easy games sometimes practice shots: technique and accuracy with power (10–15 mins)	**court shuttles/drills and hill bounding** **easy court shuttles/drills** rec/semi: 15–30 mins (high vol) **stadium/box bounding** (5–10 m) rec: 1–2 semi: 2–4 comp: 2–6 rest to recovery btwn substitute long easy games sometimes practice shots: technique and accuracy with power (10–15 mins)	During: N/A Between: .... (LSD)
LOAD/ SPEED 4	begin to 'transfer' strength to speed putting multiple 'plays' together with accuracy	**hill sprints** **hill sprints** (18 m) rec: 1–2 semi: 1–3 comp: 1–4 rest to recovery btwn throw/bat/pitch **specific resistance exercises** (10–15 mins) bat/pitch/throw/catch practical technique and accuracy with power many times (10–15 mins) maintain shuttles/run 15–20 mins (easy)	**hill sprints** **hill sprints** (11 m) rec: 1–3 semi: 2–4 comp: 2–5 rest to recovery btwn throw/bat/bowl **specific resistance exercises** (10–15 mins) bat/bowl/throw/catch practical technique and accuracy with power many times (10–15 mins) maintain shuttles/run 15–20 mins (easy)	**ghosting/court intervals, and hill sprints** **easy court shuttles (ghosting)** rec: 1–2 for 15–20 mins semi: 1–3 for 15–20 mins comp: 1–4 for 15–20 mins **hill sprints** (5–15 m) rec: 2–5 semi: 3–6 comp: 3–7 rest to recovery btwn substitute short fast games sometimes practice shots: technique, accuracy and power many times (10–15 mins)	**ghosting/court intervals, shuttles, and hill sprints** **easy court shuttles (ghosting)** reps = 15–20 mins rec: 1–2 mins on 30s off semi: 1–3 mins on 30s off comp: 1–4 mins on 30s off **hill sprints** (3–10 m) rec: 2–4 semi: 3–5 comp: 3–6 rest to recovery btwn substitute short fast games sometimes practice shots: technique, accuracy and power many times (10–15 mins)	During: N/A Between: .... (LSD)

(CONTINUED)

Sub-phase	General training theme	Sport				Heart rates
		Softball	Cricket	Tennis	Squash	
LOW SPEED 5	the beginings of speed putting multiple 'plays' together with accuracy	**accelerations and fast shuttles/run** accelerations (18 m) rec: 1–2 semi: 2–4 comp: 4–6 rest to recovery btwn practical technique and accuracy with power at speed shuttles as before (10–15 mins) **fast shuttles:** med pace (15–20 mins)	**accelerations and fast shuttles** accelerations (11 m) rec: 4–6 semi: 6–8 comp: 8–12 rest to recovery btwn practical technique and accuracy with power at speed maintain (10–15 mins) **fast shuttles:** med pace (15–20 mins)	**accelerations/shuttles court shuttles/drills** rec/semi: 15–30 mins (high vol) as for subphase 4 **accelerations** (5–20 m) rec: 2–4 semi: 4–6 comp: 4–8 vary recovery btwn technique, accuracy and power in full game simulation (10–15 mins)	**accelerations/shuttles court shuttles/drills** rec/semi: 15–30 mins (high vol) as for subphase 4 **accelerations** (5–10 m) rec: 2–6 semi: 4–8 comp: 6–10 vary recovery btwn technique, accuracy and power in full game simulation (10–15 mins)	During: N/A Between: ....(LSD)
HIGH SPEED 6	high aerobic speed, putting multiple 'plays' together at high speed with accuracy	N/A move to next sub	N/A move to next sub	**AT shuttles** **rec:** 6–8 x 20 s **semi:** 8–10 x 30 s **comp:** 8–16 x 20–40 s	AT shuttles **rec:** 6–8 x 20 s **semi:** 8–10 x 30 s **comp:** 8–16 x 20–40 s	During: ....(AT) Between: ....(LSD)
SPRINT 7	competition simulation with aerobic/anaerobic speed and accuracy	**sprints and general plyometrics** 0–10 m short sprints: 0–10 m long sprints: 36, 54 and 68 m **plyometrics:** rec: 4–6 semi: 6–10 comp: 10–20 rest to recovery btwn **sprints: (short/long)** rec: 2–4 semi: 2–4 comp: 4–6 practical technique and accuracy with power at speed and full game pressure (10–15 mins) maintain shuttles/run: 15–20 mins med pace	**sprints and general plyometrics** 0–10 m short sprints: 0–10 m long sprints: 11, 22 and 33 m **plyometrics:** rec: 4–6 semi: 6–10 comp: 10–20 rest to recovery btwn **sprints: (short/long)** rec: 2–4 semi: 2–4 comp: 4–6 practical technique and accuracy with power at speed and full game pressure (10–15 mins) maintain shuttles/run: 15–20 mins easy pace	**general plyometrics** see pages 316–22 rec: 4–10 semi: 10–15 comp: 10–30 rest to recovery btwn plus short fast games full game pressure (10–30 mins)	**general plyometrics** see pages 316–22 rec: 4–10 semi: 10–15 comp: 10–30 rest to recovery btwn plus short fast games full game pressure (10–30 mins)	During: N/A Between: ....(LSD)

(CONTINUED)

Sub-phase	General training theme	Sport				Heart rates
		Softball	Cricket	Tennis	Squash	
POWER 8	competition simulation with speed and accuracy under full competition pressure	**game-specific plyometrics:** (multi-directional) **plyometrics:** see page 316–22 rec: 4–6 semi: 6–10 comp: 10–20 rest to recovery btwn multi-directional for in and out-fielders game simulation with full speed, pressure and fast reactions (10–15 mins) **maintain shuttles** 15–20 mins fast pace	**game-specific plyometrics:** (multi-directional) **plyometrics:** see page 316–22 rec: 4–6 semi: 6–10 comp: 10–20 rest to recovery btwn game simulation with full speed, pressure and fast reactions (10–15 mins) **maintain shuttles** 15–20 mins fast pace	**game-specific plyometrics:** (multi-directional) **plyometrics:** see page 316–22 rec: 4–10 semi: 10–15 comp: 10–30 rest to recovery btwn **short fast games** break game into 3–6 parts rest to recovery btwn gradually drop reps as get closer to competition game simulation with full speed, pressure and fast reactions	**game-specific plyometrics:** (multi-directional) **plyometrics:** see page 316–22 rec: 4–10 semi: 10–15 comp: 10–30 rest to recovery btwn **short fast games** break game into 3–6 parts rest to recovery btwn gradually drop reps as get closer to competition game simulation with full speed, pressure and fast reactions	During: N/A Between: ....(LSD)
OVER-SPEED 9	competition simulation with speed and accuracy under full competition pressure aiming at fast reactions	N/A stay on previous sub	N/A stay on previous sub	N/A stay on previous sub	N/A stay on previous sub	During: N/A Between: ....(LSD)

Key: rec = recreational (club); semi = semi competitive (serious club — provincial); comp = competitive (provincial — international)

Note: Start at the bottom of the rep ranges in each subphase and gradually move the number of reps or duration as you progress through the subphase and as you feel fitter specific to that form of training. As you move from one subphase to the next maintain a little of all previously trained subphases to hold your form. This is already written into your programme.

Semi-competitive and competitive

Weekly layout:

	Mon	Tues	Wed	Thu	Fri	Sat	Sun
Training week	Day off	Speed or practice	Endurance	Strength endurance or practice	Easy	Speed or game	Long strength endurance
Playing week	Day off	Strength endurance or practice	Endurance	Speed or practice	Easy	Game	Long strength endurance

Training volume profile:

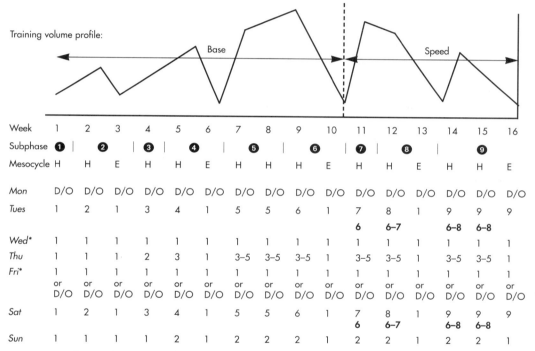

Week	1	2	3	4	5	6	7	8	9	10	11	12	13	14	15	16
Subphase	❶		❷		❸		❹		❺		❻		❼		❽		❾
Mesocycle	H	H	E	H	H	E	H	H	H	E	H	H	E	H	H	E
Mon	D/O	D/O	D/O	D/O	D/O	D/O	D/O	D/O	D/O	D/O	D/O	D/O	D/O	D/O	D/O	D/O
Tues	1	2	1	3	4	1	5	5	6	1	7 **6**	8 **6–7**	1	9 **6–8**	9 **6–8**	9
Wed*	1	1	1	1	1	1	1	1	1	1	1	1	1	1	1	1
Thu	1	1	1	2	3	1	3–5	3–5	3–5	1	3–5	3–5	1	3–5	3–5	1
Fri*	1 or D/O	1 or D/O	1 or D/O	1 or D/O	1 or D/O	1 or D/O	1 or D/O	1 or D/O	1 or D/O	1 or D/O	1 or D/O	1 or D/O	1 or D/O	1 or D/O	1 or D/O	1 or D/O
Sat	1	2	1	3	4	1	5	5	6	1	7 **6**	8 **6–7**	1	9 **6–8**	9 **6–8**	9
Sun	1	1	1	1	2	1	2	2	2	1	2	2	1	2	2	1

G = gym (strength or condition) training (this can be used as part of the programme or deleted)   D/O = day off
Numbers 1–9 in the daily workout part of the programme refer to different types of workouts which are explained in the 'Detailed Descriptions' on pages 271–4. Background information is provided in Chapter 19.
* Wed and Fri = Running technique and ball handling drills
Bold type = workout maintenance (maintain at lowest reps)
Regular type = workout emphasis (work up to max reps)

Strength or condition training:

Volleyball	HYPERTROPHY	STRENGTH	POWER	PEAK
Martial arts	HYPERTROPHY	STRENGTH	POWER	PEAK
Motor racing	MUSCLE ENDURANCE			
Sail board	HYPERTROPHY	STRENGTH	POWER/MUSCLE ENDURANCE	

See pages 323–5 for information.

Read pages 185–8 before starting.

Volleyball, Martial arts, Motor racing, Sail boarding — recreational

Weekly layout:

	Mon	Tues	Wed	Thu	Fri	Sat	Sun
Training week	Day off	Speed or practice Gym?	Endurance	Strength endurance or practice Gym?	Day off	Easy or game Gym?	Long strength endurance Gym?
Playing week	Day off	Strength endurance or practice Gym?	Endurance	Speed or practice Gym?	Day off	Game	Long strength endurance

Training volume profile:

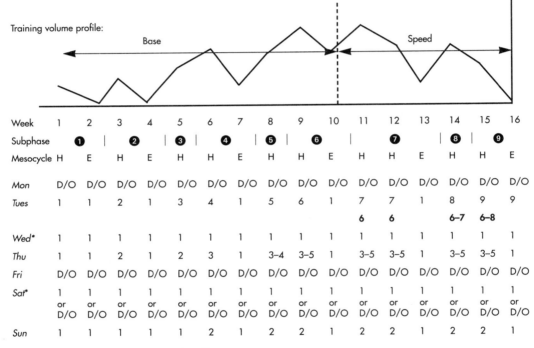

Week	1	2	3	4	5	6	7	8	9	10	11	12	13	14	15	16
Subphase	❶		❷		❸		❹		❺		❻		❼		❽	❾
Mesocycle	H	E	H	E	H	H	E	H	H	E	H	H	E	H	H	E
Mon	D/O	D/O	D/O	D/O	D/O	D/O	D/O	D/O	D/O	D/O	D/O	D/O	D/O	D/O	D/O	D/O
Tues	1	1	2	1	3	4	1	5	6	1	7	7	1	8	9	9
											6	6		6–7	6–8	
Wed*	1	1	1	1	1	1	1	1	1	1	1	1	1	1	1	1
Thu	1	1	2	1	2	3	1	3–4	3–5	1	3–5	3–5	1	3–5	3–5	1
Fri	D/O	D/O	D/O	D/O	D/O	D/O	D/O	D/O	D/O	D/O	D/O	D/O	D/O	D/O	D/O	D/O
Sat*	1 or D/O	1 or D/O	1 or D/O	1 or D/O	1 or D/O	1 or D/O	1 or D/O	1 or D/O	1 or D/O	1 or D/O	1 or D/O	1 or D/O	1 or D/O	1 or D/O	1 or D/O	1 or D/O
Sun	1	1	1	1	1	2	1	2	2	1	2	2	1	2	2	1

G = gym (strength training)   D/O = day off
Numbers 1–9 in the daily workout part of the programme refer to different types of workouts which are explained in the 'Detailed Descriptions' on pages 271–4. Background information is provided in Chapter 19.
* Wed and Sat = Skills   Note: gym (strength) training can be used on the days allotted on the weekly layout above, if you like.
Bold type = workout maintenance (maintain at lowest reps)
Regular type = workout emphasis (work up to max reps)

Strength or conditioning training:

Volleyball	HYPERTROPHY	STRENGTH	POWER	PEAK
Martial arts	HYPERTROPHY	STRENGTH	POWER	PEAK
Motor racing	MUSCLE ENDURANCE			
Sail boarding	HYPERTROPHY	STRENGTH	POWER/MUSCLE ENDURANCE	

See pages 323–5 for information.
Read pages 185–8 before starting.

DETAILED DESCRIPTIONS

(For information on exercises marked in italics, see 'Extra Information', pages 282–6.)

Sub-phase	Training theme	Sport				Heart rates
		Volleyball	Martial arts (point sparring competition)	Motor racing	Sail boarding	
EASY 1	general fitness, ball handling	*easy running* 20–30 mins basic drills ball-handling drills (see coach) work on technique	*easy running or alternate exercise* 30–40 mins **aims:** basic fitness flexibility technique strength problem solving develop new combinations **aim:** fitness	*easy fitness* (run/cycle/gym/swim,) 20–40 mins see general fitness programmes driving skills concentrate on technique and sailing skills	*easy fitness* (run/cycle/gym/swim) 20–40 mins see general fitness programmes *easy general sailing* (1–2 hrs)	.... (LSD)
LOAD 2	work on strength and basic game skills	*hill running* 20–30 mins jumping exercises with resistance/strength training (10–15 mins) combine basic techniques into 'plays' maintain accuracy	*cross-country rolling hill running* 20–60 mins begin to refine new combinations **aim:** strength	*easy fitness* 30–60 mins driving skill	*easy fitness* 30–60 mins easy general sailing (1–2 hrs)	During: N/A Between: .... (LSD)
HIGH LOAD 3	work on strength develop new 'moves' practice 'moves' with accuracy	basic *easy shuttles and stadium/box jumps* high volume to improve endurance (10–20 mins) *stadium/box bounds* high resistance (weighted) rec: 20–40 semi: 40–60 comp: 60–80 rest to recovery bhwn long easy games (can be substituted sometimes)	*high aerobic martial arts/specific circuits* (pg. 274) (high volume, high resistance) either long ints or bout length ints e.g .6–12 x 3 mins or 10–36 x 1 min move to multiple combinations **aim:** strength endurance	N/A stay on previous sub high volume	*easy sailing* (1–2 hrs) Between: *endurance pumping:* 2–5 mins rec: 1–2 semi: 2–3 comp: 2–4	During: N/A .... (LSD)

(CONTINUED)

271

		Sport				
Sub-phase	Training theme	Volleyball	Martial arts (point sparring competition)	Motor racing	Sail boarding	Heart rates
LOAD/ SPEED 4	begin to 'transfer' strength to speed putting multiple 'plays' together with accuracy	**basic easy shuttles and stadium/box jumps** high volume to improve endurance **stadium/box bounds** rec: 20–40 semi: 40–60 comp: 60–80 rest to recovery btwn **short fast 'plays'** 20–30 mins (with 20–30 'plays' in that time)	**muscle endurance high-intensity single technique exercises** to improve muscle endurance specific to the action: e.g 30 s front kick left leg 30 s front kick right leg 30 s roundhouse kick (left then right leg) 20–30 mins develop competition combinations and tactics accuracy and distancing	**easy fitness with artificial heat acclimatisation** (wear hat, gloves, socks, tracksuit, sweat shirt, etc.) to simulate heat inside vehicle watch fluids can include exercise in helmet and full racing suit	**sailing 1–2 hrs with sailing-specific strength/endurance pumping:** strength (high resistance) 5–10 pumps rec: 1–2 semi: 2–3 comp: 4–8 rest to recovery bwn	During: N/A Between: ....(LSD)
LOW SPEED 5	the beginnings of speed putting multiple 'plays' together with speed and accuracy	**competition simulation** (high volume)	**sparring** (high volume) internalise skills and combinations (30–40 mins) make sparring bout durations equal to competition bouts improve timing **aim:** speed and speed endurance spar within playing area to develop use of court/mat/ring for tactics work on distancing	N/A stay on previous sub	N/A stay on previous sub	During: N/A Between: ....(LSD)
		N/A move to next sub				
HIGH SPEED 6	high aerobic speed, putting multiple 'plays' together at high speed with accuracy	N/A move to next sub	**AT intervals** sparring for long intervals 3–4 mins to improve high aerobic ability (10–20 mins) rest to recovery btwn analyse combinations develop speed and accuracy at speed can use specific circuit (pg. 274)	**easy fitness with artificial heat acclimatisation and racing** if you can set up a computer video racing game with steering wheel, etc., at several points in the workout you have to race 1–2 laps as fast as you can go while hot and	**sailing 1–2 hrs with sailing-specific muscle endurance pumping:** high vol, medium resistance high speed 1–2 mins rec: 1–2 semi: 1–3 comp: 1–6 rest to recovery btwn and	During: ....(AT) - only martial arts Between: ....(LSD) (CONTINUED)

| | | | Sport | | | |
Sub-phase	Training theme	Volleyball	Martial arts (point sparring competition)	Motor racing	Sail boarding	Heart rates
SPRINT 7	competition simulation with aerobic/ anaerobic speed and accuracy	**general plyometrics** see pages 316–22 0–10 m rec: 4–6 semi: 6–10 comp: 10–20 rest to recovery btwn **competition simulation shuttles** under game pressure, or games (more than 20 mins)	**competition simulation** e.g. 4–6 x 3 min bouts **and general plyometrics** see pages 316–22 rec: 4–6 semi: 6–10 comp: 10–20 rest to recovery btwn **full court simulation and pressure work** (defence only or sparring with back against wall)	N/A stay on previous sub	**sailing 1–2 hrs with sailing-specific power/speed pumping:** low volume, med resistance high speed 5–10 pumps rec: 1–2 semi: 1–4 comp: 1–10 rest to recovery btwn	During: N/A Between: .... (LSD)
POWER 8	competition simulation with speed and accuracy under full competition pressure	**game-specific plyometrics** (multi-directional) see pages 316–22 rec: 4–6 semi: 6–10 comp: 10–20 **competition simulation** shuttles and game pressure with fast reactions, or games (more than 20 min)	**specific plyometrics:** (multi-directional) see pages 316–22 rec: 4–6 semi: 6–10 comp: 10–20 rest to recovery btwn short/sharp competition simulation and reaction times may break a bout into 6 x 30 s blocks or 3 x 1 min blocks **aim:** speed and competition pressure	**easy fitness with artificial heat acclimatisation** racing, and internalising try to create a distraction during 'video races' — e.g. loud music, visual distraction or counting backwards from 100; this will help internalise or make your driving 'more automatic' giving more thinking ability to decision-making and problem-solving while driving initially the distractions will slow you down but later you will improve as your responses become more automatic	**full competition simulation** race duration can break the race up into 4–6 blocks rest to recovery btwn	During: N/A Between: .... (LSD)

(CONTINUED)

| Sub-phase | Training theme | Sport | | | | Heart rates |
		Volleyball	Martial arts (point sparring competition)	Motor racing	Sail boarding	
OVER-SPEED 9	competition simulation with speed and accuracy under full competition pressure aiming at fast reactions	N/A stay on previous sub	N/A stay on previous sub	**easy fitness with artificial heat acclimatisation** racing, internalising and race pressures	**full competition simulation** short/sharp bursts of racing at full speed full competition pressure	During: N/A Between: .... (LSD)

Key: rec = recreational (club); semi = semi competitive (serious club — provincial); comp = competitive (provincial — international)

Note: Start at the bottom of the rep ranges in each subphase and gradually move the number of reps or duration as you progress through the subphase and as you feel fitter specific to that form of training. As you move from one subphase to the next maintain a little of all previously trained subphases to hold your form. This is already written into your programme.

Martial Arts Circuit (specific circuit)

Front kick   10 each leg
Block   20 each leg
Roundhouse kick   10 each leg
Punch   20 each arm
Back kick   10 each leg
Block   20 each arm
Side kick   10 each leg
Punch   20 each arm

Muscle endurance circuit is as above except:
1. Leg exercises are all grouped together separately from arm exercises.
2. 15–30 secs continuous for each exercise at fast pace.

Cycle

Weekly layout:

Mon	Tues	Wed	Thu	Fri	Sat	Sun
Day off	Bike	Day off	Bike	Day off	Bike	Bike

Training volume profile:

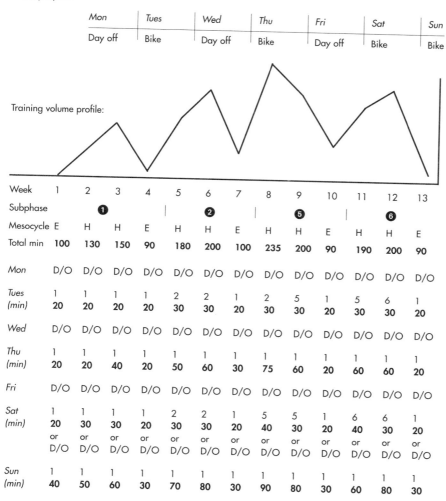

Week	1	2	3	4	5	6	7	8	9	10	11	12	13
Subphase		❶				❷			❺			❻	
Mesocycle	E	H	H	E	H	H	E	H	H	E	H	H	E
Total min	100	130	150	90	180	200	100	235	200	90	190	200	90
Mon	D/O	D/O	D/O	D/O	D/O	D/O	D/O	D/O	D/O	D/O	D/O	D/O	D/O
Tues (min)	1 20	1 20	1 20	1 20	2 30	2 30	1 20	2 30	5 30	1 20	5 30	6 30	1 20
Wed	D/O	D/O	D/O	D/O	D/O	D/O	D/O	D/O	D/O	D/O	D/O	D/O	D/O
Thu (min)	1 20	1 20	1 40	1 20	1 50	1 60	1 30	1 75	1 60	1 20	1 60	1 60	1 20
Fri	D/O	D/O	D/O	D/O	D/O	D/O	D/O	D/O	D/O	D/O	D/O	D/O	D/O
Sat (min)	1 20 or D/O	1 30 or D/O	1 30 or D/O	1 20 or D/O	2 30 or D/O	2 30 or D/O	1 20 or D/O	5 40 or D/O	5 30 or D/O	1 20 or D/O	6 40 or D/O	6 30 or D/O	1 20 or D/O
Sun (min)	1 40	1 50	1 60	1 30	1 70	1 80	1 30	1 90	1 80	1 30	1 60	1 80	1 30

D/O = day off
Numbers 1–6 refer to different types of workouts which are explained in the 'Detailed Descriptions' on pages 278–9.

Read pages 185–8 before starting.

General fitness — Walk/run/gym

Weekly layout:

Mon	Tues	Wed	Thu	Fri	Sat	Sun
Day off	W/R/G	Day off	W/R/G	Day off	W/R/G	W/R/G

Training volume profile:

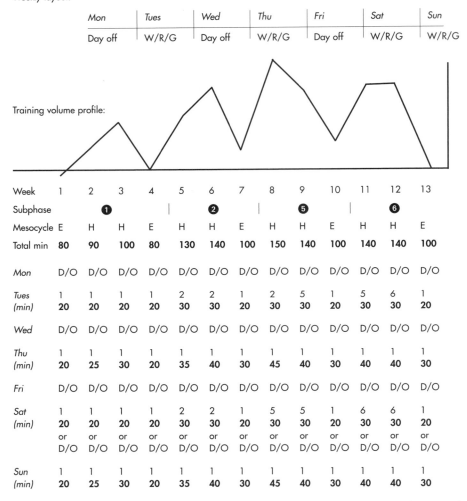

Week	1	2	3	4	5	6	7	8	9	10	11	12	13
Subphase			❶			❷			❺			❻	
Mesocycle	E	H	H	E	H	H	E	H	H	E	H	H	E
Total min	80	90	100	80	130	140	100	150	140	100	140	140	100
Mon	D/O	D/O	D/O	D/O	D/O	D/O	D/O	D/O	D/O	D/O	D/O	D/O	D/O
Tues (min)	1 / 20	1 / 20	1 / 20	1 / 20	2 / 30	2 / 30	1 / 20	2 / 30	5 / 30	1 / 20	5 / 30	6 / 30	1 / 20
Wed	D/O	D/O	D/O	D/O	D/O	D/O	D/O	D/O	D/O	D/O	D/O	D/O	D/O
Thu (min)	1 / 20	1 / 25	1 / 30	1 / 20	1 / 35	1 / 40	1 / 30	1 / 45	1 / 40	1 / 30	1 / 40	1 / 40	1 / 30
Fri	D/O	D/O	D/O	D/O	D/O	D/O	D/O	D/O	D/O	D/O	D/O	D/O	D/O
Sat (min) or D/O	1 / 20	1 / 20	1 / 20	1 / 20	2 / 30	2 / 30	1 / 20	5 / 30	5 / 30	1 / 20	6 / 30	6 / 30	1 / 20
	or D/O	or D/O	or D/O	or D/O	or D/O	or D/O	or D/O	or D/O	or D/O	or D/O	or D/O	or D/O	or D/O
Sun (min)	1 / 20	1 / 25	1 / 30	1 / 20	1 / 35	1 / 40	1 / 30	1 / 45	1 / 40	1 / 30	1 / 40	1 / 40	1 / 30

Note: If gym, see the exercise programmes on pages 280 and 281 and incorporate a programme of your own design or the programme you are currently using.

D/O = day off

Numbers 1–6 refer to different types of workouts which are explained in the 'Detailed Descriptions' on pages 278–9.

Read pages 185–8 before starting.

General fitness — Swim

Weekly layout:

Mon	Tues	Wed	Thu	Fri	Sat	Sun
Day off	Swim	Day off	Swim	Day off	Swim	Swim

Training volume profile:

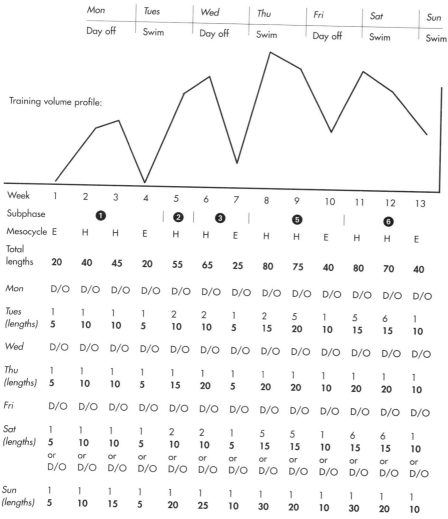

Week	1	2	3	4	5	6	7	8	9	10	11	12	13
Subphase		❶			❷	❸			❺			❻	
Mesocycle	E	H	H	E	H	H	E	H	H	E	H	H	E
Total lengths	20	40	45	20	55	65	25	80	75	40	80	70	40
Mon	D/O	D/O	D/O	D/O	D/O	D/O	D/O	D/O	D/O	D/O	D/O	D/O	D/O
Tues (lengths)	1 5	1 10	1 10	1 5	2 10	2 10	1 5	2 15	5 20	1 10	5 15	6 15	1 10
Wed	D/O	D/O	D/O	D/O	D/O	D/O	D/O	D/O	D/O	D/O	D/O	D/O	D/O
Thu (lengths)	1 5	1 10	1 10	1 5	1 15	1 20	1 5	1 20	1 20	1 10	1 20	1 20	1 10
Fri	D/O	D/O	D/O	D/O	D/O	D/O	D/O	D/O	D/O	D/O	D/O	D/O	D/O
Sat (lengths)	1 5 or D/O	1 10 or D/O	1 10 or D/O	1 5 or D/O	2 10 or D/O	2 10 or D/O	1 5 or D/O	5 15 or D/O	5 15 or D/O	1 10 or D/O	6 15 or D/O	6 15 or D/O	1 10 or D/O
Sun (lengths)	1 5	1 10	1 15	1 5	1 20	1 25	1 10	1 30	1 20	1 10	1 30	1 20	1 10

D/O = day off

Numbers 1–6 refer to different types of workouts which are explained in the 'Detailed Descriptions' on pages 278–9.

Read pages 185–8 before starting.

DETAILED DESCRIPTIONS

(For information on exercises marked in italics, see 'Extra Information', pages 282–6.)

Sub-phase	General training theme	Walk/Run	Sport — Swim	Sport — Cycle	Sport — Gym	Heart rates
EASY 1	general fitness	**easy walk/run** easy conversation pace	**easy swim** easy conversation pace	**easy cycle** easy conversation pace	**easy** easy conversation pace	...............(LSD)
LOAD 2	work on strength and basic endurance	**hill walk/run** easy conversation pace	**pull buoys** only if experienced, otherwise stay on previous sub	**hills (short)** easy conversation pace	move weights up 10%	During: N/A Between: ....(LSD)
HIGH LOAD 3	work on strength endurance development	N/A	**paddles** only if experienced, otherwise stay on previous sub	N/A	N/A	During: N/A Between: ....(LSD)
LOAD/ SPEED 4	N/A	N/A stay on previous sub	N/A stay on previous sub	N/A stay on previous sub	N/A stay on previous sub	
LOW SPEED 5	the beginings of speed high aerobic speed and cardiovascular fitness	**brisk walking or running slightly faster than easy** you should feel strong, comfortable, fast and in control; this is a pace you should be able to sustain for many hours intervals of 1–3 mins: beg: 1–2 int: 2–4 exp: 4–6	**intervals slightly faster than easy** you should feel strong, comfortable, fast and in control; this is a pace you should be able to sustain for many hours intervals of 1–3 min: beg: 1–2 lengths int: 2–4 lengths exp: 4–6 lengths	**intervals slightly faster than easy** you should feel strong, comfortable, fast and in control; this is a pace you should be able to sustain for many hours intervals of 1–3 min: beg: 2–4 int: 4–6 exp: 4–8	**intervals slightly faster than easy** you should feel strong, comfortable, fast and in control; this is a pace you should be able to sustain for many hours intervals of 1–3 min: beg: 2–4 int: 4–6 exp: 4–8	During: ....(UT) Between: ....(LSD) .... (CONTINUED)

Sub-phase	General training theme	Sport				Heart rates
		Walk/Run	Swim	Cycle	Gym	
HIGH SPEED 6	high aerobic speed and cardiovascular fitness	**very brisk walking or running** this is a pace you should be able to sustain for 1 hour, no harder! intervals of 1–3 mins: beg: 1–2 int: 2–4 exp: 4–6	**intervals at 80% effort, no harder!** this is a pace you should be able to sustain for 1 hour, no harder! intervals of: beg: 1–2 lengths int: 2–4 lengths exp: 4–6 lengths	**intervals at 80% effort, no harder!** this is a pace you should be able to sustain for 1 hour, no harder! intervals of 1–3 mins: beg: 2–4 int: 4–6 exp: 4–8	**intervals at 80% effort, no harder!** this is a pace you should be able to sustain for 1 hour, no harder! intervals of 1–3 mins: beg: 2–4 int: 4–6 exp: 4–8	During: .... (AT) Between: .... (LSD)
SPRINT 7	N/A	N/A	N/A	N/A	N/A	
POWER 8	N/A	N/A	N/A	N/A	N/A	
OVER-SPEED 9	N/A	N/A	N/A	N/A	N/A	

Key: beg = beginner (just started); int = intermediate (been exercising for six months or more); exp = experienced (been exercising for twelve months or more)

Note: Start at the bottom of the rep ranges in each subphase and gradually move the number of reps or duration as you progress through the subphase and as you feel fitter specific to that form of training. As you move from one subphase to the next maintain a little of all previously trained subphases to hold your form. This is already written into your programme.

EXERCISE PROGRAMME

Programme aim: Cardiovascular fitness / fat loss

Number of circuits: 1

Special considerations: Be careful if you have back/neck or knee trouble – consult your doctor

Warm-up   Heart rate: 60–75% HR^{max}

Exercises	Time	Sets	Reps	Rest	
Bike	5 mins				

Stretch (see stretching sheet, page 189)

Main programme   Heart rate: 75–85% HR^{max} for fitness (UT)
                            60–75% HR^{max} for fat loss (LSD)

Exercises	Time	Sets	Reps	Rest	Weights (if appropriate)
Bike	15–20 mins	N/A	N/A	N/A	
Stepper	5–15 mins	N/A	N/A	N/A	
Treadmill (walk or run)	5–15 mins	N/A	N/A	N/A	
Rower	5–10 mins	N/A	N/A	N/A	

Warm-down   Heart rate: 75–50% HR^{max} (LSD)

Bike	10 mins				

Stretch (see stretching sheet, page 189)

Note: If you feel lightheaded or do not feel well during your workout stop immediately and notify your doctor. Do not force yourself to complete the workout. Start slowly and gradually and work towards your targets (circuits, heart rate).
Consult a gym instructor regarding the exercises and appropriate technique.

EXERCISE PROGRAMME

Programme aim: Cardiovascular fitness / fat loss and tone

Number of circuits: 2–3

Special considerations: Be careful if you have back/neck or knee trouble –
consult your doctor

Warm-up

Heart rate: 60–75% HR^{max} (LSD)

Exercises	Time	Sets	Reps	Rest	
Bike	5-10 mins				
Arm circles	20				
Gentle trunk twists	20				

Stretch (see stretching sheet, page 189)

Main programme

Heart rate: 75–85% HR^{max} for fitness/tone (UT)

60–75% HR^{max} for fat loss/tone (LSD)

Exercises	Time	Sets	Reps	Rest	Weights (if appropriate)
Step ups	N/A	N/A	15 ea	N/A	
Sit ups	N/A	N/A	20	N/A	
Treadmill	N/A	N/A	1 min	N/A	
Bench press	N/A	N/A	20	N/A	
Bike	N/A	N/A	1 min	N/A	
Lat pulldown	N/A	N/A	20	N/A	
Jog on spot	N/A	N/A	30 ea	N/A	
Sit ups	N/A	N/A	10	N/A	

DO AS A FAST CONTINUOUS WORKOUT (move quickly between exercises)

Warm-down

Heart rate: 75–50% HR^{max} (LSD)

Bike	10 mins				

Stretch (see stretching sheet, page 189)

Note: If you feel lightheaded or do not feel well during your workout stop immediately
and notify your doctor. Do not force yourself to complete the workout. Start slowly and
gradually and work towards your targets (circuits, heart rate).
Consult a gym instructor regarding the exercises and appropriate technique.

Extra Information: Detailed descriptions of training

ACCELERATIONS
Accelerations are, as they state, easy accelerations up to top speed then 'pulling out'. This is used to introduce the athletes/players body to speed without being too physically demanding (in preparation for the upcoming, more physically demanding sprints). The aim is to start slow and gently accelerate up to top speed (40–80% effort, not 100%, and vary recovery between repetitions).

ARTIFICIAL HEAT ACCLIMATISATION
Using extra clothing to induce adaption to heat artificially. (See pages 62–7 for information on heat.)

AT SHUTTLES/INTERVALS (ANAEROBIC THRESHOLD)
Doing shuttles or intervals at 20 min–1 hour maximum race pace or playing pace. No faster. These intervals are designed to simulate maximum playing pace (primarily midfield or loose forward pace). The intervals are long (usually 150–200 m) and are broken into shorter blocks of effort with very short rests or activities (such as tackling, kicking or passing) in-between. Simulate game conditions: distances run, changes in pace and direction, going to ground and getting up, tackling, passing and receiving the ball, kicking, etc. Cones are often used to mark out the course of the shuttle or interval.

COMPETITION SIMULATION (AND SIMULATION SHUTTLES)
Competition simualtion is as it states, simulation of what is going to happen in competition so that the athlete/player physically and mentally begins to get fully prepared for the rigours of competition. The drills must very closely simulate the competition environment. Ghosting means simulation play with a racquet in hand, playing shots without a ball.

COURT SHUTTLES/DRILLS
Court shuttles are running exercises that involve running very short distances, stopping or changing direction and running again within the confines of the playing situation — the court. This is used to simulate the running activities in a game situation. (See also Shuttles.)

EASY (ALL SPORTS)
Easy exercise is comfortable exercise that is conducted at easy conversation pace continuously. This means that you can talk non-stop during exercise without puffing. This also applies to easy fitness, and easy non-specific exercise training.

EASY TEMPO
See Up-tempo.

EXTENSIVE SPRINTS (LONG SPRINTS)
Long sprints (100% effort) are top speed and speed endurance sprints. They are designed to improve sprinting ability over longer distances. These should replicate instances when these sprints are used in a game, e.g. changes in direction with ball, bat, racquet or hockey stick in hand, or dribbling the ball combined with passing and receiving. Vary recovery between repetitions. Don't get 'bogged down' or 'buried' by it, pull out of the effort before this happens.
aim: improve extended sprint speed

FARTLEK
Rather a rude sounding word that means 'speedplay' in Swedish. This involves accelerations up to race pace or competition playing pace and quickly dropping back down before you get tired. It allows easy conditioning to speed without being too tiring. (See also Shuttles, easy.)

FAST SHUTTLES

Fast shuttles are sport-specific running exercises that involve moving very short distances, stopping or changing direction and running again. This is used to simulate the running activities in a game situation. Fast shuttles are used to improve speed and bring the athlete/player up to competition speed. Simulate game conditions, distances run, changes of pace and direction, going to ground and getting up, passing and receiving the ball, etc. Cones are often used to mark out the course of the shuttles. Vary recovery between repetitions. (See also Shuttles).

FLAT LONG STRIDE

During your run at frequent intervals pick up the tempo slightly and extend your stride length out to a racing stride length for 100–200 m. Pull out before you get 'bogged' down (ie. stride length or rate drops or you start to puff). This is used to strengthen the full range of motion in your racing stride length.
speed: 3.5–5 min/km

GOAL MOUTH DRILLS

Goal mouth drills are drills conducted at an easy pace simulating game specific movements that would take place in a game. It is a type of shuttle where you move around the goal mouth at an easy pace while kicking, catching, passing, going to ground to save or getting back up. You or your coach should design a routine 5–15 min long.

GHOSTING

Simulation of play (see Court shuttles/drills and Competition simulation).

HIGH AEROBIC MARTIAL ARTS CIRCUITS

A series of martial arts techniques placed together in a sequence (like a 'kata') to make the athlete work hard cardiovascularly (makes them puff). This is to increase high aerobic fitness. (See page 274 for an example.)

HIGH INTENSITY SINGLE TECHNIQUE EXERCISES

This is used to build muscular endurance in a specicific muscle group in a specific action. A martial artist may work on one movement (e.g. front kick) repeating the action over and over for an extended time (e.g. 30 secs) to build endurance and move onto doing the same thing in another action. This is all within the confines of correct technique and accuracy. (See page 274 for an example.)

HILL BOUNDING

This is a combination strength/power exercise designed to develop the beginings of explosiveness. The player begins on the flat at the bottom of a hill of moderate gradient. (If it's too steep it will give you lower calf trouble). Then using long strides that player bounds up the hill driving as hard as they can off each foot in an explosive manner. In sprint sports the player aims to go as far forward and as high as possible. In a jumping sport the player trys to go as high as possible. As soon as you feel 'bogged' down as you run up the hill (stride length or stride rate drops or you start to puff) pull out and jog back down to the bottom of the hill and jog/rest to recovery before the next one. Repeat.
Full muscular effort. Gradient should be no steeper than 5–10%: it should not make you puff too much. Make sure that the terrain is sure underfoot to avoid accidents.

HILLS LONG STRIDE

Jog along the flat towards a hill and with 2–5 m to go, extend your stride out and raise the tempo of your running so that you stride out up the hill using your racing stride length to strengthen the full length of your stride. As soon as you feel 'bogged' down as you run up the hill (stride length or stride rate drops or you start to puff) pull out and jog back down to the bottom of the hill and jog/rest to recovery before the next one. Repeat.
speed: 4–7 min/km
distance: as stated in programme
gradient: shallow/moderate — the hill cannot be so steep that you cannot use a stride and action that replicates a racing running action on the flat (usually only 3–7% gradient).

HILL REPS

Hill reps are easy jogging efforts up a hill of moderate gradient to increase strength endurance.

HILL RUNNING (AND CROSS-COUNTRY ROLLING HILL RUNNING)

Running: Easy jogging up hills. Number and length of hills is important NOT how hard you do them so the aim is easy climbing. Cross-country is better as it trains the proprioception (balance) as well. Rolling hills on the grass is also good because the ascents and descents are shorter and less damaging on the muscles as is the soft ground (golf courses are good).
aim: prep for strength endurance training.
speed: 6–9 min/km on hills

HILL SPRINTS

Hill sprints are usually an extension of hills long stride and hills bounding. Hills long stride improves the strength through the full range of the sprinting motion while hill sprints makes this more specific by adding speed to the resistance exercise. The player begins on flat ground at the bottom of the hill and sprints up the hill at full speed. As soon as you feel 'bogged' down as you run up the hill (stride length or stride rate drops or you start to puff) pull out and jog back down to the bottom of the hill and jog/rest to recovery before the next one. Repeat.
Make sure that the terrain is sure under foot to avoid accidents.
Use a hill of moderate gradient (3–7%; if it's too steep it will give you lower calf trouble).
There are two way to do this:
1. Start at the bottom of the hill and accelerate up (good for acceleration).
2. Start on the flat and sprint 5–10 m on the flat before you sprint up the hill.
It is easy to overdo this — keep the sprint distances short (good for top speed).

HILL/STADIUM TEMPO REPS

Easy acceleration up stadium steps or a hill or moderate to shallow gradient (5–7%). The aim is to accelerate up to a tempo (not sprinting but not cruising) pace against a resistance to help build up strength using a 'fast break' stride length.

INTENSIVE SPRINTS (SHORT SPRINTS)

Short sprints (100% effort) are designed to improve acceleration and top speed over shorter distances. Don't get 'bogged down' or 'buried' by it, pull out of the effort before this happens.

JUMPING EXERCISES WITH RESISTANCE/STRENGTH TRAINING

This is used to increase specific jumping strength. The player will conduct maximal effort jumps with weights to create a heavier weight when jumping. This induces strength gains. Note that the landing area in this form of training must be very good/soft as the athelete could become injured.

LONG SPRINTS

See extensive sprints.

OVERSPEED SPRINTS

Overspeed sprints involves increasing muscular contraction speed. It provides slightly over paced movements of the limbs to futher increase speed. In running this may involve running down a very slight gradient (<3%). Any more and you are in danger of shin splints or hamstring pulls. So the player runs down the slight grade for 5–10 m (just enough to get up to full speed) and then along the flat for 5–20 m at 'overspeed' (faster than they could run if they started on the flat). Effort is 100%, rest to recovery between repetitions.

PADDLES

Paddles are large flat plastic boards that are put on each hand to decrease 'slippage' of the hand through the water increasing the resistance on the swimmers arms. Be careful when using paddles as they can easily create shoulder injuries if you are not used to them. Only wear them for short periods of time (100–400 m).

PLYOMETRICS (GENERAL AND GAME-SPECIFIC)

Plyometics are known as stretch-loaded exercises. This means that the exercise utilises the elasticity of the muscle to provide extra explosiveness. The player jumps off a box ($1/2$ leg length high) or bounds and as they land the knee bends stretching the quadricep muscle so that as it contracts at maximum contraction speed giving 100% effort, the recoil of the elongated quad muscle provides an extra force that increases the muscle contraction above 100% further inducing power. (See pages 316–22 for examples.)

Plyometics can occur in 2 ways :

1. General plyometircs — non-specific bounding and jumping exercises.
2. Game-specific exercises — bounding and jumping exercises that closely simulate game movements. Game-specific plyometrics must have a conversion or transfer exercise (i.e. do a plyometric exerecise immediately followed by an exercise that makes up part of the competition).

PROPRIOCEPTION TRAINING

Training used to speed up neural transmission of messages, on change in terrain (e.g. skiing) or angle of the board in relation to rider (e.g. surfing), to the brain and eliciting of response and reaction. (See page 262 for exercises.) This improves balance greatly.

PULL BUOYS

Pull buoys are floats that you put between your legs to keep your feet buoyant but stopping you using your legs which creates more drag so that the swimmer will have to use more upper body effort. This is a strength endurance exercise.

PUMPING

Pumping involves using a pumping action with your arms to generate a fan effect with a sailboard sail. Used in light wind conditions or to get up to speed having tacked or rounded a mark.

Endurance — improves the ability to pump for a long time, as might be experieneced in light winds — this involves pumping for 2 + mins.

Muscle endurance — is used to improve the ability to pump at high speed for an extended period of time, 1–2 mins.

Strength endurance — high resistance to improve strength in pumping.

Power — is used to produce near maximal pumping ability for a very short time. This may be used rounding a mark to get up to speed quickly, 5–10 pumps.

SHORT SPRINTS

See intensive sprints.

SHUTTLES (EASY)

Easy shuttles are running exercises that involve running very short distances, stopping or changing direction and running again. This is used to simulate the running activities in a game situation (e.g. kicking, passing, receiving, tackling, going to ground and getting up). Cones are often used to mark out a course or routine.

SPRINT DRILLS (RUNNING)

See page 316.

SPARRING

Competition simulation with two competitors working with each other through set techniques, attack and defence exercises, and free sparring. Progression for sparring: easy/slow, short bursts of pace, pressure, and full-pace competition simulation.

STADIUM/BOX BOUNDING AND JUMPS

This is the same as hill bounding although a box ($1/2$–$2/3$ leg length) or stadium steps can be used. Jumps are used for pure power sports such as volleyball. (See also Hill bounding.)

TECHNIQUE (ALL SPORTS)

Break your training down into the crucial movements and then develop, train and refine each specific movement. Finally bring the movements together to create the action that you use in your sport.

THROW/BAT/PITCH/CATCH PRACTICE

This involves exercises to improve technique initially, then the action is completed many times at lower than playing speeds to build up endurance and conditioning. Later resistance exercises can be implemented to improve strength through the specific action. Finally speed of movement is trained. This is all within the confines of correct technique and accuracy.

UP-TEMPO

You should feel fast, strong, comfortable and in control. This is an effort at 3-hr race pace — NO HARDER! It is only slightly faster than cruising.

A FINAL FEW WORDS

Heart rate monitors have changed the way we train — they've improved the accuracy of training as well as our ability to look at and analyse our training. Training will never be the same again. And yet this is only the beginning. While heart rate monitors have allowed athletes of all levels more advantages, there is still a lot to happen in this field.

Heart rate monitors still have a few little weaknesses, however. They don't record intensity exactly as there is a delay between when an activity is initiated and when the heart rate responds. So you can't put a monitor on an athlete in a stop/start sprint sport like soccer and record intensities exactly.

Heart rate records cardiovascular effects in training but not the muscular effects of training. Stride-outs up a hill to improve strength endurance are not going to be monitored accurately by your heart rate.

Most athletes can only do short amounts of speedwork (usually 1–3 mins). Interestingly, it takes 1–3 mins for your heart rate monitor to respond to the activity. For a lot of speedwork, heart rate monitors will not fully indicate what is happening.

What of the future? Training is moving more and more to sophisticated portable devices that record what the athlete or player is doing. Yachting uses Global Positioning Systems, cycling now uses torque meters, altimeters are now available in watch form, and wrist dive computers are available. Climbers now have wrist-worn barometers, altimeters, compasses and thermometers. Most of this is downloadable into sophisticated software for analysis.

Very soon, there will be an integration of many devices that will allow immediate monitoring of exercise and extremely sophisticated review. The physiological lab for testing today will only exist for research. As for the holy grail — immediate access to performance measurement during and after every workout — that one might take a while.

Well, I hope you enjoyed the book. Train hard, train smart, live long and perspire.

See ya,

JON

TRAINING GRAPH

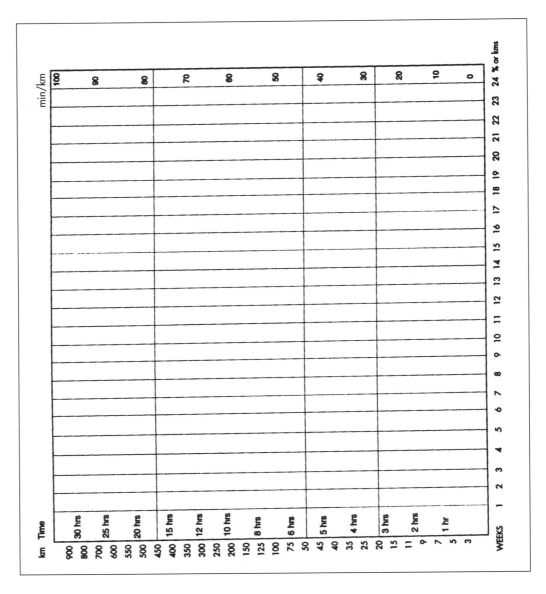

RESTING HEART RATE PROGRESS CHART

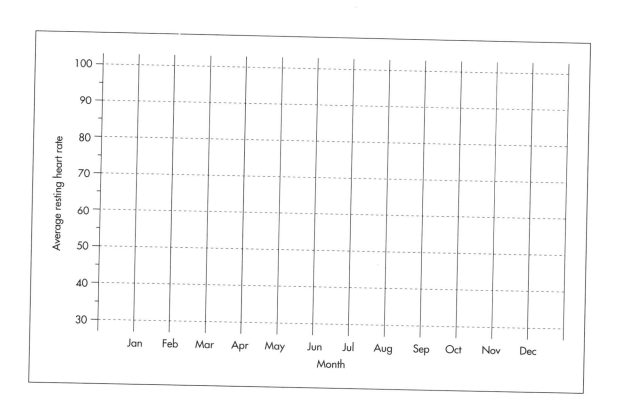

Orthostatic heart rate test

This test measures training recovery.

Resting heart rate

Take this in the morning, for a full minute.

$HR^{rest} = $ ....

Standing heart rate

Take this as soon as you get up out of bed.

$HR^{standing} = $ ....

$HR^{diff} = HR^{standing} - HR^{rest}$

$HR^{diff} = $ ....

A 5- to 10-beat difference is usual; 15 to 20 beats indicates overtiredness.

Note: you may find that the variation is greater than this, but if you use the test over a period of time you will be able to obtain an average that you can base your assessment on.

MONITORING FATIGUE/RECOVERY

MONITORING RECOVERY

You train, you get tired. You recover, you improve!

Training does not create improvements in performance. Recovery from training does. This means that if you don't recover sufficiently from each workout you will become more and more fatigued, and performance will drop.

In short, recovery (from training) is the key to your body's ability to absorb training and increase performance.

HOW DO YOU KNOW WHEN YOU HAVE RECOVERED?

The standard way to do this is to take your resting heart rate (see page 20–1). Unfortunately, taking resting heart rate does not always work. Some athletes feel tired but their heart rate remains low. And the heart rates of very overtrained athletes actually go down, not up. So, using resting heart rate to monitor recovery is problematic.

What, then, can you do to gauge recovery? You can combine resting heart rate with five other indicators of recovery from training. This gives you a rating system based on these six indicators:

♥ Life stress (the stress in your daily life).

♥ Quality of sleep.

♥ General fatigue.

♥ Muscle soreness or sluggishness (these are grouped together).

♥ Attitude to training (do you want to train?).

♥ Resting heart rate.

Each indicator is rated daily on a 1–5 scale — 1 is excellent, 3 is average and 5 is lousy. The rating of each of the first four indicators is added up to give the 'fatigue factor'. For example:

Stress	1	2	③	4	5
Sleep	1	②	3	4	5
General fatigue	1	2	③	4	5
Muscle soreness	1	2	3	④	5

Fatigue factor = 3 + 2 + 3 + 4 = 12

Attitude to training is rated either excellent, good, average or poor. Resting heart rate is recorded every morning.

If the fatigue factor and resting heart rate go up and attitude to training goes down, you are overfatigued and should have either a day off or an easy day.

The interesting thing is that often the fatigue factor goes up and attitude comes down about 24 hours before resting heart rate goes up. This tells us that the psychological indicators react before the physiological indicators. This is very useful as it acts as an early warning system, allowing you to react to fatigue before it manifests itself in training. This, in turn, means less training time and energy are wasted by training when you are overfatigued.

In order to use the rating system, you will need to establish a baseline score (average score over two weeks). Recovery can then be gauged with reference to the baseline score.

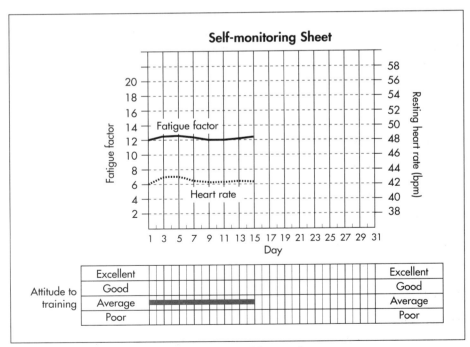

FIGURE APP 4.1: Baseline measurement of fatigue during training

The rating system also allows you to monitor underfatigue (not training hard enough), illness, jet lag, environmental adjustments (altitude, heat acclimatisation) and peaking.

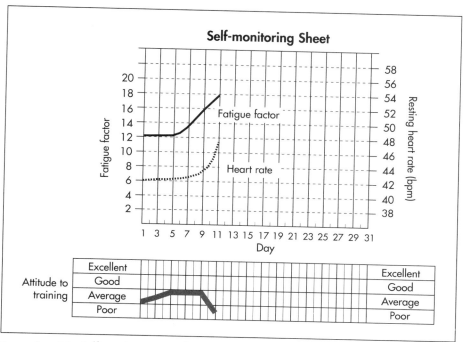

FIGURE APP 4.2: Self-monitoring graph, indicating fatigue

Underfatigue means getting scores that are better than your baseline. Illness, jet lag and environmental factors will give scores worse than the baseline, meaning a need for reduced training until the fatigue factor comes back to normal (this can also help you to determine the time it takes to acclimatise to environmental factors).

Peaking would be indicated by an excellent score in reference to the baseline.

Try the rating system out. It will help you train more effectively by ensuring that more of your training is being absorbed.

(Adapted from Angie Calder's 'Self-monitoring sheet' and 'Training Logs: An Effective Method of Monitoring Overtraining and Tapering' by L. MacKinnon and S. Hooper.)

Self-monitoring Sheet

Resting heart rate (bpm)

Fatigue factor

20
18
16
14
12
10
8
6
4
2

Day 1 3 5 7 9 11 13 15 17 19 21 23 25 27 29 31

Excellent
Good
Average
Poor

Attitude to training

FIGURE APP 4.3: Self-monitoring sheet

INNOVATIONS, ADVANCED FEATURES AND FUNCTIONS OF HEART RATE MONITORS

HEART RATE MONITORING TECHNOLOGY

Heart rate monitors have come a long way, and in this chapter we touch on the latest advances in heart rate monitoring. Let's talk about some innovations first.

♥ The first real innovation, which has been around for a while now, is the timers on heart rate monitors. Timers allow you to set a time, and the monitor counts down and beeps at you when it reaches it. It will then automatically resume the countdown all over again. In the case of racing an Ironman, say, you can set the timer to count down every 15 minutes and beep to remind you to drink and eat. Mine gives a beep to remind me to drink every 15 and 45 minutes and 2 beeps to remind me to eat and drink every 30 and 60 minutes. This allows you to calculate exactly how much to eat and drink every 15 minutes (see *The Power to Perform* for calculations). This in turn means better fluid and nutrition strategies for race day and less chance of forgetting to drink and eat enough (believe me, it happens when you get tired later in the race), and provides a better race outcome. The combination of stopwatch (some products have 30- to 44-lap memories), timer (2–3 alternate timers) and heart rate monitor in one watch for endurance racing is excellent.

♥ There are also heart rate monitors that give a calorie count, telling you the number of k-Calories burnt during a workout. This is good for weight management. Programmable calibration correction factors for the type and intensity of exercise, based on your bodyweight, allow some degree of accuracy.

♥ Coded transmission is a new and particularly useful innovation. A problem in the past was that two athletes training together would have difficulty because both chest straps were transmitting on the same frequency (the normal chest straps transmit to around 1 m). You either didn't exercise with a heart rate monitor in a group or you stayed away from each other so the transmissions didn't get 'tangled'. There are actually two innovations: first, you can set a shorter transmission distance, and second, you can change the transmission frequency so your own and your training partner's heart rate monitors do not interfere with each other. There are 30 code alternatives — two rugby teams could train together! Before this innovation, rowing eights were having nightmares monitoring heart rates.

♥ Night vision is another good idea. In the past, heart rate monitors did not have night lights, which was a major design fault. Most people who can afford heart rate monitors have to work. If they have to work they have to train before or after work. The problem is that before and after work it's often dark, particularly in winter, and in the past it was difficult to see your heart rate — you had to wait until you went under a street light, which can be hard to find on country roads. Night vision allows an athlete to press a button and a backlight illuminates the monitor's screen for a few seconds.

♥ Relaxation rate is an interesting development. This is a way of working out how relaxed you are, not just how hard you are working. How hard you are working is measured by heart rate, whereas how relaxed you are is measured by the variations in time between heart beats in milliseconds (ms). Wow!! The greater the variation in heart beats, the more relaxed you are. Ideally, the lower the heart rate and the higher the variation the better you are performing for a certain speed (relaxation during exercise generally means you will be

FIGURE APP 5.1: Relaxation rate

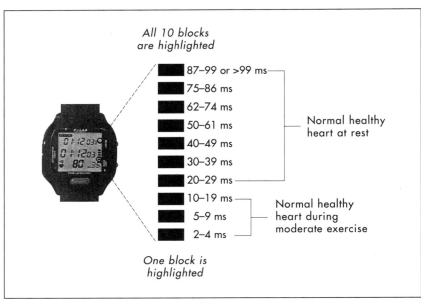

All 10 blocks are highlighted

87–99 or >99 ms
75–86 ms
62–74 ms
50–61 ms
40–49 ms
30–39 ms — Normal healthy heart at rest
20–29 ms
10–19 ms
5–9 ms — Normal healthy heart during moderate exercise
2–4 ms

One block is highlighted

performing better). Figures above 29 ms mean a normal healthy resting heart; from 19 ms down to 4 ms means a healthy heart during moderate exercise. During strenuous exercise, variation can disappear entirely.

This is ideal for monitoring your physical condition at rest, during daily activities and during mild exercise. Heart rates vary widely — although as you get older the variation becomes less — so you have to see how it works for you, but you will soon find your individual average. Variations will decrease from the average (ms time drops) if you are tired, getting fatigued during a workout, stressed, ill or have not slept well. States of mind such as anxiety, tension, anger and concentrating hard will increase heart rate and decrease variation. Stress, whether it be physical or mental, has the same effect — it tires you out. This is a new way to monitor this. As to its validity, I have seen no real evidence but it appears to work and, as with a lot of new technology, quite often the product is available before it can be validated independently.

♥ Heart rate recording is available in continuous recording or sample recording set-ups. Continuous recording means recording heart rate every 5, 15, 30, 60, or 330 seconds for a continuous period (depending on the brand). The current products can record for anywhere from 33 hours to 134 hours 46 minutes! Individual heart rate recording (that's recording every beat) ranges from 4,000 to 8,000 heart beats. I've worn mine for 24 hours to see how many times my heart beat in one day (see page 129).

Sample recording means that you press a button and the monitor takes a 'snapshot' of your heart rate at that time (44–730 samples). This allows you to see what is happening in your training. Both continuous and sample heart rates can be played back over the watch, and there are programmes available where heart rates can be manually keyed into a computer for data storage, graphing and analysis. But wait, there's more!!

♥ Heart rate monitor interfaces combined with heart rate monitors that can record training heart rates and download them onto a computer have been out for a while but they have always been more of a product to be used in testing labs or a toy. You download your heart rates and you get a graph, a distribution and a list of your heart rates. This does not mean much and is not particularly useful to 'Joe Athlete'. The technology was great but the software let it down. But, enter the latest heart rate monitor software.

Training heart rates can be downloaded into an excellent computer training log-book that allows the facility to put in other training data (distance/duration of the workout, how you felt, how you slept, etc.). You can store all your training data, training heart rates and test results, change the training intensity terminology to suit you, and even plan your training. The best part

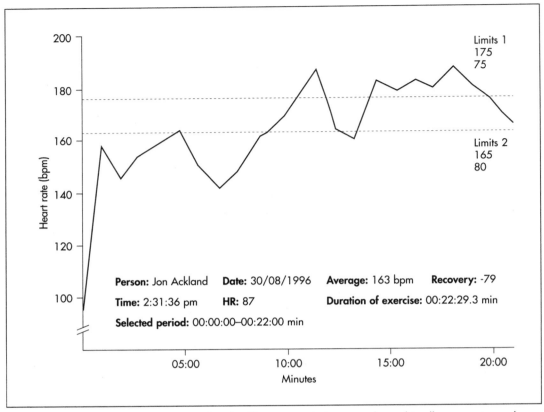

FIGURE APP 5.2: Graph of heart rate during a workout: this allows you to see how your workout progressed, pace judgment, etc.

FIGURE APP 5.3: Time spent above, in and below target training zones. This measures the quality of your workout. How much time did you spend doing what you planned to do? In this case, 64 percent of the total.

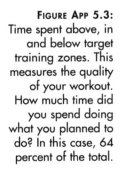

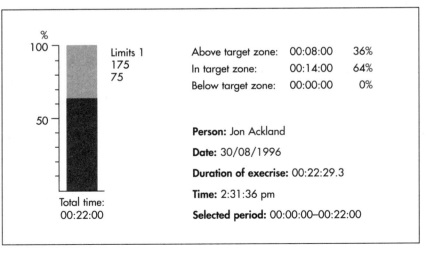

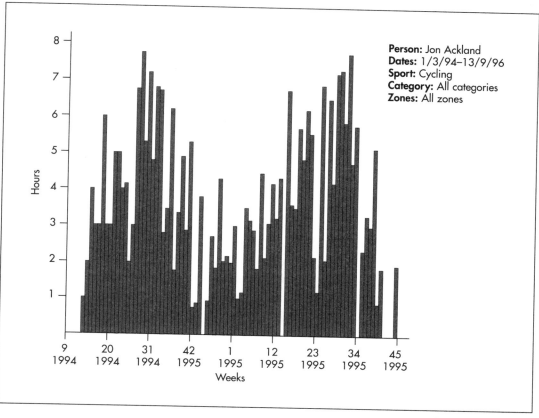

Person: Jon Ackland
Dates: 1/3/94–13/9/96
Sport: Cycling
Category: All categories
Zones: All zones

FIGURE APP 5.4:
Graph showing
weekly training
volume

of the programme is that you can see exactly what you did in training and analyse it — what was going on, what you did right and what you did wrong. Here are some examples.

1. You can assess individual workouts — see figs app 5.2 and 5.3.

2. You can monitor training volume for a build-up or over a number of weeks. This allows you to look back at your training to see what you did last time or what has been happening in your current build-up (see fig app 5.4).

3. You can measure the proportions of training intensities as part of your total training. This allows you to see exactly how much of a particular intensity you did (see fig app 5.5 and 5.6).

4. You can monitor resting and orthostatic heart rates (see pages 289–90). This allows you to see whether you are training well, have little variation in resting heart rates (not getting too tired), and are getting fitter (resting heart rate gets lower) (see fig app 5.7).

5. Heart rate distribution, trends in training, scatter diagrams, environmental conditions and other features are also able to be monitored (see fig app 5.8).

6. You can assess other parameters of your performance: stride length, stride rate, speed, cadence, watts (work), lactate (see page 307).

♥ Some products now have 'on-line' or 'real time' recording. What does that mean? It means that you can exercise in a stationary situation (on a treadmill or a stationary bike trainer) and the heart rate monitor chest strap will transmit to an interface/receiver (it must be within 1 m) and will display heart rate on your computer screen as it happens. Pretty cool!

♥ If you are conducting a physiological test on a treadmill or cycle trainer (Conconi, interval or walking tests) you can record on-line and then convert the test data on the screen to assess the test. These tests can also be conducted outdoors with a minimum of hassle. The tests are set up so well in the whole record/interface system that the testing is exceptionally easy. All it takes is a thorough read-through of the manual.

The tests that can be done using these products are on pages 303–10. Remember, always try to complete them in the same conditions.

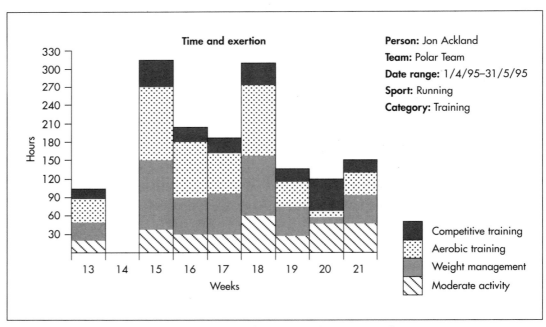

FIGURE APP 5.5: Volume of training and proportion of time spent at each training intensity

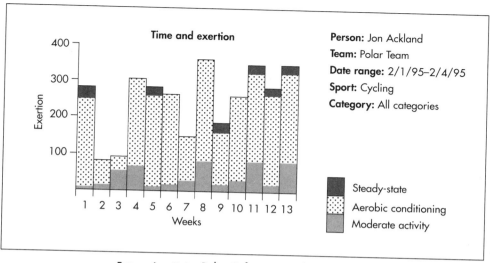

FIGURE APP 5.6: Polar Software graph depicting amount of training load (exertion count) that the athlete is under and how much is apportioned to each training intensity (see pages 310–2)

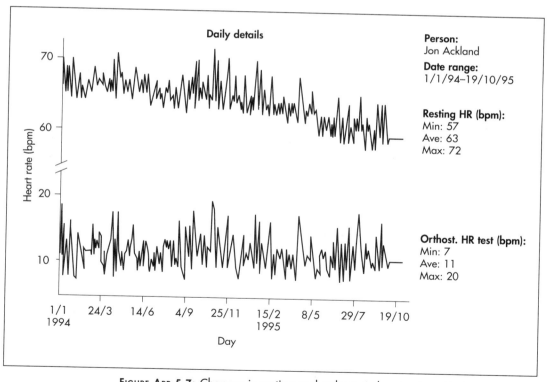

FIGURE APP 5.7: Changes in resting and orthostatic heart rates with time

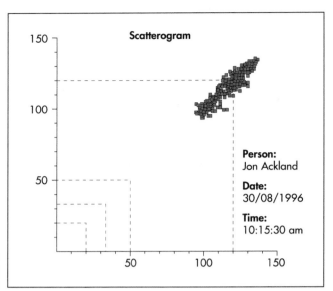

FIGURE APP 5.8:
Scatter diagram indicating
training intensities

♥ Another exciting innovation that has been around for a while but still hasn't quite made it is telemetry. In this case a rower could be training out on the water wearing a heart rate chest strap. The chest strap has a boosted transmitter on it which sends the heart rates to the coach in the following boat. If this ever really gets going you could monitor an athlete in a competition from the sidelines. Exciting stuff.

♥ Finally, another product is now available. It's a rather bulky heart rate monitor that cleverly interfaces with a computer over phone lines. The system involves buying the watch and being linked by phone to a personal trainer. You get a programme sent to you, do your training, and when you have finished you dial up the computer, put the watch up to the mouthpiece and press a button. The watch sends the data by audible beeps and pips down the phone line and into the trainer's computer. The data appears on the trainer's screen and you can then discuss it. It's a great idea for health/fitness people but not as good for athletes/players.

OTHER FUNCTIONS THAT CAN BE INCORPORATED IN HEART RATE MONITORS

♥ **Setting of target training zones** (which can include AT, AeT). Feedback of time above, in and below training zones. You set the alarm to beep if you go out of your training zones. I find the beeping drives me crazy, although a choice of visual indicator or 'vocal' indication are features in some watches.

♥ **Time of day** (12/24 hour or dual time).

♥ **Daily alarm**.

♥ **Calendar**.

♥ **Water resistance** (swimming is in; diving for sunken treasure below 20 m is out).

♥ **Bike adaptors/straps.** These are great — if you are cycling it is far more intelligent to put your heart rate monitor on the bike in front of you where you can see it.

Some heart rate monitors are 'clip on', while others are 'strap on'. 'Strap on' bike adaptors are a great idea, but the straps are very hard to get. When a monitor is put on a bike it needs to be attached quite tightly, and it is hard to prevent it bouncing around and ending up face down, where it is obviously hard to read. After a while the strap also starts to get damaged — particularly the little holes for the buckle. With the new protective straps, the monitor strap is fed into protective sleeves so the buckle is not used and therefore not damaged. The monitor is attached with Velcro which is tight and safe. It's great for Ironman triathlons, too, as all you have to do when you get off the bike is pull the Velcro strap off and slap it on your wrist.

♥ **Event markers/intermediate times.** These allow you to check a split time for a lap or at a mark and to see the heart rate at the mark. Excellent.

♥ **Heart rate recovery time.** This is used to see how long it takes your heart rate to drop to a certain level or the interval your heart rate drops in a certain time. The fitter you get the more quickly your heart rate drops. This is a good measure of improvements in fitness.

♥ **Average heart rate.** This feature gives you the average intensity that you have been working at for the duration of the workout. This is excellent (probably the most important feature after heart rate); combined with time spent above, in and below your target training zones, this can be very good in terms of stats on your workout. Lower average heart rates for the same run, in the same conditions and the same time mean you are getting fitter (see figs app 5.2 and 5.3).

TESTS WITH HEART RATE MONITORS

1. THE CONCONI TEST (SEE CHAPTER 12)

The Conconi test is useful as it allows you to assess not only AT (anaerobic threshold) but to calculate all your training intensities. This is how it works. You

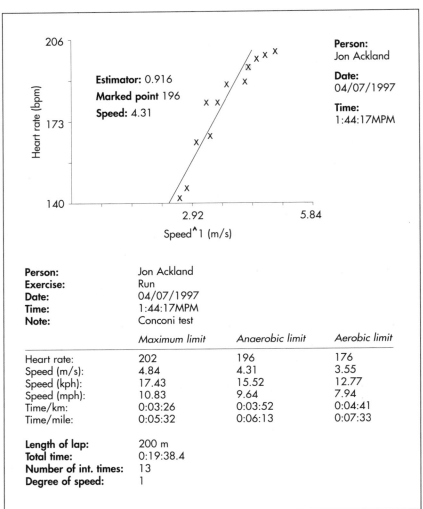

Estimator: 0.916
Marked point 196
Speed: 4.31

Person:
Jon Ackland

Date:
04/07/1997

Time:
1:44:17MPM

Person: Jon Ackland
Exercise: Run
Date: 04/07/1997
Time: 1:44:17MPM
Note: Conconi test

	Maximum limit	Anaerobic limit	Aerobic limit
Heart rate:	202	196	176
Speed (m/s):	4.84	4.31	3.55
Speed (kph):	17.43	15.52	12.77
Speed (mph):	10.83	9.64	7.94
Time/km:	0:03:26	0:03:52	0:04:41
Time/mile:	0:05:32	0:06:13	0:07:33

Length of lap:	200 m
Total time:	0:19:38.4
Number of int. times:	13
Degree of speed:	1

FIGURE APP 5.9:
Conconi
test data

cycle or run a set distance (333 m, 200 m) on a track. Set the heart rate monitor to record at 5-second intervals, starting the stopwatch on the monitor as you start the test. Start very slowly, and with each set distance covered gradually increase the speed all the way to maximum. As you complete each set distance press the store/recall button (you need at least eight intermediate times for the calculation to work). This information can then be downloaded and the computer will assess anaerobic threshold (see fig app 5.9).

How to 'zap up' a running Conconi test
Do the Conconi test described counting:

1. Steps taken for each 200 m.

2. Time to complete 200 m.

3. Record heart rate at end of each 200 m.

Do the following calculations to determine speed, stride length, stride rate and heart rates.

Speed (kph) = ((distance (m) x 0.001) ÷ (time (mins)) x 60 x 60

Speed (min/km) = (Time (secs) ÷ 60) ÷ distance (m) x 0.001

Stride rate = no. steps ÷ (time (secs)) ÷ 60

Stride length = (distance (m) x 100) ÷ 133

Heart rate is already recorded.

The data and the calculations provide a table like this:

Person: Jon Ackland

Date: 04/05/1997

Starting time: 1:44:17.0 PM   Total time: 0:19:38.4

Final time: 2:03:55.4 PM

Num	Intermediate	Lap Time	Speed	Stride Rate	Stride Length	HR
1.	0:01:17.0	0:01:17.0	6.4	152.0	102.0	142
2.	0:01:29.3	0:01:12.3	6.0	146.0	113.5	147
3.	0:03:36.4	0:01:07.1	5.5	166.0	107.5	163
4.	0:04:36.6	0:01:00.2	5.0	170.0	117.5	167
5.	0:05:35.9	0:00:59.3	4.9	168.0	120.5	181
6.	0:06:31.2	0:00:55.3	4.5	172.0	127.5	181
7.	0:07:23.2	0:00:52.0	4.2	176.0	131.5	189
8.	0:08:10.8	0:00:47.6	3.7	182.0	140.5	190
9.	0:08:57.2	0:00:46.4	3.7	182.0	143.0	196
10	0:09:42.0	0:00:44.8	3.7	186.0	144.0	199
11.	0:10:24.8	0:00:42.8	3.5	190.0	148.0	201
12.	0:11:06.1	0:00:41.3	3.3	190.0	154.0	202
13.	0:11:36.0	0:00:29.9				

For your own assessment of speed, stride rates and stride lengths, use the Conconi test information on page 119–24 and combine with this.

Here are two examples of how this information can be used. The first is a comparison of performance in early season and a few months into training; the second is a comparison between two different people.

Comparison 1:

Testing myself early season (Test 1) and later in the season (Test 2).

♥   Running speeds are better (see A graphs).

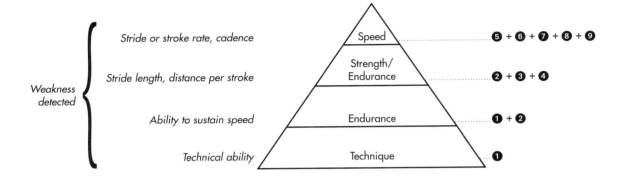

Test 1 (end of test) = 3.7 min/km
Test 2 (end of test) = 3.3 min/km

♥ Test deflected better (HR plateaux better in the anaerobic threshold test, see B graphs). In Test 1 there was no HR plateau at the end of the test, indicating that I did not have enough strength endurance or 'grunt' to sustain higher intensities. As I got fitter, I was able to keep going and my legs took longer to 'blow up' (Test 2).

♥ I was able to calculate my training HRs based on the AT point of deflection.

Jack Daniels, a noted sports scientist, discovered that top endurance athletes' stride rates were almost always around 180–190 strides per minute at race pace (see C graphs). The athlete with the longest stride usually won the race. My stride rates towards the end of the test were good (Test 1 = 194, Test 2 = 190) but my stride length let me down (Test 1 = 138.5, Test 2 = 154). I can't improve my stride rate as it is optimal. I had a strength endurance problem.

The above diagram shows the various areas where an athlete/player has a weakness and which subphases to emphasise.

Comparison 2:

Here is a comparison between myself and a friend called Russell (see graphs D and E). It was conducted to solve a problem. At the time of these tests, I could beat Russell in a 50-m sprint. We were fairly even in a 5–10 km race with Russell having the edge and being a certainty to win if it came to a sprint. At marathon and Ironman distance, I again had the edge. Our tests showed similar top speeds (3.3 min/km at the end of our tests, see graphs D). Why?

If you look at how we achieve speed, there is quite a difference. I have a high stride rate (190) and a short stride length (154) whereas Russell has a low stride rate (174) and a long stride length (166.5; see graphs E).

So how does this explain the mystery?

In the 50-m sprint, because I have a higher leg turnover rate, I can get up to

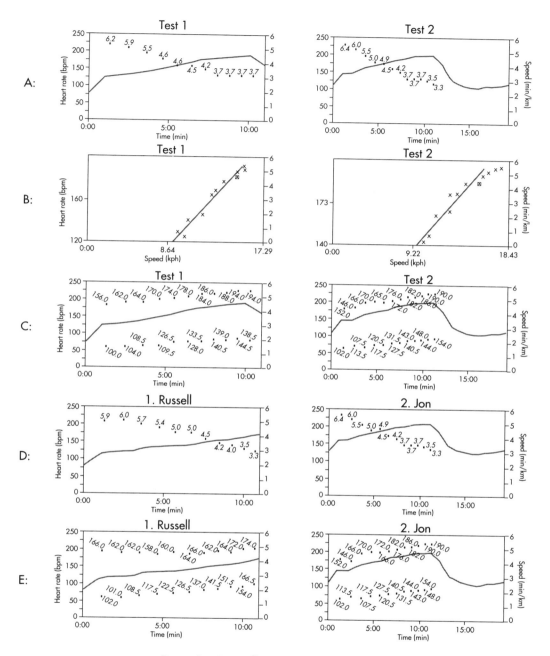

FIGURE APP 5.10: Conconi test comparisons

top speed quicker while Russell is taking much longer strides and has difficulty accelerating. I'm quicker off the mark because of my stride rate.

Over 5–10 km, Russell is stronger because of his long stride length. Over a marathon distance (42 km), I am again quicker because turning over such a long stride for 42 km will mean Russell's legs will start to 'blow up'. My higher turnover rate (stride rate) saves the 'grunt' in my legs for longer so my legs don't 'blow up' as early. Problem solved.

How do we modify our training to improve our respective weaknesses?

My stride rate is good but I need to work on my stride length (subphases 2, 3 and 4). Russell's stride length is good but he needs to work on his stride rate (subphases 5 and 6).

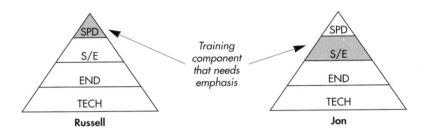

This test was conducted on a 200-m stretch of road on a flat footpath in a street in Forrest Hill, Auckland — nothing 'flash'! It took approximately 20 minutes for each test and the data that came out was:

1. Performance Test — Speed.

2. Anaerobic Threshold & Maximum Heart Rate — can calculate training heart rates.

3. Fitness Change.

4. Assesses what the performance weakness is.

Tests must be specific enough to measure both athletic potential and performance change so as to allow modification of training.

2. ENDURANCE TEST

This test involves 2–6 repetitions of 1 km. The aim of undertaking the endurance test in running, for example, is to assess whether you can sustain the required stride rate and stride length. The test can be applied to most sports (e.g. stroke rate and distance per stroke in rowing, cadence and gear in cycling). Sprinting is exactly the same as running but over shorter distances.

For a runner: Speed = Stride length x stride rate (+ technique). A runner might have very good stride rates and stride lengths but if he or she can't hold them for the duration of the event, these are meaningless. The table below shows that in a 3 x 1.2-km time trial, I could achieve a relatively good stride rate (184) and stride length (151) but could not hold them for extended periods of time. I needed to improve my endurance.

Person: Jon Ackland

Exercise: 3 x 1.2 km

Date: 16/07/1997

Starting time: 6:27:19.0 PM   Total time: 0:21:28.0

Final time: 6:48:47.0 PM

Num	Intermediate	Lap Time	Speed	Stride Rate	Stride Length	HR	Dist.	Aim
1.	0:06:34.5	0:06:34.5	5.4	160.0	113.5	145	1.2 km	Easy
2.	0:10:54.7	0:04:20.2	3.6	184.0	151.0	185	1.2 km	Race pace
3.	0:15:32.3	0:04:37.6	3.7	180.0	145.0	179	1.2 km	Race pace
4.	0:20:10.9	0:04:38.6	3.7	180.0	144.5	186	1.2 km	Race pace
5.	0:20:18.6	0:00:07.7						

3. THE INTERVAL TEST

This is a test for fitness based on recovery (how quickly your heart rate drops) between intervals. You might want to do five intervals of five minutes with a two-minute rest between. You have two timers to do this. Set the first timer on five minutes, for example, and the second on two minutes. Set the monitor to record at five-second intervals; do the interval when the first timer beeps (5 minutes) and rest when the second timer beeps (2 minutes). Repeat this for as many intervals as you wish. You start the stopwatch at the start of the test and stop it at the end, download it and, other than typing in the interval times, the computer takes care of the rest.

The idea is that the higher your average recovery value (the amount your heart rate drops) the fitter you are becoming. I wouldn't rave about this test, but it's okay for recreational athletes/players .

4. THE WALKING TEST

This test looks very good for fitness enthusiasts. It involves a brisk 2-km walk on a flat course to assess fitness index. This is a combination of your age, height/weight vs your heart rate, and the time it takes to complete the distance. It gives you a fitness index, classification of fitness and VO_{2max}.

Set the monitor to record at 5-second intervals; in this case you start the stopwatch and press the store/recall button and stop the stopwatch at the end of the test.

This seems like a very good test for general fitness enthusiasts but it's not useful for fit athletes/players and it can be affected by environmental changes (such as different temperatures or a head wind).

5. TRAINING LOAD

Training load is another useful measure which can be worked out easily with the software that is now available. Training load is usually defined as intensity multiplied by volume.

Training Load = Intensity x Volume

In other words, you can go out and work at a heart rate of 160 bpm (intensity), but that is only half the story; you also need to take into account how long or far you went (volume). The combination gives you load. A combination of effort/intensity and duration/distance will tell you what the total load of the session or sessions would be.

This doesn't entirely work; for example, a swim at a heart rate of 160 bpm for 60 minutes is not as hard as a run at a heart rate of 160 bpm for 60 minutes. The swimming has far less muscular impact on the body than the run, and it will take longer to recover from the run because it takes longer for the muscles to recover. (The limiting factor to how much training you can do is generally based on how fast the muscles recover and not how fast the cardiovascular system recovers.)

This built-in extra muscle recovery (impact) factor is called an exertion factor (see fig app 5.11). The harder you exercise, the more impact and therefore the greater the exertion factor. Exertion factors are low at low intensities but rocket up at high intensities due to the muscular stress involved, so training load = intensity

FIGURE APP 5.11: Exertion factors increase markedly at high intensities (heart rates) due to muscular impact and longer muscular recovery times required.

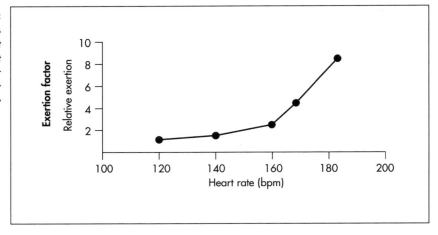

310

PRECISION TRAINING

x volume x exertion factor (see fig app 5.12).

The more muscular impact the sport has (e.g. swimming has less impact than running), the higher the exertion factors and the more markedly they increase at higher intensities.

To allow for the different muscle impact involved, it is necessary to put in a correction factor for each sport. The running load exertion factors will be higher than those for swimming. As you change intensities the exertion factor changes because the muscular impact increases exponentially as you move into higher

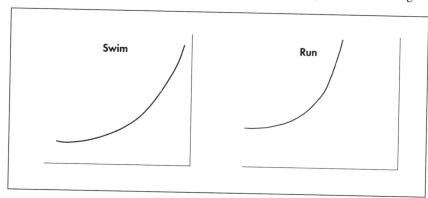

FIGURE APP 5.12:
Heart rate vs relative exertion factors: note that the exertion factors are higher for running than for swimming as running has more impact on the muscles

training intensities, so an exertion factor specific to the sport and the intensity is needed. (This may sound complicated but it is all in the software.)

The formula for working out training load is:

Intensity (heart rate) x Volume (duration) x Sport factor/100
= Training Load (work done)

So, for example, you will use a different exertion factor for a swim vs a run:

Run: 180 (AT) HR x 64 (mins) x 2.5/100 = 288
Swim: 180 (AT) HR x 64 (mins) x 1.5/100 = 172.8

(where 1.5 and 2.5 are the respective exertion factors for each sport — see fig app 5.13).

Measuring training load allows you to compare the load across sports, and compare how much load you are under during a week of speedwork vs Base training, for example. It is useful for analysis.

For instance, you can work out that 69 minutes at a heart rate of 166 is equivalent to exercising for 130 minutes at a heart rate of 147. This also enables you to assess approximately how long it will take to recover from the workout.

147 (UT) x 131 (mins) x 1.5 /100 = 288   Low intensity for a long time

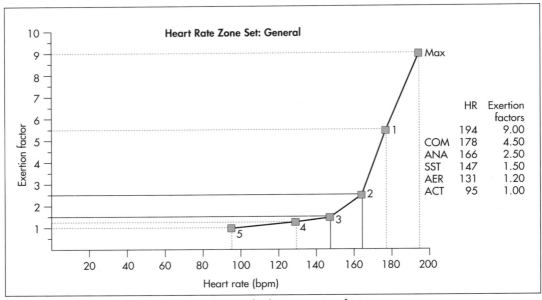

FIGURE APP 5.13: Assessed relative exertion factors

166 (AT) x 69 (mins) x 2.5/100 = 288   High intensity for a short time

This is not super accurate but it does provide a useful measure to compare different forms of training.

	Exercise 1					
		Exercise 2				
			Exercise 3			
				Exercise 4		
					Exercise 5	
				288		
1	100	200		300	400	
					Exertion count	
0	8	16	21	24	32	
					Recovery time (hr)	

HR	Time	Exertion score	Expected recovery time
160	120	288	21 hours
180	54	288	21 hours

FIGURE APP 5.14: A comparison of exertion and recovery time

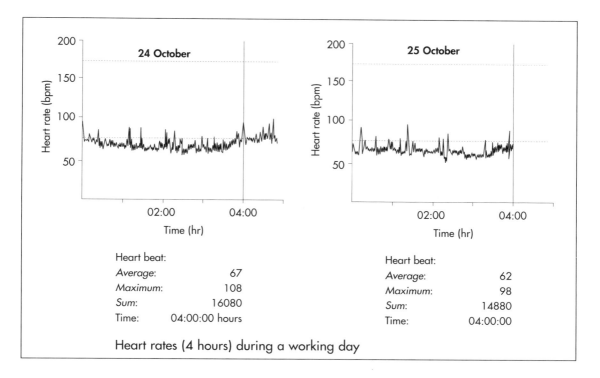

Heart rates (4 hours) during a working day

6. Measurements of cumulative heart rate

Another good idea is to measure cumulative heart rate by recording the total number of beats in a workout or a day. This is easy with continuous recording — you just set your monitor going and record.

Why is this so interesting? Because small variations in heart rate cannot be picked up in one reading. For example, let's say you took your resting heart rate in the morning. It's usually 50; this morning you took it three times and got 54, 50 and 52. Are you tired or not?

Now let's say you measured your heart rate for four hours during the day and recorded it. You know that your heart usually beats 15,600 times over four hours; today it beat 16,080 times — an extra 480 beats. You are probably a little tired.

A 2- to 3-beat difference taken in 1 or 2 heart rate checks actually turns out to be a 480-beat difference over 4 hours. Instead of a 'snapshot' of what your heart rate is, you get a more accurate 'trend'. Sometimes your resting heart rate may be up in the morning (stressed about work) but settle during the day, so a single heart rate check in the morning may not be useful.

The tiredness check becomes more sensitive if taken over a longer time. It can also be used to see if you are tired during a workout. There is no real rule of thumb figures for what equates to tired and what doesn't, partly because this

Figure App 5.15: In the graph on the left, I was tired; the graph on the right shows a normal day.

procedure is quite new, and also because heart rates are quite individualised depending on fitness, physical make-up and the physical/mental stress of the working day or workout. (You can also use the heart rate monitor to measure degree of acclimatisation.)

SOFTWARE AND OTHER PRODUCT INNOVATIONS

♥ **Fitware**. This is a new heart rate monitor-compatible product. Functions include exercise testing to determine VO2max and other data, prescribing general health-based training programmes, and a facility to monitor and analyse the training conducted.

Clever features include assessment of whether the person is exercising in the correct training zone, calculating energy expenditure (kCal — fat burning) for weight loss, and methods of assessing the level of physical work stress. The physical work stress is assessed by wearing your heart rate monitor at work and then downloading it into the computer to see what happened. All aspects of this software package are tied up with a heart rate monitor with memory and interface.

♥ **Endurance training manager.** This is a software package designed to allow a coach or athlete to design a training programme. It takes a reasonable understanding of training to design the programme but it does a very good job. The graphics, programme writing part and log book are very good. Heart rate monitors can be interfaced and downloaded to a computer. Report summaries are also available. For the coach or experienced athlete in endurance sport.

♥ **SRM cranks (bike computer)**. SRM cranks are the latest and greatest in cycling. There are bike computers that do the usual bike functions (speed, distance) and record heart rate, but SRM cranks have strain gauges in the chain rings of the bike to assess all the other functions plus work done in watts. This is a very useful data analysis system. All data can be downloaded into a computer to be assessed. Costly and only for the really committed.

♥ **Rowing computers.** These now allow far greater collection of training information than previously. Distance, speed and a number of other rowing-specific factors (as well as heart rate) can be measured. All data can be downloaded to a computer. Once again, for the serious rower.

More and more of this type of hardware and software is becoming available. Keep an eye out.

PERCEIVED EXERTION

What if you don't have a heart rate monitor? Is your training doomed to failure?

Not at all. A lot of athletes have performed very well without a heart rate monitor. You can, instead, use the surprisingly accurate method of perceived exertion. This is a system whereby you subjectively assess how hard the training intensity is. You can then apply this to a scale known as the Borg scale, which allows you to quantify the intensity that you are exercising at.

Rating of perceived exertions	Description	Intensity level equivalent (% maximum heart rate)	Heart rate equivalent (bpm, 20-year-old)	Intensities
6–8	very, very light		80	
9	very light		90	AR
10			100	
11	fairly light		110	
12		60	120	LSD
13	somewhat hard		130	
14		70	140	UT
15	hard		150	
16		80	160	AT
17			170	
18		90	180	ES
19			190	
20			200	IS/PWR

FIGURE APP 6.1: Rating of perceived exertion

The formula becomes more inaccurate as you get older and fitness declines. It is also less accurate at the lower intensities as it is difficult to determine the difference between light intensity and very light intensity. Nevertheless, it remains a useful guide for assessing training intensities.

One other problem when discussing differing forms of training is that the cardiovascular intensity may be medium but the muscular intensity may be hard. For example, in the case of load/speed training on a bike, you might be doing flat, big gear work, which has a high muscular load but a medium cardiovascular load.

PLYOMETRIC TRAINING

RUNNING AND SPEED

Many athletes train a lot but fail to become faster through poor form (biomechanics). In addition to sprint training, some consideration should be given to good running form.

Running and sprint drills are best learnt 'practically' from an expert, not from a book. My suggestion is to approach a sprint or running coach and get them to teach you the drills.

PLYOMETRIC TRAINING TIPS

1. Warm-ups

A thorough warm-up is essential prior to plyometrics. This should include jogging or simple callisthenics to raise muscle temperature, and thorough stretching. Because of the need to maintain correct form, plyometrics should be performed when the athlete is still fresh, not at the end of a training session. A warm-down should follow each session.

2. Specificity and Individualisation

The plyometric programme should involve actions and intensities similar to those involved in the power actions of specific sports. The programme should also be specifically designed to suit the particular abilities of each athlete.

3. Progressive Overload

By controlling the heights from which athletes drop, the weights used and the distances covered, the intensity at which the muscle must work can be varied. The resistive overload should be large enough to produce the desired adaptation. Excessive overloads may increase strength but have little effect upon power.

Most plyometric exercises use momentum and gravity as the overload, but medicine balls or light dumbbells can be employed for some drills. Progression, in terms of the overload and the number of sessions per week, should be made very gradually and carefully, particularly at the start of a plyometrics programme, in order to avoid injury.

4. Strength Bases

The fact that power should be developed for most sporting actions does not negate the need for strength. A well-balanced strength development should be achieved before a high volume of plyometric training is attempted. Without good strength development, the athlete runs the risk of injury from the high tensions developed in muscle and tendons during plyometric actions. A good strength base is also necessary for the maximum returns from plyometric training. Consider these factors when planning the sequencing of the yearly training programme.

5. Maximal Intensity

Speed of execution and maximal effort are crucial for optimal plyometric training effects. The rate of muscle stretch is more important than the magnitude of the stretch. Therefore, all actions in plyometrics should be performed at maximal intensity and speed.

6. Rest

Because correct form and maximal intensity are essential for plyometrics, it is important to take adequate rest between successive exercise sequences; 1–2 minutes between sets is normal. A training day involving plyometrics should preferably be followed by an aerobic training day and there should be no more than 2–3 plyometrics sessions per week.

7. Optimal Number of Repetitions

Plyometric exercises vary in the overall effort they require. The intensity of the drill will determine the number of repetitions, but most exercises involve 8–10 repetitions. The number of repetitions should also be governed by the athlete's capacity to perform quality actions. As soon as the movement becomes sluggish and poorly executed, the benefits to the neuromuscular system will be reduced and the set should be terminated. For the the intense jumping drills, 3–6 sets are recommended, and 6–10 sets for the less intense hopping and skipping exercises.

8. Technique

Correct technique must be observed at all times. One of the most important aspects of technique concerns foot contact with the ground. The best way to land is on the ball of the foot with the ankle locked. Holding the hands in the 'thumbs-up' position helps counteract the tendency for the shoulders to drop forward during jumps, hops and leaps.

9. Equipment

Quality athletic footwear, in good condition, is essential. Some individuals may also require ankle support. Hard surfaces are potentially hazardous and most of the exercises for legs and hips should be performed on resilient gym mats or grass.

10. Sessions Structure

A plyometric session could involve just one exercise, or a circuit of 2–3 exercises. In either case the complete session should involve no more than 100 explosive 'touches'. The session should be terminated if the working muscle group becomes weak or sore.

(The above tips are adapted from 'Plyometric Training — What it is and how to use it effectively', which appeared in the Summer 1991 issue of *Coaching Focus*, the technical journal of the British National Coaching Federation.)

Leg Power - Plyometrics

Basic Principles: Rapid stretching (loading) of a muscle activates a reflex, resulting in stronger muscular contraction. Therefore muscles respond to changes in length more quickly and with greater power.

Action: Each repetition should be performed at 100 percent effort, allowing enough rest between repetitions so that muscle fatigue does not limit performance.

The focus is on speed off the ground/box, distance and height gained.

All techniques should be performed on dry grass or a padded surface.

Technique in Landing: Important to minimise time spent on ground.

Right   Wrong   Wrong   Right

Landing   Foot Placement

If shin tenderness or lower back pain occurs, stop power training immediately.

Here are some examples of plyometrics that can be used for training. Try to use the exercises most specific to your sport or develop your own sport-specific plyometrics.

Power Circuit
1. Alternate/double leg bound drill

a) Alternate
ACTION: Start in $\frac{1}{2}$ squat with arms at side. Jump upwards and outwards thrusting arms forward. On landing, start sequence again!

REPS

b) Double

ACTION: Start with one foot ahead of the other. Initiate movement with back foot pushing off. Drive knee of back foot to chest then reach out as far as possible just prior to landing.

REPS

10 m

2. Side Hop Over Cone

ACTION: Jump sideways over first cone and then immediately over the second. Without hesitation change direction and reverse drill. Use arms.

REPS

3. Squat Jump Drill

ACTION: Start with hands behind head. Drop to $\frac{1}{2}$ squat position; quickly stop, then drive upwards explosively. On landing repeat sequence.

REPS

4. Leg Speed Hop Drill

a) Single

ACTION: Start in relaxed position. Jump as high as possible, driving arms upwards. Bring legs up in a flexed position; work as rapidly as possible.

REPS

10 m

b) Double

ACTION: Hold one leg flexed throughout movement. Jump as high as possible bringing knees forwards and arms upwards. Land on same leg as takeoff.

REPS

10 m

5. Lunge Jumps

ACTION: Start with one leg extended forward in lunge position. Explode upwards from flexed leg. Change legs. Repeat.

REPS

6. Acceleration Drill

ACTION: Stand on box (about 70 cm high). Step off box to land on grass or padded surface. Immediately on landing, explode into 10-m sprint.

REPS

7. Jump Off and Up Drill

ACTION: Stand on box (about 70 cm high). Step off and land on both feet simultaneously. Explode straight upwards on landing. Emphasise height and speed.

REPS

8. Box Jump Drills

ACTION: Using arms to add an initial burst, jump upwards and forwards onto box, both feet landing simultaneously. Immediately jump back to starting stance: add variations to initial movement.

REPS

IMPORTANT: 100% intensity

Minimise contact time with ground and/or box.

Stretch lower back, calf, front thigh and hamstrings upon completion.

(Adapted from New Zealand Institute of Sport material by Kate Rhind)

STRENGTH TRAINING

I'm not going to talk too much about strength training as that is a book in itself. I will provide some basic information and then you should talk to your coach, an experienced athlete or a strength conditioning expert.

Firstly, what are the different types of strength?

Type	Sets	Reps	Rest	Days/Weeks	Intensity	Speed	Weight % RM
Hypertrophy	3–5	8–20	1–2 min	3–6	LOW	SLOW/MED	60–75%
Strength	3–5	2–6	3–5 min	3–6	HIGH	SLOW/MED	MAY
Power	3–5	2–3	3–5 min	3–4	HIGH	FAST OR SLOW ECCENTRIC/FAST CONCENTRIC	30–100%
Peaking	1–3	1–3	3–5 min	2–4	VERY HIGH	FAST	50% TO CONTROL
Active Rest	Light Physical Activity						

(Adapted from a tabular summary by Mark Sutherland)

There are many other possibilities (specific to each sport), but these are the basic training types and periods of strength training, muscle endurance and power endurance. Strength conditioning can fall anywhere in the triangle below.

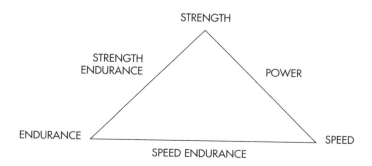

Strength training can be run in the standard linear fashion (hypertrophy then strength then power then peaking) or in a non–linear set up (more cross-over). Example of non-linear (during strength phase of training)

	Monday	Wednesday	Friday	Saturday
Intensity (RM zone)	8–10	3–5	8–10	12–15
Sets	3–4	4–5	3–4	3–4
Rest	2 min	3–4 min	2 min	1 min
	STRENGTH	POWER	STRENGTH	HYPERTROPHY

Non-linear training occurs within a week or several weeks.

OTHER POINTS:

♥ Be as specific to the sport as possible. The more I deal with athletes, the more I realise that a lot of effort is wasted in the gym.

This is mainly to do with something known as 'transfer' or 'cross–over'. Perfect (100%) transfer (what you do in the gym goes into making you perform in your sport) must use the same muscles, in the same action, through the same range of motion, for the same number of times at the same resistance at the same speed. You can't follow this totally (resistance must be increased), but the further the strength exercise moves away from what is completed in the sport the more your 'transfer' drops. An athlete may spend a lot of time in the gym and say that they are strong, but my question is: 'strong for what?' It must help you perform and a lot of gym time may be a waste of time. Be specific!

♥ Try to incorporate your sport into the strength training. (Perhaps do a strength exercise and immediately perform your action in the sport to aid transfer, e.g. leg press then immediately get off a cycle to help muscle endurance).

♥ Keep your workouts short and to the point. Don't spend hours doing exercises that will give you minimum performance gains for your effort.

♥ Technique is everything!

♥ Not everyone uses the same rep and set ranges.

Because an endurance athlete will generally fatigue more slowly than a sprint athlete because of their muscle tissue type, they should require more reps and sets than a speed/sprint athlete.

Also, more used and larger muscle groups may require more reps than less used, smaller muscle groups.

♥ It's the final few reps that generate strength, not the lead–up reps. Pay attention to times. Good technique in the last few reps will greatly improve your strength training results.

♥ Strength training should be individualised to the athlete/player, sport, and position.

♥ Sequences of exercises and exercise specifics are best left to the experts. Talk to an expert regarding your strength training and let them set the programme for you.

BIBLIOGRAPHY

Ackland, J., with B. Reid, *The Power to Perform*. Reed, 1996.

Baechle, T.R., *Essentials of Strength Training and Conditioning*. Human Kinetics, 1994.

Balyi, I., 'Keynote Address, Coaching New Zealand: Periodisation & Integration of Training', 1996.

Bompa, T.O., *Theory and Methodology of Training*. Kendall/Hunt, 1994.

Brick, M., *Precision Multisport*. Polar Electro Oy, 1994.

Dintiman, G., B. Ward & T. Tellez, *Sports Speed; #1 Program for Athletes*. Human Kinetics, 1997.

Edwards, S., *The Heart Rate Monitor Book*. Polar Electro Oy, 1994.

Gummerson, T., *Training Theory for Martial Arts*. A & C Black, 1992.

Hellemans, J., *Triathlon: A Complete Guide to Training and Racing*. Reed, 1993.

Janssen, P.G.J.M., *Training, Lactate, Pulse Rate*. Polar Electro Oy, 1987.

Johnson, R., *Travel Fitness*. Human Kinetics, 1995.

Reaburn, P. & D. Jenkins, *Training for Speed and Endurance*. Allen & Unwin, 1996.

Sleamaker, R. & R. Browning, *Serious Training for Endurance Athletes*. Human Kinetics, 1996.

Supplementary Reading

Burke, E.R., *Serious Cycling*. Human Kinetics, 1995.

Craig, N., *Scientific Heart Rate Training*. Pursuit Performance, 1996.

De Castella, R. & W. Clews, *Smart Sport: The Ultimate Reference Manual for Sports People*. RWM Publishing, 1996.

Dick, F.W., *Sports Training Principles*. A & C Black, 1989.

Evans, M., *Endurance Athletes Edge*. Human Kinetics, 1997.

Friel, J., *The Cyclists Training Bible*. Velo Press, 1996.

Hodge, K., G. Sleivert & A. McKenzie, eds., *Smart Training for Peak Performance: A Complete Sport Training Guide for Athletes*. Reed, 1996.

LeMond, G. & K. Gordis, *Greg Lemond's Complete Book of Bicycling*. Perigree Books, 1990.

Lydiard, A. with G. Gilmour, *Running with Lydiard*. Hodder and Stoughton, 1983.

Niles, R., *Time-Saving Training: for Multisport Athletes*. Human Kinetics, 1997.

Noakes, T. & S. Granger, *Running your Best*. Oxford University Press, 1996.

Noakes, T., *Lore of Running*. Human Kinetics, 1991.

Paish, W., *Training for Peak Performance*. A & C Black, 1991.

Rushall, B. & F.S. Pyke, *Training for Sports and Fitness*. MacMillan Education Australia, 1993.

Sharkey, B.J., *Physiology of Fitness*. Human Kinetics, 1990.

Town, G. & J. Kearney, *Swim, Bike, Run*. Human Kinetics, 1994.

INDEX

ALSO FROM REED PUBLISHING

SMART TRAINING
A COMPLETE APPROACH TO PLANNING FOR PEAK PERFORMANCE
Edited by Ken Hodge, Alex McKenzie and Gordon Sleivert

While many specialist resources focus on single aspects of training, *Smart Training* incorporates all the sport sciences, including sport psychology, physiology, biomechanics, medicine and nutrition, in a single, easy-to-use, personalised training plan that can be tailored to each person's specific sporting needs. It is written by experts in straightforward language and is directed specifically at athletes and coaches for practical use in their training. Each package includes a training planner wall chart.

The authors are all members of the staff at the Human Performance Centre, School of Physical Education, University of Otago.

TRIATHLON
A COMPLETE GUIDE TO TRAINING AND RACING
Dr John Hellemans

John Hellemans brings together the experience and skills he has developed through years of top-class competition, coaching and the practice of sports medicine in this definitive guide for triathletes. *Triathlon* places a strong emphasis on practical training, including planning, peaking and recovery, plus specific exercises for the individual disciplines of swimming, cycling and running. Close attention is given to the effects of triathlons on the body, and there are chapters on nutrition, overtraining, mental attitudes, women in triathlon and the relationship of ageing and competition.

John Hellemans is a sports doctor who has competed successfully in triathlons throughout the world. He guided Erin Baker to international success in triathlons in the 1980s.

EAT TO COMPETE
Jeni Pearce

The link between good nutrition and sports performance is widely recognised. In this best-selling book, Jeni Pearce shows how sound nutrition, body composition, weight control, exercise performance and good health can give the athlete the all-important winning edge. For recreational athletes, too, good food and nutrition can help to improve times, endurance, concentration and enjoyment.

Jeni Pearce is well known as a dietician and sports nutritionist, and has advised many top athletes on their nutritional requirements. She is the author of several food books including *The Eat to Compete Cookbook*, *Eat Your Stress Away* and *Jeni Pearce's Healthy Pasta Cookbook*.